Between 1933 and 1945 the Nazi regime in Germany tried to restructure a 'class' society along racial lines. This book deals with the ideas and institutions which underpinned this mission, and shows how Nazi policy affected various groups of people, both victims and beneficiaries.

The book begins with a discussion of the origins of Nazi racial ideology, and then demonstrates the thoroughness and purposiveness with which this was translated into official policy. The book deals not only with the systematic persecution of the Jews, the largest group of victims of Nazism, but also with the fate of Sinti and Roma, the mentally handicapped, the 'asocial', and homosexuals. Finally, the book examines the racially-motivated social policies of the regime which affected every German 'national comrade'. Their primary objective was to realise a racially-organised state and society. It argues that the 'polycratic' and chaotic character of the regime, described so frequently by recent historians, neither hindered nor slowed down the ruthless way in which the regime pursued and destroyed its victims. The Third Reich was fundamentally different from other totalitarian regimes precisely because of the all-encompassing nature of its racial policies.

THE RACIAL STATE: GERMANY 1933–1945

MICHAEL BURLEIGH
University of Wales, Cardiff
and WOLFGANG WIPPERMANN
Freie Universität, Berlin

CAMBRIDGE
UNIVERSITY PRESS

PUBLISHED BY THE PRESS SYNDICATE OF THE UNIVERSITY OF CAMBRIDGE
The Pitt Building, Trumpington Street, Cambridge, United Kingdom

CAMBRIDGE UNIVERSITY PRESS
The Edinburgh Building, Cambridge CB2 2RU, UK
40 West 20th Street, New York, NY 10011–4211, USA
477 Williamstown Road, Port Melbourne, VIC 3207, Australia
Ruiz de Alarcón 13, 28014 Madrid, Spain
Dock House, The Waterfront, Cape Town 8001, South Africa

http://www.cambridge.org

First published 1991
Eleventh printing 2004

Printed in the United Kingdom at the University Press, Cambridge

British Library Cataloguing in Publication data
Burleigh, Michael
The racial state: Germany 1933–1945
1. Germany. Social list, 1933–1945
I. Title II. Wipperman, Wolfgang
943.086

Library of Congress Cataloguing in Publication date
Burleigh, Michael, 1955–
The racial state: Germany 1933–1945
/ Michael Burleigh, Wolfgang Wippermann.
p.   cm.
Includes bibliographical references and index.
ISBN 0 521 39114 8. – ISBN 0 521 39802 9 (pbk.)
1. Germany – History – 1933–1945. 2. Minorities – Germany –
History – 20th century. 3. Germany – Race relations. 4. Germany –
Social policy. I. Wippermann, Wolfgang, 1945–   . Title.
DD256.5.B93 1991
323.1′43′09043–dc20   90–20209   CIP

ISBN 0 521 39114 8 hardback

The racial state: Germany 1933–1945

Contents

ILLUSTRATIONS

FOREWORD

FROM the moment the National Socialists came to power on 30 January 1933, the regime they established has been the subject of bitter controversy. Scholars have argued over whether the Nazi state was the natural outcome of some of the principal features of the historical evolution of Germany in the modern period or whether it was a catastrophe which could have occurred in any society subject to the stresses which the German people experienced after 1918. They have disputed over whether the 'Thousand-Year Reich' was backward-looking, aiming to preserve what were felt by its ideologists to be the values of a pre-industrial idealised past, or whether it was a painful stretch of the way the German people traversed on the road to the establishment of a modern state. Was it part of the general phenomenon of fascism and right radicalism, was it, indeed, merely one aspect of the drive to totalitarian structures which have been such a feature of the twentieth century, or can it be understood in terms of characteristics which are unique to itself?

This book analyses these issues lucidly and with great skill. Its principal virtue, however, does not lie in the way it enables the reader to assess these problems and make up his own mind. What makes it new and especially valuable, in the plethora of books on National Socialism, is its interpretation of the Nazi phenomenon. The authors see the Nazis as bent on creating a barbaric, racially-based utopia. It is the desire to create this 'barbarous utopia' which links all aspects of Nazi social policy from the persecution of Jews, Sinti and Roma to the suppression of homosexuality, the treatment of mentally ill and physically handicapped people, the organisation of women, and the handling of crime. In this context the book is also a significant contribution to the vexed question of the 'uniqueness' of the Holocaust. As emerges clearly from the arguments of Burleigh and Wippermann, the mass murder of the Jews *was* unique in that every Jew, man, woman and child, assimilated or deeply orthodox, was singled out for destruction. But it was not unique in that it grew out of a view of the world which regarded individual life as of no value, except in so far as it contributed to the health of the ethnic collectivity as defined by the regime's leaders. It has often been said that historical exposition is an inadequate tool to capture the uniquely appalling character of the Nazi regime. This is a book which succeeds in doing just that. Its pages analyse dispassionately and rigorously, but stir us to passionate anger and shame, not least because they show how difficult it has been to root out the mind-set which made Nazism possible.

Antony Polonsky

Acknowledgements

B OTH authors would like to take this opportunity of thanking William Davies of Cambridge University Press for his encouragement of this Anglo-German 'joint venture', and Ludwig Rost, Hans-Georg Stümke, and Paul Weindling for their expert advice on certain chapters. We are also indebted to the secretarial staff of the Department of International History at the London School of Economics and Political Science for their assistance in keeping this project on schedule.

November 1991

The Press's decision to reprint *The Racial State* has enabled us to correct a few misprints and minor errors, and to incorporate some very recent publications into the bibliographical essay.

Michael Burleigh and Wolfgang Wipperman
London and Berlin, June 1992

INTRODUCTION: WHY ANOTHER BOOK ON THE THIRD REICH?

THERE is already an immense secondary literature on the Third Reich, which even historians working on the subject find daunting. However, although this period of German history has been intensively studied, the general conclusions drawn remain highly controversial. Debates between historians working on this subject are not simply concerned with matters of detail, but rather, deal with central questions, including the following. Was the Third Reich the more or less inevitable outcome of a German 'separate path' of historical development, or an aberrant departure from the course of German history? Does the regime belong with Communist and Fascist states in a general category of totalitarian regimes? Were there sufficient similarities with Mussolini's Italy for it to be described as Fascist? Who had power in the Third Reich: Hitler and the Nazi Party or the captains of industry? Was the regime monolithically totalitarian, or a 'polycratic' dictatorship, characterised by internecine conflicts between competing agencies, individuals, and institutions? Should one characterise the Third Reich as 'the Hitler state' or Hitler as a 'weak dictator'? Did the regime pursue modernising rather than profoundly atavistic and reactionary policies?

We regard the question concerning the modernity or anti-modernity of the Third Reich as among the most crucial problems confronting modern historical research. Concepts like modernity or modernisation are notoriously nebulous. They stem from a North American, non-Marxist attempt to find a theoretical common denominator which accounts for the transformation of 'traditional' into 'modern' societies. The common processes of development include greater social differentiation and a more complex division of labour; an enhanced capacity for the institutional resolution of social conflict; and a quantitative growth of the goods and services on offer. Although political scientists and historians writing about the Third World have come to regard modernisation theories as intellectually redundant, historians and more recently sociologists writing about the Third Reich have yet to catch up with them. Older titles like *Hitler's Social Revolution* are joined by *Modernity and the Holocaust* as the unique horrors of the Third Reich disappear within a fog of relativising, sociological rhetoric. The fact of Nazi Germany's murder of millions of Jews, Sinti and Roma, and others at a specific point in time is obscured by talk of general genocidal impulses allegedly latent beneath the thin civilised crust of all 'modern' societies. In a curious way, this inability to digest the fact of the murder by Germans of millions of Jews and others at a particular moment in time mirrors commensurate attempts by a minority of German historians to argue that there is no moral difference between Auschwitz, the Soviet Gulags, and Hiroshima.

Our object in writing this book has been to counteract attempts to relativise this subject, either through perversely formulated, and politically purposive, comparisons, or through the application of theories long since regarded as heuristically redundant by any self-respecting social or political scientist. Principally, we have tried to establish whether the modernisation theory works in relation to the Nazi regime. Our answer to this question – which is to say that the word 'modern' only fits the Third Reich if one strips it of all connotations of 'betterment' or 'improvement' to an extent which renders it utterly meaningless – forms the core of this book.

Proponents of modernisation theories conventionally point to Nazi social policy. They claim that this pursued modernising aims and achieved more or less intentionally modern, or even social 'revolutionary', results. One author, David Schoenbaum, claimed a quarter of a century ago that there was a 'social revolution' in the Third Reich. Opponents of this theory, who argue that the Nazi regime was profoundly reactionary, usually refer to the barbaric racial policies pursued by the Third Reich. Was Nazi social policy therefore 'modern', and Nazi racial policy 'reactionary'? What were the relations between these two areas of policy? Were they, as will be argued here, merely two sides of the same coin? Were they based upon comprehensive plans for a new, global, racially-based social order, or the product of *ad hoc* initiatives? These questions are of crucial importance to an understanding of the Nazi regime, yet in our opinion they have been relatively neglected, or inadequately answered, by existing research. As yet, there has been no attempt to analyse the totality of Nazi racial and social policy in the light of a great deal of detailed recent research on its various aspects.

Our approach to these questions has been as follows. Chapter 1 discusses some of the issues which have preoccupied historians of the subject since the 1940s. The emphasis in our discussion is upon those who have detected modern features in the policies of the Nazi regime. The second chapter provides an overview of the development and functions of racial ideology, beginning with the late eighteenth century and concluding with Adolf Hitler. We have called this chapter 'Barbarous utopias' to convey the idea that these barbaric notions were usually concerned with how to fashion an indeterminate future. These various racial utopias acquired a prescriptive character under the Nazi regime, although the route from earlier thinkers and theorists to the industrialised mass murder of Auschwitz is complex and fraught with difficulties. In chapter 3 we discuss how racialism became the official doctrine and policy of the Nazi state. Notwithstanding marked differences in the theoretical content of the racism avowed by the regime's individual agencies, the object was to create a utopian society organised in accordance with the principles of race.

A key concern in this endeavour was the 'purification of the body of the nation' from 'alien', 'hereditarily ill', or 'asocial' 'elements'. Racial 'purification' was an integral part of wider 'social' policies designed to create a 'healthy', performance-orientated, 'Aryan' 'national community'. What this entailed, not least for the victims and 'objects' of these policies, is discussed in Parts II and III of this book.

Part II is concerned with the fate of all those whose lives or reproductive capacity were ended as a result of Nazi racial policy. It deals with Jews, Sinti and Roma, and members of other ethnic minorities categorised as 'alien', as well as the 'hereditarily ill', 'community aliens', and homosexuals. The object of these chapters is to demonstrate the comprehensive character of Nazi racism, the brutally efficient way in which it was implemented, and, not least, what policy entailed in the way of suffering for its victims. Both the comprehensiveness of racial policy and, regrettably enough, what these measures involved in terms of individual human tragedy are sometimes missing from the intellectually elegant syntheses devoted to debates concerning the bureaucratic chaos of the Nazi regime. We have deliberately opted for an approach which includes the perspective of the regime's many victims. The final part of the book is devoted to the Nazis' attempt to create a new 'national community'. This endeavour was principally guided by racial considerations. For this reason we have decided to employ a classificatory scheme based upon anthropological and biological categories rather than social class. This has become common in studies of youth or women. Since some areas of Nazi racial policy particularly affected women, there are good reasons for treating them separately, beyond the dictates of current fashions in historical writing. Since other areas of racial policy, not to speak of the pronouncedly male-dominated character of whole agencies of the regime, exclusively concern men, we have decided to include a separate chapter devoted to this half of the population.

Nazi racial and social policy must be studied as an indivisible whole. It is a travesty of a complex reality to write in terms of either allegedly progressive social policies or reactionary racial policies. Both were merely different sides of the same coin. Nazi racial and social policy was simultaneously modern and profoundly anti-modern. There is little evidence to suggest significant changes in the relationship between the social classes, notwithstanding Hitler's occasional aspersions about degenerate and effeminate aristocrats, or the emergence of functional elites of amoral 'new' men. However, there is much evidence to suggest that race was meant to supplant class as the primary organising principle in society, with a narrowing of existing social divisions and a widening of the division between 'healthy', 'Aryan' 'national comrades' and those 'elements' which the Nazis designated as being racially inferior, 'unfit', or 'alien' and hence destined for exclusion and eventual extermination. The realisation of this racially-determined cleavage self-evidently received priority over whatever cosmetic and piecemeal changes in the existing organisation of society the Nazis attempted during a twelve-year period. The millions of victims are a reminder of the purposiveness with which the regime went about realising the most crucial part of its desolate agenda, namely the creation of a functioning racial state.

PART ONE

THE SETTING

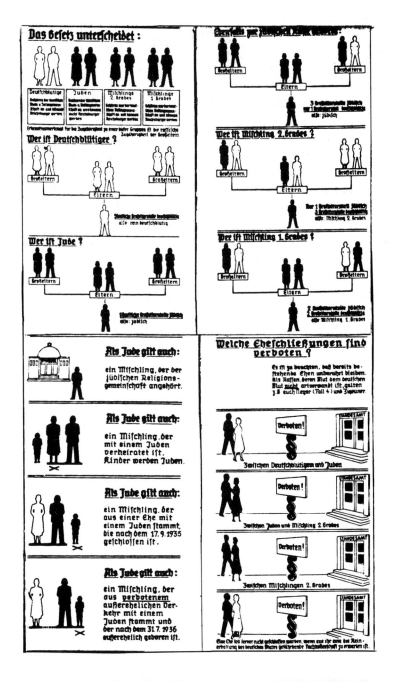

HOW MODERN, GERMAN, AND TOTALITARIAN WAS THE THIRD REICH? SOME MAJOR HISTORIOGRAPHICAL CONTROVERSIES

'WHAT the author seems above all to want to prove, is, that Nazi Germany exhibits most clearly the sicknesses of modern civilisation.'[1] These words appeared in a wartime review in *The Times* of Karl Otten's *A Combine of Aggression: Masses, Elites and Dictatorship in Germany.*[2] As a German pacifist and anti-fascist, Otten had left Germany in March 1933, emigrating via Spain and France to London. In 1942 he published the above-mentioned book, in which he explicitly argued that the Third Reich was the result of a general development towards a technological, mass society, and by no means an exclusively German phenomenon.

As might have been anticipated, Otten's book was not a success. At the time, the 'Battle of Britain' may have been won, but victory in the war against Hitler's Germany was far from certain. Two years before, German Dorniers, Heinkels and Junkers had 'eradicated' Coventry, while heavily bombing London and other British cities too. In view of this, the thesis that the British were not victims of German aggression, but rather, like Germany, of the general development of a technological, mass society seemed absurd. The explanation favoured by Robert Vansittart, whereby German fascism was a specifically German phenomenon, seemed more cogent.

Commentators in countries allied with Britain also adopted the Vansittart line.[3] In the USA, William Montgomery McGovern pointed to a German historical development which had somehow gone awry on a trajectory 'from Luther to Hitler';[4] Henry Morgenthau recommended that a perennially aggressive and undemocratic Germany be transformed into a backward pastoral society;[5] while Theodore Kauffmann simply stated: 'Germany must perish!'[6] Similar lines of thought prevailed in the Soviet Union, Germany's erstwhile ally. However the Soviet variant of Vansittartism, if one will, did not emphasise Germany's lack of a democratic political tradition, but rather a timeless, German *Drang nach Osten* which had culminated in Nazi Germany's 'Operation Barbarossa',[7] the subtleties of early Soviet Marxist historiography having long since been superseded by the Stalinist version of the 'national story'.[8]

In view of the horrors of the war begun by Germany, and of the barbarities perpetrated by Germans in every corner of occupied Europe, it is not surprising that to former members of the wartime alliance, war and fascism seemed synonymous with Germany, and not, as Karl Otten had maintained, a reflection of a general trend towards a mass, technological society. However, this 'modernising theory' was not quite as absurd and eccentric as it appeared at the time.[9] Already in the 1920s and early 1930s, various writers had stressed that both Italian and German Fascism were pursuing 'modernising' aims in economic, social, and cultural policy. According to the former Communist Franz Borkenau, Fascism represented a form of 'developmental dictatorship' for the creation of an 'industrial capitalist' society.[10] However Germany, at least, already indubitably disposed of a highly-developed capitalist economy. This led Borkenau to argue that while the prospects for Fascism in 'underdeveloped' Italy were good, the chances for Fascism in Germany were not so high. By the time Borkenau's essay appeared, the Nazis were already in power in Germany and the author in exile.

Experiences like this did not dispel the attractions of 'modernisation' theories. These continued to be espoused, in an indirect form, by Marxist theoreticians concerned with Fascism. It was they who regarded Fascism as a general phenomenon, by no means restricted to any particular country. They defined its essence with reference to its pro-capitalist social function. Fascism, in general, was an 'agent', 'tool', or 'instrument' of particularly influential capitalist circles, which therefore made it a modern phenomenon *per se*.[11] Debates then revolved around the question of whether Fascism was the most modern, or ultimate, guise assumed by the capitalist state before a general, worldwide Communist revolution.

For many liberals and conservatives, Fascism was also a 'modern', and by no means specifically Italian or German, phenomenon. It was profoundly anti-bourgeois, indeed revolutionary, and shared many characteristics with Bolshevism. According to Luigi Sturzo, the leader of the Italian Popolari, Fascism was a form of 'right-wing Bolshevism', and Bolshevism itself, a 'communist dictatorship or left-wing fascism'.[12] These terminological confusions, which involved establishing an identity between Fascism and Bolshevism, were transformed into a ramified theory of totalitarianism by the Italian liberal Francesco Nitti.[13] As he wrote, 'Fascism and Bolshevism are not based upon contradictory principles, they both represent the denial of the same principles of freedom and order.'[14]

Many German conservatives and liberals agreed with the analysis of their Italian ideological confrères. Like the latter, they stressed the similarities between National Socialism and Bolshevism. Both phenomena were novel developments on the political landscape, evident wherever radical modernisation had occurred, and the 'masses' had displaced traditional elites. According to the historian Friedrich Meinecke, a self-professed 'republican by reason' but 'monarchist at heart', Bolshevism and Fascism not only pursued comparable political goals, but also had common 'sociological causes'.[15] Here he was in agreement with the Catholic conservative publicist Waldemar Gurian.[16] The latter also emphasised the similarities with Bolshevism, and made specifically modern, indeed, democratic, tendencies responsible for the rise of National Socialism, which he characterised as a form of 'democratic Caesarism'. According to Hermann Rauschning, who, as a National Socialist himself, reached the position of President of the Senate in Danzig before leaving the Party, National Socialism was *more* revolutionary than Bolshevism.[17] It represented a 'revolution of nihilism'. Writing in exile in 1938, Rauschning was trying to convince conservatives in Germany and elsewhere of the dangers of their flirtation with Nazism. Hitler would make an alliance with the latter merely to be in a better position to destroy them.

In summary, it can be said that some Marxist and 'bourgeois' theorists saw in the Third Reich a 'modern', and by no means specifically German, phenomenon. However, these interpretations were criticised, and partially rendered redundant, by Germans writing in exile. Noteworthy in this context was an essay by Rudolf Hilferding, entitled 'The Historical Problem', which appeared in France in 1940, shortly before the (exiled) author was murdered by the Gestapo.[18] Hilferding was perhaps the most important Marxist theoretician of the SPD during the Weimar Republic. His theories concerning 'organised capitalism' are still discussed within the SPD today, and employed in the writing of social history in Germany. In this essay, Hilferding threw down the gauntlet to all existing Marxist-Leninist 'instrumental' analyses of Fascism. During the Third Reich the power of the state had become 'independent', in ways which could not be explained with the aid of Marx and Engels' notions of a 'causal connection' between base and superstructure, or between the economy and politics. Rather, developing their analysis of 'Bonapartism', Hilferding argued that the totally new phenomenon of the National Socialist 'total state' required commensurately novel heuristic approaches.

Here, two German émigrés, Ernst Fraenkel and Franz L. Neumann, responded to his call. In a book published in 1940, devoted to the 'dual state', Fraenkel claimed that the Third Reich represented a 'symbiosis' between the Nazi Party and the representatives of capitalism.[19] The latter had renounced direct control over the exercise of political power in favour of the former, because only with the help of a strong state, which would emasculate the working-class movement, could they hope to surmount the Depression. Despite this strong state, the capitalists continued to insist on the maintenance of certain legal norms without which a capitalist economy could not function. Therefore, some traditional institutions continued to operate in the fields of law, economy, and society. Fraenkel referred to these as the 'normative state'. However, there were continual conflicts and disputes over competences between this 'normative state' and the 'prerogative state', consisting of the newly-created agencies and institutions of the Party. This, he thought, would finally have a debilitating effect on the whole of the National Socialist 'dual state'.

Franz Neumann, another German exile working in the USA, similarly pointed to conflicts over competences in the apparently monolithic National Socialist 'Führer state'.[20] Where Fraenkel saw two blocs of alliance partners, Neumann saw four: the Party, army, bureaucracy, and industrialists. However, conflicts between these four 'pillars' of the Third Reich did not necessarily involve a weakening of the regime. All four power blocs mentioned above were always ready to compromise, and their conflicts were not prejudicial to the terroristic efficiency of the 'totalitarian state'. This was particularly the case in the field of racial policy, where the Party succeeded time and again in realising its inhuman, and thoroughly illogical, goals. For this reason, despite its modern capitalist structure, the Third Reich was a novel, but in no sense a 'modern' state. In order to conceptualise both this admixture of the modern and reactionary and the brutal efficiency of the regime, Neumann proposed the epithet 'Behemoth'. Behemoth was the mythical beast whose appearance during the Apocalypse would herald the onset of the last days. This was an allusive way of saying that the Third Reich represented a simultaneous regression and progression into barbarism.

Does the danger of a progression into barbarism threaten all 'modern' states, or was it only restricted to the German dictatorship? Was Behemoth a general, or a specifically German, phenomenon? Answers to these questions, which are still central to discussions of the Third Reich, can also be found in the writings of exiled German authors. Here one should mention the German Social Democrat Curt Geyer, who in a book which appeared in 1939, entitled *The Party of Freedom*, pointed to specifically German characteristics manifest in the prehistory and structure of the Third Reich, and explicitly rejected analyses based upon the 'class state in the Marxist sense'.[21] Comparable quasi-Vansittartist opinions were adumbrated by other German Social Democrats and liberals in exile. This applies to individual Communists too, notably Hans Günther, who in 1935 published a book in Moscow entitled *Der Herren eigener Geist*.[22] Unlike most Communist writers, Günther not only took Nazi ideology seriously, but also explained it through reference to particular aberrant developments within German intellectual history. However, perhaps the most significant attempt to combine Vansittartist with Marxist approaches stemmed from Ernst Bloch.[23] According to Bloch, Germany was 'deficient in simultaneity', with very modern and very reactionary modes of thought coexisting in an uneasy and unstable relationship with one another. This was principally apparent among the young and the middle classes. National Socialist ideology exploited this 'deficiency in simultaneity', this confusion of the modern with 'older modes of being', for its own purposes.

Both Neumann's 'Behemoth' and Bloch's insistence upon a specifically German 'deficiency in simultaneity' have been mentioned here because both contain important elements which can be used to clarify the history of the Third Reich. Specifically, three points in their analyses warrant closer attention. Firstly, they stressed the ambivalent, partly modern, partly reactionary nature of the regime. Secondly, they recognised the combination of general and specifically German characteristics, and finally, they realised that notwithstanding its 'polycratic' characteristics, the Third Reich was both totalitarian and terroristic.

In our opinion, none of these three points has been treated with the attention it deserves in post-war research. This is a reflection not merely of not knowing, but often of a politically-motivated 'not wanting to know', for there is hardly another field in contemporary history which is so subject to political interests as the history of the Third Reich. This is obviously particularly true of the German-language historiography, as we will try to indicate in the following sections.[24]

After the war Vansittartist interpretations were as prevalent among German historians and publicists as they were among the victorious powers. This may be exemplified by a book entitled *The German Catastrophe*, published in 1946, by the then doyen of the historical profession,

Friedrich Meinecke.[25] While Meinecke certainly drew attention to 'analogies' between the Third Reich and 'authoritarian systems in neighbouring countries', whereby he meant French Bonapartism, Italian Fascism, and above all Russian Bolshevism, he also stressed the specifically German preconditions and causes of National Socialism. Among these preconditions he included tendencies in the history of German thought from Hegel to Hitler, as well as the historical social structure of Prussia–Germany. Here, he particularly stressed the role of 'rabble-rousing big industrialists', 'bureaucratic squirearchs', the imperialistic lobbying of the Pan-German League, and the nationalistic agitation of the Eastern Marches Association. All of these contributed to the outbreak of the First World War and the rise of Hitler, and therefore to the 'German catastrophe'.

Although Meinecke was not alone in his self-critical and quasi-Vansittartist opinions, he was not able to prevail against his conservative critics. It is worth noting that these were principally historians who, like Hans Rothfels and Hans-Joachim Schoeps, had left Germany 'for racial reasons', or, like Gerhard Ritter, had been members of conservative resistance groups. After the war they vehemently and successfully attacked the idea of a German *Sonderweg* which culminated in Hitler's regime. According to Gerhard Ritter, the Austrian Hitler represented a sort of 'industrial accident', while National Socialism itself was 'not a specifically German phenomenon which can be adequately explained by reflections on German history'.[26] Possibilities for the establishment of a totalitarian dictatorship 'existed wherever the destruction of all traditional authority is followed by revolts of the masses resulting in direct rule by the people'. Therefore, the Third Reich stood in line with a European revolutionary tradition going back to the Jacobins, and was not the product of specifically German conditions.

Up to the late 1960s, the prevailing view in the Federal Republic was that the Third Reich was a variant of totalitarianism, or a state controlled by an omnipotent and ever-present dictator.[27] From the German point of view, this was a very convenient image, for it spared people the problem of having to think about their own guilt and responsibility. If Hitler was responsible for everything, then why should anyone else feel responsible too? If the Third Reich was only a variant of a thriving and threatening totalitarianism in the Soviet Union, eastern Europe, and the DDR, it was self-evident that the defence of the new German democracy should take precedence over the process of overcoming the defunct German dictatorship.

The ideological function of this 'Hitlerist' and totalitarian approach is so obvious that one must ask why it was so pervasive, and why non-German historians hardly criticised it. The answer is somewhat banal. These theories served to cement the North Atlantic alliance, which with surprising speed included West Germany as a member. Nazism was no longer the danger; the threat came rather from the highly actual communist system. In East Germany, what appeared to be a diametrically opposite view in fact turns out to be analogous. Initially, as elsewhere, Vansittartist views were dominant: the Third Reich was the more or less necessary final product of a German 'false turning', and of a specifically German *Drang nach Osten*. However, self-critical theories like these, propounded above all by Ernst Niekisch and Alexander Abusch, were soon traduced as 'misery-concepts', which the regime increasingly no longer needed.[28] In the dominant reappraisal it was not 'the Germans', or even the so-called 'little Pgs' (minor Party comrades), but the 'most reactionary, chauvinistic, and imperialistic elements of finance capital' who were responsible for the creation and direction of the 'fascist dictatorship'.[29]

Discussion in the former DDR revolved around the question of whether this or that individual capitalist or more or less anonymous 'groups of monopolists' ('elements of finance capital') were responsible for the regime and its actions. By contrast, there was never debate about whether or not the KPD was the central object of Nazi persecution, or the most important and successful resistance organisation, which then in 'brotherly agreement' with the Soviet Union liberated Germany from the 'fascist yoke'. The language employed was as leaden as the thinking which underlies it. Although the Russians and other peoples in eastern Europe were well aware that they had been invaded and enslaved not by a handful of capitalists but by vast German armies, they nonetheless tolerated the self-justifying ideologies of their East German comrades. Fears concerning the NATO alliance, of which West Germany was a member, determined this exercise in purposive self-delusion.

If one considers these inner-German attempts to employ western totalitarian and eastern 'instrumental' theories of Fascism in order to slip away from any historical responsibility for German National Socialism, it is all the more extraordinary to discover the lack of criticism they have encountered either from victims of National Socialism or from citizens of the victorious Allied countries. The work of historians like A. J. P. Taylor, Edmond Vermeil, or the Pole Marian Friedberg,[30] who all drew attention to the specifically German causes and properties of Nazism, was, and is, virtually ignored in modern discussions of the subject. However, in the

1960s a change took place, which in West Germany at least resulted in a challenge to the predominant national historical mythology. This was largely motivated by current political considerations. To begin with, it became apparent that by no means all of the crimes of the Nazi regime had been discovered, and that many of the murderers and their accomplices were living, not underground as pariahs, but as respectable citizens, often occupying important political, economic, and social positions.[31] These disturbing facts, and the reemergence of a neo-fascist movement called the NPD, which managed to gain seats in various provincial parliaments,[32] made it clear that the National Socialist past had not been 'overcome', as was maintained in prayer-mill fashion at every available opportunity. A new generation of schoolchildren and students began to ask their parents whether they had really 'known nothing', and discovered disturbing personal and institutional continuities between the Third Reich and Germany's Second Republic.

The ensuing political debate was keenly followed in the USA, western Europe, and Israel. Although up to then the Federal Republic had been constantly praised as a trustworthy military and economic partner, now it was more than distressing to discover how, rapidly after the regaining of sovereignty, the Federal Republic had terminated 'denazification', released former Nazis from their prison sentences, and indeed restored them to positions in the civil service.[33] In view of the increasing frequency of anti-Semitic incidents and the emergence of a neo-Nazi movement, the self-satisfied claim of the Federal Republic not merely to have broken with the past, but to have finally 'overcome' it, met with increasing criticism. Finally, many people could not understand how a state which could pass retrospective laws to combat terrorism could at the same time not only obdurately refuse to do the same in the case of Nazi criminals, but for a long period seriously countenanced an amnesty and statute of limitations for those involved in the unparalleled crimes of the Nazi period.

This revived political discussion of the Nazi period, and of how memory of it had been repressed in the Federal Republic, affected historical writing on the subject. From the mid-1960s historians addressed themselves to the following questions: was the Third Reich a 'works accident', or the more or less inevitable end product of a German *Sonderweg*? Did the Third Reich have a totalitarian character, exhibiting correspondences with the Soviet Union? Did it pursue modern or reactionary policies? As a glance at any of the interpretative syntheses on offer will make plain, these questions still dominate current debate. All three questions were investigated simul-taneously, and are obviously interconnected. Here they will be treated separately. The most salient aspects of the recent historiography on these subjects will be critically examined, with some indication of which questions are still open to research, and how future scholars might consider approaching them.

Renewed discussion about a German *Sonderweg* was above all occasioned by the Hamburg historian Fritz Fischer.[34] Fischer was one of the first German historians to concede, and some would say prove, that Germany had intentionally begun the First World War. This provoked an incensed response from his conservative German colleagues. However, his views were supported by young social historians like Hans-Ulrich Wehler.[35] They stressed that there were major continuities between the domestic and external policies of the Kaiserreich and Third Reich which were largely attributable to pressures resulting from a deliberate refusal to adopt political structures commensurate with a rapidly developing industrial society. Simultaneously, the hitherto almost universally dominant theory of totalitarianism came under attack from a number of directions. With the aid of a method derived from the history of ideas, the historian Ernst Nolte demonstrated correspondences between Italian Fascism, the French Action Française, and National Socialism which entitled one to describe these regimes and parties as Fascist, and to speak of a 'fascist epoch' in general.[36] This reintroduced into Western discussions of Fascism, dominated hitherto by theories of totalitarianism, a concept which had been dismissed as a device of Communist propaganda. Totalitarianism theories also came under attack from historians and political scientists working on contemporary eastern Europe. In particular they noted, not without a degree of exaggeration, changes which ensued in Russia after the death of Stalin, and the 1956 twentieth plenary session of the Communist Party of the Soviet Union. Obviously there were appreciable differences between the partially de-Stalinised Soviet Union and the auto-destructive regime of the Third Reich.[37]

Moreover, various liberal and left-wing historians, who in the meantime had rediscovered the almost forgotten theories of Fascism developed by exiles in the inter-war period, emphasised that right from the start there were significant differences in the socio-economic preconditions, ideological objectives, and methods of rule employed by the regimes of Hitler and Stalin. In contrast to Bolshevism, National Socialism came to power in a highly industrialised society. It did not abolish the private ownership of the means of production. While Stalin endeavoured to bring about the industrialisation of Russia, and at least propagated the idea of a classless society, Hitler sought to translate a fundamentally inhuman racial ideology into reality. These major differences, of which there are many more, out-weighed any similarities in the terroristic methods adopted by both regimes.

Finally, other historians of National Socialism demonstrated that the structure of the Third Reich was by no means as monolithically totalitarian as the devotees of theories of totalitarianism, like Carl Joachim Friedrich or Zbigniew Brzezinski, liked to maintain.[38] From the beginning, the policies of the Third Reich were shaped by conflicts over competence between various institutions and individuals. Policy was not planned in accordance with an ideological programme, was not determined by Hitler alone, and did not advance at an even tempo in every area. This line of argument has led some historians, most notably Hans Mommsen, to claim that Hitler was 'a weak dictator'.[39]

Closely connected with the view that the Third Reich was a form of 'polyocracy', an argument first essayed by Ernst Fraenkel and Franz Neumann, was the rediscovery and development of 'modernisation' theories. These had also been discussed by German-speaking scholars in exile during the inter-war period. Referring back to the work of Franz Borkenau, the German sociologist Ralf Dahrendorf argued that despite itself, so to speak, the Third Reich had pursued 'modernising' policies.[40] Despite the profoundly reactionary goals reflected in its ideology, the Nazi regime had resulted in a 'push into modernity', by 'finally abolishing the German past as it was embodied in Imperial Germany'. This argument was developed by the American historian David Schoenbaum, who drew attention to a number of 'modern' effects apparent in Nazi social policy.[41] The combination of the rhetoric of an anti-industrial, anti-bourgeois revolution with a reality which accelerated the development of an indus-trial society resulted in the destruction of the traditional class structure and both actual and notional social mobility on an unprecedented scale. According to Schoenbaum, the latter entitles one to speak of a Nazi 'social revolution'. The English socio-economic historian Tim Mason agreed with many of Schoenbaum's findings.[42] However, he went on to attribute the modernising aspects of Nazi social policy to a form of covert class struggle waged by the German working class. Although their own politi-cal parties and trade unions had been destroyed, the German working class nonetheless understood how to achieve both de facto wage increases and improvements in their standard of living. In order not to endanger either domestic tranquillity or increased armaments production, the Nazi regime had to make concessions in these areas. According to Mason, pressure and counter-pressure would have ineluctably resulted in the collapse of the

German economy had war not broken out. The latter represented a form of 'flight forwards', with the twofold object of staving off the bankruptcy of the Nazi regime and of integrating the working class through classical social–imperialist devices. Both Schoenbaum and Mason made extensive use of hitherto unknown or under-used sources. However, most of the latter stemmed from relatively low-level institutions in the Third Reich, and were exclusively concerned with one area of policy, namely social policy. The same criticism applies to other historians who purport to detect 'modernising' tendencies in Nazi policy towards youth, women, or the arts. Their selective findings are in obvious contradiction to massive evidence of the reactionary character of Nazi policy in the same areas, not to speak of its ideology and propaganda. To take one example treated more extensively below, one can find evidence of 'progressive' policies towards women provided one studies only the provision of maternity clinics, education, or the employment patterns of some women, and not what happened to unmarried mothers, women who were regarded as being of 'lesser value', or women 'foreign workers' in Germany.

The ambivalent relationship between the modernising and reactionary, or as Karl Dietrich Bracher has it, 'traditional and revolutionary', elements in the policies of the Third Reich[43] has been explained by Henry Ashby Turner in terms of the relationship between means and ends.[44] The Nazis had to practise a form of 'modernisation' in order to achieve their reactionary goals. By contrast, the literary historian Hans-Dieter Schäfer, who also purports to find modern – or, as he puts it, 'American' – elements in the social history of the Third Reich, argues that these stood in 'deep contradiction' to the reactionary, or *völkisch*, goals of the regime.[45] Translated into everyday social reality, this confusion of the modern and reactionary resulted in a form of 'split consciousness', already apparent in the 'schizophrenic reaction' of the Germans to modernity in general. A similar thesis has been argued by Detlev Peukert in his book *Inside Nazi Germany*.[46] Again, Peukert drew attention to various modernising tendencies, most of them negative, apparent in the social policy of the regime. In his view, the Third Reich reflected the symptoms of a wider 'modern pathology' and of a 'crisis in German industrial class society'. Without obviously being aware of it, Peukert came remarkably close to the ideas of Karl Otten mentioned at the beginning of this chapter.

All of the historians mentioned hitherto agree that the social, economic, and cultural policies of the Third Reich had certain modern characteristics. They would also agree that both the principles and the practice of Nazi racial policy were inhuman and profoundly reactionary. This last point, however, has recently been questioned by, *inter alia*, Götz Aly, Susanne Heim, and Karl-Heinz Roth.[47] These authors belong to a group of younger historians, sociologists, physicians, and the unemployed, working in Berlin and Hamburg. They work without any connection with university institutions and receive no research funds from state sources. Their research is either self-financed or subsidised by the philanthropic industrialist Jan Reemtsma. They are self-conscious outsiders on the West German historical scene, regarding organised academic life as corrupt and corrupting, and rarely passing over a chance to assail established historical scholarship. Specifically, they claim that historians have neglected the 'inner structures of the Nazi state', and have so overlayered the tracks of desk-bound Nazi criminals with academic debate that continuities between the social policies of the Third Reich and those of the Federal Republic are virtually ignored. In effect they are saying that historians themselves have contributed to the 'continuation of Nazi methods of rule', by failing to interest themselves in longer-term perspectives.[48] These strictures apply as much to *marxisant* 'structuralists', blind to issues of individual human culpability, as to inveterate conservatives. These are serious accusations, expressed in commensurately strong language. The work of these 'alternative' historians might be dismissed out of hand as a form of personalistic muck-raking, were it not for the fact that they have made remarkable contributions to the history of health and social policy in the Third Reich, achieving a depth of research which would embarrass most university academics. Their findings may not be as novel as the authors would like others to believe, but the sources they use invariably are, reflecting a massive trawl through archives in Poland, the USSR and Germany. Karl-Heinz Roth, for example, has edited 5,250 sides of documents (with another 40,000 on microfiche) from the former Scientific Labour Institute of the German Labour Front, while finding the time to make important contributions to the history of psychiatry in Nazi Germany, and, presumably, to the lives of his own patients. With the aid of hitherto untapped sources, Götz Aly, Susanne Heim, and Karl-Heinz Roth claim that Nazi racial policy reflected 'modernising' goals too. Most controversially, they have argued that these were apparent in the Nazis' search for *Lebensraum* in the East, and in the 'Final Solution' of the 'Jewish Question'. In other words, there was a 'connection between economic modernisation and the murder of superfluous people'.[49] The extermination of the Jews represented a form of 'developmental' policy, the removal of an obstacle in the way of the transformation of the Polish or Ukrainian rural proletariat into Germany's future industrial proletariat.

The 'Final Solution' was not a matter of 'destruction for destruction's sake', or the implementation of an irrational racial utopia, but a means to rationally conceived ends.

All of these relatively recent directions in research have encountered considerable criticism. This applies to the idea of a German *Sonderweg*; to totalitarianism theory and its antipode of a Nazi 'polyocracy'; and, finally, to the claim that the regime pursued overall, or partially, modernising goals, including its racial policies.

Proponents of the view that a German *Sonderweg* inevitably resulted in the Third Reich have met with powerful criticism from the British historians David Blackbourn and Geoff Eley.[50] With considerable intellectual subtlety, they argue that the notion of a German *Sonderweg* presupposes a 'normal' path of historical development from which Germany allegedly deviated. By looking at the question comparatively, they claim that there was no 'normal' path, and that other European nations, including Britain, may be said to have pursued 'separate paths' too. In other words, Germany's national 'peculiarities' are not as 'peculiar' as the advocates of a German *Sonderweg* like to maintain. These criticisms of the 'prevailing' liberal–social democratic 'orthodoxy' have been adopted – and adapted – by the German historian, and quondam adviser to Chancellor Kohl, Michael Stürmer, who claims that imperial Germany was neither as undemocratic nor as 'Bonapartist' as historians like Hans-Ulrich Wehler have maintained.[51] Throughout the *Kaiserreich* there were tendencies towards parliamentarism. The latter not only managed to come to the surface in 1918–19, but were sufficiently strong to contribute to the downfall of the Empire. Using his characteristically florid idioms, Stürmer argues that the 'restless Reich' collapsed because of a surfeit, rather than a lack, of democracy.

Stürmer, and his colleagues Hagen Schulze, Klaus Hildebrand, Andreas Hillgruber, and the American David Calleo, 'explain' the belligerence of Prussia–Germany through reference to allegedly powerful 'democratic' tendencies in the domestic sphere and the central position of Germany in the 'middle of Europe'.[52] Despite the publicity these discoveries receive, all they signify is that old-fashioned geopolitical theories, thoroughly discredited through their association with National Socialism, have come back into vogue with a vengeance. However, self-professed 'leaders of opinion' like Stürmer encounter some difficulty when they deal with the Third Reich. This is interpreted either as representing a total break in the continuity of German history, or as a form of totalitarianism, alien to the German character. This accounts for why some German historians have begun to defend theories of totalitarianism at the expense of general theories of Fascism which they themselves first formulated. This affords them the chance to make comparisons with Stalin's regime, and hence to relativise the singularity of the Holocaust. This is most notoriously the case with Ernst Nolte, who has recently argued not only that the Gulags pre-date the 'SS state', but that the former were far worse than the latter.[53] Moreover, the SS state came into being because, as Nolte maintains, Hitler felt threatened by Bolshevik aggression, a claim which may well reflect Nolte's own anxieties about radicalised students rather more than it explains what motivated the Nazi Führer. These and other equally provocative theories resulted in the so-called *Historikerstreit*, whose details need not detain us here, beyond remarking the temporary revival of the electoral fortunes of the German radical right, shortly after conservative historians rediscovered these rather sterile, if perversely formulated, ques-tions. Nolte was not the only historian to first reject, and then go on to employ – in a radicalised form – theories of totalitarianism as an ill-concealed political weapon. For example, the American historian Henry Ashby Turner has argued along similar lines. Specifically, he has used the following political argument against proponents of Marxist theories of Fascism: 'If the widely held view that fascism is a product of modern capitalism corresponds with the facts, then this system cannot be defended.'[54] Theories of totalitarianism are also indispensable to historians like Karl Dietrich Bracher. Political freedoms, he argues, are under threat from right- and left-wing extremists. Here he principally means left-wing intellectuals. According to Bracher, they stray beyond constitutionality when they employ 'radical-left' theories of Fascism, and not 'democratic' theories of totalitarianism.[55]

However, the rejection of a general theory of Fascism, i.e. one not restricted to the Italian regime, is not solely motivated by political con-siderations. Historians like Gilbert Allardyce, Renzo De Felice, Saul Friedländer, Klaus Hildebrand, Turner, Bernd Martin, and Bracher himself claim that the differences between Italian Fascism and National Socialism were far greater than their similarities.[56] As yet, however, they have failed to produce the evidence to support this claim. This can only be done through comparative studies, but none of the historians mentioned above has undertaken them.

The position regarding criticism of the view that Nazi Germany was a 'polyocracy' is rather different. The debate concerns issues of fact. The so-called 'programmatists' accuse their 'revisionist' opponents of exaggerating the extent of conflicts over competence, and hence of seriously underestimating the personal power of Adolf Hitler.[57] In their view, Hitler was anything but a 'weak' dictator. His ideological presuppositions were not merely cosmetic or integrative in purpose, but rather comprised a structured programme which must be taken seriously. Anti-Semitism and the conquest of *Lebensraum* in the East lay at the heart of this programme, which was implemented to terrible effect, and in a systematic, step-by-step manner, above all in foreign policy and policy towards the Jews.

Remarkably enough, modernisation theories have not been so extensively criticised, despite the fact that their proponents pay scant attention to the backward-looking and racist aspects of Nazi policy. Interestingly, such theories have long since been regarded as intellectually redundant by historians, sociologists, and political scientists who work on the 'modernising' and murderous dictatorships of Latin America. The Chilean example should warn one about the dangers of attaching too much value to the emergence of an incipient urban bourgeoisie or a quasi-modern governmental apparatus. By contrast, much critical energy has recently been directed to the views put forward by Götz Aly, Susanne Heim, and Karl-Heinz Roth. The historian Dan Diner has stressed that the Holocaust was not a means to a 'rational' end, but rather, represented 'destruction for destruction's sake'.[58] Similarly trenchant criticisms have been made by Christopher Browning, who has pointed to the contradictory and shifting character of Nazi policy, a series of more or less explicit signals from the centre interacting with accommodation and receptivity at the periphery, and to the economic illogicality of the final goals themselves.[59] Jews were not killed from Rhodes to Odessa on behalf of the social mobility of the Polish rural working class or in the interests of rationalising backward and overpopulated economies. The pseudo-rational gloss put upon this process at the time by academic economists was – and is – no more cogent than the 'sanitary' or 'security' arguments used by their medical or police equivalents to rationalise race-hatred.

If one surveys the various historical controversies mentioned above, one is immediately struck by the polemical way in which they are conducted. This is particularly the case in Germany, where both domestic and foreign policy considerations interact with academic debate. As the recent *Historikerstreit* has amply demonstrated, this can result in the acrimonious exchange of theories and counter-theories by historians who have long since ceased, or have never embarked upon, studies of the Third Reich. Alternatively, historians concern themselves with issues of such detail that the bigger questions cease to be asked, or knowledge of the details indisposes them to ask them. Furthermore, with a highly developed historiography which requires interpretative syntheses as guides, there is always the risk that students can become so tantalised with debates that they forget what is being debated. The present work merely endeavours to provide a factual basis from which students can then approach wider questions such as whether there was a German *Sonderweg*, whether the Third Reich pursued modernising policies, or finally, whether the regime was totalitarian in character. We have chosen the racial and social policies of the regime as our starting point, partly because in our opinion these issues were at the heart of the Third Reich, and partly because we think they have not received commensurate or uniform attention in recent research. Whole areas of the subject, notably policy concerning women, the 'asocial' homosexuals, and Sinti and Roma, remain virtually unexplored.

CHAPTER TWO

BARBAROUS UTOPIAS: RACIAL IDEOLOGIES IN GERMANY

RACIAL ideologies and theories were not an exclusively German discovery. The word *Rasse* (race) is thought to derive from the Arabic *ras* (meaning 'beginning', 'origin', 'head'). It entered the German language in the seventeenth century, as a loan word from English and French, and until the mid-nineteenth century was spelled with a 'c' as *Race*.[1] However, in Germany racial ideologies enjoyed the widest currency and the greatest political salience: the Third Reich became the first state in world history whose dogma and practice was racism. Was this predictable? Was there a form of German *Sonderweg* in the development and diffusion of racial ideologies? If so, when did this begin? What does one mean by 'race' and 'racism'?[2]

RACIAL-ANTHROPOLOGICAL THEORIES

'Blacks and Whites are not distinct types of people, for they belong to one tribe, and yet to two different races.'[3] With these words, written in 1775, Immanuel Kant both defined, and at the same time delimited, the concept of race. There were obviously different human races, however these belonged to a single 'genus', because they 'constantly produce fruitful children with one another, regardless of the great varieties which can otherwise be found in their form'. It followed that the differences between the various human races were no guide to their 'value'. Most subsequent racial ideologues ignored this last crucial qualification. They assumed that physical and psychological differences between individuals and races were an indication of their relative worth, and went on to construct racial hier-archies reflecting this assertion. In the late eighteenth century these claims were largely based upon external physical criteria. For example, the German theologian Johann Kaspar Lavater (1741–1801) attempted to deduce spiritual and psychological characteristics from physiognomy.[4] The Dutch anatomist Pieter Camper (1722–89) measured the 'facial angles' of members of different races, in order to categorise them according to corporal stature and beauty.[5] The German physician Franz Joseph Gall (1758–1828) employed cranial measurement, in order, with the aid of this so-called phrenological method, to categorise the races in terms of intelligence, morality, and beauty.[6] In a book published in 1798, entitled *Outline of the History of Humanity*, the Göttingen philosopher Christoph Meiners (1745–1810) categorised the peoples of the world according to their 'beauty' or 'ugliness'.[7] The 'fair' peoples were superior to all others, in terms of both beauty and intellectual achievements. By contrast, the 'darker coloured peoples' were 'ugly' and 'semi-civilised'. A similar line of argument can be found in a book published in 1848 by the philosopher Carl Gustav Carus (1789–1869).[8] According to him, the universe was endowed with a soul which gradually took on material form: first, interstellar ether, then the solar system, and finally the planet Earth. In turn, the latter underwent a series of metamorphoses leading to the creation of Man. The complexions of the various human races reflected their degree of 'inner illumination'. The four great races were those of the dawn (yellow), day (white), sunset (red), and night (black). These races were also 'related' to bodily organs; the Whites to the brain and the Blacks to the genitals. Following on from this, Carus attributed 'the capacity for the highest spiritual development' to the 'peoples of the day'. The latter were therefore entitled to extend their 'power over all inhabited parts of the world', and to hold sway over the uncivilised, and ugly, 'peoples of the night'. These few examples suffice to demonstrate that the transparent objective of these representatives of anthropological racism was to legitimise European colonialism. The claim that Blacks are less beautiful, and less intelligent, than Whites is still axiomatic to racist discourse in Europe and North America. In this respect Germany was hardly unique. However it is worth noting that German racial ideologists propounded the view that Africans and Asians were of 'lesser racial value' at a time when the German states possessed no colonies, nor had any desire to do so.

Racial-anthropological theories also served to legitimise claims to hegemony among the European races themselves. This resulted in a very specific form of racist discourse, which developed in the late eighteenth and early nineteenth centuries. It had three distinct points of origin, which in the beginning were only loosely connected with one another. The first was a by-product of the value attached to ethno-cultural diversity by Herder, in his case as an attempt to redress the effects of French cultural and political hegemony.[9] Herder was anything but a racist. He explicitly rejected the concept of race, subscribed to a form of cultural relativism, detested everything that involved coercion and conquest, and believed that the various peoples of the world would one day come together like the branches of a tree. However his claim that each 'nation' disposed of a specific 'national character' and 'national spirit' gradually acquired exclusive overtones. Specifically, it became interlinked with a much older tradition of 'Teutomania'.[10] Teutomania, and its attendant ideology, had a long prehistory, commencing with the rediscovery of Tacitus' Germania. Humanists in the fifteenth and sixteenth centuries regarded Tacitus' descriptions of the ancient Germans as accurate rather than metaphoric. They failed to recognise that Tacitus' principal objective was to hold up a mirror in which his Roman fellow citizens would be able to reflect on their own moral shortcomings. In the literal, Renaissance, reading, the ancient German tribesmen were assumed to have been brave, simple, pure, and self-disciplined, as well as tall, blond, and blue-eyed in appearance. Although there were adherents of this ideology of the ancient Germans in Sweden too, its principal proponents were the Germans themselves. Herder also celebrated the 'tall, strong, and beautiful bodies' of the Germans, their 'enormous blue eyes filled with the spirit of restraint and loyalty', and their 'heroic cast of mind and great physical strength'. Moreover, the Germans had laid the foundations of European freedom, civilisation, and well-being, while defending it from the barbarians. It is important to bear in mind that these sentiments did not close his mind to the virtues of other peoples, most notably the Slavs, among whom his writings were highly esteemed. Put slightly differently, one could describe Herder's proto-nationalism as essentially cosmopolitan and emancipatory in character and intention.

Nonetheless, stereotypical representations of the ancient Germans multiplied in the form of vulgarised clichés like 'Germanic loyalty' or 'Germanic fortitude', which had unmistakably racist overtones. This Germanic cult fulfilled a twofold ideological function. Firstly, it represented a rejection of French claims to cultural and political hegemony. According to Arndt, Fichte, Jahn, and other national ideologists, the Germanic peoples were superior to the Latin French in corporal stature, beauty, bravery, and love of freedom. Secondly, the alleged cultural superiority of the Germans was also used to legitimise German rule over former West Slav and Polish territories. In this case, a number of ethnic stereotypes, some of which originated in the Middle Ages, were imbued with racist aspects. An example of this is the conceptual journey undergone by the slogan 'polnische Wirtschaft', or 'Polish mismanagement'. This was first used by the German Jacobin Johann Georg Forster (1754–94), as a means of encapsulating his distaste for the anarchic and oppressive character of the Polish noble Commonwealth.[11] However, his strictures upon a particular class soon slid into criticism of the Polish people as a whole. For in addition to his strictures upon the Polish *szlachta*, Forster condemned the 'Sarmatian brutality' of the Poles in general, including the peasant victims of noble arbitrariness. National stereotypes like these proliferated in the following period, chiefly as a means of legitimising Prussian rule over part of partitioned Poland. For example, in 1801 the Prussian historian Johann Georg Friedrich Reitemeier claimed that the 'uncleanliness' of the Slavs 'was notorious from the earliest times'.[12] Therefore the Slavs, and in particular the Poles, should consider themselves fortunate that the Germans had brought them 'civilisation and the comforts of luxury'. Conquest by the Germans was 'a revolution of the most beneficent sort'. This cultural–political form of imperialism was given an historical-messianic quality through the claim that the Germans had a 'mission' to resettle territories once inhabited by ancient Germanic tribes. Looked at in this way, the Slavs were history's squatters. Thus, in 1818, the historian Karl Adolf Menzel argued that the Germans had legitimate claims to those territories which 'were already inhabited by the Germans in primeval times', by which he meant those territories once inhabited by eastern German tribes.[13]

The notion that the Germans were 'bearers of civilisation' to areas once settled by the 'ancient Germans' became interconnected with Hegel's assertion that the Slavs, with the exception of the Russians, were 'peoples without a history'. The germanisation of former Slav territory was seen as an inevitable consequence of a presumptive 'cultural gradient', declining from west to east, and of a 'German drive to the east' which gradually assumed quasi-biological aspects. According to Moritz Wilhelm Heffter's *World Struggle of the Germans and Slavs* (1847), this last process was 'the necessary consequence of the cultural-historical, intellectual and moral superiority which the cultivated always enjoy over the uncultivated'.[14] Similar claims figured in a series of articles, by Heinrich Wuttke, published in the *Augsburger Allgemeine Zeitung* during 1846.[15] In a piece entitled 'Germany's Neighbours on the Slavic Frontier', Wuttke argued that 'a Germandom more mighty in force of arms, more dominant politically, and superior intellectually than the Slavs' would always push against, and prevail over, the latter. Similar arguments were employed by German liberals, who in the 1830s had lionised Polish *émigrés*, in the course of debates during the Frankfurt Parliament which disavowed the claims of resurgent Polish nationalism.[16] A putatively 'timeless' German 'drive' to the east was gradually imbued with the character of a gradual, but unstoppable process, akin to the regular migration of birds. An unreflective Social Darwinism also began to influence the terms of historical argument. This was clear in the case of Heinrich von Treitschke, who in an essay published in 1862 celebrated the 'pitiless racial struggle' which the 'Germans' had once waged against the heathen Prussians, Lithuanians, and Poles.[17] A form of 'magic' emanated from 'eastern German soil', for the latter had been 'fertilised' by 'the most noble German blood'. Although Treitschke's object was to give historical legitimisation to the process of 'germanising' Prussia's Polish minority, rather than to license further imperialist conquests, his racialist celebration of a (mythical) 'genocide' allegedly once practised against the Prussians and Slavs would soon become a means of legitimising claims to further territories in the east.

In addition to legitimising, and, in the Social Darwinian strain, 'proving' the necessity of European imperialism and intra-European nationality conflicts, racial-anthropological theories also served to legitimise claims to hegemony by particular classes within societies. This was notably the case in France. In his *Essai sur la noblesse de France*, published in 1735, the Count Henri de Boulainvilliers argued that the French nobility was descended from Frankish–Germanic conquerors, while the townsmen and peasantry were the descendants of the ancient Gauls.[18] This 'Frankish legend' was adopted by reactionary ideologists of the Restoration, notably Louis de Bonald and Joseph de Maistre, as well as by historians like Augustin Thierry, to underwrite the position of an insecure aristocracy. Among those who subscribed to this Frankish legend was the Count Joseph Arthur de Gobineau (1816–82). Gobineau claimed that his own family was descended from this ancient Frankish aristocracy. Despite the fact that this claim was false, Gobineau clung to it with considerable tenacity, probably in order to divert attention from the present painful realities of the Gobineau family. He had had an unsuccessful career as a middle-ranking diplomat, in the service of the parvenu Louis Bonaparte and, in his eyes, the equally detestable Third Republic. Gobineau regarded the latter as being symptomatic of a general decline. The question of why this decline had occurred was the main preoccupation of his *Essai sur l'inégalité des races humaines*, which was published between 1853 and 1855.[19]

In line with received racial-anthropological discourse, Gobineau claimed that the White, Yellow, and Black races were of 'unequal' value. However, he then proceeded to argue that the rise and fall of civilisations was racially determined. All high cultures in world history were the work of 'Aryans', and were based upon an aristocratic mode of rule. Cultures declined when this 'Aryan' ruling caste interbred with members of the 'racially less valuable' lower orders. This resulted, ineluctably, in rebellion by the 'racially less valuable' against the 'Aryan ruling race'. Rebellions of this sort had occurred in ancient Egypt, Greece, and Rome. Likewise, the French Ancien Régime had been destroyed by a revolt of the Gallic plebs against a ruling elite descended from the Frankish nobility. A similar fate awaited every civilisation in the world, as a consequence of general racial interbreeding, although the effects of the latter, it should be stressed, were construed in socio-cultural rather than biological terms. A society which acknowledged no racial or social differences would make no progress in the field of culture. Gobineau described the terminal state of decline in the following bleak terms: 'The peoples, no, the herds of people, would then be overcome by a dark desire to sleep, living insensitively in their nothingness, like the buffaloes ruminating in the stagnant puddles of the Pontine marshes.'[20] Initially, Gobineau's essay was virtually ignored. This was hardly surprising. His pessimistic outlook on the world, and the associative, unscientific, and ahistorical methods he used to rationalise his own social anxieties, were out of joint with the liberal, empirical, scientific spirit of the times.

RACIAL-HYGIENIC THEORIES

Unlike Gobineau, whose work initially only appealed to a handful of reactionary aesthetes, Charles Darwin's *On the Origins of Species by Means of Natural Selection, or the Preservation of Favoured Races in the Struggle for Life* enjoyed massive success after its appearance in 1859.[21] Darwin was a reclusive Victorian gentleman scholar of a liberal, progressive cast of mind. He was opposed to slavery, and strongly supported ideas of human equality by avoiding references to 'lower' or 'higher' races. He was concerned about poverty and established Friendly Societies in Kent. *The Origins* did not contain racial theories, and was almost exclusively concerned with plants and animals. Nonetheless, Darwin, rather than Gobineau, was the involuntary progenitor of racist ideology, for he was responsible for the theory of natural selection as the mechanism of evolution. Selection was to become central to all subsequent racist discourse.

It is important to emphasise here that Darwin himself was too intelligent and responsive to criticism to adhere to a fixed set of ideas, and that his theories themselves were composite and not intended for application to human society in a prescriptive sense. This was the 'achievement' of Social Darwinians, who unlike Darwin himself used terms like 'betterment' or 'progress' in a morally-loaded manner. Contrary to popular belief, Social Darwinism was not an exclusively right-wing concern. Social theorists who were politically antagonistic to each other could call themselves Darwinians simply by referring to different tendencies in Darwin's thought. This, and a generalised belief in science and progress, accounts for the existence of Social Darwinians who could be conservative, liberal, socialist, or Fascist.

According to Darwin, there was a constant struggle for existence in the plant and animal kingdoms. It would be won by those species which demonstrated that they were the most capable of adaption. These would be capable of reproduction. This process of natural selection would lead to the further development of the individual species. In order to counter criticism of the application of this theory to man, Darwin wrote *The Descent of Man*, in which he accounted for some human attributes by resorting to a theory of sexual selection. He also noted the counter-selective effects of modern civilisation, and suggested that breeding could make up for the diminishing impact of natural selection. This shift in his thought reflected the increasing influence upon him of his cousin Galton and the German zoologist Ernst Haeckel.

The extension of Darwin's theories to human society lent an air of scientific legitimisation to the various utopias involving selective breeding which had been propounded from antiquity onwards by, *inter alia*, Plato, More, and Campanella. Francis Galton (1822–1911) took the principle of selection further, in the interests of improving the biological health of the *human* race.[22] Healthy parents, by whom he meant members of the middle classes and the learned professions, should be encouraged to marry early and have as many children as possible. These should be issued with certificates of hereditary health. By contrast, those persons who failed this 'Passed in Genetics' test were to be encouraged to emigrate to the land of 'Cantsayanywhere'. Man, in other words, was to take control of his own evolutionary processes. Galton was the founder of hereditary health care, for which in 1883 he coined the term 'Eugenics', a programme for improving the human race by genetic means. The prescriptive measures were not confined to the question of 'judicious mating', but encompassed education, public health, and welfare. Darwin and Galton's ideas were gradually diffused throughout Europe and North America, where through the mediation of Herbert Spencer the notion of the 'survival of the fittest' was used to legitimise *laissez-faire* capitalism. Although the rampant individualist strain of Social Darwinism was not so successful in Germany, its collectivist and state interventionist variety was. The zoologist Ernst Haeckel (1834–1919) attempted to propagate Darwin's teachings, while converting them into a comprehensive quasi-humanist philosophy called 'Monism'.[23] This 'new philosophy' was to be 'based upon the real foundations of comparative zoology'. Its 'application to practical human affairs' would 'open up a new path to moral perfection'. Haeckel's 'Monism' encountered considerable criticism from conservatives, and enthusiasm from the Left who saw in him a champion of academic freedom, anticlericalism, and collectivist solutions to social problems. However, neither his detractors nor supporters appeared concerned with Haeckel's racist presuppositions. These were much in evidence in his *History of Natural Creation*, a book which enjoyed considerable popularity within the German labour movement.[24] According to Haeckel's brand of anthropological racism, the 'central races' were the 'most highly developed and perfect': 'No other types of people can be compared either physically or intellectually with the central peoples. They alone have actually made history. They alone have been responsible for the cultural achievements which appear to raise the human race above the rest of nature.'[25] Within the 'central types of people', the 'indogermanic' race was superior to the 'hamosemitic' peoples. By virtue of their 'more highly developed brains they would triumph over all other races and in the struggle for existence', and 'cast the net of their dominion over the entire world'. However, in order to achieve this hegemony, selective breeding measures would be necessary. The model here was above all ancient Sparta, where the newly born were subjected to physical examination and selection:

> All of the weak, sickly, or physically deficient children were slain. Only those children who were completely healthy and strong were allowed to live, and only they were later allowed to reproduce. Therewith the Spartan race was not merely maintained in selected strength and virtues, but rather with each generation their physical perfection was increased. Certainly, in large measure, the Spartan people owed their unique level of masculine strength and tough heroism to this artificial selection or breeding.[26]

This was not merely intended for metaphorical effect. Haeckel sincerely believed in the necessity for, and possibilities of, racial selective breeding.

In a book, entitled *The Riddle of Life*, published in 1904, he explicitly advocated the killing of the sick:

> What profit does humanity derive from the thousands of cripples who are born each year, from the deaf and dumb, from cretins, from those with incurable hereditary defects etc. who are kept alive artificially and then raised to adulthood? . . . What an immense aggregate of suffering and pain these depressing figures represent for the unfortunate sick people themselves, what a fathomless sum of worry and grief for their families, what a loss in terms of private resources and costs to the state for the healthy! How much of this loss and suffering could be obviated, if one finally decided to liberate the totally incurable from their indescribable suffering with a dose of morphia.[27]

Haeckel was not merely a harmless and uninfluential ideologist-cum-scientist. His eccentric 'philosophy' was propagated through the 'Monist League', which he founded in 1906; and his ideas concerning racial selective breeding began to filter into rather more respectable scientific circles. The physician Wilhelm Schallmeyer (1857–1919) was particularly significant in this last respect.

In 1900 Schallmeyer had won first prize in a competition sponsored by the industrialist Friedrich Alfred Krupp, in response to the question 'What can we learn from the principles of the theory of evolution for application to domestic political development and the laws of the State?'[28] Schallmeyer's response was published in 1903 as *Heredity and Selection in the Life of Nations: A Study in Political Science on the Basis of the New Biology*. According to Schallmeyer, the state had the duty to secure the biological capacity of its people. This would involve measures designed to increase the birthrate and the racial quality of its people. In this connection, Schallmeyer specified encouraging early marriage, the introduction of earnings-related child allowances, special payments to mothers, and licensed polygamy for especially racially 'valuable' men. However, all of these measures were only to be available to those who had been examined by physicians expert in 'socio-biological sciences'. By contrast, those who failed the examination, and who were hence not to be issued with a certificate of fitness to marry, were to be prevented from reproducing. Schallmeyer thought that those of 'lesser hereditary value' should be isolated and compulsorily sterilised. It should be noted, however, that Schallmeyer made no attempt to relate his 'social biology' to racial-anthropological teachings. According to him, there were no pure races in Europe, and attempts to produce racial 'thoroughbreds' were as meaningless as the preferential treatment of the 'Nordic race'.

This last matter preoccupied Alfred Ploetz (1860–1940). His central concern was reflected in a book entitled *The Efficiency of our Race and the Protection of the Weak*, which was published in 1895.[29] 'Our' race was the 'West Aryan' or 'Germanic race', which was the 'most outstanding civilised race', an assertion 'about which there is nothing more to say'. However, the 'efficiency' of this 'Germanic race' was threatened by 'growing protection of the weak'. Various measures would have to be taken to halt this last process. The conception of a child was 'not to be left to accident, or to an over-excited moment, but rather regulated according to the principles which science has determined for the circumstances and times'. If, despite these 'principles', a deformed child should still be produced, then a 'college of physicians, which decides concerning issues of citizenship, should prepare a gentle death, shall we say through a small dose of morphia'. During wartime, only inferior persons should be sent to the front. Ploetz described these measures as 'hygienic'. Since they were ostensibly designed to improve the 'qualities of our race', he coined the term 'racial hygiene'. Other scientists continued to use the term 'eugenics'. Both tendencies ultimately reflected changing scientific conceptions of heredity. The hitherto dominant Lamarckian theory on the hereditability of environmentally-acquired characteristics, which influenced Darwin's theory of evolution, was superseded by others, which stressed genetic factors. The most extreme statement of the independence of heredity from the environment was August Weismann's theory of an autonomous, immutable 'germ plasm'.[30] Put simply, these discoveries ruled out the prospect of improving the mental or physical abilities of successive generations through education or sport, while emphasising the predeterminedness of, for example, criminality or alcoholism. In this view of things, human beings became aggregates of 'negative' or 'positive' biological materials, their value as individuals being increasingly overshadowed by their contribution to the future of the collective, which could be construed as either the human 'race' in general or one 'race' in particular. Again, it is important to stress that there is no automatic correlation between these scientific ideas and types of political persuasion. Alfred Grotjahn (1869–1931), a theoretician of social hygiene with links with the right wing of the SPD (to whom he owed his appointment as professor of social hygiene at Berlin University in 1920), advocated a combination of environmental improvement, isolation, and sterilisation as a means of 'amortising' those elements who did not fit the socialist's profile of the 'respectable' working classes. This included the insane, the 'workshy', people with sexually-transmitted diseases, alcoholics, accident victims and so on. Where science led, socialism followed. Unfortunately, these tendencies in the German labour movement have not received the attention they deserve from 'labour' historians.[31]

These scientific ideas did not unfold in a social void, and nor, as we shall see, were they the exclusive property of professional scientists. The scientists discussed above, and their adherents in applied health care, came from particular social classes, belonged to increasingly ramified professional structures, and lived within societies undergoing profound social and economic change. Specifically, these members of the educated bourgeoisie saw their urban 'living space' threatened by hordes of fecund proletarians bearing the physical and psychological imprint of deplorable living and working conditions. Eugenics and racial hygiene were one response to the 'social question'.[32] While, socialist or otherwise, these responses also undoubtedly reflected genuine concern for suffering humanity, they also mirrored the frustrated modernising arrogance of the educated bourgeoisie towards people apparently impervious to the verities of human betterment and progress, whether espoused by right-wingers or socialists. The debate about the origins and solution of the problem assumed ever narrower forms, while the areas of professional medical competence broadened into schools, prisons, or welfare services. Social Darwinists contributed the identification of low social position with 'unfitness', or in other words, the idea that the poor must be 'unfit' because they had failed in the 'struggle of life'. In some circles, concern about differential rates of fertility between the upper and lower social classes was related to the 'counter-selective' impact of modern medicine and welfare, a notion which bore the imprint of Darwin as mediated by Galton. Put simply, welfare was obstructing the 'natural' elimination of the 'unfit'. Questions of quality also began to enter the orbit of questions of cost. Long before the health and welfare system faced a financial crisis, some pundits were applying cost:benefit calculations to the 'asocial' and 'handicapped'. For example, in 1911 an essay competition solicited responses to the question: 'What do inferior racial elements cost the state and society?' Although eugenicists differed about the comparable merits of 'negative' and 'positive' measures, the balance of opinion began to tilt towards the former. The North American example, specifically the introduction of a Sterilisation Law in 1907 by the state of Indiana, appeared to lend this questionable practice an air of modern, democratic reasonableness. However, debates in Germany on these questions were overtaken by events. Specifically, the outbreak of the First World War resulted in a renewed emphasis upon population quantity rather than quality. The question of whether or not chronic alcoholics or habitual criminals should be sterilised was hardly the burning issue of 1914–18, when numbers counted. The issue of quality resurfaced in the early 1920s. This was partly because of concern about the perceived 'qualitative imbalance' resulting from the war's 'mass annihilation of our genetically most valuable elements', partly a reflection of paranoia over the fecundity of neighbouring races. Renewed debate also occurred because interested parties deliberately forced 'negative' eugenics on to the political agenda. Specifically, in 1923 the Zwickau District Health Officer, Gerhard Boeters, went public with the information that surgeons in his district were already sterilising the mentally handicapped without legal sanction. Boeters tried to prompt the legislature into retrospective legitimisation through the draft *Lex Zwickau*. Although his draft was rejected by the Reichstag in 1925, the onset of the Depression further reduced the gap between scientific and demographic advocates of 'negative' eugenics and those engaged in the making of policy in an austere financial climate. Mass unemployment and a corresponding fall in tax receipts at all levels of government raised questions concerning the allocation of resources. Questions of cost served to lower the ethical threshold of politicians, who were also confronted by the 'weight' of professional scientific opinion and the irrefutably gloomy prognostications of their own statisticians and demographic planners. By July 1932, the Prussian government had formulated a draft Reich Sterilisation Law, which it forwarded to the Reich government that winter. By the time it arrived, the Reich government was in the hands of Adolf Hitler.

With Hitler very much in mind, it must be stressed that discussion of these questions was not confined to scientists, politicians, or government experts. Alongside, and often drawing from, the ideas we have been considering, were a host of scientifically illiterate pundits who subscribed to selective breeding in the interests of various types of utopia. Bereft of 'objective' scientific legitimisation, the ideological and inhuman nature of their work is immediately transparent. This is clear in the case of the philosopher Friedrich Nietzsche. Prescriptively, in 1880, Nietzsche wrote that 'the tendency must be towards the rendering extinct of the wretched, the deformed, the degenerate'.[33] He ventured the following 'activist' recommendations:

> Satisfaction of desire should not be practised so that the race as a whole suffers, i.e. that choice no longer occurs, and that anyone can pair off and produce children. The extinction of many types of people is just as desirable as any form of reproduction . . . Much more so: marriage only 1) with the aim of higher development; 2) in order

to leave behind the fruit of such persons. Concubinage is enough for all the rest, with measures to prevent conception. – We must do away with this crass lightheartedness. These geese must not marry! Marriage must become much less frequent! Go through the towns and ask yourselves whether these people should reproduce! Let them go to their whores![34]

Eight years later he outlined a series of measures for racial selective breeding.

Notwithstanding Nietzsche's interest in hyper-aristocratic quality, he accompanied the eugenicists along a dirigiste, technocratic, and inhuman route, albeit to a different destination. Beyond him and the scientists were a host of outright cranks, two of whom warrant some attention. Willibald Hentschel recommended the creation of 'stud villages', in which men selected according to racial criteria should be encouraged to produce as many 'highly valuable' little Germans as possible, through the good offices of up to ten women.[35] Naturally this sounds misogynistic and ridiculous. However, there was sufficient overlap with 'serious' racial-hygienic and eugenic science for this lunacy to gain a certain purchase. Hentschel became the leading ideological light of the Artamanen League, whose members included, *inter alia*, Heinrich Himmler, Walther Darré, and Rudolf Hoess, the later commandant of Auschwitz, all of whom were indebted to the racial utopia propagated by their erstwhile mentor. Jorg Lanz, who preferred to style himself Lanz von Liebenfels, was somewhat further out in a paranoid, occultist darkness.[36] Lanz recommended the selective breeding of blonde, Aryan supermen. To this end, all suitable candidates were to be subjected to a stringent racial test. These fantasies were propagated through a journal called 'Ostara: Newspaper for Blond People'. Although these ideas were abstruse and their advocates crazed, they nonetheless had a certain political effect. For example, many members of the Thule Society, who later supported the NSDAP, knew and respected Lanz's ideas. This may also have been the case with Adolf Hitler.

Were there direct connections between this scientific, philosophical, and pseudo-scientific preoccupation with racial selective breeding and the racial policies of the Third Reich? This question is bound to arise from an *ex post facto* perspective, given the undeniable efforts of the Nazi regime to implement selective breeding while eliminating those who failed to correspond with their criteria of racial 'value'. However the question is wrongly posed, or rather artificially abstracted from a further important development, namely racially-motivated anti-Semitism.

RACIAL ANTI-SEMITIC THEORIES

By no means all of the racial hygienicists and eugenicists were either politically conservative or anti-Semites.[37] This last qualification applies to many of the scientists, pseudo-scientists, and for that matter Nietzsche too. Responsibility for fusing racial-hygienic and Social Darwinist ideas with anti-Semitism may be attributed to the (elective German) Englishman Houston Stewart Chamberlain (1855–1927).[38] According to Chamberlain, the Germanic peoples, but especially the Germans in the narrow sense, were superior to all other peoples in every respect. This superiority, which was based upon intellectual abilities rather than physical characteristics, was being threatened by another race, namely the Jews. For Chamberlain, the Jews were the Devil incarnate. They represented a demonic threat to the chosen German race. The reason for this was that, in contrast to the Jews, the Germans had no religion identical with their race. Christianity was essentially Jewish.

This rather unoriginal, racially-motivated attack upon Christianity had consequences for both the Churches and the Jews. Instead of energetically refuting this nonsense, many Protestant and Roman Catholic theologians appeared to accept Chamberlain's views, for they themselves held the Jews responsible for liberalism, socialism, and Communism, not to speak of anti-Semitism itself. All of these evils were the product of secularisation and modernisation promoted by the Jews. The latter were once again made the whipping-boys for all adverse secular developments. This in itself was hardly new. However, the way in which racial anti-Semitism closed the only alternative option, namely that of conversion to Christianity, was an entirely novel development. Baptism no longer 'liberated' the Jews from a racially, rather than confessionally, defined 'Jewishness'. The Jews were thus defined, and hence excluded, as the embodiments of general evils. Old legends and prejudices, notoriously that concerning ritual murder, were revived, and combined with more up-to-date conspiracy theories like the falsified 'Protocols of the Elders of Zion'. As the embodiment of evil, the Jews were literally capable of anything and everything. This included responsibility for the alleged racial deterioration of the German people, and the deliberate sabotaging of racial-hygienic solutions to the 'social question' made available by modern science.

Racial anti-Semitic theories were not an exclusively German phenomenon. However in Germany they appear to have enjoyed especially wide currency and a high degree of political instrumentalisation.[39] Although in contrast to eastern Europe Germany's Jews were highly assimilated, their

Emancipation, i.e. the achievement of formal legal equality, occurred relatively late, in 1869–71. Emancipation coincided with an equally belated, and comparatively rapid, industrialisation of the German economy, and hence (partial) modernisation of German society. The first great crisis of the German capitalist economy, the *Gründerkrise* of the early 1870s, coincided and was connected with the first wave of political anti-Semitism. The allegedly powerful and wealthy Jews were held responsible for the negative accompaniments of rapid industrialisation and modernisation. This convenient fiction found silent assent among Germany's ruling elites, for this modern strain of anti-Semitism had a negative, integrative utility in so far as fear of enemies, within and without, would bind the majority population more closely to the existing social order. This particularly affected the Jews after the First World War. Germany's Jews were held responsible for the 'stab in the back' and the Revolution which had allegedly resulted in Germany's defeat, despite the fact that cemeteries were lined with the graves of young Jews who had fallen for their Fatherland. The Jews were also held responsible for the deployment by the French of colonial occupation troops on the Rhine, who then proceeded to seduce German women, thus undermining the 'purity' of the 'German race'. German and foreign Jews were also allegedly involved in prostitution and the white slave trade, through which they hoped to encourage the spread of syphilis and other sexually-transmitted diseases which would damage the 'hereditary properties' of the 'Aryan–Germanic race'. Finally, 'Berlin Jews' were even attempting to prevent the racial-hygienic improvement of the German people. The writer Artur Dinter plumbed further depths in racial conspiracy theory.[40] In a novel, published in 1918, entitled *Sin Against the Blood*, he told the story of a 'racially pure', blonde, blue-eyed German woman who was seduced by a Jew. Although she later managed to get away from him, and subsequently married an 'Aryan', she and her husband nonetheless produced 'typically Jewish-looking' children. Her 'hereditary properties' had been permanently corrupted by a casual encounter with a Jew. This salacious and quasi-pornographic nonsense was sold in hundreds of thousands of copies. Writers like Dinter, Lanz, and scores of others found a sympathetic readership in Germany after the First World War. One of them was probably Adolf Hitler.

HITLER'S RACISM

It is not certain which racialist works Hitler actually read.[41] There is no 'man who gave Hitler his ideas' in a simplistic teleological sense. However, it is certain that Hitler knew the most important racial-anthropological, racial-hygienic, and racial anti-Semitic theories, and in *Mein Kampf* turned them into a comprehensive, self-contained, if totally insane, racial-political programme. His racial discourse began with the following 'truths':

> Even the most superficial observation shows that Nature's restricted form of propagation and increase is an almost rigid basic law of all the innumerable forms of expression of her vital urge. Every animal mates only with a member of the same species. The titmouse seeks the titmouse, the finch the finch, the stork the stork, the field mouse the field mouse, the dormouse the dormouse, the wolf the she-wolf, etc.[42]

On a first reading, these observations seem involuntarily comic. In reality, both this passage and the paragraphs which follow contain three axioms fundamental to racist thought. The first is the claim that only those living things which produce healthy offspring with one another constitute a race – a definition of race which can already be found in the works of Kant. Secondly, Hitler presupposed the existence of 'higher' and 'lesser' races, a notion common to virtually every racial ideologist since the late eighteenth century. Following Gobineau and others, Hitler claimed that the 'Aryans' alone were the 'culture-creating race'. The Chinese and Japanese were merely 'culture-bearing'; the other races, i.e. Blacks and Slavs, of lesser value, while the 'Jewish race' was the embodiment of evil. The third axiom was that among humans as well as animals there was, and should be, an 'urge towards racial purity'. Interbreeding between the races would result in 'bastardisation' and a deterioration of racial 'value'. This idea can also be found in the work of reactionary aestheticians from Gobineau onwards, and it is expressed in a 'scientific' guise in the research of men like Eugen Fischer. In 1913 Fischer published a study of the Rehoboter Bastards, or the children of Boers and Hottentots in South-West Africa.[43] Without the slightest evidence, Fischer claimed that the children of so-called mixed marriages were of 'lesser racial quality'. Their intellectual achievements increased or decreased according to the proportion of European blood. However, they would never create their own culture, for they required constant European leadership.

In the course of a chapter devoted to 'Nation and Race', Hitler dwelt upon the need to prevent 'miscegenation' while promoting racial selective breeding. Since there were still 'considerable remnants of unmixed Nordic–Germanic people' in the 'body of the German people', one should 'not only gather together and maintain the most valuable remnants of primeval racial elements, but slowly and surely lead them to a commanding position'. Although Hitler mentioned no names, it is clear that here he was indebted to the ideas of racial-hygienicists. It is not particularly important whether he had actually read the work of scientists such as Haeckel, Schallmayer, and Ploetz, or whether, more probably, he derived his ideas from the sub-scientific undergrowth of tracts produced by Hentschel, Lanz, and Dinter. In a subsequent chapter, entitled 'World View and Party', Hitler summed up his racial–ideological presuppositions. The 'völkisch world view . . . by no means believes in an equality of the races, but along with their difference it recognises their higher or lesser value and feels itself obligated, through this knowledge, to promote the victory of the better and the stronger, and demand the subordination of the inferior and weaker in accordance with the eternal will that dominates this universe'.[44]

How was this 'victory of the better and stronger' to be achieved? In *Mein Kampf*, Hitler outlined a catalogue of measures which can be found in racial-hygienic and eugenicist literature from Galton, Haeckel, and Schallmayer onwards. However, the terminology employed was rather different. Hitler eschewed technical scientific terms like Weissmann's 'germ plasm' or Mendelian 'hereditary properties' in favour of calls for the 'maintenance of the purity of the blood'. Firstly, care should be taken 'to ensure that only those who are healthy produce children'. The 'obstruction of the reproductive capacities of those with syphilis, tuberculosis, the hereditarily burdened, cripples and cretins' was unavoidable. He repeated this last point, which again can be found in the work of Haeckel, Ploetz, and Schallmayer, in countless speeches and writings before 1933. The corollary of these negative eugenic measures, involved 'positive' attempts to increase the birthrate. Again, in both *Mein Kampf* and subsequent speeches and writings, Hitler recommended a number of measures, which some historians have mistakenly regarded as 'modern', or even 'socially revolutionary'. These measures included the introduction of child allowances, public housing projects, the promotion of equal education opportunities for working-class children, and so forth. In reality, all of these projected measures were motivated by racial considerations, firstly, because both 'alien races' and the 'less valuable elements' of the German population were excluded from the benefits of Nazi 'social policy', and secondly, because all of these social improvements were designed to encourage the reproduction of certain types of people.

Again, in *Mein Kampf*, Hitler made no secret of this objective. He advocated the acquisition of 'outlying colonies', which were to be settled by 'bearers of the highest racial purity'. The latter were to be selected by especially constituted 'commissions of racial experts'. Only those applicants deemed to be 'racially valuable' were to receive an 'attestation (of the right) to settle'. Again, Hitler refrained from acknowledging his intellectual debt to those eugenicists and racial-hygienicists who had argued along precisely these lines for several decades. In contrast to racial-hygienicists, Hitler expected no immediate results from these measures. The initial object was 'at least to eliminate the germ of our present physical and intellectual decline'. Only after the 'six-hundred-year obstruction of the reproductive capacities and possibilities to reproduce of the physically degenerate and the mentally ill', and through 'the consciously planned promotion of the fertility of the healthiest bearers of the nation', could a level of recovery be achieved 'which is hardly imaginable today'.[45]

However, recovery would only be possible if victory were achieved in the 'struggle' against the Jews. This struggle was both absolutely necessary and indeed willed by God. As Hitler wrote, 'I believe today that I am acting in the sense of the Almighty Creator: by warding off the Jews, I am fighting for the Lord's work.' The alternative outcome was distinctly bleak. For should 'the Jew, with the help of his Marxian creed . . . conquer the nations of this world, his crown will become the funeral wreath of humanity, and once again this planet, empty of mankind, will move through the ether as it did thousands of years ago'. This plangent, pseudo-eschatological vision reflects the second and most important element in Hitler's racism, namely racial anti-Semitism. Virtually everything Hitler thought about the Jews was contained in this passage. Unlike other anti-Semites, Hitler made no distinctions between German and foreign, rich and poor, liberal, conservative, socialist, or Zionist, religious or non-religious, baptised or unbaptised Jews. In his eyes, there was only 'the Jew'. 'The Jew' was striving for mastery of the peoples of the world. His most pernicious weapon was 'Marxism', whereby Hitler made no distinction between its Communist and socialist variants. If 'the Jew' should manage to win this ongoing 'struggle', then the result would be the downfall not only of the Germans, but of all peoples, and indeed of the world as a whole. 'The Jew' represented evil incarnate, performing for Hitler much the same function as the Devil does for many Christians. It was not fortuitous that in this connection Hitler used religious terms like 'creed', or that he employed apocalyptic language to describe the threat represented by 'the Jew'. The latter was the embodiment of absolute evil: the 'struggle' against 'him' was both righteous and good.

According to Hitler, the Jews in Germany and elsewhere were the champions of 'Marxism', the 'dictatorship of the proletariat', 'democracy' and the 'majority principle'. Jews were responsible for the outbreak of the First World War, and for the war's catastrophic outcome, namely Germany's collapse in 1918. They were the 'wire-pullers' behind the German Revolution, and the 'fathers' of the Weimar Constitution. Following the Revolution, they exercised their baleful influence in every political party – excepting the NSDAP – within the bureaucracy, the economy, cultural life, and the mass media. Other countries were either ruled by 'the Jew', like 'Jewish-Bolshevik Russia', or controlled by Jews, through their alleged dominance of 'world finance'. Both of these apparently polar opposites – namely Communism and 'finance' capitalism – were merely instruments designed to further plans for Jewish 'world domination', as essayed in the Protocols of the Elders of Zion. Even the propagation of the 'Jewish universal language' of Esperanto was a device designed to achieve this same end.

There was little in this Jewish conspiracy theory that was new, or which could not be found in the ravings of anti-Semites in other countries. Again, there was little originality in Hitler's coupling of the Jews with the question of prostitution, although in this case one would have to go back to the semi-pornographic tracts of Lanz and Dinter to find the same degree of obsessional and prurient concern with this issue. Hitler devoted twenty pages to this problem in *Mein Kampf*. He regarded prostitution as the 'pace-setter' of syphilis. Indeed, for him, in 1925–6 (!), 'the struggle against syphilis . . . was the task facing the nation', and indeed, humanity as a whole. This 'struggle' was one of the 'touchstones of the racial value' of a nation. The race which failed this 'test' would 'die out, or forfeit its position to healthier or hardier races capable of greater resistance'. In order to prevent this unhappy outcome, Hitler proposed a series of measures, ranging from 'the pitiless isolation' and 'sterilisation of the incurably ill', through the 'iron hardening' of youth in order to eradicate their sexual desires, to the facilitation of early marriage, and philogenerative welfare measures. However, these measures would be otiose unless the struggle against 'the Jew' was radicalised. 'The Jew' was responsible for prostitution, the spread of syphilis, and the 'spiritual prostitution' of the German people. Directly and indirectly 'he' sought to achieve the 'racial decomposition', 'bastardisation', and 'poisoning of the blood' of the 'body of the German nation', either through surrogates, notably French colonial troops 'planted' upon the Rhineland, or directly through 'his' own marital or extra-marital relations with 'Aryan' women. Assuming the sexual passivity of the latter, Hitler emulated Dinter's quasi-pornographic and prurient interest in this subject: 'With satanic joy in his face, the black-haired

Jewish youth lurks in wait for the unsuspecting girl whom he defiles with his blood, thus stealing her from her people. With every means he tries to destroy the racial foundations of the people he has set out to subjugate.'[46] In this oft-cited but sometimes underrated passage, Hitler both fused and developed the ideologies of anti-Semitism and racism. The Jews were accused not only of trying to subjugate the German nation politically, but now of systematically undermining its 'racial foundations'. Racial-hygienic measures would therefore only be meaningful once the 'Jewish Question' had been solved. What was the point of improving the racial health of the German population, if it was continually liable to subversion by the racial arch-enemy? In other words, Hitler had succeeded in combining and radicalising all previous strains of religious, social, and racial anti-Semitism: 'the Jew' was evil personified, therefore all means were appropriate and necessary in the fight against 'him'. The language used to describe 'the Jew' suggests one of the means he had in mind. They were 'spongers', 'parasites', 'poisonous mushrooms', 'rats', 'leeches', 'bacilli', 'tuberculosis bacilli' and so forth. Although some historians like to imagine that these metaphors were merely used for rhetorical effect, unaccountably ignoring the palpable inner violence of the man using them, the terms employed suggested one possible fate for the Jews, namely extermination.

Hitler's racism therefore consisted of the following elements. Firstly, there were differences in the value of individual races. Secondly, the 'Aryans' were the most 'valuable' race. Thirdly, if the 'Aryan' race inter-bred with 'less valuable races', it would inevitably decline into extinction, a development which would have to be prevented. Fourthly, not only the purity but also the health of the 'Aryan' race, had to be maintained and improved. This would entail measures designed to increase the numbers of children born to healthy members of the 'Aryan' race, while preventing the reproduction of sickly or criminal 'elements'. Lastly, this would only be meaningful if, at the same time, the Jews as both the absolute enemy and subverters of the 'Aryan' race were isolated and eliminated either spatially or physically. Hitler's racism was neither original nor without inner contradictions, either in its parts or as a whole. However, there can be no doubt that Hitler believed in what he said and wrote, and that, notwith-standing any shifts in emphasis due to the exigencies of elections, his racism had a programmatic character, namely the realisation of a particu-larly barbarous utopia. It must also be stressed, however, that this racial programme was in no sense implemented by Hitler alone, and that his initial responsibility may well have consisted in lending the authority of a charismatic and popular dictator to pre-existing scientific, political, and publicistic forays into an ethical void. Which persons and institutions were responsible for designing and implementing policy in a climate which was at once amoral and authoritarian?

CHAPTER THREE

BARBARISM INSTITUTIONALISED: RACISM AS STATE POLICY

RACIAL LEGISLATION

'Above all, I charge the leadership of the nation, as well as its followers, to a rigorous adherence to our racial laws and to a merciless resistance against the poisoner of all peoples – international Jewry.'[1] This was one of the last sentences Hitler committed to paper. It is from his 'Political Testament', dictated in a bunker beneath the ashes and collapsing masonry of Berlin. Which racial laws did he have in mind, shortly before the end? Certainly, those which were directed against the Jews, described here as 'the poisoner of all peoples'.[2] The first anti-Jewish laws were promulgated in April 1933, in the wake of the unsuccessful boycott action earlier that month. Legislation was designed to fulfil the twofold objective of assuaging rabid grassroots Party activists, while not alienating either Hindenburg, or the Nazis' conservative coalition partners, by appearing to license disorder. Legislation commenced with the Law for the Restoration of the Professional Civil Service of 7 April 1933, followed by measures against Jewish physicians, teachers, and students, on the 22nd and 25th of the same month.[3] The former sanctioned the dismissal of both the politically undesirable and 'non-Aryans' from the public service; the latter attempted either to remove Jews from, or to restrict their access too, the professions, while encouraging 'Aryans' to dispense with the services of Jews. All of these measures were hastily cobbled together, with a number of concessions to Hindenburg regarding categories of exemption, notably war veterans. The Nazis seem to have been taken by surprise by the number of Jews who could claim exemption on these grounds. Between 1933 and 1939 these measures were then extended to cover the 'dejewification' of other occupational groups, a process which will be described in detail in the chapter on the persecution of the Jews below.

The next wave of anti-Semitic legislation, in 1935, was designed to achieve legal discrimination, segregation, and precision in the question of who was a Jew. Discrimination began with the Military Service Law of May 1935 which made 'Aryan' ancestry mandatory for service in the armed forces.[4] The Nuremberg Laws, promulgated after hasty consultations during the Party Rally that September, were the product of several circumstances:[5] firstly, Hitler's desire to announce something more substantial to the Party faithful than a law forbidding Jews to hoist the national flag; secondly, the desire of the legal profession and registry officials for greater clarity concerning how to define a Jew. As a commentator in the journal of the League of German Jurists crisply observed:

> While logic and consistency have traditionally been a special province of jurists and lawyers, it appears that since the seizure of power these faculties have eluded them. In looking through our racial laws it becomes apparent that we are lacking a certain conceptual clarity in using such terms as 'race', 'racial hygiene', 'eugenics', and others which fall into the same category. They are frequently used with different and contradictory meanings.[6]

Finally, the Party leadership was under pressure from both grass-roots activists and committed anti-Semites like Streicher, or the Reich Physicians Leader, Gerhard Wagner, to regulate marital and sexual relations between 'Aryans' and Jews. Under the ensuing Law for the Protection of German Blood and Honour, Jews were forbidden to marry or have extra-marital sexual relations with 'Aryan' partners. Under the Reich Citizenship Law, Jews were redefined as 'subjects', while 'political rights', which by this time were notional, were restricted to 'citizens of the Reich'. Although the official spokesmen of German Jewry were relieved that years of insecurity and uncertainty were apparently over, the Nuremberg Laws had officially rendered the Jews second-class citizens. These laws were accompanied by intensive discussions upon who was to be considered a Jew. The result was the First Supplementary Decree of the Reich Citizenship Law of 14 November 1935, which specified the criteria for determining who was a full or part Jew.[7] Ironically enough, these criteria were based upon a religious, rather than a scientific, definition of race.

These anti-Semitic laws, and the subsequent decrees on their implementation, continue to preoccupy historians. This interest is warranted, for in addition to shedding light on the *ad hoc* way in which the regime legislated, these measures ultimately created a pseudo-legal basis for later policies, including mass murder. However, while Hitler may have regarded these laws as being the most significant creation of his regime, they were not unique. Anti-Semitic legislation was accompanied by other laws and decrees, whose object was the 'racial-hygienic improvement' of the 'body of the German nation'.[8] Both 'alien' races and 'racially less valuable' members of the German population were excluded from their positive provisions. 'Elements' of 'lesser racial value' in the German population were subject to a series of 'negative' measures, ranging from compulsory abortion, castration, and sterilisation, via commitment to asylums, and on to murder. These racial-hygienic laws and measures were part of a continuum ranging from the progressively more covert measures taken against the Jews to initiatives in social policy and welfare which the regime publicised at every opportunity. The connections were both immanent, and central to the thinking of the politicians and experts in racial hygiene who were responsible for these measures. Consequently, it is impossible to study either anti-Semitic or racial-hygienic measures in isolation; the two were indivisible parts of the whole. Hence the following account of initiatives in 'social policy' is designed to bring out the underlying racial objectives.

One of the earliest, and most popular, initiatives in this field was the Law for the Reduction of Unemployment of 1 June 1933.[9] This introduced marriage loans which couples could then pay off by having children. However, the loans were conditional upon the woman giving up paid employment. This had been the goal of a campaign against so-called 'double-earners' waged by both the Nazis and the Catholic Centre Party during the Weimar Republic. However, the desire to disburden the labour market of married women workers, in the interests of reducing the number of unemployed men, was no longer the primary object of policymakers. The Law was also designed to force women back into their 'original' role as wives and mothers, in line with Nazi and conservative thinking about the 'natural' role of women. However, the Law also had a racial objective. According to the first decree on its implementation of 20 June 1933, loans could be refused 'if one of the prospective marriage partners is suffering from a hereditary or mental or physical illness which renders their marriage undesirable to the whole national community'.[10] A second supplementary decree, issued a month later, stipulated that all applicants for a marriage loan would have to undergo medical examination.[11] This opened a way for the racial registering of the population. Further philogenerative welfare measures, such as travel concessions and tax benefits for large families introduced in October 1934 and September

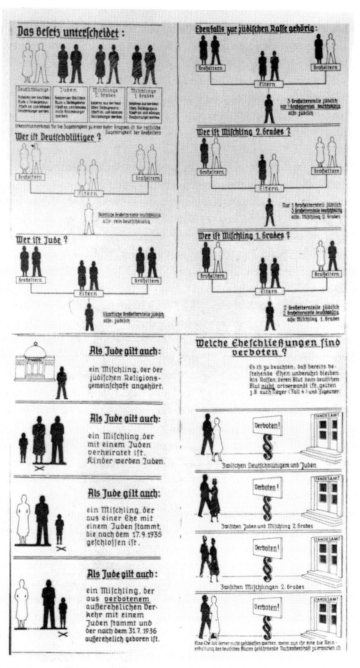

3.1 Diagram illustrating the ways in which the Nuremberg Laws (1935) defined who was a Jew; bottom right: marriages which were prohibited under the terms of the Laws.

1935, were explicitly denied to persons deemed to be of 'lesser racial value'.[12] A general decree dated 26 September 1935 stipulated that only 'citizens of the Reich according to the Reich Citizenship Law of 15 September 1935 and their children, in so far as they are free from hereditary mental or physical illnesses' should be allowed to take advantage of these welfare measures.[13] From this time onwards, social policy was indivisible from the 'selection' of 'alien' races and those of 'lesser racial value'.

Initially, members of 'alien' races were 'only' subject to discrimination, loss of civic rights, and progressive economic ruination. By contrast, those sick and socially disadvantaged persons who were classified as being of 'lesser racial value' immediately suffered physical and psychological terror. The legal basis for this was supplied by the Law for the Prevention of Hereditarily Diseased Progeny of 14 July 1933, which came into force on 1 January 1934.[14] This permitted the compulsory sterilisation of persons suffering from a series of allegedly hereditary illnesses as well as chronic alcoholics. Applications for sterilisation could be made by the persons themselves, but also by their legal guardians, physicians, and asylum or public health authorities. The decision to sterilise a person was taken by the newly-established Hereditary Health Courts, whose verdicts could only be challenged in a Higher Hereditary Health Court. If the appeal failed, then the sterilisation operation was carried out, regardless of the wishes of the person concerned or of those who raised objections on their behalf. In reality, persons were sterilised who were neither ill nor 'hereditarily ill', in the senses specified by the law. Their 'illness' consisted in being classified as 'asocial' or 'community aliens'. The law contained no provision for this last practice. Plans to include the 'asocial' within its provisions had been explicitly shelved, because of the imminence of separate legislation concerning these categories of person. The drafting of a law on the 'asocial' was under way when the law on compulsory sterilisation was promulgated.[15]

The Law against Dangerous Habitual Criminals, which was promulgated on 24 November 1933, was a first step in this direction. This permitted the detention and compulsory castration of certain types of criminal as defined by 'racial-biological' investigation. Similar measures were then incorporated into the Law on the Punishment of Juvenile Offenders of 22 January 1937. A 'racial-biological' examination determined the duration and conditions of the sentence, a practice which was then applied to adult offenders too. To this end, a number of 'criminal-biological research centres' were established in various cities. Along with the illegal misapplication of compulsory sterilisation, measures like these were to be incorporated into the projected law on the 'asocial'. However, like its analogue – a law on 'Gypsies' – no comprehensive law on the 'asocial' was ever promulgated. This was due not to the collapse of the Third Reich, but rather, as was the case with the Jews, to the fact that the regime preferred to solve the 'question' without resorting to formal legislation or decrees.

The transition from the pseudo-legal to the totally illegal persecution of both 'alien' races and those of 'lesser racial value' occurred from approximately 1935 onwards. In that year the regime introduced two important racial-hygienic laws. The Law for the Alteration of the Law for the Prevention of Hereditarily Diseased Progeny of 26 June 1935 sanctioned compulsory abortion, up to and including the sixth month of pregnancy, for women who had been categorised as 'hereditarily ill' by the health courts.[16] This law represented a qualitative radicalisation of existing racial-hygienic measures. The Law for the Protection of the Hereditary Health of the German People, issued on 18 October 1935, was designed to register, and hence more effectively exclude, 'alien' races and the 'racially less valuable' from the 'national community'.[17] The law made possession of a 'certificate of fitness to marry' mandatory for all prospective marriage partners. The certificate was issued by public health authorities. They could refuse a certificate to those who were allegedly suffering from either 'hereditary illness' or contagious diseases, notably those which were sexually transmitted. This practice gradually made it possible to register and hence 'select' the whole German population. It also enabled health and registry offices to encompass statistically members of 'alien' races not covered by the Nuremberg Laws. Therefore this so-called Marriage Health Law represented an important link between the racial-anthropological and racial-hygienic measures of the regime. This connection requires some elaboration.

The first supplementary decree on the Law for the Protection of German Blood and Honour of 14 November 1935 stipulated that not only Jews were forbidden to marry or have sexual relations with 'persons of German blood'.[18] More generally, marriages could not be contracted if 'offspring likely to be prejudicial to the purity of German blood' were anticipated. A circular issued by the Reich and Prussian Minister of the Interior on 26 November 1935 on the implementation of the law specified which marriages the regime had in mind, namely those between persons of German or related blood, and 'Gypsies, negroes or their bastards'.[19] This point was taken up by Stuckart and Globke in their

Die richtige Gattenwahl
ist die Voraussetzung für eine wertvolle und glückliche Lebensgemeinschaft

3.2 *'The right choice of marriage partner': display chart showing the importance of investigating the racial background of a prospective marriage partner. The 'correct' choice is shown on the right; a 'wrong' choice on the left.*

official commentary on the Nuremberg Laws.[20] According to them, 'in Europe', 'Gypsies, negroes, or their bastards' were normally counted alongside Jews as 'carriers of non-German or related blood'.

In the following period, further social legislation was promulgated, all of which contained racial-anthropological and racial-hygienic provisions, i.e., the exclusion of both 'alien' races and those of 'lesser racial value' in the German population. These measures included decrees on child benefits, the Income Tax Law of 27 February 1939,[21] and the decrees 'for the protection of marriage, the family, and motherhood' issued in 1942 and 1943 which increased maternity benefits.[22] By contrast, no further racial legislation was promulgated. There were various reasons for this. Firstly, existing decrees and legislation were formulated so elastically that they could simply be applied to further groups of people without having to introduce new laws. Secondly, the Nazis did not regard it as either necessary or opportune to advertise their persecution of 'alien' races or the 'racially less valuable' through formal legislation. Finally, to legislate would have involved introducing order into the struggle over competences

3.3 Registering people deemed to be of 'lesser racial value' on index cards. An office in the Rhineland Provincial Institute for Neuro-Psychological Eugenic Research.

taking place between the rival agencies involved in racial policy, an issue which will occupy us below.

RACIAL RESEARCH

From the beginning, many academics and scientists were involved in the formulation and implementation of Nazi racial policy.[23] Racial anthropologists, biologists and hygienicists, economists, geographers, historians, and sociologists created the conceptual framework and scientific legitimisation for the implementation of Nazi racial policy. Having imposed a logical structure on various forms of hatred and irrationality, the same academics and scientists voluntarily and enthusiastically put their skills at the service of the regime. For many disciplines, the advent of the Nazi regime was coterminous with the onset of 'boom' conditions. No one asked or compelled these academics and scientists actively to work on the regime's behalf. Most of them could have said no. In fact, the files of the regime's many agencies bulge with their unsolicited recommendations. They, and the card indexes, charts, diagrams, maps, books, articles, and statistics which they produced, were partly responsible for the clinically comprehensive and devastatingly effective manner in which Nazi racial policies were carried out. The application of skill and technical expertise extended from such details as the design of the electrified fencing and watchtowers at Auschwitz to the employment of modern data-gathering and demoscopic techniques to encompass and control the whole population, thus facilitating the 'eradication' of the 'alien' and 'less valuable'. Unlike many of the mindless sadists who worked in concentration camps, most of these 'desk-bound criminals' simply passed back into academic, professional, and public life after 1945, unless their profile was so high as to make Allied retribution unavoidable.

Not unnaturally, these opening observations are particularly pertinent in the case of racial anthropologists and racial hygienicists. The two main associations of racial hygienicists were 'co-ordinated' in the summer of 1933.[24] This included the German Society for Racial Hygiene, which at the time had 1,300 members and twenty local groups. Many of the members were academics, including some who were also functionaries in the Racial Political Office of the NSDAP. From this time onwards, the association and its periodical, the *Archiv für Rassen- und Gesellschaftsbiologie*, served to enlighten others about the racial policies of the regime. The German Society for Anthropology, renamed the German Society for Racial Research in 1937, fulfilled a similar function. Moreover, members of both societies took part, either as individuals or as members of research institutes, in the drafting and implementation of racial policy measures. The most important institute was the Kaiser Wilhelm Institute for Anthropology, Heredity and Eugenics, which was established in 1928 under the auspices of the Kaiser Wilhelm Society.[25] The KWI's directors, Eugen Fischer, Fritz Lenz, and Otmar Freiherr von Verschuer, were willing and enthusiastic conformists. They raised no objections when one of their colleagues, the Jesuit Muckermann, was hounded out of his post on 'political' grounds, and rewrote passages in their books to conform with the dogma of the regime. They also responded eagerly in May 1933 to an invitation to join the Committee of Experts for Population and Racial Policy in the Reich Ministry of the Interior. By July 1933 they were assuring the Interior Minister that the Kaiser Wilhelm Society in general, and their institute in particular, would put themselves 'systematically in the service of the Reich with regard to racial hygienic research'. Consequently, they also requested that the leader of the Racial Political Office of the NSDAP, Walter Gross, become a member of the Institute's executive committee.

So much accommodation and goodwill was soon rewarded. The

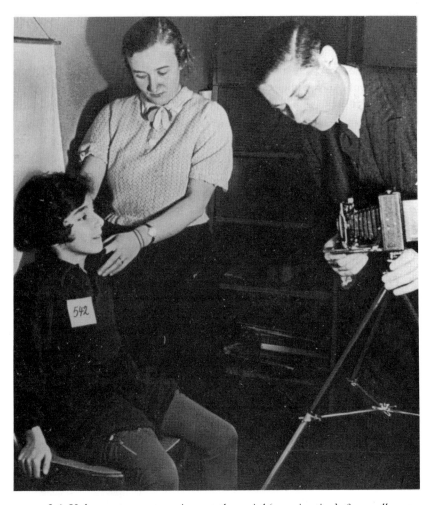

3.4 Unknown persons carrying out the racial 'examination' of a small girl.

Institute received fresh funds, new posts, and new tasks. The latter included the training in racial studies and eugenics of medical students, practising physicians, and members of the SS. Nazi racial legislation brought further benefits. Private individuals, as well as the courts and administrative authorities, sought their expert advice concerning whether a person was 'hereditarily ill', 'Aryan', or 'non-Aryan'. This trade in expert testimonials was a highly lucrative one. However, for the objects of the testimonials, it could be a matter of life and death, or of the right to have children. Members of the KWI were responsible for reports on the so-called Rhineland Bastards, shortly before the latter were compulsorily sterilised. this matter will be discussed in greater detail below.

In this case, racial research was part of racial policy. The same applies to the research of members of the Institute like Wilhelm Abel who, in addition to his work on Jews in eastern Europe was much preoccupied with Sinti and Roma in Rumania and even Scotland. However, in general, the Institute's direct influence may be said to have consisted in assisting in the scientific elaboration of the regime's guidelines on racial policy. It should be remembered, however, that the Institute's personnel also included a man whose name has become synonymous with 'medicine without humanity'. Dr Josef Mengele worked as Verschuer's assistant while functioning as a camp physician at Auschwitz. From there he sent the eyes of murdered Gypsies, the internal organs of murdered children, and the sera of others he had deliberately infected with typhoid back to the KWI for analysis. Not far from the KWI, in Berlin-Dahlem, was another institute which was even more closely involved in the regime's racial policies. This was the Racial-Hygienic and Heredity Research Centre in the Reich Health Office.[26] It was established in 1936 under the direction of the psychologist and physician Dr Robert Ritter, and was principally concerned with the 'Gypsy question'.

Ritter's professed object was to close a 'gap' in existing Nazi racial legislation. As we have seen, from 1935 onwards Sinti and Roma were classified as being 'carriers of non-German or related blood', and therefore as being on a par with the Jews. This did not resolve the question of who constituted a 'Gypsy' or 'part-Gypsy', a matter which could not be solved through the application of religious criteria. The Sinti and Roma had been Christians for several centuries. Using genealogical, 'biological', and anthropological methods, as well as threats and coercion, Ritter and his research assistants investigated virtually all of Germany's 30,000 Sinti and Roma, and classified them according to degrees of racial 'purity'. On the basis of this information, Germany's Sinti and Roma were either compulsorily sterilised or deported to concentration camps. Ritter's research was literally a matter of life and death for the persons who were its 'object'. Among those to recognise the significance of his labours was Heinrich Himmler, who provided Ritter with financial support and then appointed him director of the newly established Criminal-Biological Institute of the Security Police. Having despatched the Sinti and Roma, Ritter carved out a new empire for himself in the field of juvenile delinquency, an area to which he returned after the war. There were other institutes for racial

3.5 A 'Gypsy' being interrogated in Cologne about his family's genealogy by a member of Robert Ritter's office staff. Such investigations served to trace and locate who was a 'Gypsy', an essential precondition for their eventual deportation and extermination.

research which had a comparable political significance: one was the Provincial Office for Racial Questions in Jena, under Karl Astel.[27] Along with other academic institutions, the Provincial Office was involved in the biological encompassing of the German population. Astel was also in charge of a major research project, commissioned by Himmler, concerning the heritability of homosexuality. Himmler was also an enthusiastic patron of the Danish SS scientist Vaenert, who endeavoured to 'cure' homosexual concentration camp inmates with male hormonal implants. A further research institute was the Institute for Heredity and Race Care in Giessen under the direction of Wilhelm Kranz.[28] This was principally concerned with the 'asocial' and 'Gypsy' questions. How far members of the Institute were involved in the preparation of the projected 'Law on the Asocial' or in policies towards this group remains unexplored.

Two institutions dominated by historians, namely the Publikationsstelle in Dahlem, and the North-East German Research Community with its regional analogues, were closely involved in policy towards Slav ethnic minorities within Germany, and later in the provision of a scientific basis for policy in occupied Poland and the Soviet Union.[29] Both of these groups were in turn closely involved in the creation of research institutes in occupied eastern Europe, for example the Institut für Deutsche Ostarbeit in Cracow, the Reinhard-Heydrich-Stiftung in Prague, and the Reichsuniversität, Posen. The totally instrumentalised nature of 'scholarship' in the occupied east is most obviously symbolised by the fact that the crematoria in the cellars of the Institute for Anatomy in Posen were used by the Gestapo to dispose of the corpses of over 4,000 Polish victims, with the professors operating a lucrative trade in the products of autopsy with their academic colleagues in Germany. Economists and historians attached to these centres provided the intellectual rationalisation for the regime's exterminatory policies. In general, it can be said that there were few areas of Nazi racial policy which did not involve academics in its formulation and legitimisation, and that many of the latter were culpably involved in its implementation. Not all of these men and women were convinced or fanatical National Socialists. Many of them were conservatives or simply apolitical, although it is worth asking oneself how this consensus of professional political opinion had been achieved. Virtually all of them, however, were absolutely convinced of the value of their research and of the sciences it served, with no wider moral or critical perspective on what they were doing. They were convinced that their work was in the interests of both scientific and general progress. Moreover, a training which set a premium on 'objectivity', unencumbered by moral 'value judgements', in itself encouraged the idea that human beings were merely aggregates of functioning parts, or of more or less imperfect genetic 'material'. This reinforced other sorts of 'distancing' between the physicians and scientists and the human beings who were the 'objects' of their research. In the case of psychiatrists, the resort to compulsory sterilisation and murder may in part have reflected a belief that the resources of modern therapy should be concentrated on cases where a conventional 'cure' could be anticipated. Killing became the pendant of healing. Imprisoned in the little worlds of their laboratories, libraries, and institutes, and captive to professional hierarchies, careerism, the quest for 'fame', and petty professional animosities, many of these professionals failed to see the barbaric and inhuman goals which their research served. These tendencies, latent in most disciplines, combined with the regime's pseudo-Nietzschean contempt for the life of the mind in all but its most utilitarian guises, to give a new, sinister meaning to the quest for 'relevance'. Contrary to the notion that Nazism somehow corrupted and distorted the temples of learning – which of course it did – one could argue that a corrupt and inherently distorted science lent Nazism a specifically 'academic' and 'scientific' character.

AGENCIES, INSTITUTIONS, AND RACIAL POLICY

From the beginning of the Nazi regime, a number of State and Party agencies and institutions were keen to concretise and implement a racial political programme which Hitler had merely outlined. This resulted in conflicts over areas of competence. Although Hitler reserved all fundamental decisions for himself, he rarely intervened in the details of policy-making, and then only when planning had reached an advanced stage. It was therefore important that the plans of a host of interested agencies be co-ordinated at an early stage.

This was the role envisaged for the Committee of Experts for Population and Racial Policy, which was established by the Interior Minister Wilhelm Frick on 28 June 1933.[30] Its members included leading politicians (Himmler, the Reich Peasant Leader Darré, and the Reich Physicians' Leader Wagner), academic experts (Professor Fritz Lenz), and civil servants (the director of the Reich Office for Statistics, Friedrich Burgdörfer). The committee was sub-divided into three working parties. The first was concerned with the statistical registering of poverty and with policy towards families with large numbers of children. The second group was involved in racial hygiene, eugenics, and racial policy, and was responsible for 'health policing' issues like compulsory abortion, castration, and sterilisation. The final group was concerned with education and welfare, with particular reference to mothers and women. This last group sought to promote 'a spiritual renewal of womanhood' and, specifically, 'the ennoblement of the desire to reproduce'. In reality, the Committee of Experts failed to become the central clearing-house for Nazi racial policy-making. Only the second working party was involved in either the making or implementation of policy, namely the drafting of the law on (compulsory) sterilisation and, in 1937, the sterilisation of the so-called Rhineland Bastards. In other words, the Committee of Experts became progressively more insignificant. For example, it played no collective part in the drafting of the Nuremberg Laws, which was done in great haste by *ad hoc* committees consisting of representatives of interested ministries, and an emissary despatched by Gerhard Wagner. At the last moment Hitler chose from a number of differing drafts. The Committee of Experts also lost control over the implementation of the sterilisation programme it had helped formulate. This function was assumed by the Public Health Offices and the Hereditary Health Courts.

The implementation of racial-hygienic policies presupposed the existence of a public medical bureaucracy, both administratively and legally empowered to pursue racial-hygienic policies. However, the health system which the Nazis inherited from the Weimar Republic was decentralised and inefficient. It lacked co-ordination at the Reich, State, and communal levels, and this problem was compounded by friction between a semi-public health insurance system and a privately incorporated physicians' lobby. The Law for the Consolidation of the Health System of 3 July 1934 represented an attempt to centralise the administration of public health, while also institutionalising the regime's racial-hygienic preoccupations.[31] Various figures coveted the role of the Third Reich's medical supremo. Their ambitions were stymied by the workings of political patronage, their hatred towards each other, and Hitler's preference for leaving them suspended in limbo between Party and State. The first would-be supremo was Arthur Gütt, the Chief of the Department for the People's Health within the Ministry of the Interior. Gütt was displaced in 1939 by Dr Leonardo Conti, an ex-SA fighter who had successfully attached himself to the SS. Conti inherited Wagner's mantle as Reich Health Leader, a position he combined with a State Secretaryship in the Ministry of the Interior. However, having seen off Wagner, Conti found his position threatened by the aspiration of Ley's German Labour Front in the field of industrial health, and by the physician to Hitler's retinue, Karl Brandt. The Department for the People's Health and its subordinate public health offices were responsible for carrying out compulsory sterilisation, the issuing of 'certificates of fitness to marry', and for the 'hereditary-biological encompassing' of the German people in general. However, in this last field they were not alone. So-called 'proofs of ancestry', which were mandatory for candidates for office in the Party, were issued by the Office for Kinship Research within the Ministry of the Interior.[32] This office, which was controlled by Dr Achim Gercke, developed from an NSDAP card index used to destroy political opponents. Gercke fused various societies for genealogical research into a Reich Association, which he then 'co-ordinated' along Nazi lines. Finally, from 1931 members of the SS were subject to a stringent racial test – which from 1935 included tracing the ancestry of the ranks back to 1800 and that of officers back to 1750 – which was carried out by in-house experts, who eventually formed the SS Main Office for Race and Settlement. These specific nets of information were cast ever more widely by, *inter alia*, the Reich Office for Statistics, which began to collate information on the population as a whole from work books, police registration records, identity papers, and information gleaned through the misuse of the 1939 official census. A supplementary card accompanied the census form. It inquired whether 'one of your grandparents was or is a Jew'. The card came with a special envelope and the assurance that anonymity would be respected. The cards went to a Department for Jewish affairs in the Security Service of the SS, where they were used to close 'gaps' in their existing card index on Jews. The department was led by Adolf Eichmann. His card index would materially assist the smooth 'evacuation' of Jews.[33]

Following the outbreak of war, the significance of the Health Offices, Reich Health Office, and the Department for the People's Health waned. From 1939 compulsory sterilisation largely ceased, on account of the conscription of suitably trained medical personnel. For the same reasons registry offices began to issue 'proofs of no objections to marriage' rather than the more time-consuming and expert-intensive 'certificates of fitness to marry'. Conti compensated for this loss of function by temporarily combining with Brandt and the Chief of the Chancellery of the Führer, Philipp Bouhler, to form the Reich Committee for the Scientific Registration of Serious Hereditarily- and Congenitally-based Illnesses.[34] This committee assumed responsibility for the children's 'euthanasia' programme. A further *ad hoc* grouping, the Reich Association of Asylums, which operated under the code name 'Aktion T-4' after the address on Tiergartenstrasse 4, was responsible for the implementation of the adult 'euthanasia' programme. *Ad hoc* panels of scientists, psychiatrists, and physicians made the decisions concerning whether an individual patient was to live or die.

These examples, which will be discussed in greater detail below, show that *ad hoc* groups were formed for particular aspects of Nazi racial policy; in the last case, for the systematic mass murder of the mentally and physically handicapped. Intra-bureaucratic chaos served further to brutalise and radicalise Nazi racial policy. In every area of Nazi racial policy, State institutions – ranging from the ministerial to the communal level – frequently worked against, rather than alongside, a parallel hierarchy of Party agencies, whose relative influence waxed (Ley's German Labour Front or Himmler's SS-Police complex) or waned (the Racial Political Office of the NSDAP or the complex of agencies under Rosenberg).[35] As the evolution of policy towards the Jews makes abundantly clear, this intra-bureaucratic chaos invariably radicalised, rather than tempered, the effects of the policies adopted.

However, in the course of time one man, Heinrich Himmler, seemed to gain power and influence in all areas of racial policy. He eventually succeeded in either gaining control of or co-ordinating virtually every institution involved in both racial policy and organised terror. In the beginning, Himmler was a relatively uninfluential Nazi functionary. From 1929 he commanded the SS, which by January 1933 consisted of some 52,000 men.[36] It was technically subordinate to the SA leader Röhm. Himmler came away empty-handed from the earliest division of the political spoils. He received his first State appointment in March 1933, when he became Commissary President of the Munich police. However, by the close of 1933 he controlled not only the Bavarian political police but those of every German state, with the significant exception of Prussia. There, Göring had transformed Department 1a of the Berlin Police Praesidium, under Rudolf Diels, into a separate state agency, although one still subordinate to Frick's Ministry of the Interior. The new agency was called the Secret State Police, or Gestapo.[37] In the autumn of 1933 this agency was directly subordinated to Göring. One by-product of Göring's rivalry with Frick was Diels' replacement by Himmler, on 20 April 1934, as Inspector of the Gestapo. Within a few months, Himmler had succeeded in shaking off Göring's tutelage and in merging the Gestapo with the political police in the other states of Germany. Disposing of a ramified local and regional apparatus, Himmler embarked upon the struggle against the regime's political opponents.

The same function was performed by the Security Service of the SS, the SD. The SD was established in 1931 as an internal Party intelligence service. Like the Gestapo, the SD disposed of local and regional departments, the so-called Upper and Lower Sectors, but in contrast to the Gestapo it remained an organisation of the Party. It was commanded by Reinhard Heydrich, who also exercised executive authority over the Gestapo on Himmler's behalf. Both the SD and the Gestapo performed similar functions, namely the combating of political opposition to the regime. Since this resulted in an unnecessary duplication of activities, from 1934–5 the two organisations were allocated separate, though related, spheres of activity. This partially reflected the different backgrounds of the members of both services. While the Gestapo consisted of men who were professional policemen, the SD contained a large number of graduates and technocrats, for example Reinhard Hohn, Otto Ohlendorf, and Walter Schellenberg, whose ideological commitment and keenness to instrumentalise their learning compensated for their amateurishness as policemen. The Gestapo retained responsibility for executive actions against political opponents. Their methods ranged from interrogation to consigning persons to concentration camps. Neither practice was based upon judicial decisions or subject to judicial review. By contrast, the SD became primarily responsible for intelligence concerning the regime's ideological

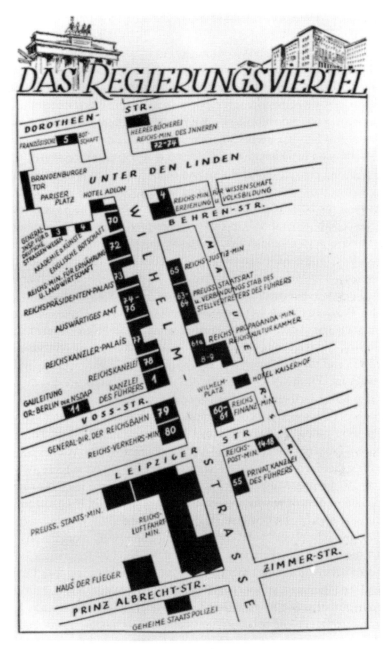

3.6 *Map printed in 1936 showing the location of the main government buildings in Berlin. The headquarters of the Gestapo is on Prinz-Albrecht-Strasse in the bottom left of the picture.*

opponents. The latter included proscribed organisations of the labour movement, both churches, freemasons, and Jews.[38] The SD's surveillance activity gradually assumed routine forms, resulting in the schematised 'Reports from the Reich', which were circulated to a restricted group of State and Party leaders. Reflecting the instrumentalisation of certain trends in sociology, these demoscopic reports – which were extrapolated from the reports of spies and informers – were a seismograph of changing public moods, and hence a means whereby decision-makers could take note of public opinion in a climate which denied it all formal expression.[39]

Following the murder of Röhm and other SA leaders on 30 June 1934, the SS was removed from the aegis of the SA, becoming an independent agency of the NSDAP, directly subordinate to Hitler. The SS consisted of the so-called 'general SS', in other words part-timers, who combined a regular job with evening and weekend voluntary service in the organisation. By contrast, members of the SD and of the SS militarised formations (*Verfügungstruppe*) were fully paid employees of the Reichsführer-SS. Initially, the militarised units consisted of Hitler's SS bodyguards, who from 9 March 1933 were organised as the Adolf Hitler Bodyguard (Leibstandarte Adolf Hitler). Further armed units were formed in the following years. From 1938 these enjoyed a separate constitutional identity, and they took part in the Second World War as separate military formations. From 1940 onwards these military units were called the Waffen-SS. A further group permanently on the SS payroll after 30 June 1934 were the guards of concentration camps. From 1936 onwards these units were called the Death's Head Formation. In 1939 the Totenkopf Division became the nucleus of the field units of the Waffen-SS. The Death's Head Formations were commanded by Theodor Eicke, who on 1 July 1934 became Inspector of Concentration Camps. Their training was designed to destroy any feelings of humanity they might have had towards their prisoners. It was obviously highly effective.[40]

Existing official and 'wild' concentration camps were reorganised in line with the model pioneered by Eicke at Dachau. His regime included a gradated system of punishments, up to and including execution by firing squad, and the use of prisoners as forced labour. In order to maximise their labour potential the SS established stone quarries and brickworks in the immediate vicinity of concentration camps. A company was established, the German Excavation and Quarrying Company Ltd., to control production, distribution, and profits. The company's workforce consisted of persons who had been arrested by the Gestapo and sent to concentration camps. Initially these were mainly political prisoners, i.e. Communists and

3.7 Discussion on the first floor of the Gestapo headquarters. From the left, Werner Lorenz, the head of the SS 'Ethnic German Liaison Office'; Reinhard Heydrich, head of the Security Police and SD; Heinrich Himmler, Reichsführer-SS and Chief of the German Police; Karl Wolff, chief of Himmler's 'Personal Staff'.

Social Democrats, but from 1934 they included ever-larger numbers of the 'asocial' who had been abducted from the streets, shelters, and doss-houses. This practice became the rule following Himmler's appointment as Chief of the German Police on 17 June 1936. Henceforth, not only the Gestapo could detain people in 'protective custody', but also the regular and criminal police, who could now keep the 'asocial' in 'police preventive custody'. This practice was retrospectively legalised on 14 December 1937 when Himmler issued a 'decree for the preventive fight against crime'.

In the ensuing period, the State police – i.e. the Gestapo, criminal, and regular police forces – drew ever closer to the various formations of the SS. On 27 September 1939 Himmler fused their upper echelons into one Reich Main Security Office. This was in turn sub-divided into a series of main offices, including the Gestapo and the domestic and foreign intelligence services of the SD. Apart from Heydrich's RSHA complex, other important SS departments were the Economic and Administrative Department under Oswald Pohl, which encompassed concentration camps, brickworks, mineral water marketing, military supplies, and of course the 560,000 soldiers who in 1944 comprised the Waffen-SS.[41]

Acknowledging the hegemonial aspirations of the SS-Police complex in the field of racial policy, Göring commissioned Heydrich on 31 July 1941 with the preparation of 'an overall plan covering the organisational, technical, and material measures necessary for the accomplishment of the final solution of the Jewish question which we desire'. Representatives of the SS and various ministries then gathered to discuss Heydrich's proposals at a conference in the Berlin suburb of Wannsee on 20 January 1942. The representatives of the ministries agreed with Heydrich's overall suggestions, although the precise course and tone of the ninety-minute discussion were not reflected in the resulting minutes, notwithstanding a recent attempt to 'reconstruct' the discussion on film. Although the meeting was not the starting-point of the Final Solution, it was the moment at which the SS gained formal control of the measures they had already embarked upon. This was probably one of the principal objects of the conference, and hence why secure telephone lines were installed in the villa to relay the successful outcome to the Reichsführer-SS.

The same SS ascendancy can be seen at work in other areas of Nazi racial policy. Persecution of the Sinti and Roma became the province of the Criminal Police. Special departments for 'Gypsy questions' were established in every local and regional Criminal Police Office. Building upon existing police records on 'Gypsies', the Criminal Police played a key role in the registering, 'criminal-biological investigation', arrest, and deportation of Germany's Sinti and Roma. Their activities were co-ordinated by a Reich Central Office for the Combating of the Gypsy Nuisance, which in turn drew upon the expertise of the Criminal-Biological Institute of the Security Police under Robert Ritter.[42] The Reich Criminal Police Office was also host to a Reich Central Office for the Combating of Homosexuality and Abortion, whose object was to persecute those members of the 'national community' who failed in their duty to increase and improve the 'stock' of the German 'race'.[43] Two further agencies, directly subordinate to Himmler, were 'Ancestral Heritage' ('Ahnenerbe') and the 'Well of Life' ('Lebensborn'). The former, founded in 1935, provided a pseudo-scholarly forum for the substantiation of Himmler's aberrant, ahistorical, holistic cultural-political vision, while satisfying the SD's more pragmatic desire to extend its control into the nation's intellectual life. In addition to archaeological digs and research on early German history, 'Ancestral Heritage' also sponsored expeditions to Tibet, homeopathic cures, and attempts to scientifically validate 'world ice teaching' or the belief that the

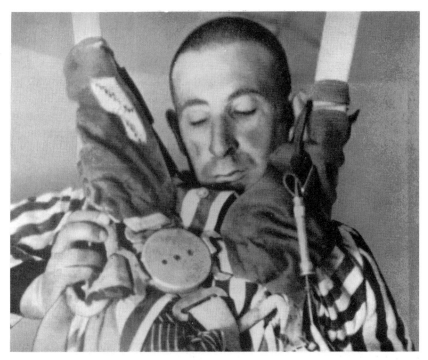

3.8 Prisoner in the concentration camp of Dachau killed in the course of 'research' into human tolerances of high altitude flying. The photograph was taken by the SS doctor Sigmund Rascher in 1942.

'Aryans' had arrived fully-formed from 'heaven', being preserved in 'eternal ice' before stalking the earth armed with superhuman 'electrical powers'. During the war, scientists working under the aegis of the 'Ahnenerbe's' Institute for Applied Military Research carried out lethal research on concentration camp inmates to evaluate human tolerance of high altitudes and prolonged immersion in freezing temperatures. Anatomists and anthropologists availed themselves of the *Kommissarbefehl* and the gas chambers of Auschwitz to collect the skulls of Jews and central Asians for a projected 'museum'.[44] The SS 'Well of Life' agency was also founded in 1935, being directly attached to Himmler's staff office in January 1938. Its costs were defrayed by the NSV and membership dues were obligatory for all SS leaders. The agency ran maternity homes in various parts of Germany, where single and married mothers who had been subjected to a racial test could give birth. Their children were in turn racially 'selected', with those who failed being subsumed in the 'euthanasia' programme. Those who passed were either given to foster-parents or remained in the homes if their mothers were unable to look after them. These homes were mainly used by single women in order to bear illegitimate children away from the attention of neighbours and relatives. Married women availed themselves of the facilities for reasons of cost or because their husbands were SS members.[45] At the time, rumours abounded that the homes were sanitised brothels, where chosen SS men could produce children or where female Nazi zealots could present 'their' Führer with a child. These totally unfounded rumours were perpetuated by sensationalising journalists after 1945.

A prurient preoccupation with this last theme has led to the neglect of the 'Well of Life' agency's activities in occupied Europe. On 28 July 1942 the Nazi Reich Commissar in Norway, Josef Terboven, granted 'Well of Life' the right to care for the illegitimate children of German soldiers and Norwegian women. Through a secret order dated 8 August, Himmler instructed the agency to contribute to the 'increasing of Nordic blood' in Germany by bringing about the 'germanisation' of 'racially suitable' Norwegian children, who were then removed from their mothers in Norway to be raised in the Reich. The abduction of children was practised on a vast scale in occupied eastern Europe. The 'Well of Life' agency established a 'children's home' at Kalisch in the so-called 'Warthegau', where children up to six years of age, who had been stolen from their parents, were 'germanised' through physical labour and harsh discipline. Some of them did not survive the experience. Children whom SS 'experts' categorised as 'racially valuable' were transported to 'Well of Life' homes called 'Pommern', 'Hochland' and 'Alpenland', where they were subjected to a further round of racial tests. Those who 'failed' were sent back to Poland; those who passed were farmed out to German foster-parents. At least 350 Polish children were disposed of in this way.

Himmler regarded this 'fishing for blood' as necessary for the 'strengthening of ethnic Germandom'.[46] A similar goal was served by the 'resettlement' of Poles and Jews from occupied territories adjacent to Germany, and their replacement by ethnic German repatriates. Himmler assumed control of this vast operation following his appointment on 7 October 1939 as Commissar for the Strengthening of Ethnic Germandom. SS units carried out the resettlement and repatriation actions, which for the Jews involved led to their deaths, as it did on a minor scale for those ethnic German repatriates who failed to pass a form of 'racial sieving' carried out by teams of SS racial experts. Finally, units of the SS and Security Police formed the core of the task forces, or *Einsatzgruppen*, which carried out

Aufn. Hoffmann

**Ein Volk steht und fällt mit dem Wert oder Unwert
seiner blutgebundenen rassischen Substanz.**

Juni **Brachet**

11 **12** **13** **14** **15** **16** **17**

Sonntag Montag Dienstag Mittwoch Donnerstag Freitag Sonnabend

Kalender „Neues Volk" 1939
Zentralverlag der NSDAP Frz. Eher Nachf., München

3.9 'A nation stands or falls according to the greater or lesser worth of
its blood-bound racial substance.' SS-officer and baby, from a calendar
produced in 1939.

mass shootings and gassings in the occupied eastern territories. Specifically they shot millions of Jews, 'Gypsies', mental patients, members of the Polish intelligentsia, and Soviet functionaries. This occurred in the immediate proximity of the German army.[47] Friction which occurred between army and SS during the Polish campaign was superseded by smooth co-operation when German forces fell upon the Soviet Union. By this time, the ultimate objective of Himmler's SS state had become apparent; namely, the systematic murder of Jews, Sinti and Roma, Poles, Russians, and others deemed to be of 'lesser racial value'. Futuristic plans being proposed by Himmler's academic planners, notoriously the 'Generalplan Ost', suggest that what happened was in the order of a prelude to something more nightmarish.[48]

It would be misleading to imagine that the SS was solely responsible for the conception and implementation of racial policy. Even apparently innocuous organisations had the same inhuman vocation. After the German Labour Front, or DAF, the National Socialist People's Welfare, or NSV, was the second largest Party organisation, with some sixteen million members in 1942. The NSV was fêted as the 'social arm' of the Party and, notwithstanding evidence of corruption, enjoyed a relatively high reputation in the populace at large.

The origins of the NSV were modest. In September 1931 a Nazi municipal councillor in Berlin-Wilmersdorf, Erich Hilgenfeldt, founded an emergency aid group whose activities soon encompassed Greater Berlin. It was designed to provide relief for Party members during the Depression. Benefiting from the patronage of Joseph Goebbels, the NSV grew in influence and stature after 30 January 1933, receiving Hitler's mandate for 'all questions of charity and the people's welfare' in May of that year. Hilgenfeldt used Hitler's endorsement to usurp the place of both private and public welfare agencies, effectively subordinating organisations like the German Red Cross. The NSV was organised according to the 'Führer' principle, with branches ranging down from the Gau to block levels. It spawned a host of specialist sub-agencies, including 'Winter Relief', 'Mother and Child Relief', 'Tuberculosis Relief'. 'Dental Relief', and so on. In sum, the NSV constituted a large empire, disposing of millions of Marks and millions of members. It was also omnipresent in the lives of ordinary people, with the NSV's jangling street collection-tins being among the most widespread memories of the period. Although rumours of corruption were rife, with the claim 'There goes the Winter Relief' accompanying every passing Party car, and although 'voluntary' contributions were docked from salaries and wages, with failure to give

3.10 Civilians being summarily shot in Lithuania by members of an SS task force. The gathering of interested onlookers to the right should be noted.

generously being reported to higher authorities, nonetheless the NSV encountered surprisingly little adverse criticism, with many former Social Democrats having no scruples about joining the organisation.

In reality, the NSV was not solely or primarily a welfare organisation.[49] It was designed to strengthen the collective biologically and politically and not to assist needy individuals. Joseph Goebbels made this clear at a Party rally in 1938:

> Our starting-point is not the individual, and we do not subscribe to the view that one should feed the hungry, give drink to the thirsty or clothe the naked – those are not our objectives. Our objectives are entirely different. They can be put most crisply in the sentence: we must have a healthy people in order to prevail in the world.

The NSV did not pursue social policies of the classical type. Instead, it participated in the political indoctrination of the 'national community' and in the 'purification' and 'strengthening' of the 'body of the nation' in accordance with racial criteria.

Most obviously, the items of clothing and money collected under the aegis of 'Winter Relief' were not made universally available to the needy.

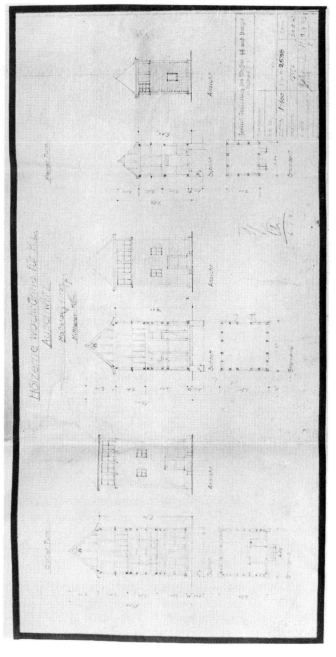

3.11 *Technical drawings for watchtowers in Auschwitz from the SS construction office in the camp.*

Jews were excluded from the start, and had to create their own welfare agencies. Sinti and Roma, the 'asocial', and the 'hereditarily ill' were also disqualified from 'Winter Relief'. Racial objectives were also pursued by the NSV's 'Mother and Child Relief'. A draft policy document from 1936 specified that only the 'biologically valuable parts of the German people' should receive support. Women who were allegedly 'hereditarily inferior' or of an 'asocial disposition' were disbarred from post-natal care. Making its records freely available to both welfare and police authorities, the NSV 'Youth Relief' itself became involved in dealing with 'community unfit and refractory youths'. By 1942 it was responsible for 92 'youth hostels' where difficult juveniles were 'raised' in a National Socialist manner and categorised according to whether they were 'worthy of help', 'hereditarily healthy', or 'of lesser value'.

Racial-political objectives were also evident in the NSV's intervention in the field of adoption. In 1935 it took over the Leipzig-based German Adoption Service, a year later, the adoption facilities of the German Red Cross. By 1937 the new NSV 'Reich Adoption Service' was proudly advertising that it only made available 'healthy children'. The criteria included 'establishing the racial characteristics of the child and . . . information on the hereditary health of its siblings, parents, and grandparents'. During the war, the NSV's attempts to appropriate the field of adoption led to conflicts with the SS 'Well of Life' agency. Questions of respective competence were settled in a spirit of compromise. In the occupied Netherlands, Reich Commissar Seyss-Inquart ruled that the NSV was responsible for the care of children born to German soldiers by Dutch women. To this end, the NSV established confinement centres, which by July 1943 had registered the thousandth birth. In occupied Norway, as we have seen, the 'Well of Life' agency secured a monopoly, establishing a total of eight homes. In practice there was little difference between the two separate organisations, both being concerned with the 'germanisation' of mothers and children in their care. This was sometimes highly coercive, with Dutch or Norwegian mothers being forcibly resettled in the Reich, or their children being put out for adoption to German foster-parents. Like the SS, the NSV was also involved in kidnapping in the occupied eastern territories. This was publicly acknowledged in an article published in July 1944:

> our historical task is not only the reconquest of territory taken from us, but also . . . the recovery and cleansing of the blood of all of those people of German origin in the liberated territory which has been overlain and submerged by Polendom. It is the present task of Party

3.12 Electrified fencing and a watchtower in the camp today.

and State to ensure that not a droplet of German blood is allowed to
go under in an alien people.

The 'recovery and cleansing of the blood' involved the NSV in the
greatest abduction of children in human history. Orphans were taken from
Polish children's homes or from their foster-parents. Children were taken
away from Polish parents who refused to be entered on the 'ethnic
German lists', or were simply abducted from Kindergarten, schools, or off
the streets. They were placed in NSV kindergartens, of which by 1942
there were 600 in the 'Warthegau' alone, and following racial 'selection'
were sent to NSV 'germanisation' centres in the 'old Reich'. There they
were given new names and papers and were forbidden to use their native
language. According to reliable estimates a total of 200,000 children were
abducted in eastern Europe, with a mere 15–20 per cent being reunited
with their parents and relatives after the war. The NSV was also involved

in a further barbaric enterprise, namely the abduction and murder of the children of Polish and Soviet female forced labourers. Initially, pregnant forced labourers were repatriated in order to minimise the costs of confinement and post-natal care. After 1942 this policy changed, with the establishment of so-called 'Eastern Confinement Homes' or 'Child Collection Points'. In these, the NSV and SS subjected the newly-born children to racial 'selection'. Racially 'especially valuable' children were taken by the SS 'Well of Life' agency; the racially 'valuable' by the NSV, which then farmed them out to adoption. The racially 'worthless' were starved to death in 'Care Centres for Foreign Children'. Their corpses were packed into cardboard boxes and incinerated. On 11 August 1943, Hilgenfeldt wrote to Himmler about the need to kill these children more rapidly:

> In my opinion, the present handling of the question is impossible. It is a case of either/or. Either one decides that the children are not to live – in which case one should not allow them to slowly starve, thereby still denying many litres of milk for general consumption, for there are ways in which this can be done without pain and suffering. Or, on the contrary, one's object is to raise the children in order to use them later as a source of labour. In which case, it is necessary to feed them so that one day their labour will be of value.

In conclusion it can be said that the social policies of the NSV were enmeshed in the regime's overall racial grand design. The jangling collection-tins and well-advertised welfare activities were a façade for the all-pervasive racism of the Nazi state.

PART TWO

THE 'PURIFICATION' OF THE BODY OF THE NATION

NORDSEEBAD NORDERNEY · IST JUDENFREI ·

CHAPTER FOUR

THE PERSECUTION OF THE JEWS

FOLLOWING the so-called 'Machtergreifung', many National Socialists were no longer content to confine their hatred of Jews to verbal calumnies. In some cities department stores owned by Jews were ransacked, and Jewish judges and lawyers were forcibly barred from the courts.[1] SA hooligans were particularly exercised by Jews who were Communists or Socialists, or who had distinguished themselves in the struggle against Nazism. These people were taken by SA and SS 'auxiliary police' to 'wild' concentration camps.[2] The latter were established in former barracks, factories, breweries, water towers, trade union and Socialist Party buildings, ships, restaurants, bars, and private residences. There were about 100 'wild' camps in Berlin alone, the most notorious being the Columbiahaus, and a barracks on General-Pape-Strasse in Tempelhof, where the abducted were abused, tortured, and sometimes murdered. Neither the police nor the judiciary made any attempt to bring those responsible to account. The international press, however, reported these SA atrocities in considerable detail. This foreign 'horror propaganda' provided the leadership of the NSDAP with a pretext to organise a 'boycott of Jews'.[3] The victims, in other words, were held responsible for the negative international response to the actions of their persecutors. The boycott took place on 1 April 1933, and affected practically every Jewish business in Germany. Crowds gathered outside Jewish businesses, which were adorned with posters reading: 'Germans, defend yourselves, don't buy from Jews!' or 'Beware, danger to life, Jews out, beware Itzig, go to Palestine.' Similar posters appeared outside the practices and chambers of Jewish physicians and lawyers. However, despite the threatening postures of the ever-present SA men, many people ignored the boycott and demonstratively continued to patronise Jewish businesses. It is impossible to speak of a widespread aggressive antipathy to Jews at this time. Despite this, the Nazis emphasised to their conservative allies and foreign governments that the boycott was a response to anti-Semitic 'public opinion'.

The Law for the Restoration of the Professional Civil Service of 7 April 1933 was of far greater long-term significance than the boycott.[4] Although principally aimed at actual or suspected political opponents of the regime, it also encompassed Jewish civil servants, in so far as these had not fought at the front in the First World War. This last point was a minor concession by Hitler to President Hindenburg, the latter being outraged at the treatment meted out to Jewish judges and lawyers who were war veterans. The so-called 'Aryan clause' of this law, sanctioning the 'retirement' of Jewish officials, both retrospectively legalised the hounding from office of Jewish judges, lawyers, teachers, and officials and supplied a pseudo-legal justification for the exclusion of Jews from other professions.[5] Naked professional self-interest was much in evidence in the cases of lawyers and physicians. In Berlin, Nazi physicians used a particularly repellent combination of anti-Semitism and pornography worthy of *Der Stürmer* to bring about the removal of their Jewish 'colleagues' and competitors. The presence of Jewish judges at beauty contests, or the 'attitude' of Jews towards 'German women' revealed in 'filthy erotic literature', apparently justified the dismissal of Jewish gynaecologists. In April 1933 Jewish physicians were forbidden to work for public insurance schemes, and the local authorities refused to send patients to hospitals with Jews among their administrators.[6] At the same time the regime introduced a law against the overcrowding of schools and colleges which restricted the number of Jews to a maximum 1.5 per cent of the total number of students attending schools and universities.[7] On 4 May all 'non-Aryan' public sector employees, as distinct from tenured civil servants, were dismissed.[8] A further decree issued on the same day prohibited promotion of Jews whose jobs were 'protected' by the war veteran clause.[9] This last measure was symptomatic of the ways in which the regime sought to circumvent its earlier, tactical concession to Jewish war veterans.[10] Nazi propaganda maintained that Jews had left the fighting to others. This point can be easily dispelled by anyone who cares to visit the Weissensee cemetery in East Berlin, with its rows of headstones commemorating some of the 12,000 Jews who had fallen for their Fatherland.[11] A further 35,000 Jews had been decorated for bravery. However, facts like these counted for little in the face of professional self-interest combined with dogmatic racist assertion. The range of professions from which Jews were excluded was

4.1 Shop door with a sign 'Jews not welcome'. The shopowner describes himself as a 'German businessman'.

progressively extended. On 2 June Jews could no longer work for public insurance schemes as dentists or dental technicians.[12] On 17 May this ban was extended to all medical personnel married to 'non-Aryan' partners.[13] From 26 July they could no longer work as university teaching assistants.[14] In December Jewish pharmacology students were no longer allowed to sit their final examinations, and from 13 December Jews were no longer permitted to submit work entitling them to work as university lecturers.[15] These formal legal measures were accompanied by a no less invidious process of informal social ostracism. Jews were 'encouraged' to give up their membership of associations of industrialists, regimental veterans' associations, student societies, or humble skat clubs. Informal ties with Jews were cut.[16] A detailed history of this process of social disassociation has yet to be written.[17]

While the self-interested purpose of many of the measures mentioned above is fairly transparent, further anti-Semitic legislation and decrees issued between 1933 and September 1935 were designed to exclude Jews from the 'national community' as a whole. This was the case with the law of 14 July 1933 which made it possible to revoke naturalisations which had occurred between 9 November 1918 and 30 January 1933.[18] This was particularly aimed at the so-called 'Ostjuden'.[19] The latter were Jews who had either fled pogroms in Russia and eastern Europe from the 1880s onwards, or, in the case of 30,000, who had been brought under duress to work in Germany during the First World War. By rendering these people stateless – as well as robbing them of their livelihoods by restricting their right to trade – the regime paradoxically frustrated its own objective, namely to force them to leave the Reich. Most states refused to take refugees, unless the possibility existed of being able to make them some-one else's problem. Jews were further excluded from the 'national com-munity' through so-called 'Aryan paragraphs' incorporated into general legislation. This applied to the Law on Entailed Estates,[20] the law for the 'Ordering of National Labour',[21] and the Armed Forces Law whereby Jews were exempted from conscription, and those still in the services could no longer become officers.[22] These laws expressly excluded Jews from both the duties and rights mentioned in them, and, in the case of the Armed Forces Law, presupposed the active collusion of agencies by no means dominated by convinced National Socialists.[23]

These examples of legal discrimination were accompanied by the public defamation of Jews by members of the Nazi Party. The works of Jewish authors figured prominently in the public burning of books on 10 May 1933.[24] In addition to the literary products of the Weimar Republic,

4.2 Memorial in the Weissensee cemetery in (East) Berlin to the sons of the Berlin Jewish community who gave their lives in the First World War.

students consigned the works of such authors as Marx, Einstein, and Freud to the flames. Prophetically, the poet Heine had once said that 'where one burns books, one ends up burning people too'. His own works soon joined blacklists of proscribed 'non-German' authors. As a result of the worsening political climate a 'brain-drain' ensued, with about one-third of university teaching staff having to flee the country, including some twenty-four Nobel Prize laureates.[25] Cultural life was also impoverished by the departure of, for example, the film directors Fritz Lang, Otto Preminger, and Billy Wilder, and the movie actors Peter Lorre and Oskar Homolka. Members of the NSDAP were also instructed not to solicit the help of Jews in courts or in dealings with the authorities. Anti-Semitic posters and placards, and copies of *Der Stürmer*, displayed in so-called 'Jewish show-cases', appeared in practically every town and village. This anti-Semitic propaganda – notoriously the May 1934 'ritual murder' issue of *Der Stürmer* – was causally connected with attacks by members of the NSDAP and its agencies upon individual Jews and their property, reported throughout Germany.[26]

This was the background to both the Reich Citizenship Law,, which denied Jews equal civil rights, and the Law for the Protection of the Blood, which prohibited marriages and extra-marital relations between Jews and 'Aryans'.[27] The objects of the Nuremberg Laws of 15 September 1935 were twofold: firstly, to legally enshrine racially-justified political and social inequalities, which were then extended at will through 'decrees for the implementation' of the Nuremberg Laws, and secondly, to curb a recent resurgence of 'wild' terror directed at Jews by NSDAP activists, including a number of prominent *Gauleiter*, who were apparently dissatisfied with the 'conservative' drift of Hitler's government. By introducing legislation, the regime would also retain the exclusive right to set the pace of discrimination and its own systematic form of terror. Although these laws were cobbled together in an *ad hoc* manner, and were the result of activist pressure, it should be remembered that shortly before the 1935 Nuremberg rally Hitler had said that the Jews must be 'removed from all professions, ghettoised, restricted to a particular territory, where they can wander about, in accordance with their character, while the German people looks on, as one looks at animals in the wild'.[28] How legislation was made is undoubtedly highly important, but so too were the ever-expanding vistas in Hitler's mind. Activist pressure and the bloodless, pragmatic labours of the bureaucracy are only part of the equation.[29]

Following the promulgation of the Nuremberg Laws, and, in this context, the equally significant decree on the implementation of the Armed Forces Law of 25 July 1935, which 'released' Jews from service in the forces, the civil status of Jews was on a par with their position prior to their Emancipation. They were once again second-class citizens. On the basis of the Nuremberg Laws, Germany's Jews were removed from the positions they had achieved in state, society, and economy since the era of Emancipation. They were disenfranchised on 14 November 1935 under the first decree on the implementation of the Reich Citizenship Law.[30] At the same time, those tenured Jewish civil servants hitherto protected by their status as war veterans were dismissed from the public service. The second decree on the implementation of the Reich Citizenship Law banned Jewish notaries, physicians, professors, and teachers from the State service. Further obstacles to the pursuance of their professional careers were imposed soon afterwards on Jewish physicians, lawyers, apothecaries, and so on. These measures continued in subsequent years, until finally in 1938 a total 'Berufsverbot' was imposed upon all academically-trained Jewish professionals.[31] These formal measures were accompanied by ongoing social disassociation and initiatives on the part of nongovernmental agencies. Martin Broszat cites a notice sent by a health insurance agency in December 1938 to a Jewish member of the scheme:[32]

> We feel compelled to point out to you as a Jewish member, that your continued membership is highly undesirable due to your race, because on the one hand we cannot expect our Aryan members to stay on in the same organisation with you and thus possibly be forced to support you with their means in case of illness, and on the other hand our employees refuse to deal with the affairs of Jewish members after the events of November 9/10. We thus urge you to declare your withdrawal and in such case are prepared to set aside the time for notice and to effect the immediate cancellation of your membership.

By this time, even humble librarians had taken it upon themselves to purge the shelves of works by Jewish authors. In 1938 a librarians' journal proudly proclaimed:

> [We had already] begun to systematically check and catalogue the racial provenance of persons involved in German cultural life. What could be more obvious than that librarians should make available their skills and knowledge? Working together with representatives of the (Nazi) Movement, librarians checked the *curriculum vitae* in the dissertations of German doctoral candidates, as well as working through and indexing Kürschner's *World of Learning*, the *Almanach de Gotha*, Judaic dictionaries and other reference works. It was due to this effort that already by 1933 half serviceable preparatory work was on hand for the elimination of Jewish authors, editors and professors.

Jews were also excluded from simple pleasures like going swimming. The following letter was sent by the NSDAP in Hesse to the Oberbürgermeister of Frankfurt am Main on 27 July 1938:[33]

> Complaints from the population are multiplying day by day concerning use by Jews of the Niederrad bathing area. In particular the inhabitants of Niederrad and of those parts of the city near the bathing area complain that they are being forced to go a relatively long way when they want to swim, because the bathing areas near them are continually being used by Jews. Moreover, on warm days the trams to and from Niederrad are so full of Jews that it often results in unpleasant incidents. With regard to the fact that the bathing facilities here are not adequate for the German population, it is no longer acceptable that the Jews should have a bathing area at their disposal. I therefore request that Jews be forbidden to use the Niederrad bathing area as soon as possible.

The decision to reverse the achievements of the post-Emancipation era, so evident in the 1935 Nuremberg Laws, was not uniformly realised in all areas of State and society until 1938. Indeed, in 1936 and 1937, the tempo

of anti-Semitic legislation appeared to decelerate, so that these are sometimes called 'the quiet years'. This was principally on account of economic
and foreign policy considerations, which to a limited degree affected the
regime's anti-Semitic policies. During the 1936 Berlin Olympics, to take a
local example, anti-Semitic posters and placards were temporarily
removed. However decrees on the implementation of the Nuremberg
Laws continued to be issued, marginalising the Jews from both the
'national community' and economic existence. On 3 March 1936, Jewish
families could no longer claim allowances for large numbers of children;[34]
from 26 March 1936 Jews could no longer lease chemist shops.[35] From
3 April 1936 both Jewish vets and 'Aryan' vets married to 'non-Aryan'
partners could no longer practise;[36] from 29 June 1936 Jews were
forbidden to work as currency dealers;[37] from 16 July as construction site
engineers;[38] from 26 January 1937 as cattle dealers;[39] from 13 February as
notaries.[40] These measures, which undermined the economic existence of
Germany's Jews, were accompanied by apparently petty forms of discrimination. From 7 December 1937 persons married to Jews were no
longer allowed to fly the national flag; the second decree on the
implementation of the Reich Hunting Law of 5 February 1937[41] forbade
Jews to hold hunting permits; and on 4 November 1937 Jews were forbidden to use the 'German greeting'.[42] These measures were the collective
product of bureaucratic experts on the 'Jewish Question'; the existence of
the job itself being sufficient to give discriminatory measures their own
momentum. One group of experts, formed in late 1936, was to assume
particular significance in the field of Jewish affairs: section II 112 of the
Security Service of the SS under Adolf Eichmann.[43] The object of this
section was 'the centralisation of the entire work on the Jewish question in
the hands of the SD and Gestapo'. It was also ominous that a secret decree
issued by Eichmann's superior Heydrich on 12 June 1937 stipulated that
persons who had been sentenced for infractions of the Law for the
Protection of German Blood and Honour were to be sent to concentration
camps after they had served their sentence.[44] In practice, this meant that
persons guilty of 'miscegenation', an offence described in prurient detail in
the regime's press, were sentenced to death. Practices like this had not
existed since the Middle Ages.

The discussions on the Four-Year Plan, held in September 1936, also
had considerable significance for the future.[45] Not only was it decided that
the German armed forces and economy had to be ready for war in about
four years, but Hitler argued that 'the whole of Jewry' had to be held
responsible for the damage which 'individual representatives of this

4.3 Sign indicating that there were no longer Jews at the Frisian bathing resort of Nordeney.

criminaldom have done to the German economy and German people'. Specifically, he entertained the idea of a special discriminatory rate of taxation for Jews, notionally as a form of revenge for the assassination on 4 February 1936 by David Frankfurter of Wilhelm Gustloff, the Nazi Party's chief agent in Switzerland.[46] Göring managed to postpone draft measures to this effect, on the grounds that they might jeopardise the regime's relentless quest for foreign currency and raw materials. Despite this, the conceptual linking of the solution of the 'Jewish question', construed as an act of 'revenge' against a people for the act of one individual, with the amelioration of immediate economic and military problems had been achieved. The lines of thought evident here were paradigmatic for the final, most radical phase of the ongoing 'dejewification of the German economy'.

On 13 March 1938 all of the anti-Semitic laws and measures passed hitherto were extended to Austria. At the same time the regime endeavoured to exclude Jews from further areas of the economy. Jews were forbidden to work as gun dealers from 18 March;[47] as dealers, detectives, marriage brokers, tourist guides, or travelling salesmen from 6 July;[48] as nurses from 28 September;[49] as patent lawyers from 31 October;[50] and as midwives from 21 December.[51] During 1938 the so-called 'Aryanisation' of the economy, in other words the more or less compulsory alienation and expropriation of Jewish-owned businesses, reached its zenith. That this had been happening for some years can be demonstrated by the fact that whereas in 1933 there were over 50,000 individual Jewish businesses in Germany, by April 1938 the figure was about 39,532. By April 1939 nearly 6,000 of the latter had been 'Aryanised', 11,000 were in the process of or on the brink of 'Aryanisation', and 15,000 had been liquidated. In other words, about 80 per cent of the businesses which had survived until April 1938 no longer existed a year later.[52] Behind these figures lay much entrepreneurial opportunism or sheer cupidity. As one (Nazi) business-man, disgusted with the greed of his colleagues, graphically expressed it: 'To me the people seem like vultures, falling upon the corpses of Jews with watery eyes and their tongues hanging out.'[53] Measures like these, whose effect was to transform Jews into consumers of their own liquidified assets, were accompanied by tighter registration of the proportion of capital they disposed of. From 26 April 1938 Jews had to register all assets of 5,000RMs or more with the authorities.[54] False rumours, put about by a State Secretary in the Reich Ministry for the Economy, to the effect that the State planned to compensate them for any eventual expropriation militated against deliberate under-valuation on the special forms requiring details of share certificates, insurance schemes, debts, and luxury items. By the spring of 1938, 60,000 members of the Jewish community were described as permanently unemployed, despite the fact that the economy as a whole was experiencing an acute shortage of labour. During the winter of 1937–8 over 21 per cent of the Jewish population was dependent upon (Jewish) charities.[55] One does not need to have lived in Nazi Germany to appreciate the connection between destitution and becoming a 'non-person'.

4.4 Park bench designated 'for Aryans only'.

This systematic and calculated pauperisation of the Jewish population was accompanied by further measures designed to isolate and humiliate them. On 27 July 1938 streets named after Jews were renamed;[56] they were not allowed to sit on certain park benches, or from 12 November 1938 to visit the theatre, cinema, concerts, or exhibitions, or eat in certain restaurants.[57] Following a decree issued on 17 August 1938, from 1 January 1939 Jews were obliged to use the compulsory first names Sara or Israel.[58] Their travel documents were also to be surrendered to the authorities, to be stamped with a red 'J'. The philologist Victor Klemperer recorded in his notes on the language of the Third Reich what these measures involved for those affected by them. He was married to an 'Aryan' woman, a fact which meant that he survived the war working as a slave labourer in various factories.[59]

> In September 1940 I saw an advertisement from a church on a poster column '*Hero of a Nation; Handel's Oratorio*'. Printed underneath in worriedly minute print and in brackets it said: '*Judas Maccabeus, revised text*'. At about the same time I read an historical novel which had been translated from English: *The Chronicle of Aaron Kane*. The

publisher, Rütten & Loening – who had published the great
Beaumarchais biography by the Viennese Jew Anton Bettelheim! –
apologised on the first page, saying that the biblical names of the
characters were a reflection of the puritanism and local customs of the
times, and that accordingly they could not be altered. Another English
novel – I forget the author's name – is called *Beloved Son* in German.
The original title, printed in tiny print inside the book, was *O
Absalom!* The name Einstein could not be used in physics lectures, and
the unit of measurement 'Hertz' could not be described by this
Jewish name.

Because they not only wished to protect German national comrades from Jewish names, but rather much more from any contact
with the Jews themselves, the latter were carefully segregated. One of
the most important ways of achieving this consisted of making them
identifiable through their names. Whoever did not have a recognisably
Hebrew name, or one which was uncommon in Germany, for
example Baruch or Recha, had to add 'Israel' or 'Sara' to his forename.
He had to give this information to his registry office and bank, he
must never forget it when signing his name, he had to tell all of his
business associates that they must not forget it when they sent things
to him by post. If he was not married to an Aryan woman, with children by her – an Aryan wife alone did not help – he had to wear the
yellow Jewish star. The word 'Jew' on this, whose letters copied
Hebrew script, was like a forename worn on one's breast. Our names
were in duplicate on the lobby door, over mine a Jewish star, under
my wife's the word 'Aryan'. At first, my ration cards had a single 'J',
later the word 'Jew' was printed diagonally across the cards, finally the
word 'Jew' stood on every tiny section, sometimes sixty times on the
same card. If I am referred to in an official context, I am always called
'the Jew Klemperer'; if I have to report to the Gestapo, there are blows
if I do not report 'smartly' enough: 'Here is the Jew Klemperer.'

'Supplementary information', gleaned from a census carried out in 1939,
was deliberately misused to create a special card index on Jews and part-
Jews within the Reich Security Main Office of the SS.[60] Both of these
measures were vital to the identification and location procedures necessary
for later deportations and extermination, as was trust in bureaucratic
rationality on the part of the victims. In 1938, however, the regime's
objective was still emigration. Measures taken since 1933 had been
designed to compel the Jews to depart, preferably leaving their assets
behind. To this end, the Security Service (SD) of the SS had actively
persecuted Jewish organisations which promoted assimilation, while
encouraging those which stood for a separate Jewish identity and recommended emigration.[61] Several factors, including the policies of the regime
itself, cut across this last objective. Principally, restrictions on the sums

Jews were permitted to take out of the country – eventually 10RMs per person – rendered it unlikely that many countries could be prepared to admit people effectively bereft of any means of subsistence.[62] Moreover, Jewish refugees from Germany had to compete with Jews fleeing anti-Semitic regimes in eastern Europe. The reluctance of foreign countries to take unlimited numbers of Jewish refugees in turn enabled the Nazis to gloat over the alleged worldwide existence of anti-Semitism. One by-product of Nazi policy, however, was that the question of Jewish emigration from Germany became an international problem. On 3 August 1938 an international commission on refugees met at Evian, whose object was to help as many Jews to emigrate as possible, taking with them at least part of their assets.[63] Representatives of the German government totally rejected this solution to the problem their government had created, insisting instead that Jews inside Germany and abroad should provide the regime with foreign currency, to pay for German imports. In practice, this meant that foreign countries were being asked to pay a form of bounty for every Jew who was allowed to leave his or her German homeland. As was to be expected, no agreement was reached at Evian.

In March 1938 the regime of Marshal Smigly-Ridz in Poland attempted to cancel the citizenship of Polish Jews living in Germany.[64] Faced with the prospect of large numbers of stateless Jews, the Nazi regime informed the Poles that 'The German government cannot view such a development passively.' On 28 October 1938, about 17,000 Jews with Polish citizenship, many of whom had lived in Germany for decades, were arrested and taken to the Polish frontier, where the authorities refused to admit them. The operation was paradigmatic, in the sense that its execution required the smooth co-ordination of the police, railway authorities, diplomatic service, and departments of finance. The end effect of this inter-governmental inhumanity was that thousands of Jews were left on an insanitary no-man's-land on the German–Polish frontier. Some of them had been tricked into the journey by the Gestapo with authentic-seeming train tickets marked 'Palestine, one way, no return'. Among these stateless persons, interned in camps at Zbaszyn, Chojnice, and Drawski Mlyn, were the family of the seventeen-year-old Hershel Grynszpan, who by way of retaliation shot and fatally wounded a legation secretary, Ernst vom Rath, in the German embassy in Paris. This assassination provided Goebbels with a welcome pretext to unleash the pogrom, which is known nowadays by the misleadingly harmless epithet 'Reichskristallnacht'.[65] On 9 and 10 November, not only panes of glass and 7,000 businesses were destroyed. Virtually every synagogue in Germany was burned down; 26,000 Jews were sent to concentration camps; and ninety-one persons were murdered. The fire brigades were issued with instructions only to attend fires in the buildings next to blazing Jewish premises and places of worship.

The individual terror masked by these global statistics may be illustrated by the account of a rabbi in Düsseldorf, Dr Max Eschenbacher, who returned home late one night from a visit to friends:[66]

> I was barely through the door, when the telephone rang: a voice, trembling with horror, screamed: 'Herr Doktor, they are destroying the community house, smashing everything to pieces, they are beating people up, we can hear their screams even here.' It was Frau Blumenthal, who lived in the building next door. I thought of going to the community house, despite the fact that I could not do anything to help there. But almost at that moment there was loud banging at the door. I put out the lights, and looked outside. The street in front of the building was thick with SA people. In a moment they were upstairs, and had forced the hall door. I could only see that the stairwell was full of them, the rank and file and all kinds of leaders, recognisable from their caps and flashes. They forced their way into our apartment with a chorus of 'Revenge for Paris! Down with the Jews!' They pulled sledgehammers out of sacks, and in a moment breaking furniture cracked, and panes of glass in sideboards and windows smashed. Then the fellows threatened me with their clenched fists. One of them grabbed me and screamed at me to get downstairs. I was convinced I was about to be beaten to death. I went into my bedroom, took off my watch, and left my wallet and keys, and said farewell to Berta. She only said 'Chasak!' ('Be strong!')
>
> I myself do not know how I got down the stairs. Luckily, in moments like these, one is so dazed that one hardly notices what is happening around one. That explains the courage which one appears to have at such times. If one was more aware, then one would also be more afraid. Down below, the street was filled with SA men. All in all, including those inside the building, it could have been 50 to 60 men. They greeted me with the cry 'Preach a little now!' I began to speak about the death of Herrn vom Rath, that his death was more of a misfortune for us than for the German people, that we bore no guilt for his death . . .
>
> On the corner, in Stromstrasse, I saw that the street was covered with books, papers, documents and letters which had been thrown out of my windows. My typewriter lay smashed to pieces on the street. While all of this was taking place, the SA people had forced their way into the Wertheimers' on the floor below us, where they had destroyed a great deal, dragged Herrn Wertheimer and his wife out of their bed, and brought them downstairs. I was seized by an SA man, and dragged about in a great arc in front of the house. A neighbour, who witnessed this, told me afterwards, that this happened several

times. I was then thrown into the entrance of the building, and kept in the area between the wall and the lift. Then the district leader came and said, 'I am taking you into protective custody.' The march to police headquarters began. A squad of SA men went before us. Then me, escorted by two of them. Then again a squad of SA people, as well as Herrn Wertheimer, escorted in the same manner, then separated from us by a squad of SA men, Frau Wertheimer in her pyjamas, and then a further group of SA men at the rear. The whole way they sang in unison, 'Revenge for Paris! Down with the Jews!' One of them said to me: 'Now you can celebrate your Passover.' Passers-by who encountered us on the streets also shouted 'Revenge for Paris! Down with the Jews!'

After twelve days held in custody, Rabbi Eschenbacher was released on 22 November, only to discover the full extent of what had taken place:

There were many dead. What took place that night was a pogrom. Paul Marcus, the owner of the Café Karema, fled, as his restaurant was totally destroyed. He was shot during the night, and was found dead early next morning in front of the house of Dr Max Loewenberg on Martin-Luther-Platz. Frau Isidor Willner and her son Ernst were stabbed in Hilden. Furthermore, both Carl Herz and Nathan Meyer were either stabbed or shot there too. Sixty-eight-year-old Dr Sommer in Hilden, a man who lived in a mixed marriage and never bothered about things Jewish, went out into the garden with his wife and their elderly, Aryan, maid, as the house was plundered and he himself was badly mishandled. There they all took poison. The bodies of Marcus, Herz and Mayer, as well as Frau Willner and Ernst, were initially not released. Berta made strenuous efforts with the Gestapo to have them released for burial. This was finally permitted. The bodies came back from the police in sealed coffins. Sally Rosenbach said prayers because I was still in prison. Otherwise, no Jew was allowed to be present on the late evening of 15 November, almost eight days after their murder. Several officers from the Gestapo saw to it that this was so. No investigation of these murders ever occurred. The night of 10 November claimed two further victims: Stefan Goldschmidt and Lewkowitz, both in their seventies. I could not find out whether they had been beaten too, or whether they had heart attacks because of fright . . . My first port of call was the synagogue. It was ringed with a high wooden fence, the windows were broken, the dome was still on the roof, but burned out, and the rafters were exposed to the elements. During the night of the pogrom, a gang had appeared, some of them physicians from the municipal hospital, some of them counsellors from the district court. They purloined a lot of petrol from the store on Schadowplatz, and tar from elsewhere. The Tora scrolls were removed from the Tora shrine, and set on fire in the courtyard, with the murderous arsonists dancing around them, partly

clothed in the robes of the Rabbi and prayer leader. Then everything
which consisted of wood, particularly the seating and roof trusses, was
doused with petrol and tar and set alight. This is how our synagogue
was burned down. Other synagogues were blown up. The mortuary
in our ancient cemetery was destroyed.

The pogrom of 9 November represented a decisive point in National
Socialist policy towards the Jews. Firstly, because the scenes initiated by
Goebbels throughout Germany took place in full view of the public, without the latter doing much – beyond a few exceptions – to translate their
clear disapproval into action. This posture showed the regime that while
the majority of 'national comrades' were not fanatic anti-Semites –
relatively few people actively participated in the plundering and violence
perpetrated by 'Party comrades' and the SA squads – the majority of the
German people were neither willing nor able to oppose Nazi policy
towards the Jews, which here for the first time both planned and took into
account murderous violence against the Jewish minority.[67] As the insti-
gator of the pogrom, Goebbels was well placed to appreciate how he had
altered the framework of what was possible. Shortly afterwards he commented, 'The whole question has now been taken a good step further.'
The passivity of the population at large cannot be explained or excused in
terms of the degree of perfection already attained by the Nazi apparatus of
terror. With very few exceptions, representatives of both Churches
remained silent, despite the fact that at this point in time they were still in
a position to issue a clear statement of moral disapproval. Similarly, there
are no recorded public protests from those in bourgeois-military resistance
circles.

Once again, therefore, the Nazi regime could introduce further anti-
Semitic regulations, with reference to the alleged 'Voice of the People' or
the passive moral climate it had inherited. These new measures went far
beyond the existing objective of reversing the achievements of the post-
Emancipation era. In line with their ceaseless redrawing of the parameters
of what was possible, it was from now on a question of the total expropriation and plundering of the Jewish minority. One may legitimately ask
what future was envisaged for a minority which was shortly denied even the
most elementary forms of subsistence and which other countries were
indisposed to take. This question was surely posed by those taking the
decisions described below. On 12 November 1938, a conference took
place under the chairmanship of Göring which resulted in a series of anti-
Semitic laws and decrees whose overall effect was purposively brutal almost
in inverse proportion to the ghoulishly jocular nature of the discussion

which produced them.[68] Firstly, the Jews were made collectively responsible for the assassination of Ernst vom Rath. They were to pay one billion Reichsmarks to the Nazi regime by way of 'atonement' for Rath's death. This was raised in the form of a 25 per cent levy, payable in five instalments, on capital assets over 5,000RMs. In addition, by virtue of the cynically-entitled Decree for the Restoration of the Street Scene in relation to Jewish Business Premises, they had to cover the cost of all damage caused by Nazi thugs during the night of the pogrom. Money claimed by Jews under insurance policies was declared confiscated by the State.

A further consequence of the conference of 12 November 1938 was the Decree for the Exclusion of Jews from German Economic Life. The resulting closure of Jewish businesses and workshops, and the further ban on Jews in various trades, was designed to satisfy the regime's short-term financial needs as dictated by the imperatives of the Four-Year Plan. The conference also debated further anti-Semitic measures. The so-called 'Aryanisation' of the economy was followed on 3 December 1938 by a decree which permitted Jews to alienate their bonds, shares, jewellery, and works of art only to the State.[69] On 5 December the regime arbitrarily reduced pensions paid to Jews who had been dismissed from public service.[70] In February 1939, Jews were obliged to surrender all precious metals in their possession to the State.[71] The physical segregation of Jews within towns, and hence the compounding of emotional with physical distance from 'them', was facilitated by the suspension, in April 1939, of measures designed to protect the security of Jewish tenants. Jews had no right to refuse the offer of (worse) accommodation, and were obliged to take in whatever (Jewish) sub-tenants the local authorities imposed on them. The ghettoisation of the Jewish population had begun. Further measures were designed to lend the Jewish minority the characteristics of 'the enemy within'. Hence a ban on the ownership by Jews of carrier pigeons on 29 November 1938;[72] the removal of their driving licences on 3 December;[73] the creation of a zone off-limits to Jews in the government quarter of Berlin;[74] and finally, from 1 September 1939, a curfew, which kept Jews off the streets between 9pm and 5am in summer and 8pm and 6am in winter. The confiscation of their radio sets effectively cut them off from the outside world. The outbreak of war with Russia brought a new wave of repressive measures, including the decision on 1 September 1941 to extend identificatory signs from Polish to German Jews. The philologist Victor Klemperer wrote a moving account of the humiliations which wearing 'the Star' had entailed:[75]

I ask myself today what I have asked myself and the most various sorts of people again and again: what was the worst day in those twelve years of hell?

I have never had a different answer either from myself or the others except this: the 19 September 1941. From then on one had to wear the Jewish Star, the hexagonal Star of David made of yellow coloured cloth, which today still signifies plague and quarantine, and which in the Middle Ages was the identifying colour for Jews, the colour of envy and of bile in the blood; the yellow cloth with the boldly-printed letters in black: 'Jew', the word bounded by the lines of the two intersecting triangles, the word formed from thick capital letters, which in their isolation, and in the broad exaggeration of the horizontal, pretended to be Hebrew characters . . .

A conventional, good-natured-looking man came towards me, carefully leading a small boy by the hand. He stopped before me. 'Look at that, Horst! He is responsible for everything!' . . . An elegant, grey-bearded man crossed the street and bowing deeply, gave me his hand: 'You don't know me, but I have to tell you that I condemn these methods' . . . I want to get on the tram, I am only permitted to use the footplate, and only when I go to the factory, and only when the factory is more than six kilometres from my home, and only when the footplate is strictly separate from the interior of the carriage; I want to get on, it is late, and if I don't arrive punctually for work, the foreman can report me to the Gestapo. Someone drags me off: 'Go on foot, it's a lot healthier!' An SS officer, grinning but not at all brutal, merely amusing himself, as one teases a dog a bit . . . My wife says: 'It is such a lovely day, and for once I don't have to go shopping or have to stand in queues – I'll go part of the way with you!' – 'Under no circumstances! Do I have to witness how you are insulted on the street on account of me?' . . . A removal man whom I have grown fond of from two earlier removals – all decent people who reek strongly of the KPD – suddenly stands before me in the Freiberger Strasse and pumps my hand with his two paws and whispers so that one must be able to hear it across the Fahrdamm: 'Now, Professor, don't let it get you down! Before long they'll be finished, the bloody brothers!' It was intended as a word of comfort, and it does warm my heart; but if the right person hears it, then my consoler would pay for it with imprisonment, and me, via Auschwitz, with my life . . . A car brakes as it goes along the empty street, a strange head leans out: 'Are you still alive, you damn pig? They should run you over, across your belly!'

If one reads the welter of decrees and regulations, it is possible to come to the conclusion that they were the product of improvisation, or of the ambition, careerism, and rivalries of the bureaucrats responsible for 'Jewish questions' in the ministries and agencies of the party.[76] The pettiness of many of these measures also indicates the self-propelling

4.5 The 'Jewish star', introduced compulsorily on 1 September 1941. This enabled 'national comrades' to tell at a glance who was a Jew, a matter difficult to establish by other criteria. The introduction of this visible stigma also marked the formal transition from defamation and economic ruination to the total exclusion of Jews from the 'national community'.

momentum of bureaucrats whose jobs and professional expertise were inextricably bound up with solving the 'Jewish question'. In looking at the matter in this way, however, one runs the risk of overlooking both the motivating force behind these measures, and how decisions were made within a fundamental ideological consensus. Put simply, no voices were heard from the top arguing in any other direction; indeed, on the contrary they mapped out the general line which the specialists fleshed out in detail. Regardless of how chaotic policy discussions and the decision-making process may have been, policy was executed with typical Teutonic thoroughness in detail by a bureaucracy which prided itself on its traditions of 'correct', Prussian abrasiveness and insensitivity to human beings. The effect was systematically devastating for those against whom these measures were directed. The Jews were discriminated against; their human rights were abrogated; they were physically isolated from the non-Jewish population, and totally eliminated from economic and professional life. It did not require much more bureaucratic ingenuity to summon, detain in collection points, and finally deport people who had no rights, and virtually no money to call their own. All of the bureaucratic mechanisms to carry out these policies were in place, once the war displaced the moral parameters still further.

THE 'FINAL SOLUTION OF THE JEWISH QUESTION'

Historical scholarship on the genesis of the 'Final Solution' has become mired in a progressively more sterile debate between so-called 'intentionalists' and 'structuralists', with textbook summaries managing to further drain the subject of either emotion or a wider philosophical dimension. Both positions in the debate have a number of merits and demerits; both ultimately reflect different forms of historical explanation; and the ground between them is steadily narrowing in favour of a consensus which borrows elements from both lines of argument. Intentionalists confront headlong the question of human agency and motivation, and place considerable stress on the role of Hitler and racial ideology.[77] Structuralists accuse them of simplifying a complex pattern of events by explaining them as 'merely' the execution of the unchangeable programme and will of Adolf Hitler, or of 'trivialising' the horror of modern, bureaucratic genocide by searching for one clearly defined culprit.[78] They also stress the *ad hoc* and reactive nature of decision-making, and the extent to which a series of essentially local initiatives were given retrospective coherence and sanction from above, or in other words the ways in which lesser figures worked their way towards the Führer. This of course raises the question of how the lesser or local figures knew which wishes they were anticipating. 'Structuralists' have the merit of directly addressing the question of how Hitler's undeniable and pathological hatred of Jews was translated into concrete policy by a host of lesser functionaries within a complex, modern,

4.6 *Man in the street wearing a 'Jewish star'.*

bureaucratic framework. The demerit in this approach is to focus to such a degree upon the contingent and chaotic details of the regime's administrative arrangements that one loses sight of the motive force and consensual ideological climate which informed these decisions, not to speak of the devastatingly efficient way in which industrialised mass murder was implemented. A preoccupation with the details of bureaucratic chaos, as if this were some unique failing of the Third Reich, can also run the risk of overlooking the visceral hatred which drove not only Hitler, but also the 'rational' labours of the bureaucrats. The 'banality of evil', a concept based upon the fact that most of those involved were not psychopaths or sadists, but steely desk-bound functionaries bounded by routine and the division of labour, has become something of a cliché. By using these terms one runs the danger of adopting a bloodless, unimaginative literalness towards men who cloaked deeply irrational hatreds in coolly detached bureaucratic language, and who themselves were tantalised by 'structures'. Dark fantasies and paranoia are not inconsistent with the most routinised and efficient 'managerial' practice. Reading some of the more academically abstract accounts of the origins of 'Final Solution', one can easily derive the misleading impression that the regime somehow bumbled into murdering millions of people, thus overlooking the passionate hatreds of the perpetrators towards their victims, or the group intoxication with violence and the prospect of going outside the limits of received moral norms which were also part of the crimes we are considering. There is also no conceivable justification for simply leaving out of general scholarly accounts work which happens to use the language of the victims rather than that of the perpetrators, on the dubious grounds that emotion and passion have no place in scholarly debate. Finally, any discussion, however brief, of these issues should not be exclusively concerned with the perpetrators, whose deeds are relatively easy to document, but should attempt the more creatively difficult task of saying something about the people whose lives they destroyed. Both of these criticisms apply as much to people on the left of the political spectrum – with some of the German 'alternative' historians showing an unhealthy fascination with the harebrained projects of middling Nazi functionaries – as they do to historians of a centrist or conservative disposition. Serious work on the victims of Nazi policy is largely being done by film-makers or novelists rather than by historians constrained by narrowly academic considerations.[79]

How and why did the persecution of German Jews escalate into the mass murder of European Jewry? On 12 November 1938 Göring stated: 'If the German Reich becomes involved in a diplomatic conflict in the foreseeable future, then it is only natural that we in Germany shall also contemplate a major reckoning with the Jews.'[80] Nine months before this conflict broke out, Hitler spelled out what a 'major reckoning' might entail:

> In the course of my life I have very often been a prophet, and have usually been ridiculed for it. During the time of my struggle for power it was in the first instance only the Jewish race that received my prophecies with laughter when I said that I would one day take over the leadership of the State, and with it that of the whole nation, and that I would then among other things settle the Jewish problem. Their laughter was uproarious, but I think that for some time now they have been laughing on the other side of their faces. Today I will once more be a prophet: if the international Jewish financiers in and outside Europe should succeed in plunging the nations once more into a world war, then the result will not be the Bolshevising of the earth, and thus a victory of Jewry, but the annihilation of the Jewish race in Europe![81]

The war intensified Nazi paranoia about the 'enemy within', facilitated the imposition of extreme solutions in extreme conditions, dispensed with the need to take into account international opinion, and transported Hitler and his associates back to what they regarded as their authentic and elemental context. A war of racial-imperialist conquest also vastly increased the scale of the 'question' by multiplying the number of Jews under Nazi tyranny. However, the fact that the regime continued to pursue plans for Jewish emigration two years into the Second World War has led some historians to regard Hitler's pre-war threats, notably the one quoted above, as so many rhetorical 'metaphors', bearing no automatic relationship to the onset of the 'Final Solution'.[82] Certainly Schacht and then Wohltat were involved in negotiations with the American Rublee, and Ribbentrop with the South African Pirow, concerning the further emigration of German Jews. Certainly, in the summer of 1940, officials in both the Foreign Office and RSHA developed the Madagascar plan, whose purpose was the creation of a Jewish colony under the aegis of an SS governor. It should be stressed that one of the professed objects of the diplomatic negotiations was to 'export' anti-Semitism, and therefore to make life for Jews impossible anywhere. The Madagascar Plan also envisaged using the Jews as a means of blackmailing the US government, and 'undoubtedly . . . would have led to physical extermination'.[83] The expectation of massive fatalities was also built into subsequent schemes for a 'Jewish reservation' in eastern Poland, plans which Hitler himself acknowledged in March 1940 'would never represent a solution'.

While these various 'long-range' solutions were being mooted, the terms of reference for those dealing with the question on the ground were altered. Although the Einsatzgruppen, who accompanied German armies into Poland, had orders to murder 'only' members of the Polish intelligentsia, a number of them availed themselves of the opportunity to murder Jews as well.[84] Attempts by the army to bring those responsible before courts martial were quashed by Hitler, who issued an amnesty on 4 October 1939 and two weeks later removed SS units from the jurisdiction of military courts.[85] This enabled the SS to continue murdering with impunity. As Goebbels noted after a visit to Posen in March 1941: 'Here everything is being liquidated, above all the Jewish filth.'[86] The terms of reference were then broadened for the racial-ideological war launched against the Soviet Union, through an order to the army to surrender Soviet commissars to the Einsatzgruppen, or to shoot them themselves; and through operational instructions issued to the former, for the execution of all Soviet functionaries, 'less valuable Asiatics', 'Gypsies' and Jews. These instructions were relayed to individual units in the form of 'an order from the Führer' for the 'rendering free from Jews of the whole of occupied Russia'. Although the practice of each task force varied, no one doubts that their orders came from the centre.

A former Roman Catholic priest, SS-Obersturmführer Albert Hartl, who joined Einsatzgruppe C in 1941, was interviewed about the matter of what would have happened had any of his colleagues refused to obey orders, which in this case included the shooting of 33,771 Russian Jews at Babi Yar:[87]

> In my experience it had a lot to do with the intellectual outlook of the individual task force commanders. As I said, Thomas was a physician. The leaders of the individual task forces were partly lawyers, like Dr Stahlecker, partly academics like Professor Dr Six, who should have been living in Heidelberg or Darmstadt, partly political economists like Ohlendorf. Among them there were those who were highly ambitious and who wanted to report to Berlin the highest possible number of shootings, and others, who attempted as far as possible to sabotage the order to carry out shootings, in order – as soon as the final implications of their command had become clear – to get themselves recalled as soon as possible. Among the latter was Brigadeführer Schulz, who, as he told me, disapproved of these mass shootings, and therefore had himself transferred as soon as possible from the command of a task force, which I recall was stationed in the Lemberg area. As far as I know no serious consequences resulted from this. However, it was clear that in general such people could not reckon on promotion for the foreseeable future . . . I know of no instance where apart from a block on promotion, or a punitive transfer, a unit leader was sent to

a concentration camp or sentenced to death. Concerning the lesser ranks, I also know of no instance in which refusal to take part in the shooting of Jews resulted in anyone being sent to a concentration camp or being sentenced to death.

Along with mass murder perpetrated independently by regional SS and police leaders, or by local pogroms which they themselves instigated, these task forces murdered 2.2 million Jews, including Jews deported from Germany, Austria, and what was once Czechoslovakia to Minsk or Riga. These people were shot, gassed – with surplus technology from the 'euthanasia' programme – or beaten to death with axes, iron bars and spades. The death squads took no account of either the age or the gender of their victims.

The following passage is from a diary entry made on 12 July 1941 by Felix Landau, an SS man who volunteered for one of the task forces which operated in the Lemberg region:[88]

Twenty-three have to be shot, including the women I mentioned before. They are remarkable. They even refuse to accept a glass of water from us. I was posted sentry and had to shoot anyone who escaped. We went along a country road for a kilometer, and then turned off right into a wood. Presently there were only six of us, and we looked for a suitable spot for the shooting and burial. After a while we found one. The condemned were given shovels in order to dig their own grave. Two of them were crying. The rest certainly had extraordinary courage. What must have been going on at that moment in their heads? I believe that each of them had a small hope that somehow they would not be shot. The condemned were deployed in three shifts because there were not enough shovels available. Curiously, absolutely nothing disturbed me. No pity, nothing . . . Slowly the hole grew bigger; two wept incessantly. I let them go on digging, for then they would not think so much. In fact, they grew quieter while working. Their valuables, watches, and money were piled up together. After they had all been lined up together in a clearing, the two women were taken to the edge of the grave to be shot. Two men had already been shot in the bushes by our Criminal Police Commissar. I did not see this, as I had to watch over the rest. The women were seized and taken to the edge of the trench, where they turned around. Six of us had to shoot them, divided so that three of us aimed at the heart and three at the head. I took the heart. The bullets struck and brain mass burst through the air. Three to the skull are too much. They almost tear the head off. Almost all of them fell down silently together, although it did not work in two cases, where they screamed and whimpered for a long time. The revolver shots were no good. There was no failure on the part of the two of us who fired together. The penultimate group now had to throw those who had been shot into the mass grave, then they had to line up, and then fall of their own accord into the grave. The last two had to sit on the far edge of the grave so that they would fall in exactly. Then a few corpses were rearranged with a pick-axe, and we began the burial work.

With the 'Kommissarbefehl' the regime had made a 'quantum leap'.[89] The fact that this still left three million Polish Jews, in worsening conditions in purposely created ghettos, led the regime to embark upon a comprehensive 'Final Solution' of the 'Jewish Question'. The conditions which the Nazi authorities created in the ghettos reinforced the regime's propaganda stereotypes. As Alfred Rosenberg put it: 'Seeing this race en masse, which is decaying, decomposing, and rotten to the core will banish any sentimental humanitarianism.' The means and the will to commit mass murder had been demonstrated by the T-4 'euthanasia' programme, where, incidentally, there is hard evidence that the general directive to commit murder came from Hitler, with his subordinates merely transforming his expressed wishes into administrative forms. The mounting unpopularity of the 'euthanasia' programme may also explain why there is no direct written evidence connecting Hitler with the 'Final Solution'. The first mass killing of Jews by toxic gas was at Chelmno in Poland, and was carried out by the 'special commando' under Herbert Lange, which had earlier used a gas van emblazoned with 'Kaiser's Coffee Company' to kill thousands of Polish mental patients. Sometimes wearing white coats and stethoscopes to dupe their victims, this unit gassed 145,000 Jews in a fifteen-month period commencing in December 1941.

Central bureaucratic control over the project to kill the Jews was achieved gradually and retrospectively after localised killings had started. This has led some historians to stress the role of local spontaneous combustion at the expense of a centrally organised conflagration. In fact, on 31 July 1941, Göring had entrusted Heydrich with the 'making (of) all necessary preparations with regard to organisational, technical and material matters for bringing about a complete solution of the Jewish question within the German sphere of influence in Europe'.[90] Both the leading role of the SS, and the inter-bureaucratic co-ordination necessary for the realisation of this 'complete solution', were established at a conference held on the morning of 20 January 1942 in the former offices of the German branch of Interpol beside the Wannsee. Representatives from the Ministries of Justice, the Interior, Foreign Office, the Generalgouvernment, Reich Chancellery and several SS agencies gathered in this secluded lakeside villa to be informed by Heydrich:[91]

> In pursuance of the final solution, the Jews will be conscripted for labour service in the east under appropriate supervision. Large labour gangs will be formed from those fit for work, with the sexes separated, which will be sent to these areas for road construction and undoubtedly a large number of them will drop out through natural wastage. The remainder who survive – and they will certainly be those who have the greatest powers of endurance – will have to be dealt with accordingly. For if released, they would, as a natural selection of the fittest, form a germ-cell from which the Jewish race could regenerate itself.

The representatives of the ministries not only acquiesced in the SS's appropriation of the 'practical execution of the Final Solution', but also agreed with all of Heydrich's suggestions, merely adding a few of their own as to how the 'combing-out' of Europe's Jews might be achieved more effectively. Eichmann's account of the conference to an Israeli court in 1960 belies the circumlocutionary tone used in the official minutes:[92]

> What I know is that the gentlemen sat together, and then in very blunt terms – not in the language that I had used in the minutes, but in very blunt terms – they talked about the matter without any circumlocution, I certainly could not have remembered that if I had not recalled saying to myself at the time: look, just look at Stuckart, who was always regarded as a legal pedant, punctilious and fussy, and now what a different tone! The language being used here was very unlegalistic. I should say that this is the only thing from all this that has still stuck clearly in my mind.
> *Presiding Judge:* What did he say on this matter?
> *Answer:* In particular, Mr President, I would like to . . .
> *Question:* Not in particular – in general!
> *Answer:* The talk was of killing, elimination and annihilation.

The Wannsee Conference did not inaugurate the 'Final Solution', i.e. the systematic extermination of the Jewish population of Europe, for this had been under way since November 1941, when transports of Jews had been killed at Minsk, Riga and Chelmno. Some of those, like Otto Lange, gathered in the villa with the waters of the Wannsee lapping at the jetties had in fact carried out mass shootings in Russia. The object of the conference was to co-ordinate the activities of the various agencies involved, in order to maximise the efficiency of the 'Solution' as it was carried a stage further. It was also the moment at which systematic mass murder passed into SS control, an achievement which Heydrich relayed to Himmler on the secure lines installed in the Wannsee villa for that purpose. This bureaucratic *coup de main* called for a round of cognacs. Subsequent conferences, with further civil and military agencies, regulated the details of the operation. Talks with officials from the Ministry of Transport concerning available rolling-stock and railway scheduling; talks with financial experts concerning the disposition of the deportees' residual resources; talks with diplomats working in allied or occupied countries; talks with industrialists to regulate the flow of slave labour to the factories they established in the immediate proximity of extermination camps.

Before the Wannsee Conference, Adolf Eichmann had become convinced that the methods employed by the Einsatzgruppen were psychologically deleterious for the men responsible, and not commensurate with the order of murder now being contemplated. Staff seconded from the defunct T-4 'euthanasia' programme graduated from carbon monoxide to the exhaust from static diesel engines, in Chelmno, Belzec, Sobibor, and Treblinka. Ninety-two former T-4 personnel, idle since August 1941, were seconded to the extermination camps because of their expertise in mass murder. The connection between the 'euthanasia' programme and the 'Aktion Reinhard' camps was made explicitly in this account by SS-Untersturmführer Josef Oberhauser on the beginning of Belzec, although he deliberately omitted to mention that up to 1 August 1942 over 140,000 Jews had been systematically murdered there, rather than just the occasional transports he mentions in this account.[93]

> The camp at Belzec lay in a north-easterly direction from the road from Tomazow in the direction of Lemberg. Since the camp required a railway connection for the arriving transports, the camp was established about 400 metres from the railway station Belzec. The camp itself was divided into two areas, camp area 1 and camp area 2. The siding from Belzec station ran directly into camp area 2, in which there were also the disrobing barracks, as well as the gas chambers and the burial area. At the time I myself was in Belzec, the gassing installations were still housed in a barracks which was lined inside with tin and which had a capacity of about 100 persons. Camp area 1 simply contained the barracks which housed the Ukrainian guard personnel.
>
> The German camp personnel were housed outside the camp area in two stone buildings which lay to the right of the road to Lemberg. In one of these was the office, the canteen and sleeping quarters. The second building consisted of sleeping quarters only...
>
> From Christmas 1941 I was subordinate to Wirth, who at this time was commandant of Belzec. At this time I was the liaison officer between Wirth and Globocnik's staff in Lublin. My competence included ordering building materials for the further expansion of the camp as well as the occasional transfer of Ukrainian guards. Wirth's deputy was Schwarz, who along with Wirth could exercise full powers of command.
>
> Gassings of Jews in Belzec up to 1 August 1942 could be divided into two stages. The first series of experiments consisted of 2 to 3

transports at 4 to 6 wagons, at 20 to 40 persons. On average 150 Jews were delivered per transport and killed. These gassings were not yet part of a systematic extermination, rather one wanted to try out the camp's capacity and to check how one carried out gassing technically. Following these first gassings, Wirth and Schwarz, as well as the entire German personnel, disappeared from Belzec. Wirth's last official business before his departure was to have about 50 Jewish labourers, including the Kapos, shot or gassed . . . At the beginning of May 1942 SS-Oberführer Brack from the Chancellery of the Führer came unexpectedly to Lublin. He talked with Globocnik about the further implementation of the extermination of the Jews. Globocnik said that he had too few people to carry out this programme. Brack declared that the euthanasia [programme] was slowing down and that the people from T-4 were being regularly put at his disposal, so that the decisions of the Wannsee Conference could be turned into reality. Since it did not appear possible for the task forces, which cleared individual areas of Jews, also to kill the people in the large ghettos of Warsaw or Lemberg, it was decided to create two further extermination camps, namely Treblinka and Sobibor, which were to be ready by 1 August 1942. The big exterminatory action was to commence from 1 August 1942. About eight days after Brack had visited Globocnik, Wirth and his people returned to Belzec. A second series of experiments took place up to 1 August 1942. During this time a total of 5 or 6 transports (in so far as I know) with 5 to 7 wagons at 30 to 40 persons arrived in Belzec. The Jews from two of these transports were gassed in the small chamber, then Wirth had the gas chamber torn down and put up a massive new building whose capacity was far greater. The Jews from the residual transports were then gassed in these new gas chambers. While the first series of experiments and the first transports of the second series of experiments were still gassed with bottled gas, the Jews from the final transports of the second series of experiments were already being killed with the exhaust from a tank or lorry engine regulated by Hackenholt.

The staff at Auschwitz discovered the comparative merits of 'Zyklon B', a gas used hitherto against pests and parasites, and then tested it on a group of Soviet prisoners of war, before embarking on the murder of millions of Jewish victims. The SS physicians responsible for 'selections' of prisoners and incoming transports left diary entries like these, from the journal of a Professor of Medicine at the University of Münster:[94]

9 September 1942
Early today I received the highly welcome news from my lawyer in Münster Prof. Dr Hallermann that on the 1st of this month I have divorced my wife. I can see colours again; a black shroud has been

taken away from my life! Later I was present as a physician at the carrying out of corporal punishment on eight prisoners and at a small calibre shooting.
10 September 1942
Present again in the morning at a special action.
20 September 1942
Heard a concert this afternoon between 3 and 6pm given by the prisoners' choir in beautiful sunshine; the choirmaster was the conductor of the Warsaw State Opera. 80 musicians. Roast pork for lunch, baked tench for dinner.
23 September 1942
Present last night at the 6th and 7th special actions. In the morning Obergruppenführer Pohl and his encourage came to the Waffen-SS barracks. The sentry at the door saluted me first. Dinner at eight with Obergruppenführer Pohl in the commandant's house, a real feast. Baked tench, as much as one wanted, real coffee, excellent beer and rolls.
28 September 1942
Present tonight at the eighth special action. Hstuf. Aumeier told me that the camp at Auschwitz is 12km in length and 8km wide and 22,000 Morgen overall. Of this 12,000 Morgen are under the plough and the fish pond is 2,000 Morgen.
12 October 1942
Second innoculation against typhus; following this strong general reaction (fever) in the evening. Despite this, present that night at a special action from Holland (1,600 persons). Horrific scenes in front of the last bunker (Hossler!). That was the tenth special action.

The commandant of Auschwitz, Hoess, left this summary account of procedures which resulted in the deaths of two million people:[95]

The cremation of about 2,000 people in five ovens took approximately 12 hours. In Auschwitz there were two installations with 5 double ovens each, and 2 installations with 4 larger ovens each . . . All of the left-over clothing and effects were sorted by a group of prisoners who worked all the time and were quartered in the effects camp. Once a month valuables were sent to the Reichsbank in Berlin. After they had been cleaned, items of clothing were sent to armaments firms for the eastern labour working there or to repatriates. Gold from the teeth was melted down and likewise sent once a month to the sanitation office of the Waffen-SS . . . The highest number of gassings in one day in Auschwitz was 10,000. That was the most that could be carried out on one day with the equipment available.

In total, about six million Jews were gassed, shot, starved, or beaten to death before the liberation of these camps by Allied forces. The camps represent the final transformation of murder into a dehumanised, bureaucratic, industrial process. Behind the words and figures were the sort of scenes described by members of the Jewish special detachments who managed to survive:

> It was pointless to tell the truth to anyone who crossed the threshold of the crematorium. You couldn't save anyone there. It was impossible to save people. One day in 1943 when I was already in Crematorium 5, a train from Bialystok arrived. A prisoner on the 'special detail' saw a woman in the 'undressing room' who was the wife of a friend of his. He came right out and told her: 'You are going to be exterminated. In three hours you'll be ashes.' The woman believed him because she knew him. She ran all over and warned the other women. 'We're going to be killed. We're going to be gassed.' Mothers carrying their children on their shoulders didn't want to hear that. They decided the woman was crazy. They chased her away. So she went to the men. To no avail. Not that they didn't believe her; they'd heard rumours in the Bialystok ghetto, or in Grodno, and elsewhere. But who wanted to hear that? When she saw that no one would listen, she scratched her whole face. Out of despair. In shock. And she started to scream.
>
> So what happened? Everyone was gassed. The woman was held back. We had to line up in front of the ovens. First, they tortured her horribly because she wouldn't betray him. In the end she pointed to him. He was taken out of the line and thrown alive into the oven. We were told: 'Whoever tells anything will end like that.'[96]

Those responsible for creating this monument to aberrant human ingenuity had one source of authority for their actions. The source, swathed in the myth and mystique of the Führer, always argued one way with those to whom he could afford to speak bluntly. In 1942 Hitler told Himmler:

> the discovery of the Jewish virus is one of the greatest revolutions that has taken place in the world. the battle in which we are engaged today is of the same sort as the battle waged, during the last century, by Pasteur and Koch. How many diseases have their origin in the Jewish virus! . . . We shall regain our health only by eliminating the Jew. Everything has a cause, nothing comes by chance.[97]

The irony of the last sentence was no doubt unintentional. Notwithstanding attempts to construct elaborate psychological explanations for those who carried out these barbaric policies, let alone attempts to displace responsibility on to tendencies allegedly latent in all modern industrial societies, the bleak truth of the matter is that the self-appointed elite were intoxicated by the idea of actions which were secret, racially therapeutic, and which took them beyond what they regarded as an obsolete morality,

4.7 Jewish girl asleep while en route into emigration to England.

and knowledge of which would go with them to the grave. In reality there was no dilemma.

Jews were the principal victims of the destructive drives of National Socialism. However, it would be misleading to describe them simply as objects of Nazi persecution, as passive as lambs going to the slaughter. It is not for non-Jewish historians to chronicle the choices individual Jews had to make between death and collusive involvement in the destruction of others, but something should be said about Jewish resistance.[98] In addition to desperate and heroic acts by Polish Jews, notably the Warsaw uprising in 1943 and the escape attempts from Sobibor and Treblinka, Jews in Germany also endeavoured to resist the stream of measures designed to disenfranchise, ruin, and finally murder them. Individual Jewish communities tried to assist emigration through collections of money and the retraining of emigrants, while maintaining both the existence and morale of those who remained, through Jewish old people's homes, hospitals, schools, and cultural centres. Emigration, which was a realistic option only for the younger members of the Jewish community or those who could afford it, involved learning new skills and languages and being prepared to live a lonely existence in societies with different customs

4.8 *Max and Martha Liebermann in their house on Pariser Platz in 1931. Behind them is Manet's portrait of George Moore which Liebermann owned. Liebermann, himself Germany's most distinguished impressionist painter, resigned in protest from the Presidency of the Prussian Academy of Arts in May 1933. He died on 8 February 1935 aged 87; his wife later committed suicide shortly after being summoned to the Gestapo headquarters.*

and little comprehension of the circumstances the emigrants had left behind them. Letters from refugees to their relatives and friends in Germany spelled out the realities of the new life in ways which did not encourage more to follow them. The reaction to the mounting terror of those Jews who remained was governed by a number of objective and subjective circumstances. The slogan 'everyone stays at his post' reflected the disbelief of assimilated and acculturated Jews at Germany's descent into barbarism, and the conviction that the Nazi regime was epiphenomenal. For many elderly and highly assimilated Jews the end of this delusion resulted in suicide. An estimated 10,000 Jews killed themselves, as self-doubt gave way to despair.[99] The age structure of the remaining Jewish population also militated against active resistance, quite apart from the efficiency of the Nazi apparatus of terror. Of the 164,000 Jews who remained in Germany on the eve of war, half were over fifty and a third over sixty years of age. Broadly speaking, those who remained were too old, sick, or poor to leave. There were also 20 per cent more women than men in the residual Jewish population, a reflection of their decision to give men and children priority in emigration, or to stay behind to care for the elderly and sick. About 15,000 of the Jews who remained were partners in 'mixed marriages', protected by the 'race' of their spouse, until voluntary or compulsory divorce once again made them highly vulnerable.[100]

From the beginning, Jews involved with socialist or communist organisations were subject to especially vicious treatment by the Gestapo. In 1933, for example, a number of Jewish lawyers who worked for left-wing organisations were drowned, hanged, or beaten to death. Because of the risks involved, in 1936–7 the underground leadership of the KPD decided to exclude Jewish comrades from resistance groups. Although individuals certainly distinguished themselves by helping Jews, German resistance groups undertook nothing comparable with the strikes which occurred in wartime Holland, or the organisation of mass flight in Denmark. German Jews certainly participated in the resistance activities of underground socialist groups, and individual Jews put up what defence they could during the Pogrom in 1938. However, there were also a number of Jewish resistance groups which maintained hideouts, falsified identity and ration cards, and helped those sought by the Gestapo. Some of these groups managed to survive into the war. Their chances of survival were highest in big cities, with perhaps as many as 5,000 Jews living underground in 1943 in Berlin alone. Others operated in a twilight zone between the underground and a barely tolerable 'normal' existence. An electrician called Werner Scharff managed to save some Jews from deportation by providing them with false identity papers and hiding places. In 1943 he had to go underground, was recognised on the street by a Gestapo agent, and was subsequently deported to Theresienstadt. Having managed to escape, Scharff not only established a resistance group back in Luckenwalde, but entertained plans to storm the prison on Berlin's Schulstrasse to release Jewish inmates. However, he was rearrested in October 1943, tortured in Berlin, and shot in Sachsenhausen on 16 March 1944. One of the most justifiably celebrated Jewish resistance groups collected around Herbert Baum.[101] This group consisted of young Jews of both sexes from petit bourgeois and working-class families, who had a history of involvement in Communist, socialist, and Zionist groups. Historians continue to debate the precise mix of their political affiliations, a question which seems to have been thoroughly irrelevant to the individuals involved. At first, the Baum group concentrated on producing fly-sheets and leaflets, with the aid of stencils since Jews were forbidden to possess typewriters. Most of the group worked in factories in Berlin, Baum himself as a skilled electrician among the 950 Jews 'employed' by the Siemens concern. They received pitiful wages of about 16–20RMs a week, and were isolated from other workers, a fact which did not stop them making contact with both foreign and other Jewish workers. The high point, and at the same time the end, of the group's activities, consisted of an arson attempt on 18 May 1942 against the propaganda exhibition 'The Soviet Paradise' in the Lustgarten. Eleven visitors were injured and some of the displays destroyed. Some members of the group were arrested within a few days, others in July and August. Herbert Baum was tortured to death on 11 June 1942; the rest were sentenced to death by a special court and beheaded at Berlin-Plötzensee. To discourage any similar actions, 500 Berlin Jews were arrested. Two hundred and fifty were shot immediately; the rest died in concentration camps. The Reich Security Main Office informed the leaders of Jewish communities in Germany, Vienna, and Prague that similar measures could be anticipated in the event of further acts of 'sabotage' involving Jewish participants. Retaliation on this scale also explains why the opportunities for resistance by Jews were so limited. It was a matter of endangering not just one's own life, but also the lives of entirely innocent people. That individual Jews nonetheless continued to run this risk deserves more attention than it customarily received in the politically-motivated accounts of 'resistance' current in what were the two German states.

One of the most remarkable acts of resistance involved the 'Aryan' partners of Jewish factory workers who on 27 February 1943 were dragged from the factories of Berlin and interned in a number of *ad hoc* collection points, prior to their deportation eastwards. Goebbels' object was to make his Gau 'free of Jews'. When their partners failed to come home, their 'Aryan' wives began telephoning the police, the factories concerned, and each other. Sometimes accompanied by male relatives on leave from the army, the women made for the collection point on the Rosenstrasse, equipped with shaving equipment and food for their imprisoned husbands. A crowd of between 150 and 200 people gathered to exchange unpleasantries with the SS sentries, one block away from the office of the Gestapo which dealt with Jewish questions. Despite bombing raids by the RAF, the deliberate closure of the nearest S-Bahn station, and the illegality since May 1933 of all non-Nazi demonstrations, relatives picked their way across the rubble of the inner city to repeat their confrontation with the SS. The latter did not seem to know how to respond. While the SD recommended that they ignore the protests and continue the planned deportations, other elements in the Reich Security Main Office were worried about further disturbing the morale, and hence obedience, of a citizenry already severely shaken by bombing, by having to shoot several hundred of them in broad daylight. The longer the demonstrations went on, the more ordinary Germans would be publicly reminded of the regime's ill-guarded secret. More crowds gathered outside other collection points on a daily basis, dispersing when threatened by the sentries only to regroup a few minutes later. These demonstrations, which involved calling SS men 'murderers' to their faces, regardless of their threats to shoot, led Goebbels to abandon the proposed deportations. The Jews in the Rosen-strasse received papers and ration cards and were released. The Berlin Gestapo was saddled with responsibility for an 'error'. Thirty-five Jews whom the Gestapo had actually managed to send to Auschwitz were sent back a few days later, although to a work training camp in order to ensure that what they had seen there remained a secret.[102]

CHAPTER FIVE

THE PERSECUTION OF SINTI AND ROMA, AND OTHER ETHNIC MINORITIES

S INTI and Roma were called 'Zigeuner' in Germany. The origins of this word, which has analogues in other languages (*zigenare* in Swedish, *cigan* in Spanish), may be a matter of dispute, but the word's pejorative overtones are not. For this reason, those Sinti and Roma still living in Germany do not like being called 'Zigeuner'.[1] The same applies to the equivalents in the English-speaking world, who object to the term 'gypsy'. This is a corruption of 'Egyptian', the name by which Sinti and Roma were known in several countries from the medieval period onwards. As far as is known, concerning a history which has never been written down, 'Gypsies' had nothing to do with Egypt.[2]

Sinti and Roma first came to Germany in the late fifteenth century. They were originally from the Punjab region of north India.[3] They became Christians in the course of their migrations through Persia, Asia Minor, and the Balkans, although they were nevertheless frequently accused of leading an 'un-Christian' way of life. Their appearance, language, customs, and itinerant way of life – determined by a mystical aversion to the uncleanliness of the soil – further distinguished them from the settled population. Soon they were accused of being beggars, thieves, spies, and practitioners of harmful magic.[4] These manifold prejudices were both the cause and the justification for the terrible persecution which Sinti and Roma experienced in Germany and elsewhere throughout the entire early modern period.[5] In the nineteenth century, there was a temporary lull in indiscriminate persecution, connected in part with a Romantic interest in this European example of the 'noble savage'.[6] But Verdi apart, nowhere could 'Gypsies' be described as equal citizens.

When the Nazis came to power, they inherited State legislation which in this area stood in obvious contradiction to Article 104 of the Weimar constitution, guaranteeing all Germans equality before the law.[7] The object of the resulting police harassment was to keep Sinti and Roma permanently on the move, paradoxically, as a means of forcing them to settle. The pace was set by Bavaria, where from 1899 the security police kept a central register on 'Gypsies', which from 1911 contained copies of their fingerprints, and material culled from public registry offices. In 1926 the Bavarian police were further empowered by a Law for the Combating of Gypsies, Travellers, and the Workshy to send Sinti and Roma to workhouses for up to two years, if they could not prove regular paid employment. Sinti and Roma were therefore discriminated against solely and simply because they were 'Gypsies'.[8]

FROM THE BAVARIAN LAW FOR THE COMBATING OF GYPSIES, TRAVELLERS, AND THE WORKSHY OF 16 JULY 1926

Article 1
Gypsies and persons who roam about in the manner of Gypsies – 'travellers' – may only itinerate with wagons and caravans if they have permission from the police authorities responsible.
This permission may only be granted for a maximum of one calendar year and is revocable at all times.
The licence permitting them to do so is to be presented on demand to the (police) officers responsible.
Article 2
Gypsies and travellers may not itinerate with school-age children. Exceptions may be granted by the responsible police authorities, if adequate provision has been made for the education of the children.
Article 3
Gypsies and travellers can only itinerate with horses, dogs, and animals which serve commercial functions if they possess a licence to do so from the responsible police authorities . . .
Article 4
Gypsies and travellers may not possess firearms or ammunition unless they have been expressly permitted to do so by the responsible police authorities.
Article 5
Gypsies and travellers may not roam about or camp in bands. The associ-

5.1 Sinti and Roma encamped in woods in East Prussia.

ation of several single persons or several families, and the association of single persons with a family to which they do not belong, is to be regarded as constituting a band. A group of persons living together like a family is also to be regarded as a band.
Article 6
Gypsies and travellers may only encamp or park their wagons and caravans on open-air sites designated by the local police authorities, and only for a period of time specified by the local police authorities.
Article 9
Gypsies and travellers over sixteen years of age who are unable to prove regular employment may be sent to workhouses for up to two years by the responsible police authorities on the grounds of public security.

The instructions to the police on how to implement the law laid bare the racial approach towards the 'Gypsy question' which was beginning to be pursued:[9] 'The term Gypsy is generally understood, and requires no further elucidation. Racial science provides information on who is to be regarded as Gypsy'. It should be noted that the Law simply overlooked the fact that the Sinti and Roma were originally from North India and belonged to the Indo-Germanic-speaking, or as Nazi racial anthropologists would have it, 'Aryan' people. Naturally, the racial discrimination which the law licensed was totally unconstitutional. It was finally abrogated by the US military government on 28 July 1947.[10]

After 1933, the apparatus of police harassment and persecution was centralised (along with the police itself); policy was progressively radicalised; and any (limited) possibilities of legal redress were destroyed, along with the autonomy of the courts. In 1936 a Reich Central Office for the Fight against the Gypsy Nuisance was established, within the headquarters of the Reich Criminal Police in Berlin.[11] This agency took over and developed the harmful bureaucratic detritus already collected by their colleagues in the Bavarian security police, including 19,000 files on Sinti and Roma. The latter were immediately subjected to the regime's racial legislation, although they were never specified as objects of it. This was apparent in the application of the Law for the Prevention of Hereditarily Diseased Progeny of 14 July 1933 and the Law against Dangerous Habitual Criminals promulgated on 24 November 1933. Sinti and Roma were sterilised without any legal basis whatsoever.[12]

They were first mentioned expressly in a circular issued by the Reich and Prussian Ministry of the Interior on 26 November 1935.[13] It concerned 'racially mixed marriages'. Registry offices were instructed to request 'testimonials of fitness to marry' only if 'as a consequence of the betrothed belonging to different races, progeny deleterious to German blood' were to be anticipated. This would be so in the cases of marriages between those of German blood and 'Gypsies, Negroes, and their bastards'. Although Sinti and Roma were not mentioned specifically in any of the regime's major racial legislative enactments, Globke and Stuckart's semi-official commentary on the Nuremberg Laws was of the opinion that the laws applied to 'Gypsies' as well as Jews.[14] Like Jews, they were 'carriers of alien blood', and therefore could not be permitted either to marry, or to have sexual relations, with those of 'German blood'.

However, it would be incorrect to attribute the drive to persecute Sinti and Roma solely to a malevolently intolerant regime. Long before the Nazis came to power, there was much evidence of what might be called citizens' initiatives. The following is a letter from the residents of Seckbacherlandstrasse in Frankfurt to the Citizens' Committee (August 1930):[15]

> The undersigned residents of Seckbacherlandstrasse Rötheneck, and the eastern part of Vereinstrasse, both owners and tenants, request most urgently that the citizens' committee raise objections with the

municipal administration about the Gypsy nuisance in their immediate neighbourhood.

Right opposite properties number 16 to 30, Gypsies have settled themselves for some time, who represent a heavy burden upon the neighbourhood. The hygienic conditions in this area defy description. The settlement has neither a well nor a latrine and therefore every possible space is used as a latrine. On account of this, and through the depositing of bath- and washing-water on the open field, there are smells which pollute the entire neighbourhood. The conditions have come to such a point that we are worried about the spread of contagious diseases. Also, with regard to sexual conduct, these people – and even the children – have no sense of decency; our children have to watch the Gypsy children playing with certain parts of their anatomy. What will this lead to? Almost daily there are fights and the neighbourhood has become so insecure that one has to worry about walking the streets alone after darkness. Because of the Gypsies our properties have greatly depreciated, and already tenants have asked the house-owners for a rent rebate and surely court cases will soon follow concerning this question. From the points outlined above, you can see the miserable situation which landlords as well as tenants have come to through the toleration of the Gypsy camp by the city of Frankfurt. Therefore we request you to cause the administration to alleviate the problem as quickly as possible, to prevent greater damage, particularly of a hygienic and health nature.

Gypsies who refused to stay on designated sites were denied welfare payments, as this draft letter of the Mayor of Frankfurt am Main to the welfare authorities on 27 September 1930 concerning the Gypsy camp at Friedbergerlandstrasse makes plain:[16]

Concerning this matter we would like to comment that the Gypsies have already completely left the site they were allocated on the Russengelände, Friedbergerlandstrasse, corner of Berkersheimer Weg. The so-called Gypsy camp is at present completely empty. As we have already previously reported, we have no legal grounds to force the Gypsies into the designated camp. As the Gypsies have left the camp, they are not eligible for social security.

Throughout Germany in the Nazi period, both the citizenry and local authorities took it upon themselves to remove Sinti and Roma from private land, depositing them in *ad hoc* camps which gradually assumed coercive characteristics. For example, in Berlin prior to the 1936 Olympic Games, the authorities quite illegally rounded up about 600 Sinti and Roma, corralling them on an insalubrious wasteland near a sewage dump and a cemetery at Marzahn, a site which was particularly offensive to a people hyper-sensitive about cleanliness.[17] The justification for this

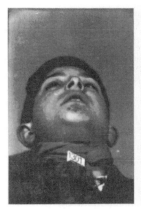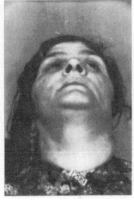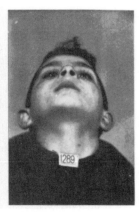

5.2 Photographs taken by Professor Robert Ritter's agency in the course of conducting 'racial-biological' research on 'Gypsies'.

measure was that the Sinti and Roma might sully the clean image of the Olympic host city. Many of them succumbed to diseases. Thereafter, the Berlin welfare authorities unsuccessfully tried to regularise this anomaly of their own making (while offloading the attendant costs of medical care) by pressing for the site's reclassification as a concentration camp. This practice would be emulated in several other German towns.

As yet the regime had still to determine who was a 'Gypsy'. Registering and classifying a group of victims was always a necessary precondition for their systematic persecution. Since the Sinti and Roma had been Christian for centuries, the ecclesiastical records which were used to discover converted Jews would shed little light upon racial provenance. However, academic 'science' came to the rescue in the form of Dr Robert Ritter, a juvenile psychologist working at the university of Tübingen.[18] His specialism 'criminal biology' was destined to become an academic growth area in Nazi Germany. In 1935 Ritter reoriented his research interests from proving that delinquency was the result of hereditary 'feeble-mindedness' to research on Sinti and Roma. In a grant application that year, he stressed that his research would be of 'decisive importance for the racial-hygienic measures of the State concerning Gypsies'.[19] For once this was not a matter of calculated exaggeration. In 1936 Ritter became director of a research unit within the Ministry of Health, whose costs were partly defrayed by the Criminal Police and the Reich Main Security Office of the SS. The unit had one task: to locate and classify Germany's 30,000 Sinti and Roma to facilitate police measures against them.

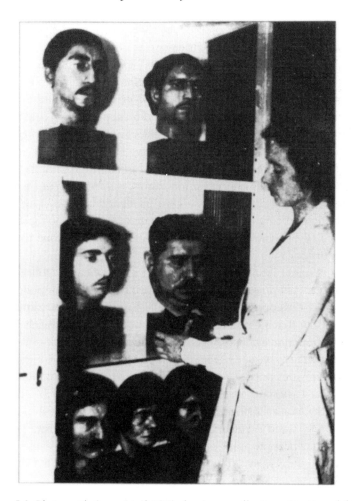

5.3 Photograph from April 1942 showing a collection of papiermâché models of 'Gypsy' heads kept by the criminal-biological department of the Reich Health Office in Berlin-Dahlem, in which Ritter and his assistants were active.

Ritter's working hypothesis was that the Sinti and Roma had certainly come from India and hence had once been 'Aryans'. However, in the course of their migrations westwards, they had interbred with 'lesser races'.[20] This applied to the majority of those Sinti and Roma living in Germany, 90 per cent of whom, he claimed, were part and not pure 'Gypsies'. Their racial characteristics inclined them towards an 'asocial' and criminal way of life. Thus while he was prepared to permit the pure

'Gypsies' further pursuance of their lifestyle under carefully controlled conditions, he advocated the resettlement in closed colonies and sterilisation of the more dangerous 'part-Gypsies'. Only these measures would stem the transmission of their criminal characteristics. Only following such a categorisation would the 'preconditions' exist for a solution of the 'Gypsy Question' on a Reich-wide basis. To support these contentions, Ritter and his assistants scoured the archives and police files in order to reconstruct each Sinti and Roma's genealogy. They also conducted interviews with the Sinti and Roma, threatening women with having their heads shaved, or men with the concentration camps, if they could not recall the names of their great-grandparents. This, incidentally, explains why Sinti and Roma detest being interviewed – particularly by anthropologists, well-intentioned or otherwise – and insist that it is for them alone to record their own history.

Ritter's research unit was soon relocated to the Central Police Head-quarters, and his findings began to percolate into government policy. This was no longer the concern of the individual Länder, but now came under the aegis of the Reich Criminal Police, with its subordinate Reich Central Office for the Fight against the Gypsy Nuisance. Both were part of the burgeoning security empire of Heinrich Himmler. Centralisation meant an end to the previous police practice of trying to shove Sinti and Roma out of their area. It became systematic. Already on 16 July 1937 Himmler instructed the Central Office 'to evaluate the findings of racial-biological research' on Sinti and Roma.[21] Doubtless he had the work of Ritter and his team in mind. The same point was made more explicitly in a circular on the Fight against the Gypsy Nuisance issued by Himmler on 8 December 1938.[22]

> Experience gained in the fight against the Gypsy nuisance, and knowledge derived from race-biological research, have shown that the proper method of attacking the Gypsy problem seems to be to treat it as a matter of race. Experience shows that part-Gypsies play the greatest role in Gypsy criminality. On the other hand, it has been shown that efforts to make the Gypsies settle have been unsuccessful, especially in the case of pure Gypsies, on account of their strong compulsion to wander. It has therefore become necessary to distinguish between pure and part-Gypsies in the final solution of the Gypsy question.
>
> To this end, it is necessary to establish the racial affinity of every Gypsy living in Germany and of every vagrant living a Gypsy-like existence.
>
> I therefore decree that all settled and non-settled Gypsies, and also all vagrants living a Gypsy-like existence, are to be registered with the

Reich Criminal Police Office–Reich Central Office for the Fight against the Gypsy Nuisance.

The police authorities will report (via the responsible Criminal Police offices and local offices) to the Reich Criminal Police Office–Reich Central Office for the Fight against the Gypsy Nuisance all persons who by virtue of their looks and appearance, customs or habits, are to be regarded as Gypsies or part-Gypsies.

Because a person considered to be a Gypsy or part-Gypsy, or a person living like a Gypsy, as a rule confirms the suspicion that marriage (in accordance with clause 6 of the first decree on the implementation of the Law for the Protection of German Blood and Honour . . . or on the basis of stipulations in the law on Fitness to Marry) must not be contracted, in all cases the public registry officials must demand a testimony of fitness to marry from those who make such an application [to be married].

Instructions on how to execute this decree, issued by the Criminal Police on 1 March 1939,[23] said that the 'requisite legal basis' for the prevention of 'racial miscegenation' and for the general regulation of the Gypsies' way of life could only be established through a comprehensive 'Gypsy Law'. The imminence of such a law was announced on several occasions, but none was ever promulgated.

Treatment of the Gypsy question is part of the National Socialist task of national regeneration. A solution can only be achieved if the philosophical perspectives of National Socialism are observed. Although the principle that the German nation respects the national identity of alien peoples is also assumed in the fight against the Gypsy Nuisance, nonetheless the aim of measures taken by the State to defend the homogeneity of the German nation must be the physical separation of Gypsydom from the German nation, the prevention of miscegenation, and finally the regulation of the way of life of pure and part-Gypsies. The necessary legal foundation can only be created through a Gypsy Law, which prevents further intermingling of blood, and which regulates all the most pressing questions which go together with the existence of Gypsies in the living space of the German nation.

A conference on racial policy organised by Heydrich took place in Berlin on 21 September 1939, which may have decided upon a 'Final Solution' of the 'Gypsy Question'.[24] According to the scant minutes which have survived, four issues were decided: the concentration of Jews in towns; their relocation to Poland; the removal of 30,000 'Gypsies' to Poland; and the systematic deportation of Jews from German incorporated territories using goods trains. An express letter sent by the Reich Main Security Office on 17 October 1939 to its local agents mentioned that the 'Gypsy Question will shortly be regulated throughout the territory of the Reich'.[25] Thenceforth, Sinti and Roma were confined to designated sites and encampments. Those who attempted to leave were sent to concentration camps. Many Sinti and Roma were actually in camps already, on account of activities deemed to be 'criminal' or 'asocial'.[26] Many Sinti and Roma were taken into 'protective custody' during the large-scale round-up of the 'asocial' in 1938.[27] In October 1939 they were joined by 'soothsayers', whom Himmler regarded as a potential threat to national morale.[28] In June 1940 the Reich Security Main Office forbade the release of Sinti and Roma serving determinate concentration camp or regular prison sentences.[29] At about this time, Adolf Eichmann made the recommendation that the 'Gypsy Question' be solved simultaneously with the 'Jewish Question' by appending 'three or four trucks' of Sinti and Roma to the trains taking Jews from Vienna to the Generalgouvernement.[30] In fact, matters did not run so smoothly, although some 2,500 Sinti and Roma were deported to Poland from the western areas of the Reich between April and May 1940 as an alleged 'security threat'.[31] A few of them managed to survive on the loose as entertainers or musicians. Most of them either simply starved to death or were used by the SS as forced labour. Those who fell sick were shot. Some 80 per cent of those deported from Hamburg alone failed to return alive. Plans to follow up these modest numbers with the wholesale deportation of Germany's 30,000 Sinti and Roma met with the opposition of Hans Frank, Hitler's satrap in occupied Poland,[32] although 5,000 were deported from the Burgenland to the Łódź ghetto, to be subsequently gassed in Chelmno in January 1942. Major deportations of Sinti and Roma were halted so as to give priority to the deportation of Jews, whose homes were needed for ethnic German repatriates. For once, an itinerant way of life reprieved the Sinti and Roma from persecution. This meant that the earlier short-term policy of corralling them in *ad hoc* camps became a long-term affair. Conditions in camps like Marzahn, and Lackenbach and Salzburg in Austria, were atrocious.[33] Those held in Lachenbach were subjected to beatings, solitary confinement, dietary deprivation, heavy manual labour, and such indignities as the shaving of their heads. The authorities' response to epidemic disease was: 'Massive loss of life in the restricted area only interests us in so far as it represents a threat to the non-Gypsy population.'[34] In the case of camps in towns or near villages, matters were made worse by the constant complaints from people living or working in their proximity that the Sinti and Roma were 'spies' or a threat to the morals of the local population. Complaints made by 'national comrades' were then used by local authorities to demand the Sinti and Roma's deportation. The Criminal Police responded by saying that a final decision in this case was pending.

5.4 *Sinti and Roma in the concentration camp at Sachsenhausen. They have 'black triangles' sewn on their trousers, indicating that they are 'asocial'. Imprisonment in a concentration camp was tantamount to a death sentence.*

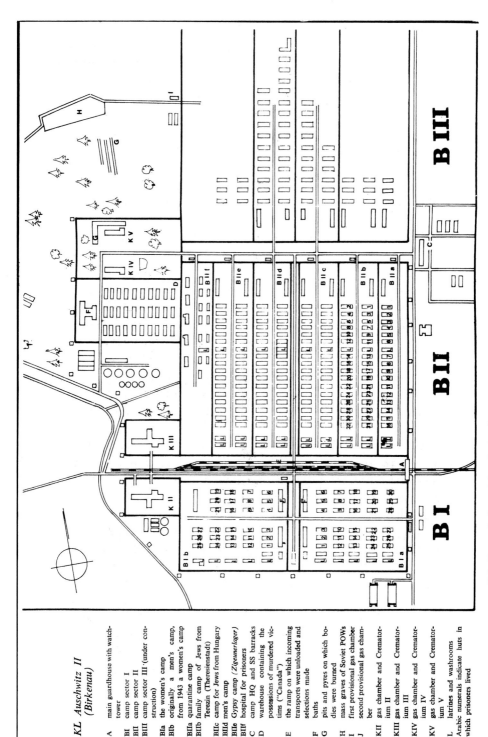

KL Auschwitz II
(Birkenau)

A   main guardhouse with watch-tower

BI   camp sector I
BII   camp sector II
BIII   camp sector III (under construction)

BIa   the women's camp
BIb   originally a men's camp, from 1943 a women's camp

BIIa   quarantine camp
BIIb   family camp of Jews from Terezín (Theresienstadt)
BIIc   camp for Jews from Hungary
BIId   men's camp
BIIe   Gypsy camp (*Zigeunerlager*)
BIIf   hospital for prisoners

C   camp HQ and SS barracks
D   warehouse containing the possessions of murdered victims ("Canada")
E   the ramp on which incoming transports were unloaded and selections made
F   baths
G   pits and pyres on which bodies were burned
H   mass graves of Soviet POWs
I   first provisional gas chamber
J   second provisional gas chamber
KII   gas chamber and Crematorium II
KIII   gas chamber and Crematorium III
KIV   gas chamber and Crematorium IV
KV   gas chamber and Crematorium V
L   latrines and washrooms
Arabic numerals indicate huts in which prisoners lived

5.5 *Ground plan of Auschwitz showing the position of camp 'BIIe' for 'Gypsies'.*

As in the case of the Jews, the invasion of the Soviet Union marked the transition from persecution to extermination. SS Einsatzgruppen and units of the regular army and police began shooting Sinti and Roma in Russia, Poland, and the Balkans.[35] Possibly as many as 250,000 Sinti and Roma died in these actions, which were legitimised with the old prejudice that the victims were 'spies'. Differences of opinion at the highest levels of government account for the final equivocations in the resolution of the 'Gypsy Question'. Himmler, encouraged by his SS 'Ancestral Heritage' organisation, wanted to keep a few token clans of pure Sinti, Roma, and Bohemian Lalleri alive on a reservation, as a form of ethnic curiosity.[36] This scheme was opposed by Martin Bormann – as the spokesman of both Hitler and the ordinary NSDAP membership – notwithstanding the very small number of people Himmler intended to keep alive. Himmler signed the order despatching Germany's Sinti and Roma to Auschwitz on 16 December 1942.[37] The 'Final Solution' of the 'Gypsy Question' had begun. The order sending Sinti and Roma to Auschwitz mentioned categories of exempt persons, which were ignored by Himmler's Criminal Police subordinates who carried out the deportations. This prompted Rudolf Hoess to remark later: 'They arrested many soldiers with high decorations on leave from the front, but whose father, mother, or grandfather were Gypsies or part-Gypsies. There was even a Party member of long standing among them, whose Gypsy grandfather had migrated to Leipzig. He himself had a big business there, and was a much decorated veteran of the First World War.'[38]

The 'B II e' camp at Auschwitz was about 1,000 m by 80 m in size, a series of wooden barracks on waterlogged soil, from which both the gas chambers and crematoria were clearly visible.[39] Entire Sinti and Roma families were sent there, chiefly to minimise the likelihood of the regime's agents being knifed or torn apart while trying to separate extended families. The camp lasted for seventeen months. Outside attempts to have people released on the basis of categories of exemption were referred to the ubiquitous Robert Ritter. They were thus doomed to failure from the start. For example, the NSDAP in Magdeburg interceded on behalf of the German foster-parents of a seventeen-year-old Sintiza in Auschwitz. The Criminal Police eventually replied: 'According to the formal testimony of the racial-hygiene research unit of the Reich Ministry of Health, [the girl's] mother is classified as a part-Gypsy. The measures taken therefore apply to the girl too.'[40] Conditions in the camp continued to deteriorate, with outbreaks of typhus, smallpox, and the ulcerative condition called Noma. Twins and dwarves among the inmates were subjected to the attentions of

Dr Josef Mengele; others fell victim to experiments conducted on behalf of the Luftwaffe, involving immersing the subject in freezing water. Beginning in April 1944, those fit for work were relocated to other camps, leaving behind women, children, and the elderly. On the night of 2–3 August 1944, the 2,987 who remained were issued with extra rations of bread and salami, and then driven under cover of darkness to the gas chambers. The vacant camp was strewn with broken pots and torn clothing, reflecting the fact that the Sinti and Roma fought to the end. A few children who had managed to conceal themselves were lured out next day by Mengele, who drove them in his own car to the gas chambers. Of the 23,000 people who had entered camp B II e, 20,078 had perished.

The Sinti and Roma's conversion into a *minorité fatale* ran parallel with their physical extermination. As we have seen, the Nazis abandoned the idea of issuing a global Gypsy Law analogous to the anti-Semitic Nuremberg legislation. This omission resulted in grotesquely contradictory circumstances. While some Sinti and Roma were already imprisoned in concentration camps, others were more or less free to move about Germany, working or serving 'their' Fatherland at the front. Various ordinances were issued to rectify these anomalies. They demonstrate that Nazi policy towards the Sinti and Roma was even more uncoordinated than policy towards the Jews. However, they also show that persecution of Sinti and Roma was similarly propelled by racial ideology. The Nazis endeavoured to bring the legal situation of Sinti and Roma into line with that of the Jews. Thus on 13 March 1942, the Reich Minister of Labour ordered that 'the special stipulations with regard to Jews in the field of welfare legislation . . . should be correspondingly applied in their present form to the Gypsies'.[41] Following an ordinance of the Reich Minister of Finance on 26 March 1942, 'Gypsies' had to pay the same special taxes as Jews.[42] Similarly, the Reich Citizenship Law of 25 April 1943 deprived Jews and 'Gypsies' of their already much curtailed rights as German citizens.[43]

> The Reich leadership of the NSDAP – Main Office for the Nation's Welfare – has decreed the following through a letter dated 21 May 1942 to the leaders of the offices for the nation's welfare in the Gau leadership of the NSDAP:
>
> Further to my communication No. V 15/39 of 2 June 1939, I make known the following:
>
> At the instigation of the Reich Main Security Office of the SS, the Reich Minister of Labour has decreed, by the order of 13.3.1942 IIIb 4656/42, that full Gypsies, and part-Gypsies with predominant or

equal parts of Gypsy blood, are to be equated with Jews with regard to labour legislation.

Dependants of full or part-Gypsies with predominant or equal parts of German blood can therefore no longer be cared for by the NSV. Only part-Gypsies with predominantly German elements in their blood are still to be included in welfare schemes.[44]

Discrimination against Sinti and Roma did not cease with the collapse of the Third Reich. In 1956, the Federal Court decided that they had only been subjected to racial persecution from the 1943 deportation order onwards.[45] This was only backdated to 1938 in the early 1960s, by which time many of the Nazis' victims were dead. Up to that point, the Sinti and Roma's 'asocial characteristics' apparently legitimated 'police and security measures' taken against them. This extraordinary claim was not unconnected with the fact that many of those responsible for 'Gypsy affairs' in the Federal Republic had been similarly engaged in the Nazi period.[46] In 1953, Ritter's files and some 24,000 'racial testimonies' were given to a newly-founded 'Travellers' Office' of the Bavarian Criminal Police, whose staff included one of Ritter's former SS associates, himself a former expert on the 'Gypsy Question'. Likewise, Ritter's research materials and findings were in evidence in many reports prepared by the Federal Republic's leading academic advisor on Sinti and Roma. He had acted as a character witness for Ritter in post-war denazification proceedings, testifying to Ritter's 'profound appreciation of the situation of the Gypsies'. This enabled Ritter to resume work as a child psychologist. Some of his female assistants and doctoral students – whose work was carried out on children who were then deported – passed upward in post-war academic and professional life, with no checks being made on precisely how they acquired their qualifications and titles.[47] The fact of Nazi genocide against Sinti and Roma was only officially acknowledged by Chancellor Helmut Schmidt in 1982, a fact which does not deter current deportations of eastern European 'Gypsies'. In the same month (November 1989) in which public agencies in West Germany were ostentatiously welcoming economic refugees from the GDR or further afield (including 'ethnic German' Poles whose sole claim on Germany is that their parents had evinced a 'positive' attitude towards the Nazi occupation of their country), the Hamburg police ejected several Sinti and Roma from their sanctuary within the former Neuengamme concentration camp and deported them to Yugoslavia. Rumanian Sinti and Roma fleeing the savagery of Iliescu's coal-miners are in turn being set upon by alienated working-class youths in both parts of Germany.

PART-NEGROES AND SLAVIC MINORITIES

Following the peace of Versailles, Allied armies were stationed in the Rhineland as an army of occupation.[48] The French forces included a small number of colonial troops: Senegalese, Moroccans, Malagasies, creoles, and a few Annamese from Indochina. German politicians of all shades of opinion were particularly exercised by their presence. Chancellor Müller inveighed against 'Senegal negroes occupying Frankfurt University and the Goethe House',[49] while President Ebert, also a Social Democrat, protested against the injustice of occupation by a 'lower culture'.[50] Outraged nationalists throughout Germany accused these troops of spreading every disease from sleeping sickness to VD, and issued postcards depicting 'gorillas' savaging German women. According to Sally Marks, who has made a detailed study of this issue, the response in the Rhineland was different.[51] The colonial troops were courteous and often popular. Unlike the French, they neither hated the Rhinelanders nor tried to lord it over them. So far from being uncontrollable rapists, the combination of exoticism and the power of the franc seems to have led to *their* complaining of being pestered by German women. The facts of the matter made no difference to German government-backed racist propaganda; propaganda, moreover, which was endorsed by the British in the interests of white solidarity. Many commentators in England were concerned lest the 'unnatural' position of 'Blacks' ordering 'Whites' about at gun-point should set precedents for them outside Europe. The children of these colonial soldiers and their female German partners were referred to as 'Rhineland Bastards' in the press of both the Weimar Republic and the Nazi regime. The numbers involved were grossly inflated by a government and public with an interest in discrediting any aspect of the peace settlement. It was not only racists who saw the existence of these children as a threat to the 'purity' of 'the Germanic race'. However, it was left to Hitler to discover a Jewish conspiracy behind this 'black curse'. As he declared in *Mein Kampf*, the Jews had 'brought the negroes into the Rhineland' with the 'clear aim of ruining the hated white race by the necessarily resulting bastardisation'.[52]

Notwithstanding the conspiracy aspect, which was Hitler's own contribution, many others joined him in expressing hatred towards children who happened to have non-European fathers. In 1920 a certain Dr Rosenberger asked: 'Shall we silently accept that in future instead of the beautiful songs of white, pretty, well-formed, intellectually developed, lively, healthy Germans, we will hear the raucous noise of horrific, broad

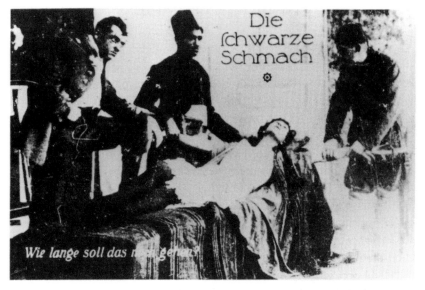

Die
ſchwarze
Schmach

Wie lange soll das

5.6 Protest placard sent to the Reich government in 1923. Entitled 'The Black Curse', the postcard asks 'how long will this continue?' beneath a picture of 'black' French troops grouped around a distressed white woman.

skulled, flat nosed, ungainly, half-human, syphilitic half-castes on the banks of the Rhine?'[53] Instead of attempting to curb the expression of racist sentiments in publicistic writing, the authorities were themselves engaged in collecting material on the number, names, and location of the 'Rhineland Bastards'. In 1927 officials in the Bavarian Ministry of the Interior recommended sterilisation, but the suggestion was turned down at Reich level because of the demoralising effects upon the children's German mothers.[54] The opinions of the fathers were not taken into account. The Nazi regime merely took over where its predecessors had left off. On 13 April 1933 the Prussian Minister of the Interior, Göring, requested the authorities in Düsseldorf, Cologne, Koblenz, and Aachen to provide accurate statistics concerning the 'Rhineland Bastards'.[55] Material relating to some 145 children was then analysed in accordance with pseudo-scientific racial criteria by Dr Wilhelm Abel of the Kaiser Wilhelm Institute for Anthropology, Heredity, and Eugenics in Berlin.[56] Abel came to the probably foregone conclusion that the 'Rhineland Bastards' were inferior to their white contemporaries with regard to their physical and intellectual capacities and behaviour patterns. Consequently, Abel appealed to those 'in whose hands it lies to prevent their reproducing'.

What this involved was spelled out in concrete terms by another academic in a pamphlet published in 1933 on 'Racial Problems in the Third Reich'. The 'black curse' could only be 'eradicated' by 'sterilisation of the half-castes'. The author, Dr Hans Macco, also called for the sterilisation of 'Gypsies'.[57] By 1934 there were intra-ministerial discussions concerning the extension of the Sterilisation Laws to 'Gypsies' and 'Rhineland Bastards'. On 11 March 1935 one of the working parties of the Committee of Experts for Population and Racial Policy met to discuss 'ways to solve the question of Bastards', by which they meant the children in the Rhineland, of whom there were estimated to be between five and eight hundred.[58] The Leader of the Racial Political Office of the NSDAP, Dr Walter Gross, recommended that the children should be sterilised following an anthropological investigation. However, the majority of those present were of the opinion that the question of whether to legalise their sterilisation had to 'be left to the Führer'. By 1937 it had been decided – whether by Hitler remains unknown – to sterilise them without legal cover. The Gestapo formed a 'Special Commission No. 3' with sub-commissions in Wiesbaden, Ludwigshafen, and Koblenz, which included representatives of public health authorities and academic experts.[59] The latter helped locate the children, who were then compulsorily sterilised. The panels of experts included the director of the Kaiser Wilhelm Institute for Anthropology, Heredity, and Eugenics, Professor Eugen Fischer, and his colleagues Abel and Heinrich Schade. No further measures were taken against the 'Rhineland Bastards'. Plans to deport them were vetoed on the grounds of the possible impact upon world opinion. The regime had either come to the conclusion that the 'problem' had been solved by compulsory sterilisation, or else had more important issues on the 'racial-political' agenda.

These issues included policy towards ethnic and national minorities, namely the Sorbs, Kashubians, and Poles.[60] The Kashubians were the descendants of a Slavic tribe which had managed to maintain its independence vis à vis the Poles and Teutonic Knights up to the fourteenth century. At the beginning of the fourteenth century their territory, which is called Pomerelia in English and German and Gdańsk-Pomorsze in Polish, was incorporated into the state of the Knights. From 1466 it became part of Poland, and then in the late eighteenth century part of (West) Prussia. Despite these three changes of regime, the Kashubians maintained their own language (or dialect) and culture, although these issues have long been the subject of nationalistically-inspired philological debate. During the Kaiserreich, the authorities endeavoured to 'germanise' the

Kashubians through such agencies as German-language schools. After 1918, the Poles essayed a policy of 'polonisation'. This in turn led to government-sponsored scholarly efforts in the Weimar Republic to foment a sense of Kashubian ethnicity. Poles and Germans fiercely debated these issues without much participation by the Kashubians themselves. The Poles wished to prove that the Kashubians were essentially Polish, the Germans that a history of Kashubian separateness had been checked by the Poles. In 1939 Hitler merged West Prussia and the Free City of Danzig into the 'Gau Danzig-West Prussia'. Unlike the Poles living there, who were driven into the confines of the Generalgouvernement, the Kashubians were allowed to stay. However, unlike the majority of 'ethnic Germans' they were not included in groups 1 and 2 of the 'ethnic German list', but were consigned to group 3 as being 'fit for germanisation'.[61] The use of the Kashubian language (dialect) and the cultivation of Kashubian customs was banned. The Kashubians were then left alone, provided they obeyed this policy and did not sympathise with their Polish compatriots. This policy did not satisfy all those Nazis who had dealings with the Kashubians. In 1939 the chief medical officer of the West Prussian provincial labour office recommended the deportation of members of the Kashubian upper classes and the sterilisation of 'less valuable elements'.[62] As far as is known, Dr Petzsch's recommendations were not pursued.

Nazi policy towards the Sorbs in Upper and Lower Lusatia was the negative mirror image of policy towards the Kashubians. The Sorbs are descendants of West Slavic tribes which once inhabited the lands east of the Elbe before the various Germanic tribes arrived.[63] The latter, once they had become literate, referred to the Sorbs as 'Wends'. Gradually the 'Wends' in central and eastern Germany lost their linguistic and cultural identity. It was otherwise with the 'Wends' in Upper and Lower Lusatia who remained resolutely Slav. During the sixteenth century, German humanists used the neologism 'Sorbs' to describe these people. The Sorbs describe themselves as 'Serbi' and dislike the term 'Wend', which has derogatory overtones in German. In the course of the early modern period the area settled by the Sorbs contracted, partly as a result of conquest, partly because the Sorbs began to adopt German in order to participate fully in religious, economic, and cultural life. The Saxon and Prussian authorities tried to promote this process by planting non-Sorbian-speaking German teachers or pastors in Sorbian villages.[64] During the early nineteenth century, Sorbian intellectuals founded societies to counteract this unwanted development through the cultivation of the Sorbian language and customs. As elsewhere, language and custom were among the main motors of national consciousness. Both Czech and Polish intellectuals assisted their 'Slavic brothers' along the road to their own identity.

A growing sense of Sorbian ethnicity resulted in German alarm concerning a 'Wendish threat'.[65] Publicists claimed that behind the Sorbs were Czechs and Russians endeavouring to bring about a Pan-Slavist union of the Slav peoples at the expense of 'Germandom'. The responsible authorities took these warnings seriously. In the second half of the nineteenth century there were deliberate and systematic attempts to suppress not only the developing Sorbian movement but also the Sorbian language and culture. The Prussian–German government's increasingly repressive policies towards the Polish nationalist movement in the province of Posen began to colour policy towards the Sorbian national movement. In reality, the latter was rather weak. Only 2,800 people belonged to the Sorbian 'Domowina', the national association founded in 1912. Only a few of the latter subscribed to the demands of the Sorbian National Committee, which in December 1918 were relayed to the peace-makers at Paris in the form of a proclamation.[66] This said: 'On the basis of the Wilsonian points, the National Committee calls for an independent Lusatian–Sorbian state, because the Lusatian Sorbs are a distinct Slavic people who, like other free people, have the right to build their own future themselves and to concern themselves with its continued independent existence and development.' The Allies did not follow up these recommendations. However the authorities in the Weimar Republic took Sorbian separatist tendencies sufficiently seriously to imprison Arnost Bart, one of the leading lights of the Sorbian national movement, briefly for treason. Likewise, in 1920, the state government in Saxony founded a secret 'Wendish department' in Bautzen to monitor Sorbian activities.

Nazi policy towards the Sorbs was constrained by a variety of circumstances. The relatively high NSDAP vote among Protestant Sorbs in Lower Lusatia did not deter the regime from interfering with the Sorbian press or from arresting some Sorbian nationalist leaders.[67] However, the negative response this generated in Czechoslovakia and Poland, namely the threat of retaliatory measures against the German minorities there, led the regime to reappraise its initial ill-considered policies. Henceforth, Sorbian separatist tendencies were condemned, but at least officially the Sorbian language and customs were to be left to die out of their own accord. Sorbian nationalists responded with a superficial, tactically-motivated espousal of some aspects of Nazi 'Blood and Soil' ideology, while continuing to organise the Sorb population.

This state of affairs may have suited both the Sorbs and the cautious elements in the Saxon 'Wendish department', but it failed to satisfy the Bund Deutscher Osten.[68] This was the 'co-ordinated' successor organisation to a plethora of Wilhelmine eastern lobby groups concerned with the plight of 'ethnic Germandom' in the East. Under the historian Theodor Oberlander, the BDO lobbied for a more aggressive policy towards the Sorbs. For example, co-ordinated efforts were made to suppress studies which would bolster Sorbian consciousness. A meeting at the Reich Ministry of the Interior on 26 April 1937 issued a series of 'Theses on the Sorbian Question' whose effect was to stifle all scholarly work on the Sorbs:[69]

1. There are no 'Sorbs' and no 'Lusatians' in the German Reich, but merely Wends or Wendish-speaking Germans.

2. The Wends do not constitute a separate nationality but are a people who, in part, speak a Slavonic language within the context of the German people and race.

3. There is no Wendei and no self-contained Wendish area of settlement. The expression 'Wendish linguistic region' is to be avoided. In case of need one should employ regional terms like Upper or Lower Lusatia or Spreewald.

4. The incidence of Wendish speaking, Wendish costume, and other manifestations of Wendish custom is no indication of a non-German nationality. The cultivation of Wendish customs within given limits is totally permissible. The Wendish language is declining through natural processes.

5. A small group in Saxony is trying to split the Wends from the German nation as a separate 'Sorbian people', a foreign national group. These efforts are supported from Czechoslovakia, Poland, South Slavia, and France. Therefore it is recommended that the Wendish Question should not be dealt with in public in the Reich either publicistically or in a scholarly way.

6. Such questions which have to be dealt with for general scholarly reasons should not be published or, if they are, only for internal use.

7. Treatment of the Wendish Question cannot be avoided in the context of academic studies of Eastern Germany, Saxony, Brandenburg, and

Silesia. In these studies the connection with the history and customs of the German people is to be strongly emphasised.

8. If, for whatever reason, for example because of hostile studies from home or abroad, it is still found to be necessary to refute the latter or to study the subject, it is strongly recommended that the manuscripts be sent to the North-East German Research Association before publication, who in turn, for their part, will get in touch with the competent authorities.

The stifling of scholarship was accompanied by the suppression of the Sorbian nationalist movement. In March 1937 the Domowina, which had refused to adopt the loaded title 'Union of Wendish-speaking Germans' in its constitution, was informed that 'all its public and private meetings and assemblies must in future be regarded as being directed against the maintenance of public tranquility, security, and order, and are therefore forbidden by authority of the police'.[70] In August the Gestapo raided the offices in the Serbski dom (Sorbian house), closing down the newspaper *Serbske Nowiny* and arresting its publisher. Sorbian teachers were transferred from Lusatia, and in 1938 Sorbian was prohibited as a language of instruction in schools. Following the occupation of Czechoslovakia, the Gestapo arrested and consigned to concentration camps leading Sorbian sympathisers. An SD report dated 30 May 1940 assessed the fruits of policy towards the Sorbs and made the following recommendations:

1. Any emphasis and promotion of Sorbian ethnicity must cease, although forcible measures of political denigration should be avoided.

2. The Sorbian ethnic splinter should be absorbed through peaceful cultural penetration. The most beneficial factors are German kindergarten, German schools, use of female labour, service in the army, or NS formations.

3. The influence of the extraordinarily thin Sorbian intellectual class must be cut out. This can be achieved, since only teachers and clergy come into question here, mostly through transfers, without needing to occasion any disquiet in the population as a whole.[71]

This relatively moderate approach failed to win the assent of Heinrich Himmler. As Reich Commissar for the Strengthening of Ethnic Germandom he began to interest himself in the Sorbs. In a memorandum on the treatment of foreign peoples in the east, dated 15 May 1940, he recommended consigning parts of the Sorbian population to the Generalgouvernement since they were of 'the same racial and human type' as the Poles.[72] There, they were to be reduced to helotry and ignorance of everything save that obedience to the Germans was 'a command from God'. Despite Himmler's ascendancy, the Sorbs were never 'resettled'. The Nazi regime contented itself with pillaging Sorbian libraries, transferring teachers and clergy, and sending Sorbian leaders to concentration camps. Himmler seems to have regarded these measures as being preparatory to 'a final solution of the Wendish question'. Towards the end of the war, plans were apparently being canvassed to move the Sorbs en masse to the mining districts of Alsace-Lorraine. Nothing came of these schemes, although the Sorbs continued to be the objects of racial researchers. The results of Nazi policy were mixed. The regime certainly accelerated a longer-term process of assimilation and germanisation, although the coercive means adopted only served to stimulate Sorbian national consciousness. This continued until recently, with the Sorbs enjoying the status of a protected minority within the former German Democratic Republic.

CHAPTER SIX

THE PERSECUTION OF THE 'HEREDITARILY ILL', THE 'ASOCIAL', AND HOMOSEXUALS

IMMEDIATELY after the seizure of power, the National Socialists left no one in any doubt that they intended to translate their plans for selective 'breeding' into reality. On 28 June 1933 Reich Minister of the Interior Frick established a Committee of Experts for Population and Racial Policy.[1] Its object was to make preparations for the promulgation of a law sanctioning sterilisation. A draft law permitting the sterilisation of those considered hereditarily ill had been prepared by the Prussian government in late 1932. This, however, insisted that either the person concerned or their guardian had to consent to the operation involved.

In clause 12 of the Law for the Prevention of Progeny with Hereditary Diseases, which the National Socialist government issued on 14 July 1933, the voluntary principle was replaced by compulsion.[2] Moreover the range of sicknesses regarded as 'hereditarily determined' was extended. Persons could now be compulsorily sterilised who were suffering from 'congenital feeble-mindedness'' 'schizophrenia'; 'manic depression'; Huntington's chorea; 'hereditary blindness'; 'hereditary deafness; and 'serious physical deformities'. Sterilisation could also be enforced against chronic alcoholics. This catalogue of sicknesses was not without problems. As some physicians pointed out at the time, it was by no means certain that some of the sicknesses were hereditary. Moreover, some of the categories were so elastic as to be meaningless. When could a person be considered to be a 'chronic alcoholic'? What did 'congenital feeble-mindedness' mean?

From the Law for the Prevention of Progeny with Hereditary Diseases of 14 July 1933:

(1) i. Anyone who has a hereditary illness can be rendered sterile by a

surgical operation if, according to the experience of medical science, there is a strong probability that his/her progeny will suffer from serious hereditary defects of a physical or mental nature.

ii. Anyone is hereditarily ill within the meaning of the law who suffers from one of the following illnesses:
1.   Congenital feeble-mindedness
2.   Schizophrenia
3.   Manic depression
4.   Hereditary epilepsy
5.   Huntington's chorea
6.   Hereditary blindness
7.   Hereditary deafness
8.   Serious physical deformities

iii. In addition, anyone who suffers from chronic alcoholism can be sterilised.

(7) i. Proceedings before the Hereditary Health Courts are not public.

ii. The Hereditary Health Court has to make the necessary inquiries; it can call expert, and other, witnesses, as well as order the personal appearance and medical examination of the person to be sterilised, compelling him to do so in cases of non-appearance without adequate excuse. The provisions concerning the conduct of civil hearings are to be applied correspondingly to the examination of and swearing in of witnesses and experts, as well as to the disqualification and rejection of members of the court. Physicians who appear as witnesses or medical experts are obliged to testify without regard to professional confidentiality. Courts and administrative authorities, as well as hospital institutions are obliged to supply information to the Hereditary Health Court on request.

(12) i. If the court finally decides upon sterilisation, the operation must be performed even if it is against the wishes of the person to be sterilised, unless that person was solely responsible for the application. The medical officer is responsible for requesting the necessary measures to be taken by the police authorities. In so far as other measures prove insufficient, the use of force is permissible.

Reasons for the law
Since the National Revolution public opinion has become increasingly preoccupied with questions of demographic policy and the continuing decline in the birthrate. However, it is not only the decline in population which is

a cause for serious concern but equally the increasingly evident genetic composition of our people. Whereas the hereditarily healthy families have for the most part adopted a policy of having only one or two children, countless numbers of inferiors and those suffering from hereditary conditions are reproducing unrestrainedly while their sick and asocial offspring burden the community . . . [3]

Questions like these were to be 'resolved' by so-called Hereditary Health Courts. These decided upon sterilisation in cases referred to them by physicians and those in charge of hospitals and asylums. A supplementary decree of 5 December 1933 made it compulsory for the latter to report their own patients and charges.[4] Attempts were made to lend the whole process an air of scientific objectivity through the use of intelligence tests. These contained questions designed to eke out the subject's educational abilities, e.g. simple arithmetic or 'who was Bismarck?' Questions like 'what is the present form of government in Germany?' were rather harder to answer satisfactorily. Was one supposed to say 'a terroristic dictatorship'? The intelligence test were also designed to 'test' the social and moral 'outlook' of the person concerned: 'Why does one learn things?', 'Why does one save?', 'What are loyalty, piety, respect, modesty?', and so forth. If one failed to give satisfactory answers, one would be categorised as 'feeble-minded', a concept which also embraced the dubious notion of 'moral feeble-mindedness'. That is to say, deviant attitudes constituted 'feeble-mindedness'. Here, those carrying out the tests usually differentiated, or in other words discriminated, between men and women. Women who had frequent changes of sexual partner were 'morally feeble-minded', but men were not. The concept of 'camouflaged' feeble-mindedness or schizophrenia was used to deal with those who got the answers right. Some 320,000–350,000 people were sterilised in accordance with these dubious criteria.[5] At least a hundred people died as a result of surgical incompetence, and many more still bear the mental scars of their private suffering.

From an 'intelligence test form' used to establish 'mental and hereditary illnesses' from 1933:

Intelligence Test Form

1. Orientation
(What is your name?)
(What are you?)
(How old are you?)

(Where do you live?)
(What year is it?)
(Which month?)
(What is the date?)
(What day of the week is it?)
(How long have you been here?)
(Where is this place?)
(Which building are you in now?)
(Who brought you here?)
(Who are the people around you?)
(Who am I?)
2. Educational ability
(Home town/village)
(Belonging to which province?)
(Capital of Germany?)
(Capital of France?)
(Who was Luther?)
(Who was Bismarck?)
(What type of state do we have at present?)
(Who discovered America?)
(When is Christmas?)
(What does Christmas mean?)
(Further questions of a similar type)
(How many days in the week?)
(How many months in the year?)
(forwards and backwards)
3. General knowledge
(Where does the sun rise?)
(Why is there day and night?)
(Why does one build houses higher in towns than in the countryside?)
(What does it mean to boil water?)
(Why do children go to school?)
(Why do courts exist?)
(Types of money?)
(What does it cost to send a letter?)
(Prices of foodstuffs?)
Differences between:
(Mistake – lie?)
(Loan – gift?)
(Parsimony – saving?)
(Lawyer – public prosecutor?)
(Stairs – ladder?)
(Pond – stream?)

4. Special questions concerning working life
Make a sentence using the following three words:
Hunter – Hare – Field
Soldier – War – Fatherland
Spring – Meadow – Flowers
School – Education – Life[6]

The Law for the Prevention of Hereditarily Diseased Progeny was not only applied to people who were in no sense either ill or 'hereditarily ill', but was also radicalised. In September 1934 Hitler advised the Reich Physicians' Leader Dr Wagner that 'pregnancies could be terminated in the case of hereditarily ill women, or women who had become pregnant by a hereditarily ill partner'.[7] The question of abortion on 'eugenic grounds' had also been both debated, and in some cases practised, in the Weimar Republic, despite the fact that it was prohibited by clause 218 of the law. The advent of the National Socialist regime at first represented no difference of policy. On the contrary, measures to combat infractions of the law on abortion were stepped up. This did not deter individual physicians from carrying out abortions on 'hereditarily ill' women. The Nazi leadership took note of this. On 26 June 1935 they promulgated the Law amending the Law for the Prevention of Hereditarily Diseased Progeny.[8] This sanctioned abortions within the first six months of pregnancy (!), in the case of women who had been categorised as 'hereditarily ill' by the Hereditary Health Courts.

From the Law amending the Law for the Prevention of Hereditarily Diseased Progeny of 26 June 1935:

The government of the Reich has decided upon the following law which hereby takes effect:

Individual clauses

The Law for the Prevention of Hereditarily Diseased Progeny of 14 July 1933 (Reichsgesetzblatt 1, p. 529) will be amended as follows:

(1) In c. 9 sentence 1, instead of 'emergency period of one month', insert 'emergency period of fourteen days'.

(2) Following c.10a insert:
(i) If, by virtue of the law, a Hereditary Health Court has decided upon the sterilisation of a woman who is pregnant at the time the operation is carried out, the pregnancy may be terminated, with the consent of the

woman concerned, unless the foetus is already capable of independent life, or unless the termination of the pregnancy entails a serious danger to either the life or health of the woman herself.

(ii) The foetus is to be regarded as being incapable of independent life if the termination takes place before the completion of the sixth month of pregnancy.

(3) In c. 11 paragraph 1, sentences 1 and 3 and paragraph 2 the words 'and termination of pregnancy' are to be inserted after the word 'sterilisation'.

(4) Clause 14 is to be interpreted as follows:
(i) Sterilisation, or the termination of a pregnancy, as well as the removal of the gonads, which are not in accordance with the stipulations of the law, are authorised and to be carried out only if a physician has decided in accordance with the dictates of medical skill that this would forestall a grave threat to the life or health of the person concerned, and only with that person's consent.

(2) Removal of the gonads of a man can be performed only with his consent, and only if this has been recommended by the medical officers of the courts or administrative authorities as being necessary to free him from a degenerate sexual drive which might result in further infringements of paragraphs 175 to 178, 183, 223 to 226 of the Penal Code. Recommendations for castration in criminal trials or custody proceedings remain unaffected.

Berlin the 26th June 1935

The Führer and Reich Chancellor Adolf Hitler
The Reich Minister of the Interior Frick
The Reich Minister of Justice
Dr Gürtner[9]

The precise relationship between these racially-motivated measures and the so-called 'euthanasia' programme has yet to be established. 'Permission for the destruction of worthless life' had been demanded by the lawyer Karl Binding and the psychiatrist Alfred Hoche in their eponymous book published in 1920.[10] This sparked off an animated public discussion. Their inhuman demands, expressed in a commensurately inhuman and utilitarian language, were not categorically or clearly refuted by physicians, theologians, and lawyers. This suggests how widespread subscription to selective breeding and racial extermination, albeit in the guise of 'eugenics' rather than the ideology of a particular political party, had become in the Weimar Republic. It is also suggested by the apparent lack of public reaction to Hitler's espousal of the most extreme elements in the 'eugenic' case. In the course of a speech to the Nuremberg Party rally on 5 August 1929, Hitler declared that 'If Germany was to get a million children a year and was to remove 700,000–800,000 of the weakest people, then the final result might even be an increase in strength.'[11] It was already obvious from these words that what Hitler envisaged had nothing whatsoever to do with 'euthanasia', if that is taken to mean painlessly ending the life of a terminally ill person either at their own request or with the consent of their relatives. Hence, throughout what follows the word 'euthanasia' is employed as a cosmetic term for murder.

The question of compulsory sterilisation continued to occupy the foreground in the years immediately after the Nazis came to power. However, Hitler held to his plans for a 'euthanasia' programme. According to the testimony of the Reich Physicians' Leader Dr Wagner, Hitler told him in 1935 that 'in the event of war he would take up the question of euthanasia and enforce it', because 'such a problem would be more easily solved in war-time'.[12] This is not the only evidence that the National Socialists planned 'to solve the problem of the asylums in a radical way' in the course of a war which would be one of racial extermination.

The 'euthanasia' programme was finally precipitated by the Knauer case in the winter of 1938–9.[13] A man called Knauer petitioned Hitler asking that his deformed child, who was in a clinic at the university of Leipzig, be killed. Hitler sent Brandt, the physician to his retinue, to investigate, with powers to authorise the child's death if the circumstances warranted it. Brandt, and the Head of the Chancellery of the Führer, Philipp Bouhler, who wished to enlarge the scope of his agency beyond answering letters to Hitler, were then authorised to deal with further requests in a similar way.

Brandt and Bouhler formed an *ad hoc* group called the Reich Committee for the Scientific Registration of Serious Hereditarily- and Congenitally-based Illnesses consisting of officials from the Chancellery of the Führer, representatives of the Reich Ministry of the Interior, and carefully selected physicians.[14] This committee constituted the clearing-house for reports on deformed births sent in by physicians and midwives throughout the Reich. The reports, ostensibly designed to 'clarify scientific questions in the field of congenital deformities', were then forwarded to three paediatricians (Professors Heinze, Werner Catel and Dr Ernst Wentzler), who marked the forms with a '+' or '−' according to whether the child was to die or survive. The children concerned were subsequently

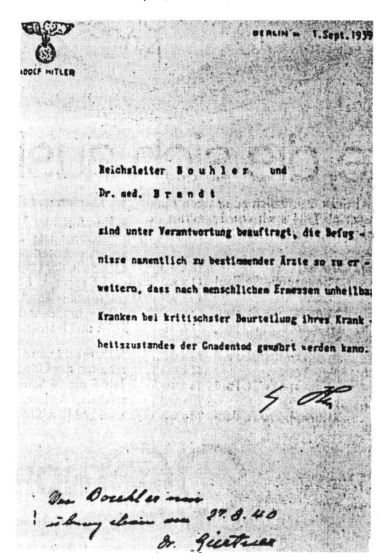

6.1 *Note from Hitler to Bouhler and Brandt authorising them to conduct 'mercy killings' in an indeterminate future. The note reads, 'Reichsleiter Bouhler and Dr. med. Brandt are charged with responsibility to extend the powers of specific doctors in such a way that, after the most careful assessment of their condition, those suffering from illnesses deemed to be incurable may be granted a mercy death.' Although written in October 1939, the note was backdated to 1 September, suggesting some unease among the T-4 operatives about the total illegality of their actions to date. Their actions remained illegal, for a note did not constitute law.*

transferred to special 'paediatric clinics' where they were either starved to death or given lethal injections. Their deaths provided research 'material' for a number of university-based psychiatrists and neurologists because, as one professor put it, 'thanks to the programme [i.e. "euthanasia"], a rapid anatomical and histological clarification can be achieved'. In the course of this initial 'children's euthanasia' programme, at least 5,200 infants, children, and adolescents were killed.

In the summer of 1939, Hitler instructed Dr Leonardo Conti, a Nazi medical-bureaucratic pluralist with positions in both the State and Party hierarchies, to organise a 'euthanasia' programme for adults.[15] His unwelcome involvement was soon short-circuited by Bouhler and his deputy Viktor Brack, who reasserted control from the Chancellery of the Führer. In the autumn, Brack and Bouhler organised a series of meetings to determine both the scope of the projected programme and the most suitable methods to be adopted. The argument that more hospital beds would be needed for a coming war apparently enabled university-based scientists to overlook the fact that the programme had no legal basis whatsoever. Their involvement in turn lent murder a spurious air of scientific 'respectability'. The question of 'how' was resolved by the Head of the Reich Criminal Police, Arthur Nebe, who set the Criminal Technical Institute to work devising the most efficient method of killing. The question of 'who' was worked out by the steering-group, which arrived at a global figure of '65,000–70,000' persons to be affected by 'rationalisation', arrived at in the following way:

> The number is arrived at through a calculation on the basis of a ratio of 1000:10:5:1. That means out of 1,000 people 10 require psychiatric treatment; of these 5 in residential form. And of these, one patient will come under the programme. If one applies this to the population of the Greater German Reich, then one must reckon with 65,000–70,000 cases.[16]

With the question of 'who' resolved in this impersonal global manner, the processes were inaugurated which determined the individual patients who were to die. The Reich Ministry of the Interior despatched forms to all asylums and clinics to be completed for each patient. These supplied details about the latter's race, state of health, and capacity to work. The completed forms were then centrally processed and duplicated, and sent in batches of 150 to expert 'assessors'.[17] The 'assessors', whose number increased, marked the forms with a red '+' if the patient was to be killed or a blue '−' if he or she was to survive. Doubtful cases, marked with a '?', were resolved by higher 'assessors', whose number included the medical

6.2 Viktor Brack, alias 'Jennerwein', a key figure in the T-4 'euthanasia' programme.

layman Viktor Brack. Some of the 'assessors', who were paid on a piece-work basis, regarded the form-filling clerical work as a worthwhile end in itself, with one, Dr Josef Schreck, congratulating himself on having processed 15,000 forms 'very conscientiously' within nine months. The 'assessors' never saw the patients.

'Form 1' of 1941 is reproduced below:

Form 1

File number:

Name of the asylum:

in . . .

Christian and surname of the patient:

Place of birth: Date of birth:

Last residence: Place: District:

Marital status: Confession: Race (1):

Address of closest relatives:

Regular visits, and from whom?

Name and address of legal guardian:

Person responsible for the costs of care:

Duration of stay in this asylum:

Duration of stay in other asylums: Where and for how long:

Ill since when

Twin: yes/no   Mentally ill relatives:

Diagnosis:

Main symptoms:

Predominantly bed-ridden: yes/no   very disturbed: yes/no

under restraint: yes/no

Incurable physical illness: yes/no   war wounds: yes/no

In the case of schizophrenia: final stage   good recovery

In the case of feeble-mindedness: debility   imbecility

In the case of epilepsy: psychological changes   average frequency of attacks

In the case of geriatric illnesses: serious confusion   incontinence

Therapy (Insulin, malaria, etc.)   lasting results: yes/no

Committed under paragraph 51, 42b Penal Code etc. by:

Crime: Previous offences:

Nature of activities: (Exact description of work and capacity to work e.g. agricultural labour, does not achieve much – metal workshop, good skilled worker – no vague descriptions like housework, but more precisely, like, for example, cleaning the rooms. Always state whether the person is constantly, frequently, or temporarily occupied.)

Can anticipate early release:
Remarks:
This space is to be left blank   Place, date:
Signature of the medical director or his representative
(1) German or related blood, Jew, part-Jew I or II Grade, Negro (half-caste), Gypsy (part-Gypsy) etc.[18]

The following is taken from the guidelines issued by Bouhler and Brandt concerning the assessment of the 'hereditarily ill' of March 1941:

(1) Elimination of all those who are unable to perform productive tasks even within the asylums, and not only those who are mentally dead.

(2) War veterans who either distinguished themselves at the front or were wounded or decorated are to be excluded. Decisions concerning distinguished service at the front or decorations are to be made by Herr Jennerwein (Brack). Cases like these which occur in our asylums are to be deferred until Herr Jennerwein has made his decision on the basis of documentary records. Otherwise, war service is no protection from inclusion in the action.

(3) In the case of geriatrics, the greatest restraint: inclusion only in drastic circumstances, e.g. criminality or asocial behaviour. In the latter cases, the records are to be consulted and photocopies of extracts are to be made available. The senile do not include patients with psychoses which themselves come within the scope of the action like schizophrenia, epilepsy etc., or who have merely grown old.

In special cases of senility the evidence will be submitted to Herr Jennerwein.

(4) Only Reich Germans shall be included in the action, therefore no Poles. The intention is to collect together all Poles in purely Polish asylums in the eastern provinces. Czechs with German citizenship in asylums outside the Protectorate can be included. Czechs with Czech citizenship should be pushed into the Protectorate. In cases where it is impossible to establish citizenship, this is to be established wherever possible by our representatives.

In cases where it is still not possible to establish citizenship, the case is to be deferred until a final discussion with Secretary of State Frank.[19]

In the course of October 1939 the ever-widening circle of those involved in the 'euthanasia' programme received authorisation from Hitler in the form of a laconic and informal note on his personal writing paper.

Backdated, symbolically to 1 September 1939, the document read: 'Reich Leader Bouhler and Dr. med. Brandt are charged with responsibility to extend the powers of specific doctors in such a way that, after the most careful assessment of their condition, those suffering from illnesses deemed to be incurable may be granted a mercy death.'[20] In fact, before the official 'euthanasia' programme got under way, *ad hoc* measures had been adopted in occupied Poland. Between 29 September and 1 November 1939, SS units shot about 4,000 mental patients in asylums in the region of Bromberg.[21] In October, the Gauleiter of Pomerania, Franz Schwede-Coburg, traded the asylums in his territory for the SS and Wehrmacht to use as barracks in return for an SS unit being deployed to shoot the inmates in discreet forest clearings. Finally, during December 1939 and January 1940, the SS Special Commando Lange gassed 1,558 patients from Polish asylums in specially adapted vans in order to make room for military and SS barracks. The SS charged 10RMs for each person thus disposed of.

The official 'euthanasia' programme, which commenced shortly afterwards, acquired a complex organisational 'front' designed to cover the wires leading back to the Chancellery of the Führer and hence to Hitler. Department II of the Chancellery formed a Reich Association of Asylums which operated from the Columbus-Haus on Potsdamer Platz, and then from April 1940 from a villa on Tiergartenstrasse 4, from which the programme took its codename 'Aktion T-4'.[22] Several of the leading bureaucrats involved used false names (e.g. Brack called himself 'Jennerwein' after a famous nineteenth-century poacher) or wrote down false job descriptions in hotel registers when inspecting out of the way asylums. The operational side of the programme was dealt with by the Community Foundation for the Encouragement of Asylums, which hired personnel and dealt with property contracts, and a phoney company called the Community Patients Transport Service Ltd (Gekrat) run by Brack's cousin, which acquired postal vans to move patients to the asylums chosen for killing. Postal vans would be relatively unobtrusive in remote areas, and they could be repaired in a nationwide network of depots.

Having selected a number of suitable asylums, including Grafeneck, Hadamar, Bernburg, Brandenburg, Hartheim, and Sonnenstein, SS personnel carried out technical 'modifications' and teams of selected medical and nursing staff moved in. In the latter case, group initiation and indoctrination were employed to minimise the likelihood of dissent. The forms marked with red '+'s were sent to Gekrat, which forwarded lists of names to the asylums concerned. The lists of names were usually longer than the number of those to be taken away, a device used to involve the

6.3 A 'Community Patients' Transport Service' postal van used to transfer asylum patients to killing centres.

asylum staff in the 'selection' of their own charges. The lists of names were accompanied by precise instructions on the patients' belongings or on the need to restrain or sedate persons who became difficult. A standard letter, notifying the patient's relatives of the transfer was to be sent out after the person had been relocated.[23]

Although at first those transferred were sometimes glad to be going on an outing, with complaints from those left behind, this mood soon gave way to terror at the regular arrival of the vans which never brought patients back. Although those involved in the programme preferred to delude themselves that those transferred were unaware of their fate, there is substantial evidence to the contrary. Long-term residents were severely traumatised by being removed from their accustomed habitat; others tried to cling on to nursing staff they knew and trusted or uttered a few words of apparent resignation; some had to be put in strait-jackets or handcuffs to get them into the vans. Asylum staff subsequently began to encounter deep suspicion in the course of carrying out injections or electro-shock therapy.

The patients 'selected' were transferred to special asylums where they were subjected to a perfunctory medical check, photographed, and killed in gas chambers disguised as shower rooms, or vans into which carbon monoxide was released from the front cab. Their corpses were burned in crematoria, whose ill-designed chimneys sometimes sent flames five metres high and which spread a pall of noxious smoke over the surrounding countryside. Relatives received notification of the patients' transfer and the information that 'he/she has arrived safely', followed a week or so later, by a schematic letter of condolence announcing the person's demise. Sometimes these were given a personal touch, as in this extract from a letter to the parents of a small girl: 'Today the asylum accounting office received your credit transfer of RM20 intended for flowers for the grave of your little daughter Irmgard . . . Concerning your little daughter, we can report that Irmgard was still overjoyed with the little coat, and above all with the lovely little dolly, which she had in her arms to the very end.'[24] Irmgard was in one of 275 (numbered) graves, each of which contained four corpses. The cause of death was usually selected from a range of diseases whose common characteristics were an absence of visible symptoms – unless they existed already – and a sudden onset. The extermination centres took elaborate precautions to conceal the large number of deaths occurring in any one place. Each had its own registry office engaged in the falsification of death certificates, and each employed couriers to post the urns of ashes in surrounding towns.

Despite these measures, the 'euthanasia' programme quickly became an open secret. The victims' clothing was returned to the original asylums. Families received two urns when they had one member in an asylum. Hairpins turned up in the ashes of males. The cause of death was given as appendicitis in cases where the patient had had their appendix removed years before. Parents who had removed their children from asylums were nonetheless notified of their unexpected death. The asylum personnel drank too much in local hostleries and made macabre jokes about the quality of local fertilisers. People could smell death. Persistent relatives lobbied the authorities to discover the truth, and sometimes used the deaths columns of newspapers to vent their dissatisfaction with the answers they were given: 'His sudden death will always remain a mystery to us' or, 'Walter R., holder of the Iron Cross for service at the Front in 1914–18 . . . Following days of great uncertainty we received news of his sudden death and of the cremation which had already taken place in Linz on the Danube.'[25] In a few asylums, ugly scenes occurred between the transport service personnel and the staff of the asylums as the latter sought to protect their charges. In one case, a crowd of local people gathered and the

6.4 The gas chamber in the cellars of the Bernburg psychiatric hospital, where between September 1940 and August 1941 8,601 people were killed. Note the fake showerheads and the reinforced glass windows.

local mayor traced the name 'Haarmann' (a notorious murderer) in the dust on the side of one of the buses. In other words, the regime's policies had come into serious conflict with ingrained moral precepts and compassion towards the weak. Of course, these seem to have subsequently gone into limbo in the case of the extermination of the Jews.

Complications multiplied as awareness of the programme spread. Relatives contacted clergymen, the judicial authorities, or contacts at various levels of the NSDAP. The judicial authorities began to ask awkward questions concerning patients who were wards of court. The following example, from evidence assembled by the higher public prosecutor's office in Dresden, is typical:

> The deaf and dumb cigar-maker Erich S., born in 1912, was committed by the courts to the Waldheim Asylum on 13 October 1937. In response to an inquiry from the higher public prosecutor, the asylum stated on 15 February 1940 that the object of the committal would be attained, if in future S. could be maintained in an institution for the deaf and dumb. The implementation of this recommendation

was impossible, however, because on 27 February 1940 S. was transferred in a group transport to an asylum whose name is not known at
Waldheim. The higher public prosecutor tried unsuccessfully to reach
the Community Patients Transport Service by telephone; the municipal relief office in Berlin had not heard of the company. However in
response to a written inquiry, Dr Schmitt of the provincial asylum in
Brandenburg informed them that S. had died as a result of pneumonia
on 16 March 1940.[26]

Although the Reich Ministry of Justice, which had misgivings about the
legality of the programme, merely confined itself to passing on complaints
to the Ministry of the Interior and the Reich Chancellery, one judge –
Lothar Kreyssig – instituted criminal proceedings against Bouhler for
murder.[27] Summoned to the Ministry of Justice, Kreyssig was shown
Hitler's authorisation, which, however, he refused to accept as an adequate
legal basis for what had been done. He was subsequently prematurely
retired. Similarly, while individual churchmen like the Protestant Pastor
Paul Braune protested against the programme, both confessions controlled asylums which co-operated in the programme, and corporate
ecclesiastical protest was confined to behind the scenes negotiations
concerning access to the sacraments of those to be killed.[28] This was to
compromise with those responsible for the programme. The churchmen's
conscience-stricken passivity was dramatically disturbed by a sermon
delivered by the Bishop of Münster, Clemens August Count von
Galen on 3 August 1941. In his passionate and embarrassingly specific
address, this conservative clergyman stated unequivocally: 'Never under
any circumstances may a human being kill an innocent person apart from
war and legitimate self-defence.'[29]

He stated further:

> If you establish and apply the principle that you can kill 'unproductive'
> fellow human beings then woe betide us all when we become old and
> frail! If one of us is allowed to kill the unproductive people then woe
> betide the invalids who have used up, sacrificed and lost their health
> and strength in the productive process. If one is allowed forcibly to
> remove one's unproductive fellow human beings then woe betide
> loyal soldiers who return to the homeland seriously disabled, as
> cripples, as invalids. If it is once accepted that people have the right to
> kill 'unproductive' fellow humans – and even if it only initially affects
> the poor defenceless mentally ill – then as a matter of principle
> murder is permitted for all unproductive people, in other words for
> the incurably sick, the people who have become invalids through
> labour and war, for us all when we become old, frail and therefore
> unproductive.

Then, it is only necessary for some secret edict to order that the method developed for the mentally ill should be extended to other 'unproductive' people, that it should be applied to those suffering from incurable lung disease, to the elderly who are frail or invalids, to the severely disabled soldiers. Then none of our lives will be safe any more. Some commission can put us on the list of the 'unproductive', who in their opinion have become worthless life. And no police force will protect us and no court will investigate our murder and give the murderer the punishment he deserves. Who will be able to trust his physician any more? He may report his patient as 'unproductive' and receive instructions to kill him. It is impossible to imagine the degree of moral depravity, of general mistrust that would then spread even through families if this dreadful doctrine is tolerated, accepted and followed. Woe to mankind, woe to our German nation if God's holy commandment 'Thou shalt not kill', which God proclaimed on Mount Sinai amidst thunder and lightning, which God our Creator inscribed in the conscience of mankind from the very beginning, is not only broken, but if this transgression is actually tolerated and per-mitted to go unpunished.[30]

Copies of the sermon were duplicated, to be leafleted eventually by the RAF, sensitive since the Nazis had made black propaganda out of the alleged bombing of the Bethel asylum. Galen's action was soon followed by a number of individual clerics. Although there was talk among Nazi leaders of hanging the Bishop of Münster, detention in concentration camps for denouncing the programme – although this reason was never given – was confined to lesser clergy who decided to emulate him. It is not clear whether the protests which ensued after Galen's sermon prompted Hitler to halt the official programme on 24 August 1941. It is unlikely that he did so because, as was later claimed, he was confronted by a hostile crowd on a Bavarian station when his train happened to halt beside a train being loaded with mentally-handicapped children. More likely, the programme was halted because the original target figure had been reached.[31] According to an internal T-4 reckoning, up to 1 September 1941 70,273 persons had been 'disinfected'. Further statistics produced later that year, which took into account persons killed other than by gassing, indicated that 93,251 beds had been 'released' from among the 282,696 beds reserved for mental patients.

Disquiet among sections of the population lent added urgency to the regime's ongoing efforts to win, if not support, then collusive passivity for the 'euthanasia' programme. The oblique approach was in evidence in these examples culled from school mathematics books:

Question 95: The construction of a lunatic asylum costs 6 million RM. How many houses at 15,000RM each could have been built for that amount?

Question 97: To keep a mentally ill person costs approx. 4RM per day, a cripple 5,50RM, a criminal 3,50RM. Many civil servants receive only 4RM per day, white-collar employees barely 3,50RM, unskilled workers not even 2RM per head for their families. (a) Illustrate these figures with a diagram. According to conservative estimates, there are 300,000 mentally ill, epileptics etc., in care. (b) How much do these people cost to keep in total, at a cost of 4RM per head? (c) How many marriage loans at 1,000RM each . . . could be granted from this money?[32]

Films stigmatising the mentally and physically handicapped were produced from the mid-1930s onwards. In October 1939 Brack commissioned one of the Gekrat staff, Hermann Schweninger, a failure with cinematic pretensions, to make propaganda films on 'euthanasia', designed for the day when the programme would operate in the light of legality.[33] The scripts, written in conjunction with physicians involved in the programme, latched on to pre-existing formats. The usual object was to contrast the expense put into maintaining 'ballast existences' with the limited therapeutic 'results' achieved. To this end, Schweninger sought out locations which would emphasise:
(1)   The marvellous situation of the asylums in the countryside.
(2)   The vast expanse of the asylum area in the case of so-called pavilion system asylums.
(3)   The attractiveness and care devoted to the gardens and grounds of the asylums.
(4)   The good ways in which the buildings have been converted.
(5)   The aesthetic value of old castles and monasteries which are still used today as asylums.
(6)   The marvellous view from the asylums.
and inside:
(1)   The almost luxurious interior settings.
(2)   Their modernity and costliness.[34]
By way of dramatic contrast, Schweninger was instructed to seek out particularly photogenic hopeless cases, some of them being given a temporary reprieve from the gas chambers situated in former palaces until the cameramen had passed through.
(1)   The most glaring and shocking types, for example, idiotic and deformed children as well as adults of a similar appearance.

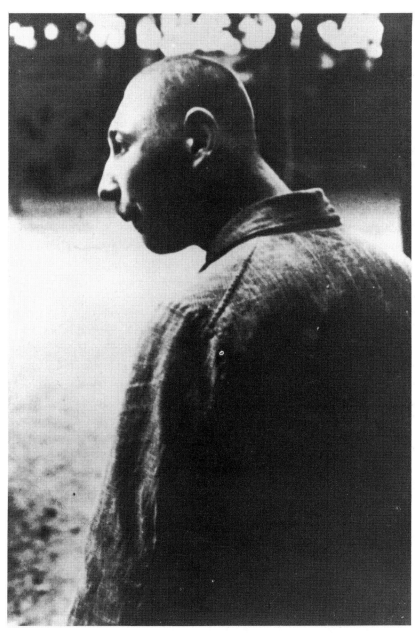

*6.5 A still photograph from an NSDAP Racial-Political Office docu-
mentary film made in the mid- to late 1930s designed to stigmatise the
mentally ill. Films like these were seen by 21 million people in 1935 and
40 million in 1939.*

(2)   Totally stunted types in contrast to the beauty of the gardens, art, etc.[35]

But preparations for the documentary approach were abruptly shelved in late 1940 as the programme encountered opposition. In line with Goebbels' dictum that the 'best propaganda works indirectly', the T-4 film-makers switched over to the feature film approach. Human interest stories would soften the stark realities of what was being done by occluding the issues in a mist of pseudo-moral dilemmas. Decisions being taken by the State in terms of cold, global statistics were thrust back on to each individual film-goer through the agency of sentiment. 'Euthanasia' was presented as everyone's choice. Those cunning considerations were apparent in the film *I Accuse*, which was released in August 1941. The main plot, which exploits the medical drama/pioneering scientist genres, concerned a professor of pathology, Heyt, whose young wife Hanna develops multiple sclerosis. This is diagnosed by the family physician, Lang, one of Hanna's former admirers. Lang is a convinced opponent of 'euthanasia' although his convictions are gradually eroded throughout the film, by, *inter alia*, his confrontation with a horrendously deformed child whose life he had managed to save as a baby. Both Heyt and Lang endeavour to alleviate Hanna's suffering, her husband by devising a cure in his laboratories. Faced with the limits of his own ingenuity, Heyt resolves to help his wife die. Hanna's brother brings an action against Heyt for murder, which allows the film-makers to rehearse the issues through the device of a concluding courtroom drama. The six jurors adopt different stances, but the spokesmen of 'consensus' argue that the law needs to be changed to permit 'mercy killings', a view which dovetailed felicitously with the regime's intentions. Lang makes his road to Damascus; the tormented scientist-hero emerges clean.

From the script of *I Accuse*:

> *Hanna* (continuing to speak): I wish that was the end.
> *Heyt:* It is the end, Hanna.
> *Hanna:* How I love you, Thomas . . .
> (*He weeps*)
> *Hanna:* I wish I could give you my hand, Thomas.[36]

The retired Major's speech from the jury scene:

> Don't get me wrong, gentlemen, but when one deploys hundreds of thousands of physicians, sisters, and nurses, and puts up vast buildings with laboratories and medicaments and God knows what, simply in order to keep a few pitiful creatures alive, who are either too crazy to get anything out of life, or a threat to the community, or in general

6.6 Still from Wolfgang Liebenneier's 1941 film I Accuse *showing
Professor Heyt consoling his incurably ill wife shortly before he kills her
with a morphine overdose.*

just like animals – and that at a time, when one doesn't have enough
people, room, or the wherewithal to keep the healthy in health, or to
properly provide for the mothers of newborn babies – then that is the
most harebrained nonsense! The State has the duty firstly to look after
the people who in general are the State – namely for workers – and as
far as those are concerned who would like to die, because they were
once healthy and now cannot endure any longer – my view is that the
State, which demands from us the duty to die, must give us the
right to die . . . I am an old soldier, and I know what I am talking
about.[37]

I Accuse was seen by 18 million people. According to a lengthy SD report,
apart from a docile press the reactions were mixed. The film was unpopular in Roman Catholic areas, where the clergy endeavoured to discourage
people from seeing it. Some regarded it as an attempt by the State to refute
charges made in Galen's sermon. Younger physicians reacted positively to
the film; lawyers were concerned about the legislative foundations for
'euthanasia'. The 'broad masses of the German people' also reacted
affirmatively to *I Accuse*, although they thought it essential that careful

controls and the consent of the person affected should accompany any State sanctioning of 'euthanasia'.

From the SD 'Reports from the Reich' (15 January 1942):

> Public Response to the film *I Accuse*
>
> All the reports to hand indicate that the film *I Accuse* has aroused great interest in all areas of the Reich. In general it can be stated that with the help of extensive word-of-mouth publicity the film has been favourably received and discussed. Characteristic of the interest this film has provoked among the population is the fact that in many towns which had not yet seen it the film was being described – even by unsophisticated people – as one which simply had to be seen. The performances were generally enthusiastically received, and the film's content has actively stimulated people to think about it and has provoked lively discussion.
>
> The film *I Accuse* raises two issues. Its main theme is the problem of *death on demand in cases of incurable illnesses*. A secondary theme deals with the question of putting an end to a life which is no longer worth living.
>
> Judging by the reports received from all parts of the Reich, the majority of the German population accepts the film's proposition *in principle, though with some reservations* – that is, that people suffering from serious diseases for which there is no cure should be allowed a quick death sanctioned by law. This conclusion can also be applied to a number of religiously-minded people.
>
> The *attitude of the Church*, both Catholic and Protestant, is one of almost total rejection. There are reports that Catholic priests have used house visits to try to stop individual members of the population from going to see the film on the grounds that it is an inflammatory film directed against the Catholic Church or a State propaganda film designed to justify the killing of people suffering from hereditary illness.
>
> In a number of cases the Catholic clergy has made only an indirect attack on the film, and according to reports has described it as being so good that it could be dangerous and 'as tempting as sin'. Despite this clear rejection of the film in Catholic circles, it has also been frequently reported that the film has in fact occasioned a conflict of opinion in the Catholic camp, with one faction supporting the principle that a person may be deprived of life if in particularly serious cases a panel of doctors has diagnosed an incurable illness and the administering of death could be considered a blessing for both parties. The other faction, however, still uses the word 'murder' in connection with the film.
>
> All reports, even those coming from predominantly Catholic regions of the Reich, refer to the fact that the celebrated statements by Bishop Clemens August of Münster have in many cases been taken as a starting-point in discussions of the film, to the extent that there have

6.7 Still from I Accuse *showing Heyt in the dock next to his defence lawyer during his trial for murder. The drift of the argument in the film is that the law should be changed to permit 'mercy killings', a decision left up to the film's audience. The human interest drama developed in the film bore no resemblance to the coldly clinical elimination of mentally or physically handicapped asylum inmates, most of whom did not receive a 'merciful' death.*

been several comments about the film referring to it as an attempt to justify the State's measures now that the Bishop has attacked them. For instance the following comments have been heard:
'The film is quite interesting, but the story's just like the lunatic asylums where they're killing off all the crazy people now.'
'You can think what you like about this, but who is going to guarantee that there won't be any abuses? As soon as laws like this are introduced it will be easy for the government to have anyone they consider undesirable declared incurable by a commission for any reason at all and eliminate them. And moreover people with enough influence or money to criticise others will soon have somebody declared insane.'

In Protestant circles the open rejection of the film is not as strongly expressed. Yet here too people often say that life, which is God-given, can and should only be taken by God.

But we have also heard of *positive* opinions in Church circles. The Superintendent of Bautzen, for instance, said the following: 'It will be the State's concern to prevent abuse, to take the responsibility and to ensure that loving kindness is extended to those incurables who are suffering. All this will be easier than the actual act of deliverance. As a Christian I must approve of this film.'

As regards *medical circles*, a mostly positive response is reported to the questions raised by the film. Younger doctors in particular, apart from a few bound by religious beliefs, are completely in favour.

Doubts are expressed among older doctors particularly, despite their agreement in principle. In many cases doctors see it as a mistake to publicise the issues openly.

Here and there the question has been raised as to whether medical diagnosis in borderline cases can really be sufficiently accurate to declare a patient incurable. For example, there are frequent cases of seriously ill patients who have been given up by all doctors and have then improved and lived on for years. Such cases are known to every doctor and every hospital. Other doctors mention that in their experience people, especially if they are seriously ill or old, talk only of their wish to die when they have temporarily succumbed to deep despair because of severe pain. However, in the moments when they have been free of pain these patients have shown remarkable spirit and have gone on hoping for recovery until the end.

Doubts have also been expressed about the film's suggestion of *medical committees*: each of the doctors serving on a committee would have to examine the patient independently. This would put an unnecessary emotional strain on the patient, who, because of the repeated examinations, would become aware of what was intended.

Many doctors consider that the decision to intervene and help a patient could be left entirely to the German doctor's sense of responsibility. In practice, this kind of mercy killing already exists. Many doctors are taking it upon themselves, in cases where there is no prospect at all of recovery and the patient is suffering severe pain, to increase the dosage of the appropriate drug and so effect a painless death.

Indeed, the *legal profession* considers it a matter of urgency to pro-vide medical practices of this kind with a basis in law. The legal difficulties which this would involve are considered to be great, since it would scarcely be possible to subject every relevant case of illness to legal examination, while on the other hand medical progress is such that an illness considered incurable today may be designated as curable tomorrow.

The *majority* of the German people has almost without exception reacted favourably to the issues raised, the following points, according to our reports, emerging as significant:

1.   An essential precondition of the decision to declare a patient incurable is considered to be the convening of a *medical committee* in the presence of the family doctor.

2.   Here and there the question has been raised as to whether

mercy killing should be applied in all cases, since even patients with only a limited time to live are often still capable of doing productive work.

3.   It is considered similarly essential where *euthanasia* is to be applied to obtain *the consent of the patient himself* or in the case of a feeble-minded mental patient *the permission of his relatives.*

4.   In every case strict standards must be applied to prevent abuse; *in no case should the decision be left to an individual.*

5.   In most people's opinion, *only the doctor* should be given the right, at his own discretion, to administer euthanasia.

On the whole the working classes are more favourably disposed to the change in the law suggested by the film than people from intellectual circles. The reason for this, according to our information, is that the socially less privileged classes are by nature more concerned about their own financial obligations. Most people respond to the film's immediate story, with the result that the theme of a long-suffering person being released from his misery is relegated to the background. Only doctors interpret the film in terms of this issue.

The negative attitudes towards the questions raised in the film are by far the minority opinion, and apart from the church's point of view they can hardly be described as fundamentally contrary opinions.

To sum up, from the wealth of material to hand it emerges that in general the practice of euthanasia is approved, *when decided by a committee of several doctors with the agreement of the incurable patient and his relatives.*

The general approval finds its best expression in the words of the Major in the film: 'The state, which demands from us the duty to die, must give us the *right* to die.'[38]

The reactions of Germans suffering from multiple schlerosis were not recorded. Although mass gassings of mental patients ceased after Hitler's halt order of 24 August 1941, the 'euthanasia' programme was in fact merely redirected to other groups of victims. In early 1941, Himmler and Bouhler had come to an arrangement whereby the capacity of asylums involved in the T-4 Aktion was employed to 'free' concentration camps of 'sick' inmates. This operation took place under the code name 'Aktion 14 f 13', 14f being the filing code for the Inspectorate of Concentration Camps, and 13 being one of a series of numbers used to describe the cause of death in the camps, in this case the 'special treatment' of sick or frail prisoners.[39] Physicians involved in the T-4 Aktion toured the camps to 'examine' prisoners whom the SS staff had pre-selected as being sick. The diagnoses scribbled beside photographs of the victims included: 'Alfred Israel, 14.11.06 Düsseldorf, married. Jewish. Businessman. Diagnosis: Fanatical Germanophobe and asocial psychopath. Main symptoms: Hard-

6.8 *'Diagnosis' by a doctor selecting prisoners in Dachau for extermi-
nation under 'Aktion 14 f 13'. It reads, 'Jew from the Protectorate.
Subversive behaviour. Miscegenation. In the camp: lazy, insolent.
Punished repeatedly by being suspended (by his arms) from a post.'*

bitten Communist, unworthy to bear arms, penitentiary sentence for high
treason: six years' or 'Schonhoff Egon Israel, lawyer, 9.4.80 Vienna.
Dachau 1938, 6069. Communist lawyer. Member of Red Aid. 1927 in
Russia. Major Germanophobe. Agitator. In the camp: presumptuous,
impertinent, lazy, obstructive. Since 1901 1st Lieutenant in the Austro-
Hungarian army. Lieutenant of the Reserve. Front-line service from start
of World War till May 1915; then Russian POW. Promoted to 1st
Lieutenant at the front, to Captain while a POW.'[40]

Judging from correspondence and diaries which have survived, the
physicians involved seem to have enjoyed their visits to Ravensbrück or
Buchenwald, constantly dilating on the quality of the canteens, the comfy
beds and the speed with which they got through the day's 'selections'.
These examples are typical: '7.40: Off I go happy hunting. This morning
I got a terrific lot done, in the two hours from 9–11 I got through 70
forms. Dr. Müller did 56 so another 126 are finished'; or 'Everything is
going perfectly. I am having my meals in the camp: for lunch in the mess
there was lentil soup with bacon and omelette for pudding. I finished at

6.9 Dr Friedrich Mennecke, a doctor responsible for selecting for extermination concentration camp prisoners already preselected by the SS as being 'sick'.

17.00 and had my supper in the mess: 3 sorts of sausage, butter, bread, beer. I sleep marvellously in my bed, it is just like in Hilmerhausen . . . I hope you are as well as I am. I feel perfect.' Up to April 1943, when the SS decided to restrict the action to inmates who were 'genuinely' mentally ill, perhaps 30,000 prisoners were transferred to the asylums used as extermination centres.[41]

A letter from Dr Friedrich Mennecke to his wife, 26 November 1941:

> Hotel Elephant,
> Weimar
> Wednesday 26.11.41 7 a.m.   Ding-ding-ding: 7.00!! Got up! A right good morning Mummykins!! Kisses! You're still slumbering, am I right? Now off we go – shave! Ahoy!
> 7.30 a.m.   Ready, ready too after a sh . . . and now off to the new day. I'll write more tonight. Kissikins! Ahoy!
>
> 7.50 p.m.   Home again, my little mouse! The first day's work in Buchenwald is over. At 8.30 this morning we were out and about. First of all I introduced myself to the officers in charge. The deputy camp commandant is SS-Hauptsturmführer Florstedt, the camp medic: SS-Obersturmführer Dr Hofen. First of all there were still about 40 forms ready to be filled in on a portion of Aryans, upon whom the other colleagues worked yesterday. Of these 40 I dealt with

about 15. When this portion had been got ready, Schmalenbach pushed off to drive to Dresden, and didn't come back until our work here was over. This was followed by the 'examination' of pat[ients]., i.e., presentation of the individual and comparison with entries taken from the records. We won't be finished here until Monday, because yesterday both colleagues only worked notionally, and so I had to 're-examine' those whom Schmalenbach (and myself this morning) has got ready and Müller his too. At noon we stopped for lunch and ate in the officers' mess (1st class! Boiled beef, red cabbage, boiled potatoes, apple compote – all for 1,50RM!), no coupons. In the course of meeting many SS officers, I came across the SS-Unter-sturmführer who in December 1940 was the adjutant in the camp at Hinzert. He recognised me too straight away, introduced himself, and asked after you too. – At 1.30pm we began examining again, but then Ribbentrop's speech came on which we listened to. He said a lot of good things, did you hear the speech too? Then we examined again until about 4 o'clock, I did 105 pat[ients]., Müller 78 pat[ients]. so that the first batch came to 183 forms completed. The second portion consisting of 1,200 Jews, who were not 'examined', but for whom it was enough to take the reason for arrest (often very extensive!) from the records and to put that down on the forms. Therefore it is purely notional work, which will certainly occupy us until Monday, perhaps longer. Out of this second portion of Jews we did: me 17, Muller 15. On the dot of 5pm I 'threw in the towel' and went to supper: a cold platter of cervelat sausage (9 big slices), butter, bread, coffee! Cost 0,80RM without coupons! At 5.30pm we got a lift with a Criminal Police officer – SS-Hauptscharführer [Leclair], who lives in Weimar, but who drives back to Weimar every day.[42]

The murder of mental patients also continued after Hitler's halt order, although the preferred methods were thenceforth starvation through a diet of potato peel and cabbage with no fats, or the administering of lethal injections and pills. Far from the programme winding down, new extermination centres were opened at Meseritz-Obrawalde near Frankfurt/Oder, Eichberg in the west and Kaufbeuren in the south.[43] The need for extra hospital beds for victims of Allied bombing raids, notably after 'Operation Gomorra' in 1943 when the RAF killed 30,000 people in Hamburg, provided a pretext to further decimate the patient population. Asylums throughout the Reich were encouraged to kill their own patients on a decentralised basis. The categories of person encompassed by the programme were also extended to include *Ostarbeiter* who had fallen ill or had nervous breakdowns; the racially 'undesirable' babies of female *Ostarbeit-erinnen*; sick or querulous inmates in 'regular' prisons; the handicapped; and, it seems, severely wounded soldiers and pilots resistant to conventional treatments for shell-shock. Killings also continued in the paediatric units set up in the 'Children's Euthanasia' programme.

The following is taken from the testimony of a female Polish deportee concerning conditions in the hospital at Kelsterbach in the Gau Rhine-Main in the summer of 1944:

> I don't know any more how long I was separated from my husband. It could have been a week, maybe longer. One morning a German physician came to our room, whose name I do not know, as well as two orderlies who were also Germans. They took the child of someone I knew, undressed it, and laid it on the table which stood in our room. It was an ordinary table, without any covering. I assume that this man was a physician, since he was accompanied by two orderlies, but whether or not he was a physician is beyond my knowledge. His face was not very intelligent. As the child lay on the table, he gave it an injection in the lower part of the spinal column, and then sucked out a white, transparent fluid, which looked like water. He squirted this fluid into a glass receptacle; I report that as the needle entered the spinal column, this fluid slowly flowed into a glass contained underneath and filled about half of it. This process took about half an hour. During the process, the child began to scream, but it was then held by the orderlies until it was quiet and had died. I stress that before this interference, my friend's baby daughter was perfectly healthy and lively; she could also speak, which meant that she was well developed for her age.
>
> When the child had died, the mother was told to carry the body into a neighbouring washroom. As she left with her child, they wanted to take mine from me. However I resisted, because I saw what had happened with the other child. This so-called physician, however, brutally pushed me aside, threw me on the bed and tore my child from my hands. At that moment I lost consciousness. When I came to, I was outside the barracks and wet. I realised that someone had thrown water over me. I went back to the room. My child was already in bed. I saw that my child had a fever, that it tossed and turned, as if it was in great pain. At about 10 o'clock my child died. During my child's agony, no one came and when it died I was ordered to take it to the washroom. In the washroom, which was not in use at the time, because it had been damaged during an air raid, there was a long, lead-covered table which earlier might probably have been used to lay out wet washing. On the table I saw the bodies of about 10 children, the oldest being at most one and a half.[44]

The cessation of mass gassings and the decentralisation of killings to the asylums themselves left a pool of experienced personnel available for mass murder on a vast scale. Although many were relocated to Russia to serve as medical personnel for the army, some former T-4 operatives were redeployed, firstly to relieve the Einsatzgruppen of the psychologically burdensome task of shooting Russian mental patients, and secondly to apply their technical expertise in the context of the Final Solution of the 'Jewish Question'. Three 'Brack's aids' or mobile gassing units were despatches to Chelmno in Poland, where 145,000 Jews were murdered. Ninety-two ex-T-4 personnel were given a crash course at the SS training camp of Trawniki and then deployed in the context of 'Aktion Reinhard' to run the technical side of the extermination camps Belzec, Sobibor, and Treblinka.[45] In the case of Belzec, this connection is made explicit in a document reproduced in the chapter on the Jews below. The lists of camp staff read like a roll-call of former T-4 operatives, with Christian Wirth (the commandant of Belzec, formerly Hartheim and Hadamar); Franz Stangl[46] the commandant of Sobibor and Treblinka, formerly Hartheim); Franz Reichleitner (the commandant of Sobibor, formerly Hartheim), and so forth. Collectively, these men and their subordinates were responsible for the deaths of 1.7 million people in the course of 'Aktion Reinhard'. Killings continued in some of Germany's mental asylums weeks after Allied troops had occupied the surrounding areas.

What became of the men and women involved in the successive phases of the 'euthanasia' action?[47] Following a brief period in the late 1940s when severe sentences were sometimes imposed, a more sympathetic political climate ensued, enabling many medical murderers smoothly to re-enter the upper reaches of civil society. Their peace of mind was henceforth only fitfully disturbed by assiduous prosecution lawyers like Willy Dressen. Once arrested, retribution invariably failed to ensue. Some of those eventually detained committed suicide in custody. Others escaped from prison. Rearrest was hampered by the failure of the West German police to take the fingerprints of men accused of up to 10,000 murders. Others were spirited abroad through the good offices of organisations like the 'Stille Hilfe', a loose association of aristocratic women and former SS officers. Medical attestations came to the aid of those who could not get away, individuals whose delicate health would have been endangered by lengthy periods in the dock, but who nonetheless could toil in their gardens into their nineties; for individuals who were described as being 'psychological wrecks', but who nonetheless could continue to treat patients. Of course, medical practitioners were well place to simulate physical or psychological symptoms. In one notorious case, a minor concession was made to the rest of humanity by removing the accused's driving licence. Some communities also colluded in repressing the past, transforming their 'own' criminals into 'victims' of 'Jewish' or 'Marxist' outsiders. Towns like Idstein rallied behind the former personnel of the nearby Kalmenhof asylum, testifying that men who had threatened to turn handicapped children 'into angels' had 'always' lived 'upright and decent lives', in order to secure their continued presence in the town. Until very recently, none of the physicians who worked within the 'euthanasia' programme ever served a day of a prison sentence. What of the T-4 film-makers? Hermann Schweninger went on to make corporate and adver-tising films. The director of *I Accuse*, Wolfgang Liebeneiner, was rehabilitated by British field security, and went on to do 'critical remakes' of Nazi films in the Adenauer era. Heidemarie Hatheyer, the actress who portrayed Hanna Heyt in *I Accuse*, had a moderately successful career on the stage and in television after the war, and retired to North Italy. In the 1970s her husband, Curt Riess, published a book on the 'golden years' of the German cinema. It was called, after a popular song, *That Happened Once Only*.[48]

THE PERSECUTION OF THE 'ASOCIAL'

In the 1966 edition of the *Brockhaus Encyclopaedia*, the word 'asocial' is defined as follows: 'The "asocial" ("unsocial") are persons who conduct themselves in a refractory manner towards the most basic legal and moral requirements of society.'[49] If we accept this definition, then every 'society', including that of Nazi Germany, has the right to describe as 'asocial', and hence to exclude, persons who will not or cannot fulfil its more or less arbitrarily established 'basic legal and moral requirements'. This view determined the policies of the courts and compensation agencies in what were until recently the two German states. Persons whom the Nazis designated 'asocial', and who wore black triangles in the concentration camps, are still not recognised as having been victims of Nazi persecution.

This is to overlook two points: firstly, the incontrovertible fact that the Nazis themselves hardly fulfilled 'the most basic legal and moral require-ments' of society; secondly, that the principles of National Socialist society stemmed from an unscientific and inhuman racial ideology.[50]

In the Nazis' view of the world, 'asocial' and criminal behaviour was not determined by either individual choice or the social environment, but rather was innate, and hence heritable. In line with many so-called 'criminal biologists', they called for the fight against crime to be conducted according to criminal-biological criteria. 'Criminal character substances', as Hans Frank put it in 1930, must be permanently excluded from the 'national community', i.e. sent into perpetual exile.[51] More important, however, was the 'elimination of the capacity to reproduce' of these 'criminal character substances'. This meant that the individuals concerned were to be either sterilised or castrated. Only in this way would it be possible 'to maintain the purity of our morality and of the race'.

The recommendations of this National Socialist legal expert, who himself was sentenced to death in 1946 by a Polish court for crimes committed while Generalgouverneur of Poland, were transformed into reality. Immediately after the 'seizure of power' the National Socialists began to solve the 'asocial' and criminal question in accordance with criminal-biological criteria. Persons who were accused of being 'asocial' or criminal were compulsorily sterilised in accordance with the Law for the Prevention of Hereditarily Diseased Progeny.[52] This was not expressly permitted by the law, but the Hereditary Health Courts found a loophole. They claimed that in addition to the 'feeble-mindedness' mentioned in the law, there was also a form of 'camouflaged' or 'social feeble-mindedness'. This meant that persons were compulsorily sterilised who were unaffected by any of the illnesses specified by the law, and who were perfectly capable of passing the intelligence tests which it prescribed. They were simply accused of deviating in some way from the 'healthy instincts of the Volk' with regard to social or sexual behaviour. As we shall see below, in view of the prevailing double morality of the Third Reich, this last point particularly affected women. Far more women were accused of 'social feeble-mindedness' than men, because of either the frequency of their changes of sexual partner or their having had illegitimate children.[53]

However, the National Socialists did not only content themselves with curbing 'criminal character substances' in this fashion. They also endeavoured to exclude both criminals and the 'asocial' as permanently as possible from the 'national community'. The first organised raids against beggars and vagrants occurred in September 1933, in order both to present an image of a 'cleaner' Germany to foreigners and to help channel charitable donations into 'worthwhile' causes.[54] As a series of guidelines issued by the Ministry of Propaganda put it:

> The psychological importance of a planned campaign against the nuisance of begging should not be underestimated. Beggars often force their poverty upon people in the most repulsive way for their own selfish purposes. If this sight disappears from the view of foreigners as well, the result will be a definite feeling of relief and liberation. People will feel that things are becoming more stable again, and that the economy is improving once more. A successful action against the nuisance of begging can have important propaganda benefits for the 'struggle against cold and hunger'. Once the land has

Die Drohung des Untermenschen.

Es treffen auf:

Männliche Verbrecher: 4,9 Kinder   Eine kriminelle Ehe: 4,4 Kinder

Eltern von Hilfsschulkindern: 3,5 Kinder

Die deutsche Familie: 2,2 Kinder   Akademikerehe: 1,9 Kinder

6.10 Illustration from a book, Nation in Danger, *showing the 'menace of the subhumans'. According to this chart, 'criminals' were outbreeding both the classical 2.2-child 'German' family and professional couples, who tended to produce even fewer children.*

been freed of the nuisance of beggars, we can justifiably appeal to the propertied classes to give all the more generously for the Winter Aid Programme now being set in motion by the State and the Party.[55]

Although the police took perhaps as many as 100,000 vagrants and beggars into 'protective custody', most of them were soon released, for the regime had not considered where to put them.[56] Still, the Nazis had scored a propaganda success, even though the homeless quickly filtered back to the streets and doss-houses, making a nonsense of the government's statistical claims to have diminished the number of vagrants. Independently of this essentially cosmetic exercise, the welfare authorities subjected the homeless to tighter controls and made benefit claims as difficult as possible. 'Orderly wanderers' received a Vagrants' Registration Book which recorded their progression through approved overnight shelters. 'Disorderly wanderers' on the other hand could be arrested and assigned to compulsory labour schemes or incarcerated. The welfare authorities used the power to issue these permits as a means of getting rid of whole categories of vagrants. Women vagrants, for example, were simply never issued with Registration Books, while in north Germany welfare agencies simply confiscated the permits of those they deemed 'unfit to wander'. The welfare agencies also played a leading part in reducing the statistics of the homeless through more drastic action. In 1933 the Hamburg Homelessness and Vagrancy Department recommended that 'Beggars registered as inhabitants of other towns must be ruthlessly removed by the police for a lengthy period into a concentration camp as far away as possible from Hamburg.' In 1936 the same department further manipulated the statistics concerning those claiming welfare by despatching single male claimants to a labour camp fifty miles north of the city where they had to work eight hours a day and sleep in mass dormitories. Those who refused to go were recategorised as 'work-shy' and excluded from benefit payments. Such measures enabled the welfare authorities to claim that between September 1934 and 1937 the number of single male claimants had fallen from 5,721 to under 1,500. The unpaid benefits amounted to savings of several millions. Finally, the welfare agencies could avail themselves of legally dubious care and custody orders to detain 'difficult cases' in closed institutions. Many of those detained in the Home for the Destitute at Farmsen were subsequently quietly subsumed into the so-called 'euthanasia' programme.[57]

Hamburg was also the scene of attempts to implement slum clearance without simply dispersing the 'asocial' inhabitants to the periphery, as had been the case with earlier, analogous measures. At first, the regime simply

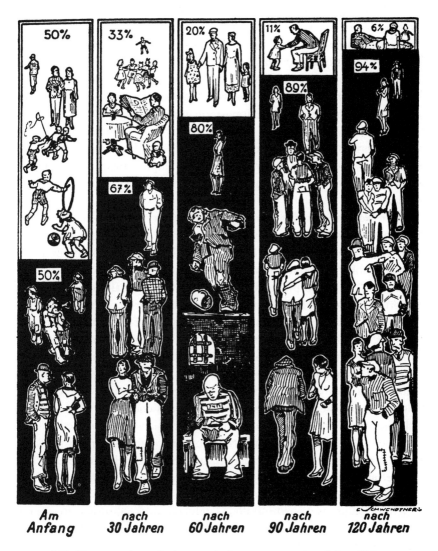

6.11 'Degeneration of the population as a result of insufficient reproduction of valuable families'. The darker lower areas show the mounting numbers of 'criminal families'; the lighter upper part of the picture the diminishing number of 'full-value families', declining from 50 per cent to 6 per cent of the total population over a 120-year period.

lashed out indiscriminately at the inhabitants of the slums in response to a strike by dockers and harbour-workers against the 'seizure of power'. Demolition teams moved in to clear up a 'hiding place for criminals, prostitutes and shady characters, and therewith a breeding ground for Communism'. Subsequently, academic urban sociologists decided to give this policy greater precision by lending their expertise to the process of sifting the biological wheat from the chaff. Electoral statistics were used to locate 'nests of Communists'. Police records were used to establish the incidence of rent disputes, family conflicts, fights, and sexual delinquency. The records of the probation and welfare agencies were combed to locate juvenile delinquents and the long-term unemployed. The object of so much assiduity was to create a 'criminal geography' which would enable the authorities to direct the demolition squads with a hitherto unknown precision, and to bring those not capable of improvement under control; and to eradicate the hereditary properties of the hopelessly 'biologically deficient'.[58]

Both policing and the penal system began to be suffused with racial-biological criteria. 'Disorderly wanderers' were among those affected by the Law against Dangerous Habitual Criminals of 24 November 1933, which enabled the police to keep persons with two or more criminal convictions in unlimited preventive detention.[59] A criminal-biological expert report determined who was to be detained, and whether or not the person could be castrated.[60] The ensuing tightening up of the criminal law, and the deterioration of conditions in 'normal' prisons and places of correction, were similarly in accordance with criminal-biological, or racist, criteria. Concretely, this meant that both the sentence imposed, and subsequent treatment in prison, were dependent upon the criminal-biological classification of the offender. To this end, from 1935 onwards all prisons and correctional institutions in Prussia were instructed to carry out 'criminal-biological investigations' on their inmates. Similar measures were applied to juvenile offenders throughout the Reich under a decree concerning the punishment of juveniles issued on 22 January 1937.[61] Special 'criminal-biological collection points' were established in Berlin, Freiburg, Münster, Leipzig, Halle, Hamburg, and Königsberg to carry out the prescribed tests. Robert Ritter's Criminal-Biological Research Unit within the Ministry of Public Health decided in doubtful cases.

Policy towards the 'asocial' and 'habitual criminals' was further radicalised following Himmler's appointment as Chief of the German Police in the Reich Ministry of the Interior on 17 June 1936. Himmler's object was clearly to remove responsibility for the 'solution' of the 'asocial question' from the courts and normal correctional institutions.[62] On 23 February 1937 he ordered that 'about 2,000 professional or habitual criminals and those who offend against public decency should be taken into police preventive custody'. Like 'protective custody', the imposition of police 'preventive custody' (*Vorbeugungshaft*) took place without any prior legal proceedings. Like persons in 'protective custody', those detained in 'police preventive custody' were sent to concentration camps and set to work in the enterprises of the burgeoning SS economic empire.

However, this practice – which was not sanctioned by either the law or any ministerial decree – soon encountered criticism from the justice authorities, who resented both Himmler's efforts to appropriate this area of activity and the Criminal Police's attempts to follow the Gestapo in evading legal controls. Himmler regularised the situation on 14 December 1937.

The following passage is taken from the circular of the Reich and Prussian Minister of the Interior of 14 December 1937 on 'the preventive fight against crime':

> Those to be considered asocial are persons who demonstrate through behaviour towards the community, which may not in itself be criminal, that they will not adapt themselves to the community. The following are examples of the asocial:
> (a) Persons who through minor, but repeated, infractions of the law demonstrate that they will not adapt themselves to the natural discipline of a National Socialist state, e.g. beggars, tramps, (Gypsies), whores, alcoholics with contagious diseases, particularly sexually-transmitted diseases, who evade the measures taken by the public health authorities.[63]

This enabled the Criminal Police to take into 'preventive custody', and hence to send to concentration camps, persons who had not been concretely charged with a criminal or political offence. It sufficed to have been sentenced for a previous offence, or as the decree significantly put it, to have demonstrated an unwillingness to conform to 'the natural discipline of a National Socialist state'. The decree also concretised and extended the circle of persons to be taken into 'preventive custody'. It spoke of 'for example [!] beggars, tramps, (gypsies), whores, alcoholics with contagious diseases, particularly sexually transmitted diseases, who evade the measures taken by the public health authorities', and of persons 'against whom it can be proved that on two occasions they have turned down jobs offered to them without reasonable grounds, or who, having taken on a job, have given it up again after a short while without a valid reason'. These persons were to be designated 'work-shy'. Persons were also to be sent to concentration camps whose behaviour, 'while not criminal, gives offence to the community', and who had demonstrated that they would not 'become a part of the community', In other words, the 'asocial' had been effectively criminalised.

The Gestapo were entrusted with the first major wave of arrests, carried out between 21 and 30 April 1938, since the operation required no particular police skills.[64] This was because the information the Gestapo required was supplied by, *inter alia*, the local labour exchanges. Apart from those with more than 30 per cent disabilities, the operation excluded members of the NSDAP, SA and SS. Those arrested were questioned and then sent to Buchenwald. By June the recently centralised Reich Criminal Police Office was ready to implement its own more comprehensive plans for the detention of the able-bodied 'asocial'. Heydrich ordered that each regional district police headquarters was to fulfil a quota of at least 200 arrests. Those arrested were to be sent to 'labour and improvement camps', or in other words Sachsenhausen, Buchenwald, and Dachau. Only 'males capable of work' were to be arrested. The raids on doss-houses, overnight shelters, and hostels began in the early hours of 13 June. In Hamburg alone, the Criminal Police detained 700 people instead of the 200 Heydrich had asked for. Judging by a list of persons abducted from one hostel in Bielefeld, the Criminal Police were far from scrupulous about whom they took away:

L. Kurt, born on 19.2.1888 in C. Worker.
Arrived 30.3.38. L has asthma and chronic bronchial catarrah, suffers from his stomach also. He required hospital treatment from 11.4–29.4.38.
S. Walter, born on 2.5.1893 in W. Barman.
Arrived: 18.5.1938. In recent years S has not had regular employment. He has been staying in various institutions because of his chronic alcoholism. In this case one is dealing with a psychopath, who because of his addiction to drink will never hold a regular job or be made to settle down.
L. Bernard, born on 3.8.1884 in B. Worker.
Arrived: 10.6.1938. L came from a job on the Reichsautobahn, from which he had to be dismissed because his papers were not in order. Before that he spent some time in the workhouse at Brauweiler. He hoped to seek work from here as soon as his papers had been put into order.
Sch. Albert, born on 2.6.1899 in O. Surveyor's assistant, has been with us since 2.6.1938. He came from a labour camp, where he had been living for about a year. His great-grandfather, grandfather, and father were drunks. He himself: rachitic deformation of the lower jaw, as a result of which he

cannot chew his food properly and therefore suffers from stomach problems. His physical condition is such that Dr Blumke thinks that hospitalisation is necessary.[65]

As we saw in an earlier chapter, these raids – which 'netted' perhaps as many as 11,000 people – encompassed Jews with previous convictions and many Sinti and Roma. The latter were arrested simply because they were 'Gypsies'.[66] The overall motivation behind these waves of arrests, which were collectively known as the 'Reich Campaign against the Work-Shy', was economic. By 1938, rearmament and preparations for war had converted the mass unemployment of the early 1930s into a general labour shortage. This was reflected in the requisitioning of 120,000 foreign agricultural labourers in early 1938, and in subsequent labour procurement measures like compulsory labour service for girls. More specifically, the rounding up of 'able-bodied' vagrants under the guise of 'crime prevention' coincided with the development by the SS of industrial enterprises as adjuncts to their concentration camp system. The Gestapo raids took place on the same day as the SS founded their German Earth and Stone Quarry Ltd, which ran quarries, granite, and brick works in the proximity of Buchenwald, Sachsenhausen, Flossenburg and Neuengamme. This point was made explicitly by SS-Oberführer Ulrich Greifelt, who was Himmler's link with the Four-Year Plan apparatus:

> The chief of the SS administration has created the ideal means in the concentration camps for achieving the productive deployment of the labour potential of criminal and political prisoners. They have established, or are in the process of establishing, production centres for costly building materials which are needed for the major construction enterprises of the Führer . . . In view of the tight situation on the labour market, national labour discipline dictated that all persons who would not conform to the working life of the nation, and who were vegetating as work-shy and asocial, making the streets of our cities and countryside unsafe, had to be compulsorily registered and set to work. Prompted by the Office for the Four-Year Plan, the Gestapo intervened with considerable energy. Simultaneously, the Criminal Police took on tramps, beggars, Gypsies, and pimps, and finally those who refused to pay maintenance. More than 10,000 of these asocial forces are currently undertaking a labour training cure in the concentration camps, which are admirably suited for this purpose.[67]

Judging by what is known of the physical condition of those arrested, and by the nature of the work they had to carry out in the camps, it seems that the 'cure' Greifelt ironically spoke of was intended to be lethal. This seems to be confirmed by the large number of fatalities among the 'asocial' inmates of Buchenwald. This apparently contradictory result can be explained by the fact that the arrests and detentions in concentration camps were designed to terrify those not arrested – and indeed the working population as a whole – into renewed efforts on behalf of the economy. Anyone contemplating dropping out was well advised to think again.

The measures taken against the 'asocial' were solely based upon Himmler's decree on crime prevention of 14 December 1937. There was never a formal law on the 'asocial'. However, there were various attempts from 1940 onwards to pass what in the Nazis' hyper-German speech was called a Community Aliens Law (*Gemeinschaftsfremdengesetz*).[68] These plans ran into difficulties with the Ministry of Justice, which wished to defend its areas of competence from Himmler's ever-expanding security empire. What this law would have entailed can be seen from a draft classificatory system on the 'asocial' by a Munich law professor, Mezger, for a conference on this issue, and from an advanced draft of the projected law, produced by the printing workshop in the prison at Tegel.

Dr Edmund Mezger
Professor of Law in the University

Munich 25 March 1944
Kaulbachstr. 89

Ministerial Director Grau
Ministry of Justice
Berlin
Wilhelmstrasse 65

Dear Ministerial Director

In the question of the 'classification' of criminals under discussion, I have decided on the following scheme:

I. Situation Criminals
1. Criminals by virtue of conflict
2. Criminals by virtue of development
3. Criminals by virtue of opportunity

II. Character Criminals
4. Criminals by virtue of inclination
5. Criminals by virtue of tendency
6. Criminals by virtue of condition

Yours faithfully
Heil Hitler
Your loyal
Dr Mezger

The experience of decades has shown, that the criminal fraternity is
continuously replenished from inferior clans. The individual members
of these clans always mate with individuals from equally bad clans.
This means that inferiority is transmitted from generation to generation, quite often intensifying into criminality. Most of these people
are neither willing to join, nor capable of joining, the national community. They lead a life which is alien to the ideas of the community,
have no feelings for society, are often incapable if not hostile to a life
within the community, and are in any case community aliens.

It is an old demand of those organisations entrusted with the public
welfare that community aliens (asocials) be compulsorily maintained;
because of their inability to become part of the community they
become a permanent burden on society. Up to now, existing welfare
legislation only recognises custody in cases of proven helplessness or
of voluntary committal . . . The social order will need a legal basis for
taking community aliens into compulsory custody, beyond the
inadequate possibilities of existing welfare legislation.

The governments of the time of the system [i.e. in the Weimar
Republic] failed in the case of community aliens. They did not make
knowledge of eugenics and criminal biology the basis of sound welfare
and criminal policies. Liberalistic thinking only saw the 'rights' of the
individual, and was more concerned with the protection of rights vis à
vis the power of the state than with the wellbeing of the community.

In National Socialism the individual does not count as far as society
is concerned.

Measures introduced by the Reich Criminal Police after the seizure
of power, based upon a gradually developing National Socialist police
law against community aliens, developed from this principle. It was
increasingly recognised that the treatment of community aliens was a
matter not so much for the welfare authorities as for the police.
According to National Socialist thinking, welfare can only be accorded
to people who are not just needy but also worthy of it. Community
aliens who only harm the national community do not need welfare,
but rather compulsion based on action by the police, designed either
to retrieve them as worthwhile members of the national community or
to prevent their causing further harm. Protection of the community is
therefore the first priority.

The draft law concerning treatment of community aliens must fulfil
these requirements, in so far as it incorporates existing police
measures, refashions them, and creates a legal basis for further judgements in criminal cases involving community aliens, as well as for the

sterilisation of community aliens if progeny deleterious to the community are to be expected.

Applying the knowledge of eugenics and criminal biology, the law categorises three groups of people as community aliens:

1. The group of failures:
People who through their personality and way of life, and in particular through extraordinary defects of intellect and character, reveal that they are not capable of satisfying the minimal requirements of the national community.

2. The group of the work-shy and slovenly:
People who are good-for-nothings and parasites, who either lead a useless, unproductive, and disorderly life, and who therefore become a burden upon others or on the community, or who have a tendency towards vagrancy and slacking, theft, deception, and other minor offences, and who lead a purposeless life. In this group we could also include people who because of aggressiveness and obtuseness repeatedly disrupt the peace of others or of the community, people whom this draft could call hooligans.

3. The group of criminals:
People who reveal through their personality and way of life that their minds are bent upon criminal deeds.

To ensure that those community aliens, who through their behaviour harm the national community, can be brought back into the community, or if this is impossible, will be prevented by the power of the State from doing more harm, this draft envisages police measures for the non-criminal community alien. This would be mainly along the lines of police surveillance; surveillance can be coupled with particular conditions, stipulations, and prohibitions. If those surveillance measures prove inadequate, then this draft will provide the legal basis for the admission of community aliens into regional asylums or institutions of correction. If this stronger curtailment of liberty still proves inadequate, then the community alien is to be detained in a police camp. Thus the idea of detention, which has been developed in welfare law, will be extended into the field of protecting the community.

Particular importance has to be accorded to the fight against criminal community aliens. Therefore in addition to police treatment of the community alien, the law regulates the courts' handling of criminal community aliens. The task of reintegrating the criminal community alien as a positive member of society is not for the police but a matter for the judiciary, as is their being rendered harmless in so far as this is possible under the terms and conditions of sentence.

Punishment of the criminal community alien must not merely be a matter of retribution for their deeds, but rather has to be concerned with their resocialisation, and therefore has to be suited to the character of the criminal community alien. As the length of time necessary to influence the hereditary or biological constitution of the criminal community alien to the extent that he is no longer a burden or danger to the national community cannot be foreseen, the sentence has to be of indefinite duration.

The draft envisages that just as the police may detain persons for an indefinite period, so the courts must have powers of indeterminate sentencing at their disposal. Thus, in line with long-term demands of both criminal lawyers and criminal biologists, the draft equips the police and courts with a weapon which goes beyond the Law for Habitual Criminals of 24 November 1933. Indefinite sentence not only has the advantage over a determinate sentence that it can be adjusted to the moral and mental development of the prisoner during his period in custody, but it also increases our hold over the man himself. It does not allow him to do his time more or less uninvolved, but rather shakes him up and forces him to change his ways so that he earns his release from the institution through inner transformation.

In particular, the draft distinguishes between criminals who according to their lifestyle and personality have a strong inclination to commit serious crimes, and others who have a lesser inclination to commit (minor) crimes of all kinds. For the former, the draft envisages a minimum indefinite sentence of five years. For the latter, the draft threatens a prison sentence of not less than one year according to the seriousness of his offence.

Judges should separate out hardened criminals right from the start, and deliver them to the police, whose task it is to protect the national community from these elements. They will be declared to be persons of lesser legal standing. Because of their inferior disposition, they will be sent for a form of treatment which is primarily concerned with incarceration. This draft also envisages surrender to the police of vagrants, professional beggars, and similar good-for-nothings who are more burdensome than harmful. The reason for this is that this group of community aliens is closer to the group of parasites because in both cases, their behaviour is based upon work-shyness and slovenliness. Therefore for those groups the same kind of treatment is suitable. By contrast, criminals by virtue of inclination, in whose case improvement and reform can be expected after firm education in work, should be subjected to a process of resocialisation in prison. If this fails, then this draft both enables and requires the prison authorities to surrender the inmate at that late date to the police. This regulation of the treatment of the criminal community alien signifies a considerable but absolutely necessary change in the criminal law because it rejects the concurrency of punishment and detention in favour of punishment designed as re-education. Detention *per se* is recognised as a task for the police.

The draft also extends the practice of castration in the case of sexual offenders, to persons who have a predilection towards their own sex. Recent medical findings show that castration is also a powerful weapon against these persons.

In the case of minors, we have to take into account that their education is mainly a matter for borstal training and probation, and in the case of criminal youths, prisons for young offenders. The police measures in the law should only be applicable in cases where the educational authorities have decided that reintegration into society through youth welfare agencies is impossible. Youth should only be sentenced to indefinite detention when the preconditions of the Decree against Young Professional Criminals of 4 October 1939, RGBl. 1.S. 2000, or the Decree for the Indefinite Detention of Youth of 10 September 1941 RGBl. 1.S 567 apply. Community aliens, particularly failures and layabouts, are very frequently members of clans who either as a whole, or as individual members, demand the continuous attention of the police and courts, and so are a burden upon the national community. This draft makes it possible to sterilise community aliens if undesirable progeny are anticipated. Whether undesirable progeny can be expected from a community alien is a decision for the Hereditary Health Courts. The detailed implementation of the law will be regulated by decrees on implementation issued by the ministers concerned.[69]

The worsening position of the Ministry of Justice within the Nazi governmental polyocracy, symbolised by the advent of the fanatical Nazi Otto Thierack, resulted in what amounted to capitulation in the inter-bureaucratic struggle. On 18 September 1942 at a five and a half hour conference in Himmler's field headquarters in the Ukraine, Thierack expressed his readiness to exclude all 'asocial elements' from the penal system, and to hand them over, to the Reichsführer-SS 'for extermination through labour'.[70] Among those to be handed over were all 'Jews, Gypsies, Russians, and Ukrainians', as well as Poles who had been sentenced to more than three years' detention in 'normal' prisons. Germans were only to be sent to the camps if they were serving sentences of eight years or over.

A letter from Reich Minister of Justice Otto Thierack to the Chief of the Reich Chancellery Martin Bormann of 13 October 1942 states:

> With a view to liberating the body of the German nation from Poles, Russians, Jews, and Gypsies, and with a view to making the lands in the east which have come to the Reich free for German settlement, I intend to hand over the criminal prosecution of Poles, Russians, Jews, and Gypsies to the Reichsführer-SS. My assumption here is that the justice authorities can only contribute in small measure to the extermination of members of these peoples . . . There is no point in conserving such persons for years on end in German prisons and houses of correction.[71]

Senior members of the Ministry of Justice toured the nation's prisons to select those inmates who were to be sent to the concentration camps. Since by 1 April 1943 5,935 of the 14,700 prisoners deported had already died it seems probable that the prison authorities availed themselves of the Ministry of Justice officials to rid themselves of sick or otherwise 'difficult' inmates.

The fact that racial discrimination was practised against the prison population demonstrates that in the Third Reich the 'asocial question' was solved in line with racial criteria. The Nazis made no secret of this. The official judicial letters of 1 June 1943 said that the campaign against major felons and the asocial had a 'racial-hygienic' goal, namely to contribute to 'a progressive purification of the body of the nation' through the 'ruthless removal of criminals unworthy of life'.[72]

From the 'judicial letters' of 1 January and 1 April 1942:

> In the course of time the criminal law has gradually taken on the task of cleansing the body of the nation in addition to the punishment of individual felons, especially criminals who mostly consist of asocial, sick, or degenerate clans. It therefore stands in close organisational proximity to the major fundamental laws of the National Socialist State, which serve the selection, purification, and maintenance of the health of our people.[73]
>
> In so far as they have to do with the fight against crime . . . punishments in our time must fulfil the racial-hygienic task of progressively purifying the body of our nation by ridding it of criminals unworthy of life.

Naturally, in the Third Reich there were persons who would be regarded as criminals in our societies too. However, it is important to remember that in Nazi Germany both criminals and the criminalised 'asocial' were sentenced by a fundamentally criminal regime. Many of them ended their lives in concentration camps, without any formal legal proceedings, and without any legal justification whatsoever. Their 'crime' was to have been on the deficit side of the Nazis' racial-biological balance sheet. These policies were aimed not just at criminals, but at the poor and 'feckless' in general.

The following comes from a circular of the Reich Minister of the Interior of 18 July 1940 concerning 'guidelines for the determination of hereditary health':

(a) (1) Asocial persons and members of asocial families are to be excluded from all of the measures in question, and disqualified from all public welfare expenditure. Asocial progeny are totally undesirable to the racial community, therefore asocial families with many children can never be regarded as being 'rich in children'.

(2) Persons are to be regarded as being asocial (community aliens) who by virtue of a hereditarily determined and therefore irremediable attitude of mind:

1. continually come into conflict with the law, the police, or the authorities.

2. are work-shy, and who perpetually try to burden public or private charitable foundations, in particular the NSV or WHW, with the maintenance of themselves and their children. Included in this category are families who obviously regard their children as a source of income, and therefore regard it as legitimate to avoid regular employment themselves, or

3. [who are] particularly unproductive and unrestrained, and who in the absence of a sense of responsibility do not conduct orderly domestic lives or raise their children to be useful racial comrades, or

4. who are drunks, or who are conspicuously dissolute in their way of life (e.g. whores, who earn their living wholly or in part by immoral earnings).

(3) In cases like the above, adequate information can be acquired from the records of the welfare and juvenile agencies, the police or, should the need arise, other authorities.

(4) Families are to be described as being asocial when several of their members are asocial (community aliens) and when the family as a whole is regarded as being a burden on the racial community.

(b) Between asocial families and families which in terms of the following stipulations are to be regarded as being part of the average population and hence are worthy of assistance, there are a number of families whose progeny can certainly not be regarded as a benefit to the racial community, but who do not represent a serious burden on the latter, and who are therefore to be regarded as being accepted families.[74]

THE PERSECUTION OF HOMOSEXUALS

A homosexual recalls 1933:

> Then came the thunderbolt of the 30 January 1933, and we knew that a change of political climate had taken place. What we had tried to prevent, had taken place.
> Over the years, more and more of my political friends disappeared, of my Jewish and of my homosexual friends. Fear came over us with the increasingly co-ordinated pressure of the Nazis. For heaven's sake

not to attract attention, to exercise restraint. 1933 was the starting-point for the persecution of homosexuals. Already in this year we heard of raids on homosexual pubs and meeting places. Maybe individual, politically uneducated homosexuals who were only interested in immediate gratification did not recognise the significance of the year 1933, but for us homosexuals who were also politically active, who had defended the Weimar Republic, and who had tried to forestall the Nazi threat, 1933 initially signified a reinforcing of our resistance.

In order not to mutually incriminate ourselves, we decided to no longer recognise each other. When we came across each other in the street, we passed by without looking at one another. There were certainly possibilities for us to meet, but that never happened in public.

For a politicised homosexual, visiting places which were part of the homosexual subculture was too dangerous. Friends told me that raids on bars were becoming more frequent. And someone had written on the wall of the subway tunnel of the Hamburg S-Bahn between Dammtor station and the main station, 'Street of the Lost'. That was some sort of film or book title. We found this graffiti very amusing, for most of us tried to cope with the thing by developing a sort of gallows humour.[75]

Homosexuals were not recognised as victims of Nazi persecution in either post-war German state.[76] This is despite the fact that those who were forced to wear the pink triangle in concentration camps were particularly harshly treated by guards and fellow inmates alike. There are several reasons for this unsatisfactory state of affairs. Firstly, it is a reflection of widespread continuing prejudice against homosexuals, and of the natural reticence of the victims to publicise persecution posited upon sexual preference. Secondly, it is a consequence of the fact that the Nazis' harsher 1935 interpretation of paragraph 175 of the 1871 Reich Criminal Code, criminalising 'acts of indecency' as well as sexual intercourse between two men, was not repealed until 1969. Concretely, this meant that men who had been sent to concentration camps because of their sexual preferences could be punished after 1945 under the same law. In East Germany, the Nazis' emendations to the law were partially abrogated in 1950, and homosexual acts between consenting adults of eighteen years of age or over were legalised in 1968. However, in the GDR too, homosexuals were not numbered among Hitler's victims. Neither post-war German state has a distinguished record in this area. In a recent election contest in Schleswig-Holstein, the CDU incumbent candidate tried to smear his SPD rival with the charge that his party advocated sex with minors. The advent of Aids has also become a means to collect votes and percentage points on the pretext of restoring 'traditional morality'. Although in the GDR there were real efforts to demystify homosexual activities and to 'normalise' homosexual partnerships, foreigners determined to be HIV positive were simply deported.[77] This fact received less attention than the regime's well-publicised investment in research on Aids.

For most of the medieval and early modern periods, the penalty for homosexual acts was death. Under the impact of the Enlightenment and the French Revolution, certain German states, beginning with Bavaria in 1813, decriminalised homosexuality. The significant exception was Prussia, whose benighted legislation concerning this issue was carried over in 1871 on to the Reich as a whole.

Text of Paragraph 175 of the 1871 Reich Criminal Code:

> 1. A male who indulges in criminally indecent activity with another male, or who allows himself to participate in such activity, will be punished with imprisonment.
>
> 2. If one of the participants is under the age of twenty-one, and if the offence has not been grave, the court may dispense with the sentence of imprisonment.[78]

Since it was difficult in practice to prove what had taken place in private between two men, before the turn of the century convictions under Paragraph 175 amounted to on average 500 per annum. This does not mean that homosexuals had an easy time of it. While the number of successful prosecutions may have been limited, the opportunities for 'informal' prosecution were immense. During the Kaiserreich, homosexuals were particularly vulnerable to blackmailers, known as *Chanteure* on the homosexual scene. Blackmail, and the threat of public exposure, resulted in frequent suicides or suicide attempts. Nonetheless, gradually a recognisable homosexual subculture developed, particularly in the big cities, which afforded individuals some degree of anonymity. During the First World War, Berlin alone had about forty homosexual meeting places, ranging from elegant bars to ordinary pubs, all largely staffed by homosexuals. In Berlin there were also spectacular homosexual dances, where men were (temporarily) allowed to dance freely with other men. Otherwise, there were a number of homosexual meeting places, notably the 'queers' way' in the Tiergarten, or in Hamburg the 'Tabakgärtchen', as well as private baths and less salubrious places.[79] Most homosexuals, however, seem to have preferred small circles of the like-minded, where they could talk and socialise in the privacy of their own homes.

The beginnings of a homosexual rights movement in Germany are closely associated with Magnus Hirschfeld (1868–1935).[80] Through an

6.12 Male couple.

association called the Scientific-Humanitarian Committee, founded in 1897, Hirschfeld sought to enlighten the public about homosexuality and to bring about the repeal of Paragraph 175. A petition to this effect was supported by, *inter alia*, Gerhart Hauptmann, Rainer Maria Rilke, Karl Kautsky, Max Liebermann and the socialist leader August Bebel, the only leader of a German political party ever to bother to find out at first hand about the life of homosexuals in that country. He was also the first person publicly to reveal the existence of 'pink lists', on which the police recorded the names of homosexuals regardless of whether they had been convicted of homosexual activities or not.

This is not to claim that the political Left had a monopoly of virtue on this subject. The correspondence of Marx and Engels contains periodic aspersions against homosexuals – as it does against Poles and Jews – and in the 1890s German Social Democrats sought to make political capital out of a number of homosexual scandals involving prominent persons. This was so in the cases of Friedrich Krupp, Prince Philipp zu Eulenburg, and Kuno von Moltke, all close associates of the Kaiser himself. In 1902, for example, the SPD's *Vorwärts* ran an article under the headline 'Krupp auf Kapri', revealing that the Italian police had brought charges against the industrialist.[81]

The Weimar Republic brought an initial liberalisation of the climate of opinion, but not changes in the law. Homosexual meeting places and magazines proliferated, while books and films appeared which dealt with the subject in a comparatively open way. In 1919 Hirschfeld founded the Institute for Sexual Science, devoted to the scientific discussion of marital problems, sexually transmitted diseases, laws relating to sexual offences, abortion, and homosexuality. Greater openness concerning homosexuality resulted in an attempt by the conservative governmental coalition in 1925 to tighten up the law. Operating under the assumption that a minority of 'Ur-Homos' were using the new climate to propagate their sexual preference among heterosexual men, a group of civil servants drafted an amendment to the law known as E 1925. This attempt to turn the clock back resulted in counter-proposals from Hirschfeld's Scientific-Humanitarian Committee concerning the reform of all laws pertaining to sexual matters. The first reading of E 1925 took place in the Reichstag on 22 June 1927. The Catholic Centre, German People's Party (DVP), and German National People's Party (DNVP) coalition received vocal support from the fourteen Nazi deputies, with Wilhelm Frick claiming, 'Naturally it is the Jews, Magnus Hirschfeld and his racial comrades, who have taken the lead and are trying to break new ground, just as in general the whole

6.13 The Russian-Roman Baths for gentlemen on Potsdamer Platz in Berlin.

of Jewish morality has ruined the German people.' Despite the opposition of the SPD and KPD, the draft went through to committee stage. Following a leftwards change in the political composition of the Reichstag, the committee eventually met on 16 October 1929. Conservative committee members claimed that sexuality was not a private matter and that the object of legislation should be to maintain the generative 'powers of the nation'. They were outvoted, however, fifteen to thirteen, by representatives of the SPD, KPD, and DDP, who recommended the legalisation of homosexual acts among consenting adults. The advent of the Nazi regime soon nullified this considerable achievement. This had been made clear in an article in the *Völkischer Beobachter* on 2 August 1930 which said, 'We congratulate you, Herr Kahl and Herr Hirschfeld, on this success! But don't you believe that we Germans will allow such a law to exist for one day when we have succeeded in coming to power.' Like the conservative press in general, Nazi newspapers contained denunciations of Hirschfeld as 'the big boss of the perverts' and alarmist articles whenever he happened to speak about reform of Paragraph 175 in schools.[82]

Official Nazi party statements on the issue were another matter. This was not unconnected with the fact that the leadership of the NSDAP included at least one notorious homosexual. The SA leader Ernst Röhm openly attended homosexual bars and meeting places and belonged to the main homosexual organisation, the League for Human Rights. In keeping with a form of character assassination first explored with Friedrich Krupp, the German Left attempted to smear the Nazi movement with the charge of homosexuality, despite the fact that the SPD and KPD had recently endeavoured to decriminalise the issue. The SPD *Münchner Post* ran a series of articles entitled 'National Socialism and Homosexuality' with headlines like 'Stammtisch 175', or 'Brotherhood of Poofs in the Brown House'. The party's *Rheinische Zeitung* warned, 'Parents, protect your sons from "physical preparation" in the Hitler Youth.' Similarly, both the KPD with its claim that homosexuality was 'unproletarian', and assorted left-wing anti-fascist groups with their talk of 'Hitler's queer friend Röhm', made the mistake, as Kurt Tucholsky noted, of attempting to compete with the Nazis on a ground of which they were the acknowledged masters, namely the calculated appeal to the 'healthy instincts' of the German people.[83]

If, at first, even Heinrich Himmler was prepared to protect Röhm – 'The object of these attacks is Staff Chief Röhm whom the Jews and their lackeys have regarded as the most unpleasant and feared leader of the SA and SS since the creation of the Party' – this mood changed once the Nazis were in power. Specifically, Hitler feared that Röhm's efforts to transform the SA into a militia were alienating the army, and hence represented a threat to Hitler's own power. There is no evidence that in June 1934 Röhm was contemplating a *Putsch*. Nazi propaganda, however, justified Hitler's ensuing murder of his SA associates in terms of striking down a putative conspiracy, the restoration of 'law and order' against the anarchic gang-sterism of the SA, and last but not least, as a cleansing operation against sexual 'deviants'. Thus the *Kölnische Zeitung* reported on 1 July 1934 that the Führer could no longer tolerate the fact that 'millions of upright people should be burdened and compromised by abnormally-inclined creatures'. This perversion of the issues involved – namely Hitler's resort to murder to resolve a political power struggle – was highly effective. Many 'upright' and 'normally-inclined' members of the NSDAP and 'national comrades' found Hitler's measures against 'asocial and diseased elements' both 'upright' and 'normal'. The murder of homosexuals evidently corresponded with 'the healthy instincts of the people', including many who were otherwise totally opposed to the regime.

A report by the Social Democratic Party in exile (SOPADE), concerning public reactions to the Röhm affair (30 June 1934), observed:

> Baden . . . The immediate result of the murders was great confusion, both as regards the way they were viewed and as regards their future political consequences. On the whole, Hitler's courage in taking decisive action was stressed the most. He was regarded practically as a hero. Hitler's slandering of the victims, their homosexuality, and their 30,000-Mark meals, was at first also adjudged heroic. As to what repercussions to the events of the 30th June and their aftermath will be, an agreed and definitive answer cannot yet be given. Our comrades report that Hitler has won strong approval and sympathy from that part of the population which still places its hopes in him. To these people his action is proof that he wants order and decency. Other sections of the population have been given cause for thought.[84]

The Nazis' persecution of homosexuals predated the Röhm affair. On 6 May 1933 students of the Berlin School for Physical Education demolished the Institute for Sexual Science. The 12,000 books in the library were burned on the Opernplatz to the singing of the 'Deutschlandlied'. A bust of Hirschfeld was ceremonially hanged and then thrown on a bonfire. This is an eyewitness account of the destruction of Magnus Hirschfeld's institute for Sexual Science:

> On 6 May at 9.30 a.m. a few vans with about one hundred students and a band with brass instruments appeared before the Institute. They took up military formation and then, accompanied by music, forced their way into the building. Since the office was not open yet, they found no member of staff in the building, only a few cleaning ladies and a man who sympathised with the staff. The students demanded entrance to all the rooms; in so far as these were locked, like the reception rooms on the ground floor, which were no longer in use, or the present office of the World League for Sexual Reform, they broke through the doors. Since the ground floor rooms had nothing much to offer them, they went up to the first floor, where they emptied inkwells over papers and the carpets, and turned to private bookshelves. They took with them what appeared to be suspect, in line with what they had on so-called 'blacklists' . . . Most of the other pictures, photographs of representative types, were taken off the walls. They played football with them, so that a great mess of broken glass and crumpled pictures remained. When one of the students objected that this was medical material, another answered that it was irrelevant, that their task was not to confiscate a few books and pictures, but to destroy the institute . . . The occupants of the Institute had thought

that this plundering would be the end of the matter, but at 3pm several vans arrived with SA men, who declared that the confiscation must continue, because the Squad in the morning had not had enough time to clear everything out totally. This second troupe once again searched the whole building, and using a lot of baskets, loaded two large lorries with valuable books and manuscripts. From the insults they used it became clear that most of the authors represented in the special library were well known to the students. Not only Sigmund Freud, whose picture was thrown down the stairs and taken away, received the soubriquet 'the Jewish swine Freud', but also Havelock Ellis was called 'the pig Havelock Ellis' . . . Again and again they asked when Dr Hirschfeld would be coming back. As they put it, they wanted a 'tip' concerning when he would return. Even before the plundering took place, on several occasions SA men were in the Institute asking after Dr Hirschfeld. When they were told that he was abroad because of his malaria, they replied: 'Then hopefully he will snuff it without us; then we won't need to string him up or beat him to death.' . . . The number of books from the Institute's special library which were destroyed amounted to over one hundred thousand. The students carried a bust of Dr Magnus Hirschfeld in a torchlight parade, and threw it on a bonfire.[85]

The Röhm affair then provided Himmler with the pretext to order the central registering of all persons engaged in homosexual activities, particularly in so far as this concerned politically prominent individuals. The fruits of this police work were soon in evidence in the form of the public character assassination of General Fritsch and members of Roman Catholic religious orders. In 1935 Paragraph 175 was amended with Paragraph 175a, which henceforth encompassed any form of 'criminal indecency' between men or behaviour which was likely to offend 'public morality' or 'arouse sexual desires in oneself or strangers'. Concretely, this meant that if one man glanced at another in an 'enticing' way, he could be prosecuted under Paragraph 175a.

> Paragraph 175a:
> A term of imprisonment of up to ten years or, if mitigating circumstances can be established, a term of imprisonment of no less than three years will be imposed on:
> 1. Any male who by force or threat of violence and danger to life and limb compels another man to indulge in criminally indecent activities, or allows himself to participate in such activities;
> 2. Any male who forces another male to indulge with him in criminally indecent activities by using the subordinate position of the other man, whether it be at work or elsewhere, or who allows himself to participate in such activities;
> 3. Any male who indulges professionally and for profit in criminally

6.14 Magnus Hirschfeld's Institute for Sexual Research shortly after it had been ransacked by squads of Nazi students.

indecent activities with other males, or allows himself to be used for such activities or who offers himself for the same.
Paragraph 175b:
Criminally indecent activities by males with animals are to be punished with imprisonment; in addition, the court may deprive the subject of his civil rights.[86]

In practice, 'public morality' was interpreted by the Criminal Police. Specifically, in 1936 Himmler created a Reich Central Office for the Combating of Homosexuality and Abortion, led by Josef Meisinger, who was subsequently executed by the Poles in 1947 as the 'Butcher of Warsaw'.[87] The SS were particularly vociferous in their call for the death penalty for homosexual acts. In May 1935 their house journal, *Das Schwarze Korps*, ran an article by SS-Untersturmführer Professor Eckhardt, entitled 'Unnatural Indecency Deserves Death', which justified this demand with the arcane wisdom that 'nordic–Germanic' states had generally punished homosexuality with greater severity than the 'western–Latin' peoples – in the former case, as Himmler observed in a speech, by drowning the offenders in peat-bogs. These differences of practice, the article claimed, were a reflection of the 'nordic–Germanic people's' purer consciousness of 'the idea of race'. 'Hence', they had clearly recognised that homosexuality was a 'degenerate and racially-destructive phenomenon', and 'therefore' present-day Germany should reach back to 'the primeval Germanic point of view' by instigating 'the eradication of degenerates'.

An immediate consequence of Himmler's appropriation of this area of police activity was an incremental increase in the number of prosecutions under Paragraph 175. While in 1934 766 males were convicted and imprisoned, in 1936 the figure exceeded 4,000, and in 1938 8,000. Moreover, from 1937 onwards many of those involved were sent to concentration camps after they had served their 'regular' prison sentence, in accordance with Himmler's decree of 14 November 1937 'concerning the preventative fight against crime'. Himmler spelled out the racial-ideological arguments for his pathological homophobia in a speech to a conference of SS officers in February 1937. As a consequence of the First World War, Germany had lost two million men. There were also, he calculated, two million homosexuals in the population. This meant that Germany's 'sexual balance sheet' had gone into deficit, because 'four million men capable of sex' had either died or had 'renounced their duty to procreate' on account of their sexual proclivities. A 'people of good race' could not afford this imbalance. Instead of fulfilling its 'candidature for world power and world domination', Germany would sink into 'insignificance' within fifty years because some of its 'racially pure' and 'sexually capable' male population did not want to produce children or have sexual contact with women. Sexual behaviour was no longer a matter for the individual, for it involved 'the life and death of a people, world power or "swissification"'.

The following is part of Heinrich Himmler's speech to SS-Gruppenführer on 18 February 1937 concerning the 'question of homosexuality':

> If you further take into account the facts I have not yet mentioned, namely that with a static number of women, we have two million men too few on account of those who fell in the war, then you can well imagine how this imbalance of two million homosexuals and two million war dead, or in other words a lack of about four million men capable of having sex, has upset the sexual balance sheet of Germany, and will result in a catastrophe.
>
> I would like to develop a couple of ideas for you on the question of homosexuality. There are those homosexuals who take the view: what

I do is my business, a purely private matter. However, all things which take place in the sexual sphere are not the private affair of the individual, but signify the life and death of the nation, signify world power or 'swissification'. The people which has many children has the candidature for world power and world domination. A people of good race which has too few children has a one-way ticket to the grave, for insignificance in fifty or a hundred years, for burial in two hundred and fifty years . . .

Therefore we must be absolutely clear that if we continue to have this burden in Germany, without being able to fight it, then that is the end of Germany, and the end of the Germanic world. Unfortunately, we don't have it as easy as our forefathers. The homosexual, whom one called 'Urning', was drowned in a swamp. The professorial gentlemen who find these corpses in the peat-bogs are certainly unaware that in ninety out of a hundred cases, they have a homosexual before them, who was drowned in a swamp, clothes and all. That wasn't a punishment, but simply the extinguishing of abnormal life. It had to be got rid of, just as we pull out weeds, throw them on a heap, and burn them. It was not a feeling of revenge, simply that those affected had to go . . . In the SS, today, we still have about one case of homosexuality a month. In a whole year, about eight to ten cases occur in the entire SS. I have now decided upon the following: in each case, these people will naturally be publicly degraded, expelled, and handed over to the courts. Following completion of the punishment imposed by the courts, they will be sent, by my order, to a concentration camp, and they will be shot in the concentration camp, while attempting to escape. I will make that known by order to the unit to which the person so affected belonged. Thereby, I hope finally to have done with persons of this type in the SS, so that at least the good blood, which we have in the SS, and the increasingly healthy blood which we are cultivating for Germany, will be kept pure.

However this does not represent a solution to the problem for the whole of Germany. One must not have any illusions about the following. When I bring a homosexual before the courts and have him locked up, the matter is not settled, because the homosexual comes out of prison just as homosexual as before he went in. Therefore the whole question is not clarified. It is clarified in the sense that this burden has been identified, in contrast to the years before the seizure of power.[88]

At a subsequent conference for police officers rhetoric was translated into reality. They were to recruit barbers, porters, and public bath attendants as spies, to watch the advertisement sections of newspapers, and to encourage youths to inform on their teachers, youth group leaders, and so on. Efforts literally to eliminate homosexuals were at first confined to the SS itself. On 15 November 1941 a passage was incorporated into SS and police disciplinary procedures whereby homosexual members of the SS and police were to be executed.

What did this worsening climate mean for Germany's homosexual population? A homosexual in his mid-thirties, living in a small town called Reinbeck near Hamburg, recorded:

> With one blow a wave of arrests of homosexuals began in our town. One of the first to be arrested was my friend, with whom I had had a relationship since I was 23. One day people from the Gestapo came to his house and took him away. It was pointless to enquire where he might be. If anyone did that, they ran the risk of being similarly detained, because he knew them, and therefore they were also suspect. Following his arrest, his home was searched by Gestapo agents. Books were taken away, note- and address books were confiscated, questions were asked among the neighbours . . . The address books were the worst. All those who figured in them, or had anything to do with him, were arrested and summoned by the Gestapo. Me too. For a whole year I was summoned by the Gestapo and interrogated at least once every fourteen days or three weeks . . . After four weeks my friend was released from investigative custody. The fascists could not prove anything against him either. However the effects of his arrest were terrifying. Hair shorn off, totally confused, he was no longer what he was before . . . We had to be very careful with all contacts. I had to break off all relations with my friend. We passed each other by on the street, because we did not want to put ourselves in danger. There were no longer any homosexual meeting places. When I wanted to meet people I went to Hamburg. Each time that was a clandestine undertaking, because I had to make sure that no one was following me. I went up to the platform, waited until a train came, and let it depart. When I had seen that no one was left on the platform, I got on to the next train. At Berliner Tor I got out, went over to the tram stop, and when every one had got on, quickly ran over to the underground and went further . . . We lived like animals in a wild game park, always sensing the hunters.[89]

Raids on homosexual bars and meeting places took place from 1933 onwards. The Gestapo also used those arrested to compile lists of all homosexuals working in particular factories and firms, which enabled them to remove whole groups of homosexuals from, for example, the Hamburg power stations. Those arrested gradually filtered into the concentration camp system. Himmler himself, however, recognised that repression alone was no solution to the question of these 'demographic political dead losses'. Here academic science came to his aid. In their annual report of 1939–40, the Reich Criminal Police reported that 'In order to find further possibilities for the containment of this plague and to leave no method unexplored, the suggestions of various persons are being examined, which will deepen scientific knowledge of the problem of homosexuality.'

Among those to claim to have a 'solution' to the 'homosexual question' was a Danish SS doctor called Vaernet.[90] He had been experimenting with artificial gland implants since the early 1930s. His subjects were 4,000 mice. He then operated, unsuccessfully, on 180 human beings. Vaernet patented a hormonal implant capsule, and endeavoured to sell his findings – which were based on the totally false assumption that homosexuality is a consequence of male hormone deficiency – to the SS. They provided him with a large salary, laboratory facilities, and access to concentration camp prisoners, in return for which he was to give them sole licensing rights for the commercial exploitation of his 'discovery' at home and abroad. Vaernet carried out his operations on a number of prisoners. This involved the surgical insertion of a capsule which released the male hormone testosterone. One of the first to be operated upon was a Roman Catholic cleric who had served an eight-year jail sentence for offences under Paragraph 175. Precise medical records chronicled his post-operative progression to heterosexuality. His 'erotic mental universe had totally altered'. He had even dreamed of the women in the camp brothel, but 'for religious reasons' he could not bring himself to go there.

A report by Vaernet on the case history of an inmate in Buchenwald, dated 30 October 1944, reads:

> Patient No. 1
> No. 21 686, S., Bernhard, born 1889, theologian, member of a religious order.
> Prehistory:
> Always sickly, rather withdrawn, but cheerful and helpful. Sexual maturity at 18. 1911–12 attempt to come close to a girl, but on account of fear nothing sexual came of it. At school, bad performance at first because of living conditions, then good. 1924–8 relations with young men, touching their thighs, no feelings of fear. 1932–5 again with men, then normal relations with a girl, satisfaction the same. Last emission in February 1944. 8 years' imprisonment, nothing took place there.
> Implantation of the 'artificial male hormonal gland' on 19.6.44 (dose 3a).
> Following the operation on:
> 16.9.44   Pains. Neurological, no findings.
> 17.9.44   No pains.
> 18.9.44   Erection.
> 19.9.44   Full erection in the early morning.

20.9.44   Once again full erection.
22.9.44   Erection again.
22.9.44   Erection, but weaker. No pains.
23.9.44   Erection in the morning and evening.
24.9.44   The same.
26.10.44   Surgical wounds fully healed without any reactions. No
           reactions to the implantation of an 'artificial gland'. Feels
           better and has dreamed of women.

His appearance has improved considerably. Looks younger, his
features are smoother, today he came for an examination laughing and
happy. During the first examination he was taciturn and only
answered the questions obliquely; today he talks freely and in detail
about his earlier life and about the changes which have taken place
since the implant.
Statement:
Already a few days after the implantation he slept better. Before then
he felt tired and depressed, and his thought constantly revolved
around life in the camp.

His depression has vanished – is looking forward to when he will be
released, is making plans for the future. Has mastered himself, also
psychologically, everything is better, in every respect feels more free.

Other prisoners have told him that he has changed, that he looks
younger and better.

Also his entire erotic mental universe has altered – before, all of his
erotic thoughts and dreams were aimed at young men, but now only
at women. He thinks that life in the camp is unfavourable – thought
about the women in the brothel, but for 'religious reasons' he cannot
go there.[91]

The SS were not so morally fastidious. In 1944 Himmler ordered that
Vaernet's 'patients' should be sent to the women's camp at Ravensbrück
to see, in the camp brothel, whether the operation had worked. At least
two patients did not survive Vaernet's surgical attentions. The fate of
patients whose sexuality remained unaltered is unknown.

The number of homosexuals imprisoned in concentration camps has
never been established. The usual figure given is 10,000, but it could have
been as high as 15,000.[92] However, as is clear from the accounts of
homosexual survivors and other categories of prisoner, those who wore the
pink triangle were treated deplorably by guards and fellow inmates alike.
The following is a description of the treatment of 'pink triangles' in
Sachsenhausen:

Those wearing the pink triangle had to use wheelbarrows to pile up
earth and clay as an artificial mound, to stop the bullets on the rifle
range. However, after a few days, a group of SS men appeared at the

range, to practise their shooting, while we were still emptying the earth from our wheelbarrows on to the mound. Naturally, while the shooting was going on, we did not want to bring any more earth up to the mound, in case we were hit by one of the bullets. However, with threats and blows the Kapos and SS men forced us to go on working.

The bullets started to fly between our ranks, and many of my comrades in suffering fell together, some only wounded, but many hit fatally. We soon discovered that the SS men were less happy to shoot at the targets than to use us work detail prisoners as targets, and to hunt individuals pushing their wheelbarrows up.[93]

Homosexuals also lacked any opportunities to exercise the sort of group solidarity which kept up the morale of political or criminal inmates. As a prisoner from Dachau reported, 'The prisoners with the pink triangle did not live very long; they were quickly and systematically exterminated by the SS.' The exact number of those who died remains unknown. It is clear, however, that in the Third Reich homosexuals were treated in a manner without parallel in any civilised state in the world. It is also clear that they were persecuted for racial-ideological reasons. They were held responsible for 'a deficit in the sexual balance sheet', because they had failed to fulfil 'their duty to procreate'. It should also be noted that almost half of the 50,000 convictions for homosexual activity during the Third Reich occurred between 1937 and 1939, or in other words, that in this area the regime's persecutory drives were not fuelled solely by the 'radicalising' impact of war.

PART THREE

THE FORMATION OF THE 'NATIONAL COMMUNITY'

DIE **NSDAP** SICHERT DIE VOLKS-GEMEINSCHAFT

VOLKSGENOSSEN
BRAUCHT IHR RAT UND HILFE
SO WENDET EUCH AN DIE

CHAPTER SEVEN

YOUTH IN THE THIRD REICH

THERE was scarcely another problem with which Hitler dealt so intensively, or, to use one of his favourite words, 'fanatically', as policy towards youth. In *Mein Kampf*, he treated the subject at considerable length and in pedantic detail. The call for 'a balance between intellectual instruction and physical training' enjoyed primacy of place among the 'educational principles for a (future) *völkisch* state' adumbrated in the book.[1] Here, Hitler argued that every day young people should receive physical education for 'at least an hour each morning and evening'. He was thinking particularly of boxing, for this sport developed the 'spirit of aggression', required 'lightning decisions', and trained the body in 'steely dexterity'.[2]

Hitler justified this by remarking that an 'excessive emphasis upon purely intellectual development and the neglect of physical education . . . leads to the premature onset of sexual imaginings'.[3] The premature 'satis-faction of the senses' was especially dangerous because it could lead young men to consort with prostitutes, and hence to run the risk of contracting syphilis. This was bad enough, for according to Hitler, the 'struggle against syphilis and its pace-setter, prostitution' was among the 'most immense tasks facing humanity'. But worst, and most dangerous of all, was the 'fact' that behind prostitution and syphilis lurked 'the Jew'. It was 'he' who both championed and derived a living from libertine tendencies in literature, the arts, and the press. Jews, he claimed, were predominant in the 'white slave trade', and promoted prostitution in every conceivable way, in order to further the spread of syphilis and hence the extermination of the 'Aryan race'. In order to nip these (associated) evils in the bud, it was essential that 'through sport and gymnastics . . . boys should be hardened like iron', to prevent them from succumbing to the need to 'satisfy their senses'. Therefore, the 'fundamental educational principles of the *völkisch* state' in general, and the call for more sport in particular, were ultimately aspects of a racial-ideological vision. As Hitler wrote in *Mein Kampf*:

> If, as the first task of the State in the service and for the welfare of its nationality we recognise the preservation, care, and development of the best racial elements, it is natural that this care must not only extend to the birth of every little national and racial comrade, but that it must educate the young sapling to become a valuable link in the chain of future reproduction.[4]

The task of turning 'little national and racial comrades' into valuable members of the 'national community' principally devolved upon the Hitler Youth. Like most of the political parties of the Weimar Republic, the NSDAP disposed of a youth organisation.[5] Founded as early as 1922, as the Youth League of the NSDAP, after the 1926 Party Rally in Weimar, it was redubbed the Hitler Youth – League of Working German Youth. Males over fourteen years of age could join; at eighteen they progressed to the SA. In addition to the Hitler Youth, from 1929 there was also an NS-School League, consisting mainly of grammar school children, and from 1930 a League of German Maidens. On 30 October 1931 these organisations were subordinated to the newly appointed Youth Leader of the Reich, Baldur von Schirach, who was also leader of the NS-League of Students.[6] In March 1932, the Hitler Youth was briefly banned along with the SA. This was justified, for Hitler Youth members often took part in street battles against political opponents alongside SA men. A few of them were killed in the process, rapidly becoming honoured as martyrs of the Nazi movement. Despite, or perhaps because of this, the membership figures of the Hitler Youth continued to grow. By October 1932, 80,000 members of the Hitler Youth paraded past Hitler on the so-called 'Day of Reich Youth' at Potsdam.[7]

Following the 'seizure of power', the membership figures rose incrementally. By the end of 1933, 812,038 of the 7.5 million Germans in the fourteen to eighteen age group belonged to the Hitler Youth or the League of German Maidens.[8] By the end of 1934 the figure was 1.25 million. The reasons for this rapid growth in membership were various. Many young people joined because of their enthusiasm for Hitler, and in the hope that their free time would be purposively and rewardingly occupied in the organisation, others as a result of more or less direct pressure exerted by both the Hitler Youth and the Party upon their

7.1 Hitler photographed with a group of children.

parents, teachers, or employers, or because of anxieties about their future careers or places in higher education. Parents also argued that their own jobs would be more secure through their children's contribution within the organisation.[9] The entry into the Hitler Youth of adolescents who already belonged to other youth organisations which were either dissolved or dissolved themselves and merged with the Hitler Youth, cannot be described as entirely voluntary.

The first casualties of the rise of the Hitler Youth were the youth organisations of the other political parties. Working-class youth organisations which were suppressed included the Communist Youth Association of Germany (KJVD), the Social Democratic Socialist Working Youth (SAJ) and the German Socialist Youth Association (SAP).[10] Many of the latter took part in the defensive struggle against the Nazis – a struggle rich in victims, but ultimately futile – and then became the earliest and most active members of the Communist and Socialist resistance groups. By contrast, the youth organisations of the bourgeois parties more or less voluntarily dissolved themselves and merged with the Hitler Youth.

This left the independent, *bündisch* youth groups, as well as confessional, professional, and sporting organisations.[11] The Hitler Youth soon endeavoured to 'co-ordinate' them too. They approached the problem from 'above' and from 'below'. For example, on 5 April 1933 members of the Hitler Youth simply occupied the Berlin offices of the Reich Committee of German Youth Associations, the steering group for various youth organisations with a total membership of between five and six million. In this way Schirach usurped the leadership of these organisations. Those socialist or Jewish youth organisations which still existed were excluded from affiliation to the Reich Committee by the new, Nazi, directorate. Shortly afterwards, the Hitler Youth also took over the running of the network of German Youth Hostels, enabling them to determine who could or could not spend the night in one.

These measures particularly affected the non-party-political independent youth groups, which, in the tradition of the 'Wandervogel' of the Wilhelmine era, liked to take their members on hikes, with 'guitars' and 'gear', in order to experience nature and comradeship at close quarters. Many of these groups also subscribed to a vehement nationalism and anti-Semitism, worshipped war, condemned democracy, and called for the creation of a new 'Greater German Reich' under the leadership of a commensurately powerful and authoritarian 'Führer'. Regardless of this, the Hitler Youth declared a 'ruthless war of extermination' against them too. In May 1933 a piece appeared in the broadsheet of the Hitler Youth leadership, *Young Nation*, which said:

> We proclaim a ruthless struggle against the *Bünde*, in order to be able to remain true to the historical task of the Hitler Youth, which is to be regarded as the fulfilment of the revolution of national socialist transformation in accordance with the ideas of Hitler.[12]

Concretely, this portentous passage meant that the Hitler Youth wished to realise its totalitarian aspirations, even with regard to youth groups whose political temper approximated to their own, and whose members considered themselves to be National Socialists. For the Hitler Youth, this last claim was a contradiction in terms. One could only be a National Socialist, and not 'also a National Socialist'. One could be a National Socialist youth only within the Hitler Youth. Therefore the separatism of the *Bünde* had to be 'eradicated'. Nonetheless, both the 'human material of the *Bünde*' and some of their 'particularities' could be absorbed by the Hitler Youth. Many former members of the *Bünde* were allowed to practise their 'particularities' within the Hitler Youth organisation. This was especially the case with hiking expeditions and the romanticism of the campfire, which henceforth characterised life in the Hitler Youth too, and which accounted for much of the latter's initial attraction.

Those youth groups which persisted in refusing to submit to the combination of threats and blandishments emanating from the Hitler Youth were officially proscribed by Schirach. The only exceptions to the general ban on the youth organisations affiliated to the Greater German League were the extreme *völkisch* and anti-Semitic Artamanen League, whose former members included Heinrich Himmler and Rudolf Hoess, and, with regard to international opinion, the German Boy Scouts.[13] In 1934 the Artamanen voluntarily merged with the Hitler Youth, while the Boy Scouts joined the list of proscribed youth organisations.

When, late in 1933, the 800,000 members of Protestant youth organisations were incorporated into the Hitler Youth on the initiative of 'Reich Bishop' Müller, Schirach had almost achieved his goal. All that remained outside the Hitler Youth were Roman Catholic, professional, and sporting associations. Since in 1934 it was decreed that every adolescent who wanted to join a sporting association or to win sports certificates had to be a member of the Hitler Youth, young sportspersons were effectively incorporated into the Hitler Youth too. The same aim lay behind the restriction to Hitler Youth members of the right to enter the 'National Vocational Competition', which brought material advantages, and brief fame, to younger members of the workforce.

The struggle against Roman Catholic youth organisations was more protracted, because their existence had been formally guaranteed by the Concordat of 20 July 1933 with the Vatican.[14] However, regardless of the internationally binding character of the Concordat, the activities of Roman Catholic youth organisations were progressively circumscribed. A decree issued by the Gestapo in 1935 forbade them to wear uniforms or insignia, to parade, hike, or encamp in large groups, to fly 'banners, flags, and pennants', or to practise or receive instruction in sports.[15] Although both officers of the political police and members of the Hitler Youth went to great lengths to enforce this ban, several Roman Catholic youth organisations endeavoured to continue to pursue their activities. This had deleterious personal and professional consequences for the individuals involved. Active members of Roman Catholic youth organisations forfeited their membership of the German Labour Front (DAF), and therewith access to apprenticeships and employment. Following repeated bans on Roman Catholic youth newspapers like the *Young Front*,[16] and the arrest of individual functionaries, the Gestapo decided upon a major blow. In February 1936 the headquarters of the Roman Catholic youth organisations in Düsseldorf was occupied and closed, and fifty-seven leaders and priests, including the Generalpräses Ludwig Wolker, were arrested. The Roman Catholic episcopate decided to throw in the towel. Although at Easter 1934 the Pope had extravagantly praised the 'courageous faith' of the German Roman Catholic youth organisations, because of the way they 'had stayed true to their oaths of love and loyalty to Christ and his Church', in April 1936 the German Roman Catholic episcopate effectively ordered the dissolution of Roman Catholic youth organisations.[17] Thenceforth, Roman Catholic youth work was to be pursued within the context of the Church, and on a parochial level, rather than through the hitherto existing leagues and associations. This decentralised organisational structure, which ironically was harder for the state to monitor, but easier for the Roman Catholic hierarchy to control, has continued since 1945. Representatives of the Roman Catholic Church and historians sympathetic to it continue to celebrate the resistance activities of individuals and groups who refused to conform with the dictates of both the National Socialist State and their own hierarchy, as an important aspect of the (alleged) resistance of the Roman Catholic Church to the Nazi regime.

By the end of 1936, Schirach had reached his goal. In accordance with the Law on the Hitler Youth of 1 December 1936, the Youth Leader of the German Reich was directly subordinated to Hitler and made responsible for 'the education of the whole of German youth in the spirit of National Socialism, and in the service of the people and the national community'.[18] The wider totalitarian aspirations of the regime were stated with chilling clarity by Hitler two years later:

> These young people learn nothing else but to think as Germans and to act as Germans; these boys join our organisation at the age of ten and get a breath of fresh air for the first time, then, four years later,

7.2 A collection of Nazi toys and children's books.

they move from the Jungvolk to the Hitler Youth and here we keep them for another four years. And then we are even less prepared to give them back into the hands of those who create our class and status barriers; rather we take them immediately into the Party, into the Labour Front, into the SA or into the SS, into the NSKK and so on. And if they are there for eighteen months or two years and have still not become real National Socialists, then they go into the Labour Service and are polished there for six or seven months, and all of this under a single symbol, the German spade. And if, after six or seven months, there are still remnants of class consciousness or pride in status, then the Wehrmacht will take over the further treatment for two years and when they return after two or four years then, to prevent them from slipping back into the old habits once again we take them immediately into the SA, SS etc., and they will not be free again for the rest of their lives.[19]

The claim to the total control, education, and indoctrination of German youth could not be more starkly expressed than in the words 'and they will not be free again for the rest of their lives'. These were not empty phrases. In reality, an entire generation of Germans was forced to follow the route mapped out here by Hitler.[20] Entry into the Jungvolk or Jungmädel for ten-year-olds; progression to the Hitler Youth or League of German Maidens at fourteen. Labour service, for both sexes, from eighteen; then entry into the armed forces, and more or less voluntary membership of one of the formations of the Party, like the SA, SS, or NSKK for men, or the NS-Womanhood for women. The generation which progressed through one or more of these stages is without doubt the one which was most intensively subjected to, and formed by, Nazi indoctrination. This makes it all the more remarkable when members of the 'Hitler Youth generation' like Chancellor Helmut Kohl (born in 1930) make reference to the 'blessing of being born late'.

It would be incorrect, however, to take the regime's self-estimation at its face value. The 1936 Law on the Hitler Youth, which staked out its totalitarian aspirations, contained the important proviso 'without prejudice to the parental home and the schools'.

Schools came under the aegis of the Reich Minister for Education and Science, a post occupied by the former grammar school teacher Bernhard Rust.[21] In one of the (many) struggles over areas of competence which characterised the regime, Rust succeeded in curtailing the influence of the Hitler Youth within schools. The latter threatened to undermine not only the authority of teachers – a trend incidentally encouraged by the pseudo-Nietzschean anti-intellectualism propagated by the regime itself – but also the requirements of employers for a reasonably well-educated workforce.

This does not mean that the school system was spared attempts to 'co-ordinate' it in a National Socialist direction. Both before (!) and after the promulgation of the Law for the Restoration of the Professional Civil Service of 7 April 1933, thousands of teachers and educational administrators were dismissed, because of either their Jewish ancestry or their political unreliability. In Berlin alone, during the first months of the Third Reich, 19 of the 34 municipal educational counsellors, 83 of the 622 head teachers, 130 of the 3,200 secondary school teachers, 230 of the 8,500 primary and middle school teachers, and 190 of the 1,300 persons teaching in technical schools were hounded from their posts.[22] Further waves of dismissals ensued. Certain schools which tried to practise democratic and progressive forms of education, notably the Karl-Marx-Schule in Berlin Neukölln, were subject to 'reorganisation' on the grounds that they were 'citadels of Marxist barbarism'. This meant, *inter alia*, the dismissal of 43 of the 74 teachers, the expulsion of several pupils, and the introduction of the compulsory singing of the 'Horst-Wessel Song'. The school was renamed the Kaiser-Friedrich-Realgymnasium.[23]

During 1933 the teachers' associations were 'co-ordinated'. They were either dissolved or more or less voluntarily merged into the NS-League of Teachers, which by 1935 included 25 per cent of all the teachers in Germany. A teacher in Berlin commented on this 'co-ordination' of the

7.3 A family Christmas tree with lighted swastikas.

teaching profession in the newspaper of the NS-League of Teachers on 27 April 1933:

> We know of co-ordination from electrical engineering, and we know that through it, for example, a number of bulbs can be attached directly to a cable, and that all will light up with the same intensity, regardless of how far apart they are from one another, because the same current flows through them all. Our Reich Chancellor Adolf Hitler may well have had this image in mind when he gave the name 'co-ordination' to his incomparable endeavours.[24]

It is doubtful whether Hitler's knowledge of electrical engineering was so extensive, or whether all teachers were like electric light bulbs, burning 'with the same intensity' in their zeal to transform their schools in line with Nazi educational imperatives. Notwithstanding the notoriously high incidence of teachers within the NSDAP, a fact connected with loss of status during the Depression and general public vilification of the profession, reports concerning everyday life in schools provide a mixed picture. Externally, schools built during the period, like the Dreilindenschule in Berlin's Nikolassee (1937–), bore the hallmarks of the regime's ideological fixations:[25] a combination of neo-classical and *Heimatschutz* architectural styles, the *Reichsadler* perched upon a swastika over the entrance, and reliefs depicting boxing, javelin throwing, and running. Internally, school life was subject to some transformations. Corporal punishment was reintroduced; parent and pupil participation was abolished; the introduction of the 'Führer' principle bolstered the power of head teachers at the expense of the rest; and much time was wasted with a politicised morning assembly and in observing the regime's self-celebratory calendar. Inevitably, some teachers patrolled the school corridors in Party uniform, harassing anyone who was not quick enough with their 'Heil Hitler', and generally taking it upon themselves to disseminate the 'spirit of National Socialism' in the school concerned.[26]

The question of what was taught defies easy generalisation, because both instructions from above and new curricula came relatively late and were often so self-contradictory that they had to be withdrawn. This applied above all to religious education. At first this was reintroduced in all schools. In 1933 the small number of secular elementary schools were either abolished or turned into confessional schools. One year later, the National Socialists themselves launched a campaign against confessional schools, and, in the face of bitter opposition from the Roman Catholic Church, endeavoured to transform them into 'Community Schools'. In the process, religious instruction was either abolished outright or curtailed,

Bundestracht des BDM.

Untergauführerin	Jungmädel	Untergauführerin
des BDM.	in der allgemeinen	des BDM.
in der allgemeinen	Sommertracht	in der allgemeinen
Wintertracht		Sommertracht

7.4 League of German Maidens uniforms. Left, winter kit of a BDM sub-regional leader; middle, young maiden's summer outfit; right, sub-regional leader's summer kit.

and Christian symbols and images were banned from the classroom, provoking outrage among pupils, parents, and priests in the Roman Catholic areas of Germany.[27]

Likewise, in 1933 the regime first reintroduced and then abolished the gender-specific *numerus clausus*, whereby women could comprise only

7.5 Roundel on the wall of the Dreilindenschule, Berlin showing a young drummer boy. This present-day Gymnasium is one of the few schools constructed during the Nazi period.

10 per cent of those in higher education.[28] However the regime continued to pursue educational policies which discriminated against women. The 1933 ban on co-education, which existed in a minority of schools, was maintained. Moreover female secondary school pupils had to choose between two alternative subjects on offer to them: domestic science and modern languages. The successful completion of a course in domestic science – popularly known as the 'pudding matric' – did not count towards a place at university. School graduates with qualifications in modern languages also found it difficult to gain admission, because they lacked an education in Latin, which was a language requirement for many subjects at university.

Most of the new curricula arrived rather late, and it took time to write new textbooks and teaching aids to replace those which had been withdrawn and destroyed in 1933.[29] In the case of the so-called 'liberal arts',

7.6 Ordensburg Vogelsang, one of the training centres for future Nazi cadres.

like German or history, the problem was not so acute, since these subjects were already so infused with an extreme nationalist–ethnocentric and anti-democratic spirit that they required slight alteration. However, the increased number of hours (up to five hours a week) devoted to sport, and the importance attached to this subject and its teachers, were both new. A mark of '5' (on a German scale of 1 to 5) in sport meant not being allowed to take the exams leading to university admission. The introduction of compulsory studies in 'racial science', from 13 September 1933, was complicated by both the virtual absence of appropriate textbooks on the subject and the obvious illogicality of what was to be taught. Teachers took it upon themselves to make extracts from the works of Hans F. K. 'Rassen' Günther, and to introduce cranial measuring into the classroom. Since the most prominent 'racial scientists' often contradicted each other, mistakes in this field were unavoidable. A grammar school in Zehlendorf in Berlin which reported proudly that in 'racial studies' it taught 'The concept of race, the origins of races, the European races, the physical characteristics and origins of the different races in the German racial mixture' was courting racial-ideological disaster.[30] The problems set in subjects like mathematics could also be used to subliminally implant the racial–social goals of the regime in the minds of the young.

It would be a grave mistake, however, to attempt to relativise the significance and realities of racism in the field of education and schooling. Racial ideology was taught in the schools, and racial policy was practised in them. This principally affected Jews. Virtually all Jewish teachers were dismissed in 1933, following the Law for the Restoration of the Professional Civil Service.[31] Those who came under the so-called 'front-line veteran clause' were subject to harassment, until in 1935 they were also driven from their posts. The situation of Jewish schoolchildren, who according to the law 'against the overcrowding of German schools and universities' of 25 April 1933[32] had the 'privilege' of attending 'German' schools, was bleak. The number of schoolchildren 'of non-Aryan origin' was not to exceed the percentual 'proportion of non-Aryans in the Reich German population', or no more than 1.5 per cent. On 15 November 1938 they were temporarily, and then on 20 June 1942 finally, forbidden to attend either Jewish or non-Jewish schools.[33] However, for many of them, attendance at 'German' schools had long since become a living nightmare. They were often insulted by teachers and pupils, and subjected to malevolent injustices. They had to sit at separate desks, and were often forbidden to play with 'Aryan' children during breaks. A report in August 1933 noted:

> Jewish children come home from school depressed and deeply hurt. Here is an example of the way in which the sensitive soul of a child reacts to the atmosphere of hatred in the classroom. A seven-year-old lad began at a school in Berlin last Easter. Here he received his first impression of the boycott of Jewish children. His face streaming with tears, he came home and cried: 'Mother, I don't want to be a Jew.'[34]

Jewish children could only escape harassment if they had the chance to attend a Jewish school. Jewish communities, and the Reich Representation of German Jews, did everything possible to expand the existing Jewish schools or to create new ones.[35] In 1942, these were forbidden too.

These alternative possibilities were not open to the children of Sinti and Roma, who were hence defenceless against insults and abuse. Following the decision of various communal and regional authorities (like the Burgenland in Austria) to curtail or prohibit their attendance at school, a decree of the Reich Minister of Education on 22 March 1941 finally banned them from attendance at all state schools, on the grounds that they represented a threat to the morals of their contemporaries of 'German blood'.[36] They had to grow up as illiterates.

Schools for backward and handicapped children were subject to particularly disgraceful treatment in the context of Nazi racial policy.[37] They were subject to economy cuts on the grounds that 'false notions of humanity' resulted in costs per child being twice the sums expended on other pupils. To an extent, special schools became institutions involved in 'racial selection', because it lay within their competence to decide whether, for example, backward pupils should be compulsorily sterilised. How frequently this occurred can be inferred from a denial published on 9 April 1936 by the Municipal Health Office in Frankfurt am Main in the *Municipal Advertiser*:

> The Municipal Health Department declares that rumours to the effect that all backward pupils are to be sterilised are false. Examinations carried out to date in Germany have shown that almost half of backward schoolchildren are not hereditarily ill, and therefore do not come into consideration for compulsory sterilisation . . . There is therefore no reason for conscientious parents to keep children with learning difficulties from special schools.[38]

In general, it can be said that changes in the school system were uneven. One of the principal reasons for this was the conflict between Rust and Schirach over spheres of competence.[39] In 1936, Rust even succeeded in abolishing the 'Day of State Youth', introduced in 1933, which granted all members of the Hitler Youth a day off in the week to enable them to fulfil their duties within the organisation. Rust argued that the schools would be unable to perform their statutory duty to educate pupils, if one whole day in the week was not available for lessons. The armed forces, industry, and government agencies set some store upon having a well-educated workforce. In this fashion, Schirach and the Hitler Youth lost the influence they had aspired to within school affairs, even if the presence of uniformed members of the Hitler Youth in the classroom continued to compromise the authority of teachers. Rust and Schirach also found themselves on opposing sides in the struggle to monopolise 'elite' education. From 20 April 1933, Rust endeavoured to establish National Political Educational Institutions (Napolas).[40] These were boarding schools, on the sites of former Prussian military cadet schools, intended to train the functionaries of the Third Reich. However, by 1938 there were still only fifteen of these institutions in the whole of Germany. A year before, they had acquired an (unwanted) competitor in the shape of the Adolf Hitler Schools (AHS), established on the initiative of Schirach and Robert Ley,

7.7 'Students' of one of the Ordensburgen on a march.

7.8 In sequence: a Nazi childhood; Walter (1926–45) with his family on holiday near Fechenheim in 1931; Walter saluting the camera for his proud father.

the leader of the German Labour Front (DAF).[41] These were also designed to train the Führers of the future, and were Schirach's instrument for an 'inner transformation of the schools'. However, he was unable to establish even one AHS in each *Gau*, for in the meantime Hitler had decided upon the accelerated development of the Napolas. However, because of wartime economies, these plans were only partially realised. Ley himself was also responsible for a Nazi innovation in the tertiary sector, in the form of the Ordensburgen, established from the mid-1930s under the auspices of his DAF.[42] Based loosely upon the castles of the Teutonic knights, these were intended for young NSDAP members with seven years' post-school experience, who had demonstrated during this time 'an unwavering sense of community'. The trainees were to circulate between the romantically situated fortresses of Crossinsee (Pomerania), Vogelsang (Eifel), and Sonthofen (Allgäu) over a five-year period, culminating with six months at the 'Reichsordensburg' of Marienburg in West Prussia. They spent their time acquiring military and sporting skills while pursuing a pseudo-

academic curriculum that included racial studies and both pre- and contemporary history. The aim was to mass-produce future leaders to replace
the generation that had had the benefit of rude experience. They were also
a criticism of the traditional forms of higher education, which were perceived as being class-bound and excessively specialised, notwithstanding
the enthusiastic conformism of many university professors. Reality did not
accord with this meritocratic high-mindedness. The Ordensburgen were
stony embodiments of National Socialist narcissism. The colossal architec-
ture and rules on alcohol consumption contradicted attempts to recreate
the beery camaraderie of the *Sturm* locale, and the asceticism of the
barracks was principally designed for the edification of the curious staying
at the neighbouring 'Strength through Joy' hotels. They also failed to
achieve their aims. A report entitled 'Führers of the Future', filed by a
Manchester Guardian correspondent in November 1937, does not suggest
that the trainees were being put in the way of learning political dexterity.
'Heavens', the correspondent exclaimed, 'what an education! . . . You are
only forming brawn here, not brains!' 'We distrust words and phrases: we
prefer action', was his guide's stern reply.[43] Ley's aims were also frustrated
by a failure to integrate graduates into career structures, and by the reluctance of other Nazi leaders to allow educational reproduction to come
under any rival institutional aegis. The SS in particular ensured that those
marked out for high office by attendance at the SS-Junkerschule at Bad
Tölz had bloodied their hands during a practical period at Dachau. When
they took their midnight oaths to Hitler, they were part of the apparatus
of terror in ways that Ley's 'solid chaps' were not.

The new types of school created by the regime represented an addition
rather than an alternative to the traditional school system, which maintained its threefold division into primary, secondary, and tertiary
institutions. Really decisive changes only took place during the war, when
children from bombed-out cities and regions were evacuated to camps run
by the Hitler Youth.[44] Removed from the influence of both school and the
parental home, it was easier to carry out political indoctrination and to prepare the young for military service. Crass *obiter dicta* like 'Death is only a
departure for the sake of a higher life' ill prepared teenage boys for their
encounters with adult Allied soldiers in the rubble and ruins of Germany's
cities.

The growing political and ideological influence of the Hitler Youth was
accompanied by a clear diminution of its attraction to many young people.
It had become identified with ideological indoctrination, paramilitary
training, and the exploitation of the labour potential of young people in

7.9 Walter as a young member of the Hitler Youth ('Pimpf') in the autumn of 1933.

the service of war. The involvement of its members with harvesting, collecting old clothing, civil defence, and finally as airforce or naval auxiliaries in military action, had long ceased to be on a voluntary basis, but was rather the consequence of a stream of ordinances which were enforced by both the Gestapo and the ubiquitous Hitler Youth patrols especially formed for this purpose. Young people reacted to the onset of compulsion in various ways. While many were enthusiastic up to the end, joining special military units consisting of fourteen- to eighteen-year-olds and throwing away their lives in expectation of 'final victory', others became progressively disillusioned, recalcitrant, and rebellious. Rebelliousness was regarded as resistance, and hence a crime, by the terroristic institutions of

7.10 Walter in Hitler Youth group, photographed by his father in the summer of 1939.

the Third Reich, and was dealt with accordingly. Measures taken by the State provoked further protest and resistance, which began to assume organised forms. National Socialist youth policy therefore resulted in a specifically anti-National Socialist youth resistance movement, which was taken seriously by the leadership of police and state, who combated it with exemplary savagery and harshness.[45]

This can be illustrated by the examples of the so-called 'Swing Youth', the 'Edelweiss Pirates' and other 'wild cliques', who, severally, were regarded as a threat by the Nazi leadership, and were persecuted accordingly.[46] 'Swing Youth' were young people of mainly bourgeois origin, who, beginning in Hamburg, then in other towns, gathered together in pubs, bars, and private homes, in order – as the official argot had it – to dance to the 'decadent Jewish' and 'degenerate' prohibited music of Benny Goodman, Tommy Dorsey, Duke Ellington, Louis Armstrong, and other giants of the age of jazz. Their style of dancing and their preference for Anglo-American modes of dress, hairstyles, and idioms, offended the 'cultural sentinels' of the Nazi regime.

These were described at length in a report written by the Reich leadership of the Hitler Youth in September 1942:

7.11 Memorabilia. At Christmas 1944 Walter sent his mother sixteen views of the Masurian Lakes in East Prussia and photos taken in occupied Holland while on leave. His father received Walter's Iron Cross (Second Class) shortly after his son's death on the Eastern Front on 16 January 1945

The dancers were an appalling sight. None of the couples danced normally; there was only swing of the worst sort. Sometimes two boys danced with one girl; sometimes several couples formed a circle, linking arms and jumping, slapping hands, even rubbing the backs of their heads together; and then, bent double, with the top half of the body hanging loosely down, long hair flopping into the face, they dragged themselves round practically on their knees. When the band played a rumba, the dancers went into wild ecstasy . . . Male members gained credibility from long hair, often reaching down to the jacket collar (length of hair up to 27cm). Mostly they wore long, often checked English sports jackets, shoes, with thick light crepe soles, showy scarves, homburg hats, an umbrella over the arm whatever the weather, and as insignia, a dress-shirt button worn in the buttonhole, with a jewelled stone. Girls too favoured a long, overflowing hairstyle. Their eyebrows were pencilled, they wore lipstick and their nails were lacquered.[47]

In itself, all of this was utterly innocuous. A few members of the 'Swing Youth' listened to foreign radio stations, which was forbidden from the outbreak of war, but only a handful were interested in politics, or had contacts with opposition circles. What they wanted was simply to be left in peace, particularly by the Hitler Youth with its boring organised events. The Hitler Youth regarded this as a challenge to its authority. In Himmler and the Gestapo, who wished to prevent the development of a new youth culture outside the official channel of the Hitler Youth, they found a sympathetic audience. The Gestapo had been on the track of illegal *bündisch* youth groups who had contacts with political resistance groups both at home and abroad. But from the outbreak of war, when membership of the Hitler Youth became obligatory, they discovered to their horror that in various towns autonomous youth groups had sprung up, with only a tenuous connection with the earlier independent youth groups.

In Leipzig, for example, these consisted of young people of both sexes, calling themselves 'gangs' or literally, 'packs' (*Meuten*), who wore particular types of clothing (brightly checked ski-shirts, blue ski-trousers, or blue ski-shirts and white knee-stockings), and who greeted each other with 'Servus' or 'bye bye' instead of 'Heil Hitler'.[48] With up to 1,500 people involved, according to Gestapo reports, they met in cinemas, parks, and bars, managing to offend the National Socialist guardians of the nation's morals by engaging in what the latter described as uninhibited sexual activity. There were similar subcultural 'cliques' in Munich, called 'crews' or 'crowds', and above all in the Rhineland: the 'Kittelbach Pirates' from Düsseldorf, the 'Navajos' from Cologne, and the 'Edelweiss Pirates' based in several of the region's cities, the group which particularly attracted the animosity of the Hitler Youth and the authorities. Unlike the devotees of 'swing', these groups consisted of young people from the working class. They had left school at fourteen, were too young for the armed forces, but too mature for the Hitler Youth. They also wanted to spend the wages they earned on the objects of their choice, and not to participate in the sham collectivism of the Hitler Youth whose leadership often came from social classes above them. But like the 'Swing Youth', these groups were also hostile to service in the Hitler Youth, attacking the latter's patrols if they encountered them. A report from the Hitler

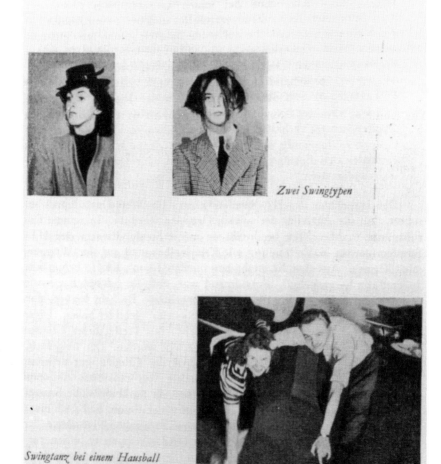

Hamburger Swingjugend 1940

Zwei Swingtypen

Swingtanz bei einem Hausball

7.12 Bourgeois 'Swing Youth' in Hamburg in 1940. These non-conformist youths were persecuted for their style of dress and penchant for American jazz.

Youth in September 1942 described these groups in the following terms:

> Since the spring of 1942 it has been established that in all areas of the Hitler Youth province of Düsseldorf, young persons of both sexes have once again formed gangs consisting of significant numbers,

which organise outings, publicly provoke the Hitler Youth, and undermine the work of its unit leaders. Sometimes groups of up to 30 persons go about the towns singing and playing guitars. Leaders of the Hitler Youth have been ambushed, pestered, and even shot at. The dress of these cliques is similar to that of the former independent youth groups. Their favourite emblem is an Edelweiss . . . This development has grown considerably in recent months. They particularly like camping trips in which boys and girls go together. Criminal convictions concerning activities in prohibited independent youth groups have become more frequent in recent times.[49]

The criminal convictions mentioned in this report were not on account of 'activities in prohibited independent youth groups', but a result of a range of new decrees designed to smash autonomous youth groups and to discipline German youth in general. This was the main object of a Police Ordinance for the Protection of Youth issued by Himmler on 9 March 1940.[50] This forbade young people to visit bars or cinemas after 9 p.m., or to 'loiter . . . on streets or public houses' after dark, or to smoke in public. A new instrument of repression called 'youth custody' was introduced to enforce this ordinance. On the basis of a decree issued by the Reich Ministry of Defence in the autumn of 1940, judges in juvenile courts, but also the police, could sentence young offenders to a maximum of four weeks' youth custody, where they would carry out forced labour. The 'shock' was made 'longer' and 'sharper'. Despite this, or perhaps because of it, the juvenile crime statistics increased, although it was the Nazis, of course, who decided what was 'criminal' in the first place.

Himmler's reaction to this development reflected the way in which the mores of the juvenile subculture challenged every fibre of his being. Casualness, disorder, self-indulgence, and physicality were a threat to his obsessions with discipline, order, and self-denial. He created a new form of camp for juveniles within the National Socialist system of forced labour camps. Here the inmates were subject to 'criminal-biological' selection, carried out by the regime's academic scientific accomplices. In two circulars issued on 21 December 1943 and 25 April 1944, Himmler ordered the creation of 'youth custody camps'.[51] One was established for male juveniles at the former provincial workhouse in Moringen (near Göttingen), which had been used as a concentration camp since 1933. The 'youth custody camp' for females was established in the immediate vicinity of the women's concentration camp at Ravensbrück. In order to prevent German 'criminals' from mixing with Polish 'criminals', a further camp exclusively for Poles was established at Łódź. The inmates of Moringen were subjected to the attentions of Dr Robert Ritter, who had

Cliquen
Bilder von der Osteraktion 1940

Wilde Clique aus Köln (Ostern 1940)

Wilde Clique (Navajos) aus Köln, festgenommen Ostern 1940

7.13 'Wild cliques' in Cologne before and after their arrest at Easter 1940.

already made a reputation for himself in the service of the regime's extermination of Sinti and Roma.[52] Juveniles in Moringen were allotted to a carefully planned series of huts according to their position in the 'criminal-biological' scheme of things. This afforded them the chance of 'finally proving themselves' through service at the front when their sentence had finished. Those about whose capacity to be educated reservations existed were housed in Block F, while 'nuisances' and the 'incapable' went to Blocks S and U. The latter were mostly compulsorily sterilised and sent to 'proper' concentration camps on their eighteenth birthday.[53]

However, even the establishment of these juvenile concentration camps failed to have the desired deterrent effect. Himmler had to concede this in a circular he issued on 25 October 1944:

> In the last few years, and recently in increased numbers, gatherings of youths (cliques) have formed in all parts of the Reich. These reveal asocial–criminal rather than political-oppositional tendencies and therefore require, particularly with regard to the absence of many fathers on account of the war, the most stringent control by Hitler Youth leaders and teachers. Cliques are groupings of juveniles outside the Hitler Youth, who lead a separate way of life whose principles are irreconcilable with the National Socialist world view. Collectively, they reject or are indifferent to their duties towards the national community, or towards the Hitler Youth, and in particular evince a lack of will to conform with the dictates of wartime.[54]

Himmler's characterisation of the cliques was not entirely correct. Among them there were groups and individuals who had contacts with political resistance groups, and who therefore pursued 'oppositional-political' goals. This was particularly the case with individual 'Edelweiss Pirates', who in Cologne made partisan-style attacks, one of which claimed the life of the Cologne chief of the Gestapo. Others, in so far as they stole to provide themselves, foreign workers, and deserters with money or food, were 'asocial-criminals' in the eyes of the Nazi regime.[55] Collectively, these 'cliques', which existed in 'all parts of the Reich' by the end of the war, represented a threat to the regime because of their unwillingness to 'conform with the dictates of wartime'; their refusal to carry out their 'duty' to the Hitler Youth and the 'national community'; the irreconcilability of their lifestyle with that propagated by the regime; and finally, their connections with underground groups in the last stages of the war. This means that the Nazis failed to realise their ultimate goal of encompassing and indoctrinating young people. They failed because of the determination of these 'cliques' to pursue an independent way of life outside the Hitler Youth and the 'national community', which clearly had nothing to offer them. If one considers the degree of ruthlessness and harshness with which the National Socialist regime endeavoured to suppress 'oppositional-political' and 'asocial-criminal' activities, culminating in the public hanging in Cologne in November 1944 of the leaders of the 'Edelweiss Pirates', then these young people should be recognised at least as victims, if not as resistance fighters.

The following are some relevant documents:

1. From a decree issued by Baldur von Schirach on 22 June 1933 concerning the dissolution of the Greater German League and the Reich Committee of German Youth Associations:[56]

(1) The Great German League and its subordinate and affiliated organisations are dissolved with effect from 17 June 1933. The following are also dissolved together with the Great German League: the Volunteers of the Young Nation; the German Volunteers; the League of German Scouts; the Circle Association of German Scouts; the Circle of German Scout areas; the German Scout Corps; the Protestant Scout Volunteers.

(2) The Reich Committee of German Youth Associations is dissolved with immediate effect. The tasks carried out hitherto by the Reich Committee will be taken over under the extended competences of the Youth Leadership of the German Reich.

2. From a 'special order' issued by the Berlin area Hitler Youth leader, Artur Axmann, concerning the clothing and equipment of the Hitler Youth (1935):[57]

The following are forbidden:

(I) All use of tents and tepees, in so far as they belong to particular youth formations. These are to be surrendered to the local leadership of the Hitler Youth and sent to Area 3.

(II) In so far as these are the personal property of individual boys, their existence is to be reported to the area command before 15 November 1935.

(III) All German Young People (DJ) boys' jackets must only be worn with shiny buttons. Off duty, they should only be worn without armbands and insignia.

Black buttons are prohibited.

The wearing of parts of the uniforms of former independent youth groups, like the Werewolves, the Young Stahlhelm, the Bismarck Youth, and Marxist associations is forbidden.

Lily buttons are to be removed. The wearing of tartan shirts, with large checks, along with short trousers is forbidden.

The obtaining of military equipment from the armoury of St George is forbidden. It is forbidden to obtain printed matter, song books etc. from the Günther Wolff publishing house.

(IV) Whoever, after 15 November 1935, is found in possession of the prohibited items of uniform or the printed matter mentioned above will be handed over to the Gestapo.

Spot checks will be carried out on the former leaders of independent youth camps.

The items listed under Point I are to be handed over to the police.

3. From the decree of the Reichsführer-SS and Inspector of the Prussian Secret State Police of 1935 concerning limitations on the activities of confessional youth associations:[58]

c.1. All confessional youth associations, including those temporarily formed for special occasions, are banned from all forms of activity not of a purely ecclesiastical-religious nature, particularly activities involving politics, sport, and drill.

c.2. The following regulations apply to confessional youth associations, and their members of both sexes, including the so-called parish youth:

The following are forbidden:

(1) The wearing of uniforms (association outfits, gear, etc.), uniform-like clothing, and items of uniforms, which indicate membership of a confessional youth association. This encompasses the wearing of uniforms or items of uniform underneath civilian clothing (e.g. coats), as well as all forms of similar clothing which could be regarded as a surrogate uniform.

(2) The wearing of badges which indicate membership of a confessional youth association.

(3) Parades in closed formation, hiking and camping in public places, as well as entertainment with their own music or brass bands.

(4) The carrying in public, or display, of banners, flags, and pennants, with

the exception of when participating in traditional processions, pilgrimages, and other ecclesiastical celebrations, as well as funerals.

(5) Instruction and practice in all forms of sport and drill.

c.3. Whoever violates this decree, or calls for or encourages its violation, will be punished with either a fine or imprisonment, in accordance with c.33, 55, 56 of the law of police administration. Prohibited items of uniform and banners, flags and pennants are to be handed in.

4. The Law on the Hitler Youth of 1 December 1936:[59]

The future of the German nation depends upon its youth, and therefore German youth must be prepared for its future duties. The Reich Government has accordingly decided on the following law which is promulgated herewith:

(1) The whole of German youth within the borders of the Reich is organised in the Hitler Youth.

(2) All German young people, apart from being educated at home and at school, will be educated in the Hitler Youth physically, intellectually, and morally in the spirit of National Socialism to serve the nation and the community.

(3) The task of educating German youth in the Hitler Youth is being entrusted to the Reich Leader of German Youth in the NSDAP. He therefore becomes the 'Youth Leader of the German Reich'. His office shall rank as a Supreme Governmental Agency with its headquarters in Berlin and he will be directly responsible to the Führer and Reich Chancellor.

5. From the first decree on the implementation of the Law on the Hitler Youth of 25 March 1939:[60]

By virtue of c.4 of the Law on the Hitler Youth of 1 December 1936 I decree that:

(1) The Youth Leader of the German Reich is exclusively responsible for all tasks concerning the physical, intellectual, and moral education of the whole of German youth in the territories of the Reich, without prejudice to the parental home and school. The responsibility of the Reich Minister of Education and Science and private and State schools remains unaffected.

(1.2) The following areas of responsibility are transferred from the Reich and Prussian Ministry of Education and Science to the responsibility of the Youth Leader of the German Reich:

All matters pertaining to youth welfare, the youth hostel system, as well as accident and insurance liability in the area of youth welfare.

The question of responsibility for the year spent on the land is reserved for separate regulation.

(1.3) The Youth Leader of the German Reich together with the Hitler Youth are financially accountable to the NSDAP.

(2.1) The regular Hitler Youth exists within the Hitler Youth.

(2.2) Whoever has belonged to the Hitler Youth since 20 April 1938 belongs to the regular Hitler Youth.

(2.3) Youths who have conducted themselves well for at least a year in the Hitler Youth, and whose ancestry fulfils the conditions for admission to the NSDAP, can be admitted to the regular Hitler Youth. The Reich Youth Leader of the NSDAP will issue more precise regulations in agreement with the Führer's Deputy.

(2.4) Admission to the regular Hitler Youth can take place immediately in the case of persons over eighteen years of age who are to be appointed to the leadership or administration of the Hitler Youth.

(2.5) Only the regular Hitler Youth is an affiliated organisation of the NSDAP.

(2.6) Membership of the regular Hitler Youth is voluntary.

(3) The Reich Minister of the Interior determines in agreement with the youth Leader of the German Reich and the Reich Minister of Finance the offices subordinate to the Youth Leader of the German Reich.

(4) Members of the Hitler Youth are entitled, and in so far as it is decreed, obliged, to wear the regulation uniform.

6. From the second decree on the implementation of the Law on the Hitler Youth of 25 March 1939:

(1) Length of service

(i) Service in the Hitler Youth is honorary service to the German people.

(ii) All young people are obliged from the age of 10 to their 19th birthday to serve in the Hitler Youth. In particular,

1. Boys aged 10 to 14 in the German Young People (DJ).
2. Boys aged 14 to 18 in the Hitler Youth (HJ).
3. Girls aged 10 to 14 in the Young Maidens' League (JM).
4. Girls aged 14 to 18 in the League of German Maidens (BDM).

(9) Registration and admission

(i) All young people must be registered for admission with the Hitler Youth Leader responsible by 15 March in the year they reach their 10th birthday . . .

(ii) The legal guardian of the young person is responsible for registration.

(iii) Admission to the Hitler Youth follows on 20 April each year.

(12) Penalties

(i) A legal guardian will be liable to a fine of up to 150RM or imprisonment, if he deliberately contravenes the stipulation of c.9 of this decree.

(ii) Anyone who maliciously prevents or attempts to prevent any young person from serving in the Hitler Youth will be punished by fine or imprisonment.

(iii) Prosecution will follow only at the request of the Youth Leader of the German Reich. The request can be withdrawn.

(iv) Young people can be required by the responsible local police authority to fulfil the duties which are imposed on them by this decree and regulations for its implementation.

7. From the law 'against the overcrowding of German schools and universities' of 25 April 1933:[61]

c.4. It is to be observed, with regard to the new intake, that the number of Reich Germans who in the meaning of the Law for the Restoration of the Professional Civil Service of 7 April 1933 are of non-Aryan ancestry should not exceed among the entirety of those attending each school, or type of faculty, the proportion of non-Aryans in the Reich German population as a whole. The proportion will be set on a unitary basis for the Reich as a whole . . . Paragraphs 1 and 2 are not applicable to Reich Germans of non-Aryan ancestry whose fathers served the German Reich at the front during the World War, or who fought for one of its allies, as well as the offspring of marriages which were contracted before the law came into effect, where one parent, or two grandparents, are of Aryan origin. They are also not to be included in the calculation of these proportions and ratios.

8. From the decree of the Reich Minister of Education and Science concerning the creation of separate Jewish schools of 10 September 1935:[62]

The racial congruence of teacher and pupil is an essential precondition for all successful pedagogical activity. Children of Jewish origin represent a major hindrance to the unity of the community of the classroom, and to the untrammelled implementation of National Socialist youth education in the State schools in general. A series of random checks carried out on my orders in various districts of Prussia have shown that a not insignificant number of Jewish schoolchildren are still attending State primary schools. This is particularly the case in larger towns; but in the countryside too, where there are areas which are more or less densely settled by Jews.

Commencing with the school year 1936, I therefore plan to carry out as complete a segregation of the races as is feasible for pupils attending all types of school.

9. From a decree of the Reich Minister of Education and Science of 14 November 1938 concerning the immediate dismissal of Jewish children from 'German' schools:[63]

Following the dastardly act of murder in Paris, no German teacher can be expected to give instruction to Jewish schoolchildren. It is also self-evidently intolerable for German schoolchildren that they should have to sit in a classroom with Jews. Certainly, in recent years, racial segregation has already been widely introduced into the school system; however a remnant of Jewish schoolchildren remains, who now are no longer allowed to attend schools along with German boys and girls.

Subject to further legal regulation, I hereby decree with immediate effect:

(1) Jews are not allowed to attend German schools. They may only attend Jewish schools. In so far as it has not occurred already, all Jews currently attending a German school are to be dismissed immediately.

10. From a speech by Reich Interior Minister Wilhelm Frick on 9 May 1935 concerning the co-ordination of the education system:[64]

Liberal notions of education have totally destroyed both the raison d'être of education and our educational institutions. In line with these notions, our schools have schooled rather than nurtured. They have failed to develop all the strengths of the pupils for the benefit of nation and state, but rather have communicated knowledge for the benefit of the individual. They have not helped to shape German people, rooted in the nation and duty bound to the State, but rather free individuals . . .

The national revolution lays down a new law for German schools and their educational duties: German schools have to form politically-conscious people, who sacrifice and serve with every thought and deed, who are rooted in their nation, and who are totally and indivisibly anchored to the history and destiny of its state.

11. From the guidelines for education and instruction in the primary schools (1939):[65]

The task of primary schools is not to communicate all sorts of knowledge for the benefit of the individual. They must develop all the strengths of the young person for the benefit and service of nation and State. Only material which promotes the attainment of this goal should have a place in instruction. They must therefore be spared material which has forced its way in through outmoded notions of education.

12. From 'regulations concerning education and instruction in middle schools' (1939):[66]

With respect to the required emphasis upon relevance, middle schools must permeate their work with economic perspectives in the National Socialist spirit. They will thereby help to form a people aware of its duty to ensure that none of the nation's resources will be squandered. Conscientiousness, thoroughness, a sense of orderliness, cleanliness, frugality, and also the established habit that even the smallest task should be carried out carefully, correctly, and properly, should become the fundamental virtues of all schoolchildren.

13. From the guidelines concerning education and instruction in the higher schools (1938):[67]

Germany is poor in territory and in natural resources; its true national riches lie in the strength, faith, and talents of its men and women. Therefore, the duty of German schools is to train people, who are able, in true devotion to nation and Führer, to lead a German life, to develop their intellectual powers, and to reach the highest performance, so that they can master the tasks which Germany has given to their station . . .

Therefore, the job of the higher schools is to select, from all sections of the population, those young Germans who are capable of, and ready for, increased responsibility, and to train them in those decision-making and productive skills which they will need later to bear the responsibility of a physician, judge, officer and a teacher etc. . . .

The new higher schools will give young persons a strict training of the intellect, and will not shy away from teaching the young spirit through compulsion, facts, rules, and numbers, in order to keep them strong and supple. But they will also always bear in mind that the aim of all instruction is not dead knowledge, but a lively understanding and skill.

14. The self-image of the Hitler Youth, from the Hitler Youth manual *Joy–Discipline–Faith* (Potsdam, 1937):[68]

A Flag Parade

The squad has arrived. The duty leader reports to the camp leader.
'Heil Hitler, camp squad!'
'Heil Hitler!'
The duty leader gives the password of the day.
'Eyes – front! Today's password is: Herbert Norkus!'
A boy speaks:
'We do not mourn at cold tombs, we march in and say: he was one who dared do what we all dare to do. His voice is silent. We march in and say: comradeship is immutable.

Many die. Many are born.
The world is great, which contains them all.
However, the word to which we swore an oath,
the word which is not lost on the dead;
that is: duty is greater than the world!
The duty to remember what was before we were born.
Because we will become, when we are interred in our graves, what
from our lives is left worth reading.
That is more powerful than iron and stone!'

The camp leader says of the fallen comrade:
'On 24 January 1931 our 15-year-old comrade Herbert Norkus was struck down by Communists in the Beusel neighbourhood of Berlin. As a member of the Hitler Youth he did no more than his duty, but even that drew down upon him the hatred of the Commune. On account of our dead comrades, we know that there will never be an understanding between Bolshevism and us!'

The duty leader:
'Stand to attention!

As we hoist the flag we will sing: "A young nation arises, ready for the Storm" – first verse.
For the hoisting of the flag – eyes – right!
Hoist the flag!'

On the command the first verse of the song specified will be sung.

The duty leader:
'Eyes – front! Move yourselves!'
The leaders of the units in camp immediately give the command to march off.

15. On the self-image of the League of German Maidens (BDM), from an essay by the BDM Reich consultant Dr Jutta Rudiger (1939):

The League of German Maidens, today the largest association of girls in the world, can only be understood in terms of National Socialism. The old youth movement, whether we are talking now of the movement for boys or girls, arose at the turn of the century from a form of rebellion; rebellion against the narrow, bourgeois, petty world, against the materialistic spirit of the times. But just as the times themselves were uncreative and without a style of their own, so the youth movement itself had no ideas of its own.

Worthwhile individuals often found themselves gathered together. They forgot, however, that opposition must never become the primary object, but that only a powerful idea can overcome the old, and create new values. Hence, they often lost themselves in romantic daydreams and discussions beside the camp fire . . .

The Hitler Youth was the first and only youth movement which recognised that the death of two million soldiers in the World War signified a responsibility: namely the idea of serving Germany through deeds.

They knew that youth does not have the right to criticise and oppose, but rather that they bear the responsibility of the future of our nation . . .

Already in the time of struggle, the differences between them and the old youth associations became apparent, as was also the case with girls. Here the idea was there, the idea of Germany, which by necessity put them under its spell . . .

The fact that the Hitler Youth is the most powerful youth organisation in the world today can only be understood if we acknowledge that Adolf Hitler is our starting point. Today, we all know that men and women, and boys and girls make up the nation, and that each has to carry out his duty to the nation according to his station. Boys will be raised as political soldiers, and girls as brave and strong women, who will be the comrades of these political soldiers – and who will go on to live in their families as women and mothers, and help shape our National Socialist world view – and to raise a new generation which is hard and proud.

Therefore, we want to shape girls who are politically conscious. That does not mean women who debate or discuss things in parliament, but girls and women, who know about the necessities of life in the German nation, and act accordingly.

16. ' "Führers" of the Future: The Chosen Few.' A correspondent of the *Manchester Guardian* visits Vogelsang on 17 November 1937:[70]

The Gauschulen are placed in picturesque spots as far as possible from the towns, and there are long walks, climbs, or marches; in the course of the marches the youths are encouraged to sing hymns to the race, the regime, and the Fatherland. At night they sleep eight in a room, in superimposed bunks. They may have time to dream of a future in authority, but, I was told, it would not occur to them to analyse the text of what they had been singing with the criticisms of the regime that might be implicit in it.

'Heavens, what an education!' I said. 'You are forming only brawn here, not brains!'

'We distrust words and phrases: we prefer action', was my guide's reply. . . . Above the dining hall for a thousand is the lecture hall, also for a thousand. At the extremity of this long room is a little platform from which the head of the school addresses the students through a loud-speaker. On the right of the platform is a curtain. The curtain can be drawn back to reveal the holy of holies. Framed by swastika flags, standing out from a background of white stone, surrounded by the chiselled names of the victims of the Munich 'Putsch', and judiciously floodlit, is a statue. It is a man eight feet high, powerful, muscular, saluting with raised right arm; his left hand is clenched against his thigh. He is the typical 'Aryan'. 'Homo Germanicus' – the new god in whose image the German admires and loves himself.

I left Vogelsang profoundly disturbed, astonished at the emptiness of the teaching given there, and full of apprehension of a future that may lie in the hands of these fanatics . . . As I got back into my car I heard the sound of tramping in rhythm with a song. Impeccably aligned, uniformly shod, their forage caps crammed on their heads, the future Führers were returning to barracks. One, two; one, two – they raised clouds of dust as they hammered powerfully on the road, marching towards us. I listened for the lively song coming from all these young throats amid this ravish-

ingly sweet and gentle mountain country. They turned aside, but before they went into the distance I caught these two lines:
'And when the hand grenade explodes,
We shake with hearty laughter.'
Their evensong.

17. Some songs of the 'Edelweiss Pirates':[71]

(a) We all sat in the tavern
With a pipe and a glass of wine,
A goodly drop of malt and hops,
And the devil calls the tune.

Hark the hearty fellows sing!
Strum that banjo, pluck that string!
And the lasses all join in.
We're going to get rid of Hitler,
And he can't do a thing.

(b) The Hamburg sirens sound,
Time for the Navajos to go.
A tavern's just the place
To kiss a girl good-bye.
Rio de Janeiro, caballero, ahoy!
An Edelweiss Pirate is faithful and true.

(c) Hitler's power may lay us low,
And keep us locked in chains,
But we will smash the chains one day,
We'll be free again.
We've got fists and we can fight,
We've got knives and we'll get them out.
We want freedom, don't we boys?
We're fighting Navajos

(d) In Cologne many have fallen,
In Cologne many were there,
And though the Edelweiss Pirates may fall,
The *bündisch* youth will be free.

18. From a circular of the Reichsführer-SS and Chief of the German Police, Heinrich Himmler, of 25 October 1944, concerning 'the fight against youth cliques':

In the last few years, and recently in increased numbers, gatherings of youths (cliques) have formed in all parts of the Reich. These reveal asocial-criminal rather than oppositional-political tendencies, and therefore require, particularly bearing in mind the absence of many fathers on account of the war, the most stringent control by Hitler Youth leaders and teachers.

In future particular attention is to be paid to all gatherings of youths, who are to be proceeded against – where possible in conjunction with the offices of the Hitler Youth, the State and Party youth welfare services, and the judiciary – in accordance with the following regulations.

Nature and appearance of the cliques

Cliques are groupings of juveniles outside the Hitler Youth, who lead a separate way of life, whose principles are irreconcilable with the National Socialist world view. Collectively, they reject or are indifferent to their duties towards the national community, or towards the Hitler Youth, and in particular evince a lack of will to conform with the dictates of wartime.

Cliques use various names (clique, mob, crowd, pack, shufflers, Edelweiss Pirates, etc.). Generally there is no fixed organisational structure; the groupings are often only loose and irregular. Sometimes they wear special forms of identification (e.g. Edelweiss badges, skull and crossbone rings, coloured pins etc.). They do not raise membership contributions, but in some cases they issue membership cards. The cliques have more or less regular meeting places and territories; they often go on outings together. Sometimes there are cross-connections between the various groups, which can be of an amicable as well as a hostile nature. The cliques mostly consist of young fellows, but also some girls too.

In general, three fundamental tendencies can be ascertained in the individual cliques, whereby it is to be noted that only a minority of the cliques reveal only one of these fundamental tendencies in a pronounced form. Rather, activity in one area mostly leads to activity in another area. One must distinguish between:

(a) Cliques of an asocial-criminal character. This reveals itself through involvement in petty and major offences (boorishness, affrays, infringement of police regulations, collective theft, offences against morality – particularly with their own sex, etc.). Among members of the cliques this leads to a more or less pervasive degeneration of character and morale.

(b) Cliques of an oppositional–political character, however usually without a firmly circumscribed opposition programme. This reveals itself in a general antipathy towards the State. Rejection of the Hitler Youth and other duties towards the community, indifference towards the course of the war, manifesting itself in disturbance of Youth service duties, attacks on members of the Hitler Youth, listening to foreign radio stations and the spreading of rumours, cultivation of prohibited *bündisch*, or other, groups, their traditions, songs etc. Frequently youths of this type seek to camouflage themselves, or to gain the chance to carry out their destructive activities, by penetrating Party organisations.

(c) Cliques with a liberal-individualistic outlook, preference for English ideals, language, behaviour, and clothing (English casual), preference for jazz and 'hot' music, swing dancing etc. Members of these cliques largely come from 'the better classes', and merely want to pursue their own pleasure and sexual or other types of excess, through which they rapidly come into sharp conflict with the National Socialist world view. They resist the demands of the Hitler Youth, labour and military service, and thereby approximate to the type of clique described in point (b).

Members of the cliques may be categorised according to their level of involvement into leaders, active participants, and hangers on.

19. From a report by a senior regional court judge in Essen to the Ministry of Justice on 31 July 1944 concerning the 'police youth custody camp' at Moringen:[72]

The object of the youth custody camp, namely 'to investigate the inmates according to criminal-biological criteria, to assist those fit for the community so that they may take their place in the national community, and to detain those who are ineducable, making use of their labour, until their final accommodation elsewhere', was in evidence in the measures and facilities which we saw during an inspection of the camp.

The camp is continually under inspection by the Criminal-Biological Institute of the Reich Security Main Office, whose Director Prof. Dr Ritter frequently visits the camp, and which has detailed a permanent representative (at present Dr Abshagen) to the camp. The camp is a quarry for the Research Institute, which examines the camp trainees according to criminal-biological criteria, and which, in accordance with the camp commandant, differentiates between them on this basis. According to the regulations, every trainee is examined before he is committed. On arrival, he is sent to the admissions block (observation block), where he is criminal-biologically examined. The examination and inspection results in his transfer to another block. Namely, the trainees are divided between a number of blocks, which are kept in isolation from one another. The incapable (the feeble-minded and mentally deficient) who are not fit for the camp go to U-Block (block for the incapable), from which they will be sent to an asylum (in so far as medical treatment is necessary) or to a closed psychiatric institution. This block contains 5–10 per cent of the camp trainees.

Trainees who are difficult, deviant in character, suffering from emotional inadequacies, hyperactive, excitable, discontented in disposition, bad-tempered, incorrigible nuisances, or determined petty criminals – who are continually at odds with the community, are clear custody cases. In line with the practice of the Criminal-Biological Institute and the camp itself, these trainees are described as 'trouble-makers' and, as soon as they are identified as such, are assigned to S-Block. Between 5 and 10 per cent of trainees are assigned to this block. As soon as they have reached the appropriate age, they are either transferred to a concentration camp or, as soon as the Community Aliens Law has been enacted, will be transferred to an appropriate institution of the Land Welfare Association.

Trainees with character deficiencies, who are unsettled and lacking in motivation, who cannot pass any of the proficiency tests and have an unfailing leaning towards aberrancy, are also without exception custody cases. They are allotted to D-Block (Persistent Failures Block), and later transferred to concentration camps or to half-open or closed institutions. D-Block accounts for between 10 and 15 per cent of trainees.

Those who are primarily unstable, irresponsible, or lacking in independence, who are severely at risk and liable to recidivism, go to G-Block (Occasional Failures Block). Ten to 15 per cent of the trainees go to this block; some of them can later be released, while others will have to be taken into custody. About 20 to 25 per cent of the trainees go to F-Block (block for those possibly capable of being educated). The principal task of the camp will be carried out in this block on the ill-bred, the seriously ill-disciplined, and perhaps late developers, who are still capable of education. In the case of those discovered to be ineducable in this block, they are to be transferred to one of the other blocks mentioned above, or sent to concentration camps upon reaching adulthood. From time to time the upper age limit may be disregarded; sometimes even as far as 25 years of age in special cases, because examinations in this block are to be far-reaching. If the trainee is regarded as educable, then he is to be allotted to E-Block. The latter consists of trainees who have been immediately transferred from B-Block or, after further examination, from F-Block. Those concerned are trainees where there is the hope of successful education, the wild, pubescent educational failures etc. According to experience to date, this block will consist of 6 to 8 per cent of trainees. Trainees from this block will continually be freed i.e., mostly for the Reich Labour Service or military service.

CHAPTER EIGHT

WOMEN IN THE THIRD REICH

Hitler declared in 1933, 'in my State the mother is the most important citizen'.[1] This sentiment was endorsed by Goebbels, who added, 'a woman's primary, rightful, and appropriate place is in the family, and the most wonderful task that she can perform is to present her country and people with children'.[2] Statements like these demonstrate that the attitudes of leading Nazis towards women were profoundly reactionary.[3] Like the Roman Catholic and conservative political parties, they were hostile to what limited progress had been made towards the emancipation of women during the Weimar Republic. This hostility encompassed women politicians, lawyers, and journalists, particularly if they were also Jewish or socialist. It also extended to young single women who had taken advantage of changes in the patterns of employment, in order to eke out a falsely glamorised independent existence as clerks, typists, actresses, waitresses, or dancers in the bigger cities, without attaching much immediate priority to marriage or childbirth. However the Nazis attached no absolute value to fecundity in itself. They were also hostile to women who burdened the welfare services and the 'racial community' with an excess of biologically 'undesirable' progeny. Beyond these negative types of women, exemplified by the Polish Jewish Socialist Rosa Luxemburg and the prolific 'slut', the Nazis operated on the basis of an assumed 'natural' distinction between the sexes. Men were productive and creative actors in the big world of politics and war, women reproductive, imitative and essentially passive in the little world of the family household. This meant that women should confine themselves to their 'natural' occupations, i.e., as wives and mothers, or if they had to work, to occupations which reflected their 'natural' talents, such as nursing or social work, which would not endanger their biological capacity to reproduce. Broadly speaking, therefore, Nazi policies towards women were both illiberal and paternalistic. In the case of women who failed to correspond to the Nazis' normative assumptions concerning who was racially and socially 'valuable', policy became illiberal and actively harmful.[4]

Despite the overt anti-feminism of many of the regime's leaders, Nazi propagandists continually employed films and photographs of women frenetically acclaiming 'their' Führer. Leaving aside the implication that women are more prone to mass 'hysteria' than males, these films suggested, and in so far as excerpts are used uncritically today, still suggest, that German women not only 'worshipped' Hitler, but that in some unexplained way were responsible for putting him in power.[5] This last point is clearly false. Our knowledge of the electoral behaviour of women in the Weimar Republic is based on very fragmentary data.[6] There were no public opinion polls, and reliable data are only available from a few towns where the ballot papers of men and women were counted separately. On the basis of this information it can be said that at first, far more men than women voted for the NSDAP. However, the proportions gradually approximated to one another, so that by the Reichstag election of 5 March 1932 the same number of women as men voted for Hitler and the NSDAP. Several factors should be borne in mind when interpreting this development. Firstly, although the Weimar Republic may have given the vote to women, it certainly did not remove many forms of legalised discrimination against women, either within marriage or in the wider social and economic spheres. Moreover, all political parties in the Weimar Republic were more or less exclusively represented by men – with a higher proportion of women representatives in the parties of the left – and hence issues specifically concerning women played a subordinate role in election contests.[7] This is another way of saying that the extreme anti-feminist NSDAP should not be falsely juxtaposed against allegedly pro-feminist democratic parties. The Catholic Centre Party, for example – a party which enjoyed particularly strong support from women – pursued policies towards women and the family which at first glance were little different from those of the Nazis. During the Depression, in May 1932, the Centre Party sponsored a bill permitting the dismissal of 'double earners', i.e. married women, from the civil service in order to create jobs for unemployed men. This meant that the Constitution, in so far as it concerned equal rights for women in the civil service, was a dead letter before the Nazis came to power. It also meant that if women voted in terms of how parties treated women's issues, then the democratic parties could be

*8.1 The physicist Lise Meitner (1878–1968), Professor at Berlin
University until her emigration to the Netherlands in 1935.*

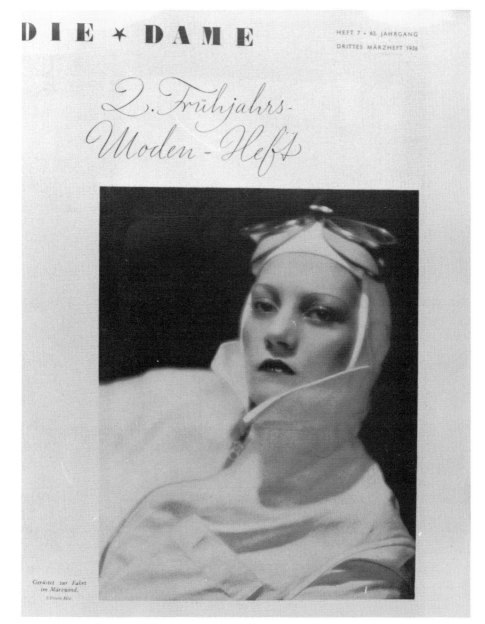

8.2 Modelling motorwear from Die Dame *(1936).*

8.3 Plaster figures displayed during the 1936 Berlin Olympics.

8.4 Woman in the shadow of a man. Modelling fur coats beneath a
statue of a man, from Elegante Welt (1940).

described as being merely the lesser of two evils. However issues specifically pertaining to women, as distinct from general political, social, or
economic questions, do not seem to have been crucial in determining how
women voted. Many women also seem to have been influenced by their
husbands, fathers, brothers, or priests as to how they should cast their vote.
The high incidence of female support for the Catholic Centre Party may
also reflect how women living and working in 'traditional' environments
reacted negatively towards pockets of accelerated female emancipation in
the big cities. The fact that the Nazis did not dispose of a comprehensive
political programme concerning women does not seem to have deterred
some women from joining or voting for the NSDAP, or as the Presidential
elections in March 1932 revealed, from a marked general preference for
the forces of 'order'. Existing studies of women in this period shed little
light on why this was so.[8]

The anti-Nazi propaganda of the KPD and SPD frequently alighted
upon the anti-feminist statements of prominent Nazis, of which Gottfried
Feder's assertion that woman should be the 'maid and servant of man' was
among the most notorious.[9] This hostile propaganda in turn prompted the
Nazis to concern themselves more with women's issues, primarily in order
to attract the female vote. A crucial step in this direction was taken in 1931,
when several pre-existing local Nazi women's groups and *völkisch* women's
organisations, of which Elsbeth Zander's Deutscher Frauenorden was
among the largest, were subsumed – with much personal acrimony – into
the 'NS-Womanhood' (NSF).[10] This umbrella organisation was intended
to co-ordinate a heterogeneous array of women's groups which had
proliferated during the *Kampfzeit*, either as auxiliaries providing first aid,
meals, uniform sewing, or prison visiting services to male Nazis, or in
reaction to the dual evils of 'Bolshevism' and moral 'permissiveness'.
Through its subsidiary umbrella organisation the 'German Women's
Enterprise' (DFW), created in 1933, the NSF set out to 'co-ordinate' all
those women's groups which remained after feminist, pacifist, and socialist groups had been dissolved, as well as the majority of German women
beyond the purview of any existing organisation or party. In order to
achieve this objective, the NSF programme made a number of concessions
towards the twentieth century. While it stated that marriage, the family,
and motherhood were women's 'most obvious service to the whole
nation', it also stressed the need to further 'the education and integration
of all female forces for the good of the nation'. This signified that female
Nazi functionaries, most of whom were younger than their analogues in
other political parties, had no intention of reversing the limited achieve-

ments of women's emancipation.[11] On the contrary, individual Nazi activists like Lydia Gottschewski, who at twenty-six became Reich Leader of the League of German Maidens (BDM) and then briefly head of the NSF, hoped to see women's political role extended under National Socialism. However, young feminist militants like Gottschewski exerted little more than a temporary appeal for male Nazi leaders, who used her ambitions to resolve a conflict of competence between the NSF and BDM. Young militants like Gottschewski also had no appeal whatsoever for older women. In Gertrud Scholtz-Klink, who became leader of the NSF in 1934, the regime found the answer to its problems. At thirty-two neither too old to repel young militants, not too young to alienate the older woman, her eleven children also reflected the 'right' order of priorities. She was, and still is, a committed National Socialist.[12]

The foundation of the NSF, which by the end of 1938 had 2.3 million, mostly non-activist, members, demonstrated that women were not formally excluded from political life in the Third Reich, even though in the same year Scholtz-Klink complained that she 'had not yet once had the chance to discuss women's affairs in person with the Führer'.[13] Notwithstanding this lack of interest in high places, the regime's totalitarian aspirations encompassed women too. Like their masculine equivalents, from 1936 girls had to join the Hitler Youth. At fourteen they advanced from the 'Young Girls' to the BDM.[14] Between eighteen and twenty-one they could join the BDM's 'Faith and Beauty' organisation, and thereafter the NSF. Some women seem to have regarded a career in these organisations as a means of escaping the oppressive tutelage of their mothers, fathers, and families. According to much subsequent testimony, some valued membership of these organisations because it enabled them to develop their self-confidence and to achieve positions of leadership and responsibility. During wartime, and much to the annoyance of other women, they enjoyed the perks and advantages of their male Party comrades.

Nazi policy towards the family particularly concerned women. Policy reflected both widespread anxiety about Germany's falling birthrate and the regime's 'qualitative' eugenic preoccupations. Groups, often associated with the political Left, which advocated birth control or provided contraceptive advice were dissolved by the police and attempts were made to restrict the supply of contraceptives to chemists. Although the regime later positively encouraged abortion for the 'hereditarily ill' and racial 'aliens' in May 1933, the penalties for persons who performed abortions upon 'healthy Aryans' without adequate medical grounds were extended to up to two years' imprisonment.[15] During wartime the penalty was death. The corollary of these attempts to control women's bodies was a number of incentives and measures designed to boost the birthrate of the racially 'sound' members of the community. Some local authorities introduced rent, water, or electricity rebates for large families, which also benefited from free theatre tickets or concessionary railway fares. Attempts were also made to raise the status of motherhood. Those with three children under ten received Honour Cards entitling them to preferential treatment while shopping, and from 1938 particularly prolific mothers received the Honour Cross of the German Mother, which meant, *inter alia*, that members of the Hitler Youth were required to salute them in public.[16] Less cosmetically, the Reich Mothers' Service (part of the DFW) organised classes for pregnant women, to educate them in child care and domestic science. These courses, which by March 1939 had been attended by over 1.7 million women, provided instruction concerning the dangers of smoking or excessive drinking during pregnancy, infant care, and with an eye to the economy, the virtues of artificial fibres or food-preserving as a means of saving foreign exchange.[17] There was also a service providing second-hand cots, prams, and children's clothing. The Law for the Reduction of Unemployment of 1 June 1933 introduced interest-free loans of up to 1,000RMs for young married couples. The capital was raised through a tax on single persons at the rate of between 2 and 5 per cent of their income. The loans, which were conditional upon the wife giving up work, took the form of vouchers which could be redeemed in the form of household goods and furniture, thus stimulating employment in these sectors. They were to be repaid at the rate of 1 per cent per month, with 25 per cent being cancelled and payment suspended for a year on the birth of each child. In popular parlance this became known as 'paying off with children'.[18]

After a poor start, the revocation, in 1937, of the prohibition on women's employment as a condition of the loans made the scheme more attractive. In 1939, some 42 per cent of all marriages contracted were assisted by these loans. However they had little appreciable effect upon the long-term trend towards one- or two-child families. More marriages may have been contracted, but whereas in 1920 they produced an average of 2.3 children, in 1940 couples had 1.8. Neither marriage loans nor gold Honour Crosses made much of an impact on this trend. This was because the loans covered a mere 20 per cent of the estimated actual costs of a three-child family, and were not accompanied by any commensurate housing policy which would have made larger families viable in urban

8.5 'Germany grows from strong mothers and healthy children.' Nazi
pro-natalist propaganda poster.

environments. New furniture made no difference to people who would have to cope with three small children in cramped and gloomy tenements. The loans were inevitably made conditional upon racial criteria, and hence were designed to channel funds towards the biologically unimpeachable. Following the Marriage Health Law of October 1935, the right to marry became conditional upon receipt of a certificate of 'fitness to marry' issued by the local health authorities.[19] Marriage loans, tax rebates, and family allowances thus became conditional upon racial criteria. Inevitably, this meant that it became dangerous even to apply for these benefits. In 1934 a couple who applied for a marriage loan found that the racial examination resulted in a recommendation that the wife be sterilised for 'feeble-mindedness'. She had apparently had to resit two classes at school.

The regime's philogenerative fixation lay behind what some historians falsely regard as an enlightened attitude towards unmarried mothers. That their principal 'protector' was Heinrich Himmler should immediately put historians on their guard. Himmler's 'sentimentality' on this issue concealed his profoundly inhuman search for more cannon-fodder for the Reich, regardless of the happiness of the women concerned and regardless of conventional morality. However, morality ensured that the regime as a whole had to move cautiously on this issue, lest they be accused of promoting 'Bolshevik' immorality. From 1937 mothers could avail themselves of the title 'Frau' regardless of their marital status.[20] Two years later, unmarried motherhood ceased to be a reason for dismissal from the civil service. The SS went further by positively advocating a number of measures to support women who bore children to men serving at the front, regardless of whether this involved marriage. The facilities of SS 'Well of Life' homes were also made available to pregnant unmarried women who had no connection with the SS.[21] Although Himmler seems to have favoured legalised polygamy, and thought in terms of his men acting as 'conception assistants' after surviving the front, the Lebensbornheime were not, as was popularly rumoured, human stud farms for disabled SS men. During the war they provided ante- and post-natal facilities for unmarried mothers and an adoption service for their babies. More sinisterly, they were also responsible for rearing 'racially valuable' children abducted from their parents in Poland and the Soviet Union. This last practice was either unknown to the population at large, or regarded as a necessary evil. As we shall see below, 'progressive' attitudes towards unmarried mothers did not encompass German women who deviated from the regime's racial norms. The divorce laws were also amended in the interests of terminating 'unproductive' marriages. Alongside adultery, the

Marriage Law of 1938 included refusal to conceive, abortion, and irretrievable marital breakdown reflected in three-year separation as grounds for divorce. These amendments were designed to enable either partner to contract further relationships which would produce children for the 'national community'. An apparently even-handed approach to alimony – working women had to support their indigent ex-husbands – ceased once the male partner assumed further familial obligations.

Most of the measures discussed above served to promote the birth of 'racially valuable' children. Some historians have taken the increased provision of maternity clinics, along with trends in women's employment to be discussed below, as 'evidence' of women's 'new status of relative, if unconventional equality'.[22] This not only overlooks the reactionary intent behind the maternity clinics and marriage loans, it also simply ignores the whole groups of women who enjoyed anything but 'equality', unconventional or otherwise. Gertrud Scholtz-Klink's organisation did not include women socialists, pacifists, Jews, Sinti or Roma, or female forced labourers from Poland and the Soviet Union. Nor did the regime's maternity clinics cater for women deemed to be racially 'inferior'. In fact, pro-natalist policies were accompanied by measures designed to prevent the latter from having children. The projected numbers involved were staggering. At a meeting of population planners on 28 June 1933, the Interior Minister, Frick, declared: 'We must again have the courage to grade our people according to its genetic value', and mentioned that 'some authors', including men sitting around the same table, claimed that 20 per cent of the German population were racially 'undesirable'. Other percentages floated by scientific 'authorities' hovered between '5 and 30 per cent'.[23]

In fact, in the five and a half years between the introduction of compulsory sterilisation on 1 January 1934 and the outbreak of war, about 320,000 people, or 0.5 per cent of the population, were compulsorily sterilised.[24] Although this was nowhere near the 'optimal' figures in the minds of the scientists and experts, its scale can be grasped from the fact that with comparable laws, thirty states in the USA sterilised 11,000 people between 1907 and 1930. In Germany, the victims were divided equally between men and women, although only the latter concern us here. The most frequent reasons given for sterilisation were either 'feeble-mindedness' (53 per cent) or 'schizophrenia' (20 per cent). Between 1934 and 1937 about eighty men and 400 women died during the operation. In Germany the victims were from poorer sections of the population, or were dischargees from asylums. Regardless of their actual state of health, the latter were alleged to have 'recessive' genes which might endanger their progeny. Of course, behind the 'objective' scientific criteria used by bourgeois, male physicians to interfere with these women's rights lay an abundance of social and gender-specific prejudice. Blanket terms like 'feeble-mindedness' or 'schizophrenia' were used regardless of their clinical meaning to disguise the fact that the victims simply deviated from 'normal' behaviour, in ways which offended the categories of their social 'superiors'. People who failed to be monogamous, thrifty, clean, efficient, tidy, responsible, and striving upwards were designated 'socially feeble-minded', on the basis of 'intelligence tests', spurious 'diagnoses', or more usually gossip and hearsay. In so far as 'disorderly' and promiscuous men were less liable to be sterilised on these grounds alone, one could argue that these measures reflect gender-specific prejudices.[25]

Gisela Bock has made a detailed study of compulsory sterilisation in Nazi Germany, which includes a number of individual case histories. Although each 'case' was different, severally they reflect, above all, the determination of people who coped with physical or emotional difficulties to resist the attempts of the medical profession, the courts, and the State to interfere with their bodies. The 'objects' of files bulging with sterilisation applications, attestations, diagnoses, records of intelligence tests, letters to other authorities, extracts from criminal records, psychiatric reports, lawyers' bills, and reports on police inquiries and of the operation itself were people like Emma F. She was twenty-nine and had had two spells in psychiatric institutions, one of which recommended, without her knowledge, that she be compulsorily sterilised as a 'schizophrenic'. In a letter appealing against the resulting decision of the Hereditary Health Court, she wrote:

> I was informed in writing by the Hereditary Health Court in Offenburg of the decision of 15 May 1934 whereby I was to be rendered infertile. I reject this decision, and raise objections to it on the following grounds. For a long time my nerves were so over-wrought that I had to obtain medical treatment in the psychiatric clinic at Freiburg. I was soon discharged from the clinic, because my condition had improved. I soon returned to my job in the cigar factory, and since then I have worked there without interruption up to the present day. I am almost the highest wage-earner in the factory, and my employers are always satisfied with my work. I request that the foreman X be questioned about my activity in the factory. He should also be asked whether he can say something about my mental state. My nerves have calmed down again, and for some time I have been as mentally normal as any other healthy person. Although today I am still entitled to invalidity pension, from the provincial insurance office in

8.6 A sixteen-year-old girl compulsorily sterilised for 'hereditary schizophrenia' by the regime.

Baden, I have voluntarily foregone this right, since I am fully capable of working. I cannot understand why they want to sterilise me, since I have done nothing wrong morally or sexually. Every person can become mentally ill, which in my opinion is a form of illness like any other illness, and which heals itself again. It would be otherwise if I pursued sexual desires and wanted intercourse with men, or wanted under any circumstances to marry. That would be something different, but I am very reserved, and do not want to know anything about men. I do not need to be made infertile, it is not necessary in my case I have never given and will never give any opportunities for sexual intercourse whereby I could become pregnant, thereby bringing suspect hereditary progeny into the world. Every person is different from another, as is every separate case. I therefore make application to the Hereditary Health Court to abrogate the decision to sterilise me. I also petition for a re-examination of my psychological state.[26]

A higher court rejected her claim that she had had a nervous breakdown, and claimed to have evidence of 'hereditary schizophrenia'. In other words, a temporary period of mental disorder 'proved' latent illness. Emma F.'s account of her life was totally ignored, and her professions of independence and celibacy, and her resort to the terminology of racial 'science', did not save her from being sterilised shortly afterwards.

The procedures for sterilising the seventeen-year-old agricultural servant girl Anna P. were set in motion on Christmas Eve 1935 by her own physician.[27] In February 1936 she and her father appeared before a Hereditary Health Court in Erlangen, where the father objected to the sterilisation of his daughter on the grounds that her 'feeble-mindedness' was a result of a hearing disability and undernourishment at the hands of her previous employer. In other words she was a little deaf and run-down. Anna added, 'What my father says is correct. I will not be operated upon.' The court began to trawl through Anna's earlier life. An elementary school teacher ventured the opinion that her 'lesser value' was 'hereditary' since he had also taught Anna's mother 'whose achievements were not spectacular'. The local police volunteered that the parents were hard of hearing, but otherwise the family was quite healthy. Of course neither the teacher nor the police were in any way competent to pontificate on these issues. Anna was sent to an ear, nose, and throat clinic at Erlangen, despite the sarcastic protest of her present employer that 'removing essential labour from farmers in summertime is not part of the battle for production'. She arrived, distraught, at the clinic. Having recovered sufficiently to take intelligence tests, she made the error of being facetious. The results were mixed. She stated that if three out of five pigeons were shot off a roof, two would remain, and also that a pound of iron weighed more than a pound of feathers. She could not sing the national anthem, read with difficulty, and could not solve riddles intended for eight-year-olds. The results of these tests, and the fact that her mother did poorly at school, were taken as evidence of 'hereditary feeble-mindedness'. Her father was duped into waiving his right of appeal, but then, following delays caused by his farming commitments and his inability to understand his rights, decided to appeal on Anna's behalf. He was told that the higher court had confirmed the decision because the report from the clinic in Erlangen left 'no doubt' about Anna's 'hereditary illness'. She was sterilised in February 1937.

A final example illustrates both how some unmarried mothers were treated in the Third Reich, and how psychiatric assessments were used to cut welfare costs. In 1940 the welfare authorities in Lörrach applied to the health authorities to bring about the sterilisation of a factory-worker called Fanny N.[28] She had six children, five illegitimate and one legitimate. The latter lived with her former husband, two of the former with her parents, and three at public expense. This last point figured in an array of evidence designed to prove Fanny N.'s 'hereditary feeble-mindedness (moral defects)'. This included a history of unemployment, frequent pregnancy, criminal convictions in the family, a brother's attendance at a special school, and so on. Something, it was assumed, was 'wrong' with her parents. When this proved not to be the case, the problem was approached from another angle. Further evidence was raked up concerning the father of one of her children, who was in a concentration camp, and about the children themselves, who although of average ability were apathetic and lazy. This enabled the authorities to circumvent the inconvenient fact that Fanny's parents lived unexceptionable lives. Her mother wrote to the courts protesting against the decision to sterilise her daughter:

> My daughter is absolutely not in agreement with this decision, and nor are we, my husband and I. Firstly, because she is not feeble-minded, but merely indifferent, and that is not a matter requiring sterilisation. The children she has had are healthy and normal, and not one of them is an idiot. I think it is absolutely unnecessary to do something like this to her. You are doing her wrong, and you will reap the consequences of it, or we will take the matter to our Führer, who himself is for the children. If the children were stupid it would be otherwise. One of them is a girl of 9 whom I have with me, who doesn't do too well at school, but there are children of well-off parents who don't do too well at school either, and therefore she is far from being feeble-minded. My daughter is marrying again this year, and then she will take the two children she has in a children's home, and I will take the other. As long as my husband and I are still alive, and we have brought up ten of our own, we can raise one more. Therefore I hope you will acknowledge this letter and think again, if you want to avoid a mishap. There are many mothers here in W. who have really stupid children, and for whom it would be more necessary to do something like this, but it isn't done to them because a man is there. Up to now, my daughter had no husband, so you are doing to her what you like. But we are still around and we still have rights over her. Many mothers would be overjoyed to have such beautiful, healthy children as she has . . . I have . . . eight lads and two girls, and all of them are healthy and right in the head, and I have

> always devoted myself day and night to the children, and I am proud
> of them, and therefore I will never allow my daughter to be
> sterilised.[29]

A court referred Fanny to an asylum for tests lasting a week. Her level of intelligence was described as 'frighteningly low', because she thought there were ten hours in a day, did not understand the significance of the SA and SS, could not name the last Kaiser, did not know how many angles were in a triangle, and thought that 'lieutenants, captains, and colonels' were 'something high up'. Since there was no exogenous reason for her limited intelligence, the conclusion was that she was 'hereditarily feeble-minded'. She was sterilised in June 1941 because 'the subject is the problem child of the family. She has never learned a trade, and latterly was a casual labourer in a cardboard packing factory. During a personal interview she was noticeably indifferent towards her shifting sexual relationships. Likewise, her knowledge and mental abilities are limited.'

Most of the measures considered so far clearly served the objective of encouraging the birth of racially 'valuable' ethnic comrades, while preventing the reproduction of the 'asocial' and racially 'worthless'. Other aspects of Nazi policy towards women were designed to integrate them into the 'national community'. Hitler's oft-quoted remark that there would 'never be another November 1918 in German history'[30] had a certain gender-specific aspect, in the sense that in 1918 it was often women who were no longer prepared to tolerate the privations of the 'home front' in the service of prolonging carnage on the battlefields. This brings us to one of the most important areas of Nazi policy towards women, namely employment.

Immediately after the 'seizure of power', the Nazis endeavoured to cut the female labour force, initially by driving women from the professions. This aim was reflected in the Law for the Reduction of Unemployment and the conditions attached to marriage loans; and through the extension of the Brüning government's campaign against 'double-earners', from women in public service at Reich level to their colleagues in state or local government. In line with one of Hitler's many fixations, women were subsequently forbidden to work as judges or lawyers. Broadly speaking, women remaining in the public sector were paid less than their male equivalents, who also monopolised all positions of authority. Access to the learned professions was also restricted by the introduction on 28 December 1933 of a gender-specific *numerus clausus*, which limited the admission of women to universities to 10 per cent of the total annual intake.[31] Many of these blatantly discriminatory measures were reversed

8.7 Women in the rest area of a chocolate factory. German Labour Front propaganda photograph designed to show improved working environments.

once a labour surplus was superseded by a labour shortage as a result of conscription and the regime's armaments policies. As we have seen, from 1937 onwards marriage loans ceased to be conditional upon the woman's renunciation of paid employment. The *numerus clausus* limiting the number of female students was dropped in 1936. Despite several measures designed to retard the academic potentialities of women – notably compulsory needlework instead of Latin or science – the conscription of males ensured that women comprised an ever-larger proportion of the student body. By the winter semester of 1943–4 27,442 or 60 per cent of students were women, regardless of the fact that the regime's own policies had ill equipped many of them for higher education.[32]

Students and professionals constituted only a small minority of women. Having extolled the virtues of motherhood and domesticity for so long, the regime now had to find a way of enticing women back into the labour market. However, despite devices like factory kindergartens, maternity leave, and greater attention to factory hygiene, the fact remained that many women saw no reason to supplement domestic work by resuming low-paid, dead-end jobs in factories and offices. One particularly unfortunate group of women had no choice in the matter. As male agricultural labourers forsook the land for better earnings in construction or manufacturing industry, much of their work devolved, by default, upon women. Following the outbreak of war, representatives of industry, the army, and NSDAP – notably Göring and Speer – demanded the mobilisation of the 'female reserve army' for employment in munitions factories.[33] Their limited success in this endeavour was reflected in the fact that the number of women in paid employment only rose from 14.6 to 14.9 million between 1939 and September 1944, with a drop to 14.1 million in 1941. As Tim Mason has suggested, the totalitarian Third Reich had considerably less success in mobilising the female population than Britain, which in 1941 supplemented voluntary enlistment with conscription and compulsion.[34] The regime's self-defeating emphasis upon the 'natural' roles of women only partially accounts for this conspicuous failure. To begin with, in order to maintain the morale of the troops, German women received relatively generous separation allowances of up to 85 per cent of their husband's peacetime earnings. Moreover, in line with policies first essayed in the First World War, the regime endeavoured to purchase quiet on the home front by satisfying its insatiable quest for labour through the deployment of foreigners. The latter were initially recruited as 'guests', although they were increasingly 'guests' who had been abducted from their own countries and were imprisoned in special camps. By 1944, 20 per cent of agricultural work was performed by foreign labour, with a mounting proportion deployed in industry also.[35] The presence of more than seven million 'foreign workers' and the absence of millions of German men afforded some female employees the opportunity to obtain better-paid and more prestigious jobs than were available to them under normal circumstances. The reminiscences of women 'foreign workers' are littered with memories of humiliation and maltreatment at the hands of petty male and female German tyrants. For example, Polish women working in the kitchens of a jute-spinning and weaving works in Bremen were subject to abuse by a woman called Veit, who held sway amidst the steaming pots and piles of plates.[36] In addition to controlling the consistency of each group of workers' soup, fishing out vegetables and replacing them with more water in the case of the 'Russians' pot', this bully regularly hit her undernourished and despondent Polish subordinates, and forbade them to use their mother tongue. Arrogance and insecurity were manifest in her making the Poles recite sentences like 'There is no Poland any more.

8.8 *Ukrainian forced factory worker in the Siemens plant in Berlin. Her overalls are marked 'Ost', indicating that she is an 'Eastern worker'.*

Poland is finished. It is forbidden to speak Polish. You must speak German. Poland is lost.'[37]

In the regime's ideational scheme of things, the arduous and dirty work was to be performed by a racially-categorised foreign workforce, which would become incorporeal during non-working hours. Many people were simply indifferent to this ghost army, which cleared up the rubble and tramped into the factories, but which was barred from cafes and swimming baths. They also apparently took it for granted that 'Eastern workers' should be treated worse than their equivalents from France or Belgium. This is indicative both of the degree to which the regime's racism intersected with prejudices in the population as a whole, and of how far racism became part of everyday life. Of course, it was impossible to decree or police contact between Germans and 'foreign workers' out of existence. Relations between German women and workers from Poland or the Soviet Union were regarded as constituting a particular 'ethnic-political threat'. At first, totally arbitrary sanctions were used against German women who had sexual relations with 'foreign workers'.[38] They had their hair shaved and were publicly humiliated, while the men involved were assaulted and sometimes lynched. Subsequently, the Gestapo took a hand in the matter, which resulted in the women being tried by Special Courts and then sent to concentration camps. In the camp jargon of Ravensbrück they were known ironically as 'bed politicals'. Draconian penalties do not seem to have deterred either the women or men involved. An SD report in January 1942 chronicled the alleged susceptibility of German women to foreign men, and the sometimes unwelcome attentions of the latter:

> Reports from every part of the Reich reveal that the deployment of millions of foreign workers has resulted in a steady increase in sexual relations with German women. This fact has had a not inconsiderable negative effect upon the mood of the people. Today influential circles estimate the number of illegitimate children German women have had by foreigners as being at least 20,000. The threat of infiltration of German blood becomes ever greater due to the conscription for military service of many millions of German men, the absence of a general prohibition on sexual intercourse for foreigners, and the increasing number of foreign workers . . . [39]
>
> In the case of women of German blood, one is often dealing with the less valuable part of the German population. These are often women with a pronounced sexuality, who find foreigners interesting and therefore make it easy for the latter to approach them. The following has been reported:
> 'In particular there are a large number of German girls of

unrestrained character, especially those working far from their home town, who throw themselves into the arms of foreigners' (Potsdam).

'There are mounting complaints that girls of German blood are running after Czech workers in order to have relations with them' (Bielefeld).

'The case of a 23-year-old telephonist from a bourgeois background is also typical, who made up to a French prisoner of war, because he had "dark hair and was a Latin type"' (Bayreuth).

'It is particularly evident that young girls are very interested in foreigners and sometimes have sexual relations with them. Despite stringent controls, adolescent girls again and again try to have relationships with foreign workers, or to hang around with foreigners' (Chemnitz).

'It can be proved that a Pole working for a miller, who was accepted into the family community, regularly had sexual intercourse with the miller's wife' (Halle).

'At this time foreign workers are billeted in a few pubs in northern Leipzig. Circumstances have arisen which are insupportable in the long term. Every girl who looks as if she is alone is smoothly ambushed, with a dictionary in one hand, in an unbelievable fashion. The girls are asked to go to the park in no uncertain terms. There, German girls are treated in an extremely vulgar and heedless manner, concerning which complaints are multiplying from day to day' (Leipzig).[40]

Clueless in the face of uninhibited male and female sexuality, the report concluded with the suggestion that brothels be established for foreign workers.

Pregnant or ailing women workers from Poland, Russia, and the Ukraine were initially despatched to collection camps, and then returned to their country of origin in order to avoid the cost of having to care for them. This practice seems to have resulted in some women deliberately incapacitating themselves in order to be reunited with their families.[41] It also resulted in the shipment of hundreds of pregnant or sick women back to Poland, where the German authorities were unwilling to take them. Seeing this barbaric practice would deter any future workers from wanting to go to Germany, so decisions were taken to solve the problem in the Reich. From 1943, abortion was encouraged for Polish or Russian women who were expected to bear racially 'undesirable' babies. If it was too late to perform abortions, then the babies were deposited in 'child collection centres' at, for example, Kelsterbach or Pfaffenwald, where they were either starved or murdered with lethal medication. The children of racially 'valuable' female 'foreign workers' were removed from their mothers and farmed out to German foster-parents by the Nazi welfare services.

'Foreign workers' who suffered psychological disorders, which were not infrequent in view of the way they were treated, were sent to 'collection points' where the likelihood of recovery was established. If their illness was regarded as 'incurable', which from 1944 meant that it was likely to incapacitate the patient for more than six weeks, they were sent to asylums like Hadamar or Kaufbeuren and killed.

The presence of millions of 'foreign workers' was clearly regarded as constituting a 'racial-political threat' by sections of the regime. However, this did not result in the adoption of the alternative option, namely of conscripting the 'reserve army' of women, which in 1939 included 1 million single and 5.4 million married, but childless, women. For contrary to the regime's relentless insistence upon the hard-working, self-sacrificing character of 'the German woman', the latter seem to have been loath to volunteer for additional work on the farms and in the factories. Various factors account for the failure to tap this source of labour. In mounting order of priority, these included the cost of providing special facilities for women workers; the general economic value attached to housewives' unpaid ingenuity in preserving foods, saving energy, and making clothes; and finally, the unpopularity of attempts to mobilise women, both among them and among their male relatives at the front. The decision taken in 1943 to conscript all women between seventeen and forty-five, and then fifty years of age was unpopular and unsuccessful. It was also hedged round with so many categories of exemption that by the end of 1943 only some 500,000 extra women had been mobilised for 'total war'. Agents of the SD reported that many women managed to circumvent this measure with various stratagems. They also reported increasing signs of 'defeatism' and opposition among women. From Frankfurt am Main it was reported that women were saying: 'if all women got together, then this madness would soon be over'.[42]

However the 'madness' continued, despite the apathy and war-weariness of a female population demoralised through queueing for non-existent food; confused shopping hours and incivil service; the terror and devastation of area bombing; the evacuation of their children and the loss of husbands, brothers, and sons in distant places. SD reports noted that previously harmonious marriages quickly degenerated into mutual antagonism when the husband came home on leave. Wives rendered nervous by the strains of the 'home front' found themselves confronted by husbands rendered abnormal by combat, who evinced no interest in the daily grind. A *dialogue de sourds* ensued, between women who lay awake at night wondering how to feed the children and men worried about going back to

8.9 'Comrades, do you need advice and help? – turn to your local
NSDAP branch.' Nazi poster.

the front. Many women sank into a dispirited mood, oblivious to the hollow determination of NSF functionaries, and unable to bear the news of defeat after defeat. Others, according to a lengthy SD report in April 1944 concerned with an alleged collapse of women's morals, apparently used their separation allowances to buy alcohol, or sought and gave sexual gratification in return for luxury items purloined from the occupied countries.[43] Interestingly, the same report indicated that women preferred what it called the 'eroticising of public life' – the authors meant romantic films and love songs – to propaganda designed to promote woman as 'the guardian of morality' or 'protectress of life'. In the end, of course, the 'madness' was not halted because of a collapse of morale, not to speak of 'morals', on the home front, but as a result of Allied force of arms. Women did not uniquely contribute towards Germany's defeat, either in the sense deplored by their detractors, or in that admired by sympathetic males who see endemic crisis on the domestic front. Like men, women were simultaneously victims of and participants in National Socialism, with some of the latter equalling their male colleagues in inhumanity and cruelty.

CHAPTER NINE

MEN IN THE THIRD REICH

W HILE many books and essays have been written about youth and women in the Third Reich, there is nothing about men as a specific category, beyond an isolated venture into the realm of male fantasies, or a few studies of homosexuals.[1] Why is it acceptable to use anthropological categories in the case of youth or women, and apparently unacceptable to employ them in the case of men? Most obviously this is because adult men were the principal political actors in the Third Reich, and as such have received massive treatment in the literature already. Beyond the dictates of current historiographical fashions, there are good reasons for treating women as a separate category. By definition, racial-hygienic laws which regulated conception, birth, and abortion primarily affected women, although the responses of their husbands or lovers need to be considered too.

The Law for the Prevention of Hereditarily Diseased Progeny of 14 July 1933 was the most obvious example of this. Although it was directed equally against 'hereditarily diseased' men and women, there were significant differences in its application. As far as one can tell from the available evidence, more women were compulsorily sterilised than men, particularly for being allegedly socially or morally 'feeble-minded'.[2] A frequent change of sexual partners was far more likely to be cited as 'evidence' of 'moral feeble-mindedness' in the case of women than in that of men. Moreover, far more women died as a consequence of compulsory sterilisation than their male equivalents, although this reflected the greater complexity of the surgery involved, and hence the risks attendant upon it. Of course, the 1935 decree legalising compulsory abortion naturally only affected women. The various pro-natalist laws and decrees penalising those who had illegal abortions or restricting the availability of contraceptives also had particular consequences for women. These measures, aimed at 'Aryan' and 'hereditarily healthy' women, compelled them to take part in the 'battle for children'. This also applies to the other measures introduced by the Nazis to increase the birthrate, described in the chapter on women. It is therefore obvious that the various 'racial-hygienic' policies of the regime particularly affected women.[3]

Matters were otherwise in the case of the regime's racial-anthropological and racist-social policies. No fundamental distinctions of gender were made in the case of Jews, Sinti and Roma, Slavs or the 'asocial'. These people were persecuted solely because of their 'lesser racial value'. However, if one studies the matter closely, differences do emerge in the treatment of the sexes. The 'offence' of 'race defilement', introduced by the 1935 Law for the Protection of German Blood and Honour could only be committed by male Jews. Although the Law made no mention of 'Gypsies', subsequently only male Sinti and Roma were executed or sent to concentration camps for this 'offence'.[4] A similar disparity of treatment between the sexes can be observed in the case of homosexuals. The Nazis' harsher amendations to paragraph 175 of the Criminal Code exclusively affected homosexual men. Lesbians were not subjected to formal persecution in the Third Reich, despite the fact that some zealous legal experts demanded this. These demands were countered by the argument that since physical affection between women was socially acceptable, the 'offence' would be hard to prove, and by the unproven assertion that lesbianism was a temporary state of mind, requiring merely the application of male sensitivity and solicitude to convince women of the blessings of heterosexuality. In a state which extolled manly, martial toughness, lesbians were less of a threat to the regime than men who subverted its crude stereotypes of 'normal' male behaviour. Some women, of course, were sent to concentration camps for reasons which included lesbianism, regardless of the formal legal position. In conclusion, one could argue that there were some gender-specific differences in both the conception and the implementation of Nazi racial policy.

By contrast, racial legislation reflected no specific class differences. Racial legislation was directed against everyone, regardless of whether they were rich or poor, or members of the upper, middle, or lower classes. In practice, as is usually the case, important differences emerged in the law's implementation. Wealthy Jews were obviously in a better position to emigrate than their poorer co-religionists. Although the law sanctioning compulsory sterilisation made no mention of social class, a

9.1 Josef Thorak's 'Danzig Freedom Monument' (1942). The figure is the embodiment of insensate, martial masculinity.

disproportionate number of the poor were affected by it. By definition, the 'asocial' were virtually synonymous with the most deprived parts of the population. In contrast, neither the 'euthanasia' programme nor the 'Final Solution' made distinctions regarding the social background of the victims, except in so far as wealthy Jews were more likely to have emigrated, or that well-off families could exert greater political influence on behalf of ailing members.[5]

This is not to claim that no social classes existed in the Third Reich, or that the Nazis were successful in replacing the received social order with one based upon racial criteria. Society remained divided into upper, middle, and lower classes. However, there is much evidence to suggest that gradually these divisions would have been replaced by a system whose primary organising principle was race. In what follows, we will look at policy as it affected each of the social classes, in full awareness that the discussion is neither comprehensive nor exhaustive.

Before 1933 the National Socialist German Workers' Party made no secret of its animosity towards Germany's traditional upper classes.[6] The Party programme of 1920 talked of nationalising large enterprises and the expropriation of big landed estates. Subsequently, however, these 'social revolutionary' demands were watered down or simply abandoned. Leading Nazis began to stress the obscure distinction between Jewish 'rapacious' and 'Aryan' 'creative' capital; demanding the destruction of the former, and the protection of the latter from the Bolshevik menace. In 1931 Hitler gave his personal assurance to Friedrich Svend, Prince Eulenburg Hertefeld, that he would never try to bring about 'the destruction or expropriation of great estates'. These distinctions and disavowals were well received by representatives of industry and the landed interest. Increasing numbers of industrialists, landowners, senior civil servants, ecclesiastics, and other members of the traditional elites either sympathised with the NSDAP or joined it. Many of the East Elbian Junker class voted NSDAP in the 1929 provincial elections. The so-called 'seizure of power' was based upon an informal alliance between the NSDAP and representatives of the traditional elites within the army, industry, agriculture, bureaucracy, and anti-Marxist elements in both Churches.[7] The common goals of these alliance partners included the destruction of the organised labour movement; the overcoming of the Depression; and the enhancement of Germany's political and military power. In order to achieve these objectives, the conservative elites were prepared to countenance the destruction of democracy, the proscription of all political parties including traditional conservatism, and even the 'co-ordination' of key bastions of power such as the army and both Churches. In the process, they forfeited their own organised political power. Like changes in a geometric figure, political power moved increasingly towards the Nazi angle in the alliance. Representatives of the traditional elites accepted this loss of political power because they retained their leading position in society as a whole. They also undoubtedly profited from the forcible suppression of organised labour and the economic upturn. The regime's foreign policy 'achievements' also corresponded with many of their traditional goals. The Nazis compensated them for their loss of political power by abandoning any intention of interfering with the overall distribution of socio-economic power. Large factories and landed estates were neither nationalised nor expropriated. New state enterprises were complementary to, rather than in competition with, existing concerns, a form of hybrid supplement to the existing capitalist economy. Schacht's 'New Plan' corresponded with the interests of many industrialists. The same applies to the new agencies created under the auspices of the Four-Year Plan. Representatives of Party and State worked closely with representatives of major companies, such as the chemical combine I. G. Farben, so that it is necessary to speak of the 'privatisation' of what, outwardly, appeared to represent growing state control of strategic sectors of industry.[8]

In sum, relations between the traditional elites and the Nazi regime were close and largely amicable. People became rich and made careers, often at the expense of Jews who were discriminated against, pauperised, and persecuted. The fact that one had once had business or social relations with Jewish fellow members of the upper classes slipped quietly out of mind. Certainly, public persecution of the Jews was unpopular, but members of the upper classes and the two Churches remained conspicuously silent about it. This was both a tactical and a moral error. The persecution of the Jews was part of a global attempt to remodel society in accordance with racial criteria, and hence to replace the existing class system with a radically novel form of society.

The main exponents of this new social order, based upon racial rather than class criteria, were the SS.[9] Before 1933 the SS was a relatively insignificant part of the SA, the party's paramilitary organisation. Following the Röhm affair, the SS ceased to be subordinated to the SA and became directly responsible to Hitler. At this time, its main functions consisted of protecting Hitler and guarding concentration camps. The guard were recruited from the General SS. They took the name 'Death's Head Formations' from the emblem they wore on their uniforms. These units were soon augmented by so-called 'militarised formations', armed units which grew out of the regiment responsible for protecting Hitler. Eventually these military formations became known as the Waffen-SS. They were never subordinated to the regular army, but rather developed into a dangerous rival. Occasionally, individuals in the regular army criticised the Waffen-SS's brutal style of ideological warfare, but mostly they admired its members' fanatical courage and unparalleled ferocity. Individual soldiers also criticised the murder of Jews, Sinti and Roma, and Soviet Commissars perpetrated by the SS task forces; others went about with photographs of mass murder in their tunics, alongside pictures of their wives and children. The SS task forces consisted of members of the general SS, the police, and

9.2 Two SS NCOs enjoying a drink in the concentration camp at Sobibor.

members of the Death's Head Formations temporarily redeployed from concentration camps. They also received the enthusiastic assistance of Ukrainians and Lithuanians, as well as members of the regular army.

All of these SS forces were controlled and financed by the Reich Main Security Office in Berlin. This consisted of a complex of agencies. One was responsible for the Waffen-SS. The Administrative and Economic Main Office controlled the concentration camp system, contracted out slave labour to both SS and private industrial concerns, and 'processed' the meagre belongings of murdered camp inmates. This encompassed the latter's spectacles, hair, and gold teeth, which were 'recycled' for gain. The Reich Main Security Office also controlled the Gestapo and the SD, the State and Party political police responsible for the surveillance and persecution of political opponents and those who were objects of the regime's racial policies. Adolf Eichmann was typical of these desk-bound murderers: keen and driven by the need to perform efficiently, and quite devoid of moral scruples. Heinrich Himmler was 'Reich Leader' of this burgeoning bureaucratic empire. His concern for his subordinates went beyond ensuring that they carried out their duties as soldiers, or technocrats of mass murder, as smoothly and efficiently as possible. Himmler regarded

9.3 Two SS men, an NCO and officer, who served in Sobibor and Belzec.

the SS as a male, martial 'order'; a bizarre and ahistorical conflation of the Teutonic knights, the Jesuits and Japanese Samurai.[10] They were to be the the elite of National Socialist Germany. 'Pure and good blood' was an absolute precondition for membership of Himmler's order. Members of the SS were subjected to a particularly stringent form of racial investigation and selection. The SS's genealogical experts enquired whether candidates, or their wives and relatives, had any traces of 'alien', 'asocial', or 'hereditarily diseased' blood. If the candidates passed these tests, then as members of the SS they were not only committed to total obedience, but were duty bound to propagate their own biological qualities by having as many children as possible.

This last point was one of Himmler's chief preoccupations. He interfered in the most private areas of his senior subordinates' lives with embarrassing zeal, demanding to know whether projected spouses were 'racially pure' or when wives were likely to expect children. He was personally responsible for the SS's abstruse and absurd marriage and birth rituals. These developed into an ersatz religion, complete with pagan kitsch symbolism, and the SS's own castle of the holy grail – the Wewelsburg, near Paderborn.[11] Although these rituals seem ridiculous, they deserve to be considered seriously. They contributed to the individual's self-estimation as part of a carefully selected racial elite superior to all existing aristocracies. This feeling was given objective confirmation by the significant number of Germany's upper classes who were members of the organisation. Its higher ranks included many representatives of blue blood, including the Princes of Hohenzollern-Emden or Waldeck and Pyrmont, and other names more redolent of the Almanach de Gotha than of Auschwitz: (von) Schulenburg, Rodern, Strachwitz, Planitz, Alvensleben, Podbielski, Treuenfeld, and so on. The fact that in 1938 18.7 per cent of SS Obergruppenführer were aristocrats has received less attention than the involvement of this class in 'resistance'.[12] Together with bourgeois lawyers and other academically-trained professionals, these men formed a functional elite. Members of the SS administered, tortured, and murdered people with a cold, steely precision, and without moral scruples. Group complicity also reinforced group loyalties. Had the Third Reich survived, the SS would have replaced all existing social elites. As Hitler said in 1941, 'I do not doubt for a moment, despite certain people's scepticism, that within a hundred years or so from now all the German élite will be a product of the SS – for only the SS practises racial selection.' The SS was a microcosm of the modern, racially organised, hierarchical, performance-orientated order with which the Nazis wished to replace existing society. The SS would have absorbed or destroyed all alternative bastions of power occupied by the traditional elites.

Twelve years were not long enough to achieve this long-range objective. During those years the Nazis had to work within a given social framework. This meant working together with the traditional elites, who continued to occupy the commanding heights of the army, bureaucracy, and industry. As long as the regime's foreign policy and conduct of war were successful, this collaboration worked without much friction. Military reverses resulted in discontent, and eventually resistance, on the part of members of the traditional elites in the army and administration.[13] Although the various groups had different aims – ranging from the utopian to the nakedly reactionary – they were united in the conviction that the Nazi regime would lead to the destruction of Germany, dragging them down with it. But their resistance was too late and merely resulted in catastrophe for those involved. The attempt to assassinate Hitler on 20 July 1944, and the failure of the rising timed to coincide with it, resulted in the obliteration of the plotters around Beck, Goerdeler, Moltke, and Stauffenberg. The Nazis exacted a considerable price. In addition to the principal actors in the plot, the regime imprisoned, tortured, and killed the relatives of the

*9.4 The SS leadership in 1932, shortly before the 'seizure of power'.
Himmler is third from the right in the front row; Heydrich second from
the right in the third row. The SS prided itself on its spirit of intense male
camaraderie, even if this 'spirit' was rarely present in the steely language
of members of its bureaucracy.*

conspirators, removing their children to orphanages. This barbaric practice reflected the regime's repressed hatred and contempt for the traditional upper classes.[14]

In 1945 the victorious Allies agreed that the residual social and political powers of Germany's traditional elites had to be destroyed.[15] Although this occurred in the Soviet occupied zone, the onset of the Cold War prevented the implementation of the Potsdam Decrees in the West. The power of traditional elites in both the administration and industry survived, or was deliberately restored. However, even in the West there was only a partial reversion to the social order which had existed prior to the 1933–45 period. Both the defunct Nazi regime, and to a far greater extent the massive territorial losses resulting from Germany's defeat in the war, resulted in a form of social modernisation. This has undoubtedly contributed to the striking performance of post-war German industry, certainly in the FRG, and – notwithstanding a corrupt and parasitic Stalinist bureaucracy and the industrial tithe collected by their Soviet Russian allies – in the former GDR too.

Before 1933, the old middle class – peasants, artisans, shopkeepers, salaried employees, and lesser civil servants – were a particular target group for the Nazi party. Many members of this class believed that the NSDAP intended to protect the 'little man' from the competition of big business or the department store; that it would release farmers from the burden of debt; and that it would provide employment for salaried employees, while abrogating the salary cuts imposed upon civil servants under Brüning.[16] The proportion of Nazi voters from this social constituency was relatively large, but we should be careful about generalisations based upon this fact. Modern research has shown that contemporary observers were wrong in assuming that the NSDAP was essentially a lower-middle-class party.[17] There were enough supporters from both the upper and working classes to justify the description of the NSDAP as a 'people's party'. Analyses based on generational, regional, or confessional factors have also shown that it was a party of the young, and of Protestants rather than Roman Catholics. A further fact which militates against the description of the NSDAP as a middle-class party is that after 1933 it conspicuously failed to pursue policies benefiting their interests. This will be illustrated by examining Nazi policies towards artisans, small businessmen, and peasants.

In 1933 it seemed as if the Nazis would pay due attention to the social and political interests of their middle-class clientele.[18] The Combat League of Middle-Class Tradespeople carried out various boycott actions against Jewish businesses and department stores with the new regime's encouragement and connivance. However, following the main boycott action on 1 April 1933, further campaigns along these lines were discouraged. The Combat League was dissolved, and its members were incorporated into the newly created 'NS-Hago', which in turn was absorbed into the German Labour Front. From the start it was clear that the powers of the NS-Hago would be strictly limited. The same applied to the principal existing middle-class economic association. This was 'co-ordinated' and transformed into a compulsory cartel called the Reich Estate for German Commerce. This was subsequently rechristened the Reich Group Commerce and subordinated to the Reich Minister of Economics. In other words, the organisations of artisans and shopkeepers were brought under closer State control. The same aim was reflected in the Law for the Protection of Retail Trades of 12 May 1933, and the Law for the Provisional Construction of German Craft Trades of 29 November 1933.

9.5 Parade of chimney sweeps and assistants on the 'Day of National Labour', 1 May 1933.

These made it compulsory for anyone wanting to operate as an artisan to prove both an ability to do so, and the existence of demand for the skills or services they had to offer. These measures reflected both the *dirigiste* thrust of the regime and the long-standing desire of artisans to regulate access to their crafts while cutting out unwanted competition from the entrepreneurially-minded unemployed. However, these concessions to the 'little man' were accompanied by the wholesale abandonment of the protectionist policies inherited from the Kaiserreich. Industrial concentration was accelerated by the regime. In the course of March 1938 a large number of small shops and workshops fell victim to a 'self-cleansing' action, designed to mobilise yet further reserves of labour. Although these measures were legitimised with much reference to the general good of the national economy, it was clear that the regime took more account of the interests of the major banks and big business than of artisans and shop-keepers.

The same trend was evident in the case of department stores.[19] Prior to 1933 artisans and tradesmen had demanded their compulsory closure, and this duly figured in NSDAP electoral propaganda. However, the Law for the Protection of Retail Trades merely prohibited an increase beyond the existing number of stores, coupled with the closure of specific in-house services, such as barbers or tailors, which competed with small businesses. Government purchases and special taxes were also employed to discriminate against this sector of the retail economy. The Nazis justified these relatively modest steps by pointing to the number of people employed by department stores who would otherwise be out of work. Following the onset of full employment, they changed the argument to one based on the greater rationality of department store retailing within the overall context of autarchy and an economy given over to war production. Although some small businesses, notably in construction or engineering, profited from this last development, in general one could claim that small business suffered, rather than benefited, from National Socialist economic policies. The weak and the marginal continued to go to the wall. It also took until 1939 for those who survived to achieve the levels of prosperity enjoyed before the Depression, levels of prosperity which both workers and employers had achieved two years earlier. 'Gloom and despondency', rather than overt discontent, apparently characterised the small business sector. One of the reasons for this was the benefit which this class hoped to accrue from the exclusion of Jews from whole areas of the economy.[20] The closure of Jewish businesses wiped out unwanted competition. As we saw above, many businesses run by Jews fell victim to the licensed greed of their 'Aryan' competitors. However, once again the principal beneficiaries were the banks and big business. Major department stores belonging to Jews, such as Tietz (the 'Hertie' and 'Kaufhof' stores), Schocken, and Wertheim, were taken over by banks and major firms rather than by the small fry of the business world. The latter could console themselves with the thought that they were the owners and masters of 'Aryan', albeit modest, businesses. Indeed in this case one could argue that Nazi racial policy was both a compensation and a substitute for socio-economic policies which ignored the interests of the intended beneficiaries. During the war, the gulf between myth and reality reached such proportions that by 1943 the SS economic expert (and mass murderer) Otto Ohlendorf advocated a return to policies which concentrated on the interests of the 'little man' and the dismantling of huge industrial concerns.

A similar gulf between aspiration and reality can be observed in the case of Nazi policies towards agriculture.[21] The structural crisis in this sector, beginning in the 1870s, became critical during the Weimar Republic. Many smaller peasant farms became unviable, while large estates east of the Elbe felt the chill wind of international competition, or in the case of East

9.6 Parade of the butchers' guild in Naumburg/Saale on the 'Day of National Labour', 1 May 1933.

Prussia, were cut off from their hinterland. Measures introduced in the Kaiserreich to protect German agriculture from North American competition became less and less effective, notwithstanding the taxpayers' money doled out for political and demographic reasons to major East Elbian landowners under Weimar 'Osthilfe' schemes. The onset of the Depression and the fall in agricultural prices threatened the existence of many farmers. Many of them had to alienate their chronically indebted properties at very low valuations. Genuine economic distress, and bitterness towards the governments held responsible for it, characterised the rural scene in large parts of Germany.

The Nazis thrived in these pockets of rural desolation. The NSDAP jettisoned those parts of its programme calling for major expropriations, and replaced them with calls for land reform, protectionism, and the elimination of Jewish rural creditors and middlemen. Both the land itself and those who lived on it also occupied a special, emotionally-laden position in Nazi ideology, best typified by the mystical slogan 'Blood and Soil'. City life was denigrated as the breeding-ground of liberalism and Marxism, and held responsible for a declining birthrate which, it was alleged, would result in a German population of 20 million in the year 2000. The peasants were the true 'aristocracy' and the 'life source of the Nordic race'. 'Co-ordination' of the various agrarian interest groups proved a relatively easy affair, given the large number of Nazi sympathisers and voters in these organisations already. The hegemonic Nazi agrarian apparatus was controlled by the Argentine agronomist Walter Darré, who became Reich Peasants' Leader, and then in June 1933 Minister of Agriculture. In September 1933 Darré embarked upon the reorganisation of German agriculture through the establishment of the quasi-corporatist Reich Food Estate, a mammoth syndicate designed to bring an entire sector of the economy under State control. Many of his ideas – notably on the key role of the agrarian sector in wartime, the demographic and strategic necessity of militarised agrarian settlements in the east, or the goal of securing Germany's future through a 'greater regional economy' – had been *communis opinio* among leaders of the conservative agrarian lobby since the early years of the First World War.

Policy was designed to satisfy the interests of the regime, and was only fitfully congruent with those of the peasantry. The latter were apparent in the solution to rural indebtedness. Interest rates were lowered, and those farms which were heavily in debt were protected against repossession. In other words, the State intervened administratively rather than financially to alleviate the peasants' plight, with the banks, insurance agencies, and private creditors bearing the real costs of peasant indebtedness. Much of Nazi agrarian policy was designed to halt a long-term flight from the land. It also combined racial and social considerations. This was most obvious in the Entailed Farm Law of 29 September 1933. Ostensibly, this was designed to maintain the number of small-to-middling peasants by insulating them from the effects of indebtedness, structural backwardness, partible inheritance, incompetence, and market forces. Some 700,000 farms of between 7.5 and 125 hectares were declared to be inalienable and impartible, provided that the entailed heirs were of unimpeachable 'racial' purity and were demonstrably competent farmers. Only 'Aryans' were entitled to become entailed farmers, and only males were entitled to inherit. This represented a radical departure from both the State protectionist policies of the Kaiserreich and even the most archaic forms of inheritance custom. Although in practice the law affected only new settlers and not existing farmers, it was regarded as a mixed blessing by many in the rural community. By precluding foreclosures for insolvency it effectively destroyed farmers' access to credit, and hence the wherewithal to modernise their operations. Deprived and unmarriageable former co-heirs swelled the numbers attracted to life in the towns, where wages were significantly higher than on the land. Thus between 1933 and 1939 the rural population continued to decline from 20.8 per cent to 18 per cent of the total, while the number of those employed in agriculture fell from 16 per cent to 10.5 per cent over the same period. The regime's rural settlement schemes failed to reverse this trend. Between 1933 and 1938 it created about 20,700 new farms totalling 325,000 hectares, an unimpressive figure when set alongside the 57,500 farms totalling over 600,000 hectares achieved by the quintessentially urban Weimar Republic. This resulted in increased reliance upon foreign seasonal labour. Whatever the official rhetoric, in 1932 German agriculture had employed about 7,000 migrants, but by 1935 the figure was in excess of 50,000.

Nor was the regime able to realise its goal of agricultural self-sufficiency, based upon both Germany's own resources and preferential trading arrangements, governed by economic-political criteria, within a wider regional economic system. Certainly, by 1933–4 'autarchy' had been achieved in the case of bread grains, with surpluses three years later. However, most vegetable and 20 per cent of animal fats had to be imported, thus contributing to the worsening foreign exchange crisis. By 1936, food imports still accounted for 35.5 per cent of total imports, a situation hardly improved by the proclamation of the so-called 'Battle for Production' two years earlier. Rural depopulation, rising agricultural wages, rigid price controls, and a lack of credit meant an inability to purchase machinery or artificial fertilisers, and hence an inability to keep up with the regime's grandiose targets. Farmers were also subjected to the *dirigiste* attentions of Darré's cumbersome Reich Food Estate bureaucracy, which *inter alia* maintained dossiers on each farm, dictated production targets, and penalised farmers for adulterating produce, black marketeering, or illicit slaughtering, while nonetheless presiding over an inefficient and wasteful system of distribution. The following report details the problems of Bavarian egg farmers in the summer of 1934.

> Recently in the town of Cham, where there is a district egg collection point, an entire wagon filled with eggs was ruined through being left standing out in the heat. The leader of the egg depot only wanted to release the train when it was fully loaded. Purchasing was sluggish. Whatever arrived each day was loaded on to the train and then left in the sweltering heat. The eggs were spoiled by the time they were transported. The peasants knew all about this, and were furious with the inept bigwigs 'who only know how to ride around in cars'.[22]

In some parts of Germany, the mood on the land turned as sour as the ill-distributed produce.

Cosmetic propaganda measures were designed to compensate the peasants in the realm of consciousness for what was an onerous and stagnating reality. They received their own date in the Nazi alternative festive calendar. Hitler and the prominent regularly attended an annual harvest festival held at Bückeberg, near Hameln. The festival, which was an attempt to detach the peasants from its Christian equivalent, was relayed into homes over the radio. Darré encouraged the press to refer to Hitler as 'the peasants' Chancellor', and Hitler was often photographed surrounded by beaming and colourfully dressed peasant women and children. This conveyed the fact that the harvest festival was also a form of fertility rite, a celebration of the generative powers of people as well as of turnips and potatoes. Based in Goslar, the Reich Food Estate also encouraged the wearing of folk costume in areas where it had long ceased to be fashionable, which may explain why farmers look so self-conscious wearing it in photographs. A sort of academic agrarianism was responsible for the introduction of supposedly time-honoured customs like presenting heirs with decorated spades – 'May it [the spade] never rust, and you never rest until you give the farm to your heir' being an unintentionally ironic attempt to solemnise back-breaking reality.

The Ministry of Propaganda forbade the press to print cartoons or stories ridiculing the mores and habits of peasants, which always had to be described in an idealised manner. The essentials of 'Blubo' ideology were also conveyed through the regime's extensive photoreportage output as well as in the novels, plays, films, and paintings of innumerable hack artists. Painters celebrated and made careers out of the ruddy hues of peasant faces or the plaited locks of their daughters. Such modern features of rural life as the bank manager, tractors, cars, radios, railways, or truckloads of chemical fertiliser were deliberately omitted in the interests of promoting a selective version of the rural 'heritage'. While art may have stressed the virtues of the past, as we have seen, the regime pioneered novel agrarian policies, based upon increased State control and the application of racial criteria to rural life. Possibly the Nazis' sole structural achievement in the realm of rural reality consisted of absorbing the organised political power of the large-scale landed interest. About 17,000 major landowners, controlling one-sixth of the area under cultivation, had managed to exercise a uniformly baleful influence upon the politics of the Weimar Republic, notwithstanding their dependence upon the taxpayers for the survival of their bankrupt and inefficient enterprises. The governments of Brüning and Schleicher had fallen, partly because of the behind-the-scenes machinations of the agrarian lobby, which had secured its lines to the reactionary conservative Hindenburg through the gift to the President in 1927 of an East Prussian estate at Neudeck. With their interest group organisations absorbed by Darré's apparatus, many members of this class settled down to years of active collusion with the Nazi regime. This was not just a matter of reviving their flagging economic fortunes, or of achieving traditional 'revisionist' territorial goals, but of active collusion in the regime's racial policies. To take one example, Hans Nagel, a prominent figure in the Reich Land League and in the conservative DNVP, was partly responsible for a 1941 document concerning policy in the occupied east which said:

> As many as ten million people will become superfluous in this area and will die, or will have to migrate to Siberia. Attempts to achieve surpluses from the Black Earth region to save the people there from starvation can only occur at the expense of provisioning Europe. This will hamper Germany's ability to prevail in the war, and will under-mine Germany's and Europe's steadfastness in the face of economic blockade.[23]

The loss of former Prussian territories after 1945 dealt a final blow to this pillar of the German establishment, whose dubious past virtues are now chiefly extolled to a wider public by one of the aristocratic editors of an otherwise renowned Hamburg weekly newspaper.

Although the NSDAP called itself a 'workers'' party, neither its aims nor its social basis corresponded with this description.[24] Long before 1933 the Party dropped the pseudo-socialist policies advocated by some of its members in favour of a programme organised around nationalism, anti-Marxism, and racism. Although the membership undoubtedly included significant numbers of workers, sometimes estimated at 20 per cent, these tended to be those employed by small firms or by local and central government – in other words, workers outside the organised labour movement. Before 1933 the Nazis were unable to make much of an impact upon the working class, notwithstanding their use of terroristic violence against the 'red' strongholds of working-class areas in Berlin or Hamburg.

However, within five months of coming to power the Nazis had destroyed the most powerful labour movement in western Europe. The very considerable courage of a few resistance groups cannot conceal the fact that by 1935, there were several regions in Germany without an organised working-class resistance worth speaking about.[25] The Com-munists, who were the main objects of Gestapo terror, were long on individual courage but short on organisational flexibility or political imagination. The conclusion of the Nazi–Soviet pact in 1939 brought Communist resistance activity to a virtual standstill. Only in the wake of Hitler's invasion of the Soviet Union in 1941 were new cells formed to augment the few that had survived the Gestapo's onslaught. The SPD leadership split over the parliamentary Party's confused strategy of opposing the Enabling Law, whilst simultaneously endorsing Hitler's professions of peaceful international intent. While the Party leadership retreated to Prague and other foreign capitals, Social Democrats in Germany tried to work through traditional and legal institutions so as to preserve a nucleus of the like-minded for the day when Hitler was no more. This low-key and unheroic strategy was more successful in the long term than the heroic and largely gestural activities of the self-appointed 'vanguard of the working class'. Some Social Democrats were involved in the 1944 plot to assassinate Hitler. With all due respect to those who resisted Nazism, it was unfortunately the case that this was a resistance 'movement' largely bereft of a popular following. There was no popular front, because of the ideological and social antagonism between Communists and Social Democrats, and hence no broad resistance movement. The conservative–utopian military plotters of 1944 were even more isolated. These cursory and unintentionally derogatory comments on the workers' resistance 'movement' need to be qualified. Workers formed the largest, most active, and most continuous element in what passed for a German resistance, and workers comprised the largest group persecuted by the Nazis for political reasons. However, although workers were subjected to the special attentions of the SS and Gestapo, they were also paradoxically the class whose loyalties the regime most endeavoured to secure through more than superficially seductive social and welfare policies. Much ingenuity went into neutralising this potential source of trouble, and a response was very evidently forthcoming.

For it is incorrect to depict the Nazi regime solely in terms of its infinite capacity for systematic brutality. The Nazis were well aware that terror alone would not suffice as a means of pacifying the working class and then integrating it into the 'national community'. To this end, they built up a State-controlled, emasculated alternative to the proscribed labour movement, and pursued social and economic policies which were both attractive and successful, even if, paradoxically, the working class were not always the principal beneficiaries.[26] The end of the socialist trade unions was shamefully unheroic. Despite the fact that thousands of Social Democrats and Communists were languishing behind barbed wire, the trade union leadership enjoined its members to participate in the Nazi 'Day of National Labour' on 1 May 1933. The leaders were trying to secure a niche for themselves in the new 'national community', a fact which many trade unionists are loath to recall. Twelve hours after thousands of workers had dutifully paraded past Hitler, the SS occupied trade union buildings and expropriated their assets. Union leaders such as Leipert and Grassmann were sent to concentration camps with Goebbels' slogan 'Honour work, respect the worker' still ringing in their ears. Following the prohibition of the socialist trade unions on 2 May 1933, many people expected the Nazi factory cell organisations (NSBO) simply to usurp the unions' vacant place. The factory cells were a form of pseudo-trade union which had been established by the 'left wing' of the NSDAP in order to attract those who took the word 'socialist' in the Party's title literally. They were also typical of the Nazi strategy of establishing parallel sectoral interest groups to infiltrate particular electoral constituencies. The NSBO pursued what appeared to be anti-capitalist policies, and had pretensions to becoming an effective and unified trade union organisation. The NSBO were hampered by the fact that in 1932 they had a mere 300,000 members, although numbers rose exponentially after 30 January 1933. They did badly in elections for factory councils held in March 1933, being unable to match the votes given to the existing socialist unions. Lack of success was probably one of the reasons why the NSBO failed to develop into a Nazi alternative trade union. The other reason was Hitler's distrust of this outgrowth from a wing of the NSDAP which he was bent on defeating, in the interests of maintaining his alliance with conservatives and industry. Industrial managers did not respond warmly to interference in their affairs by shop-floor NSBO functionaries, who sometimes backed up their demands for higher wages with threats of having the managers sent to concentration camps. It seemed as if the class struggle was being perpetuated within the context of the Nazi movement, regardless of the regime's corporatist and emollient socio-economic rhetoric. From Hitler's point of view the NSBO were dangerous and hence totally expendable. Where the regime's sympathies lay became clear from the Law for the Regulation of National Labour of January 1934. Managers and owners became factory 'leaders'; their workforce, a 'following' pledged to loyalty and obedience. Works councils were replaced by others whose members were selected by the NSBO.

Members of the NSBO and the defunct trade unions were offered a new resting place in the German Labour Front (DAF), established on 10 May 1933.[27] Although the DAF, which with 20 million members and a bureaucracy of 40,000 became one of the largest agencies in the Third Reich, scooped up the assets and property of the trade unions, it did not inherit the rights the latter had once enjoyed, and was in effect 'deunionised'. This fact was already apparent in its adoption of a structure which replicated that of the NSDAP rather than one based upon the usual branches of industry. The appointment on 19 May 1933 of Trustees of Labour meant that the DAF had no powers to negotiate wage settlements. The Trustees, who were responsible to Seldte, the Minister of Labour, froze the very low wage tariff established in 1933, and then endeavoured to ensure that these levels were respected. Removed from this crucial area of trade union activity, the DAF concentrated upon the improvement of conditions in the workplace, and raising both the self-esteem and the productivity of the individual worker. The DAF was undoubtedly assisted in this endeavour by the successful and popular economic policies of the regime. If the view that 'the lower middle class put Hitler in power while the working class maintained him there' is neither wholly accurate nor tenable, it does point to the workers' passive acquiescence under the Nazi regime, notwithstanding attempts by some historians to whitewash the chauvinism, racism, and consumerism of sections of the working class, while detecting 'opposition' or 'resistance' in every non-attended lathe or workbench. The far from reticent reports of the exiled SPD spoke another language, noting, for example, signs of exhaustion among overworked Ruhr miners 'which do not necessarily have anything to do with sabotage and passive resistance'.

Before turning to the activities of the DAF it is necessary to sketch in the outlines of Nazi economic policy.[28] According to official statistics, there were some six million people unemployed in early 1933. The actual number was probably much higher, for the figures omitted school leavers, seasonal workers and women in part-time employment. Most of those unemployed received no unemployment benefit payments and were dependent upon local welfare which failed to cover basic subsistence. Doss-houses and hostels were filled with the despairingly mobile young, as well as their regular clientele. Those still in work were subject to painful wage and salary cuts, with many public employees such as teachers being laid off in large numbers. This was a *novum* in German history. In other words, the number of people reduced to desperate straits had assumed proportions virtually unimaginable for most modern western Europeans. However, early in 1933 recovery was in sight, on both a national and an international level. Various German economic experts had predicted this, and had made plans involving the abandonment of narrow fiscalism in

9.7 A section of one of the new Autobahnen constructed by the regime in accordance with plans developed by, among others, the mayor of Frankfurt, in the Weimar Republic.

favour of counter-cyclical strategies based upon investment in the infrastructure and public housing, whose effect would be to reduce the number out of work. The Nazis, who initially hardly disposed of economic plans worth considering, latched on to these schemes, and used the existing economic bureaucracies to realise them. In other words, their much-vaunted job creation schemes, such as the labour-intensive construction of a major motorway network, merely represented the implementation of projects which were already in the filing cabinets of the agencies of the Weimar Republic. Policies like these were successful. Although there was still 10 per cent unemployment in 1935, with much higher percentages in economically depressed areas, the percentage of unemployed in the USA was still almost 25 per cent a year later. The regime picked up the credit for economic recovery and the general return to optimism about Germany's economic prospects. It aped the Italian example of militarising the conduct of the economy, with Hitler copying Mussolini's tactic of wielding the first shovel in front of the assembled photographers, without, however, following the Duce's penchant for baring his bull-like torso at harvest-time. Gradually, investment in the infrastructure and housing was displaced by expenditure on rearmament. While in 1933 5 per cent of the budget was expended on arms, in 1934 this rose to 18 per cent, in 1935 to 25 per cent, and in 1938 58 per cent or one-fifth of the Gross National Product. Expenditure on this vast scale resulted in a crisis of foreign exchange and a foreign trade deficit, which by 1934 amounted to 284 million Marks. It was therefore the Economics Minister Schacht's task to avert both inflation and bankruptcy with any means at his disposal. He enjoyed some temporary success in this endeavour before the requirements of war swept aside his brand of economic rationality. The Four-Year Plan, adopted on 18 October 1936, brought increased controls on sectors of the economy; the partial 'privatisation' of state agencies involved in strategic industries; and efforts to replace certain imports, e.g. gasoline and rubber, with synthetic substitutes. Captains of industry, like Carl Krauch of the chemical combine I. G. Farben, oscillated freely between the boardrooms and government-cum-military organisations, steering much of the ensuing business in the direction of their own concerns. The object was no longer to surmount the Depression, for that had been achieved already, but to prepare a broad economic base for a war of imperialist aggression. Any damage to the economy, and resentment at increased State control, would be compensated through future conquests.

This dangerous course was accompanied by enthusiasm rather than trepidation on the part of the German public. This was particularly the case with the German working class, who appeared to be the principal beneficiaries of the regime's economic policies. By 1936 there was not only full employment, but also a labour shortage in certain arms-related industries. It followed that the workers in these sectors were able to exploit a shortage of labour in their own interest. While workers in agriculture or consumer industries such as porcelain continued to receive derisory wages, with the former being overworked and the latter subject to short time and layoffs, workers in arms-related industries could use the threat of their departure to extort supplementary bonuses and other inducements, despite the fact that these were forbidden by the Trustees of Labour. Despite the sums arbitrarily deducted from wages in the name of the regime's extended list of worthwhile causes, there can be no doubt that some workers enjoyed considerable wage increases. There were a number of drawbacks. Firstly, given the regime's concentration upon armaments, there was a shortage of consumer goods available for purchase. Secondly, the movements of the workforce were subjected to increasing controls. 'Work books', detailing family circumstances, employment history, qualifications and any past difficulties with employers, were introduced in 1935. Factories were riddled with Gestapo and SD agents, while the SS patrolled the assembly lines and corridors. Absenteeism or malperformance began to be construed as evidence of biological deficiency. This last point reflected a wider attempt to break down the group solidarity of the workers by introducing divisive measures based upon competition and individual performance. This practice is best exemplified by a car plant which introduced 'self-inspectors' and 'self-calculators'.[29] The former were awarded a plaque to keep on their workbench denoting that they worked assiduously without supervision. The 'self-calculators' were entitled to set their own piece-work rates, although this simply meant that management would apply their levels of performance to the rest of the workforce. Rewards based upon individual achievement served to keep overall labour costs low while increasing worker productivity. In the case of the car plant mentioned above it also cut the costs involved in employing supervisors and foremen. In other words, working-class solidarity was destroyed while production increased. Many workers, and in particular the young and upwardly mobile, were prepared to forfeit class solidarity if the reward appeared to be an escape from an hereditary class ghetto. Only the most obtusely romantic labour historians would deny them the right to do so.

In addition to these meritocratic strategies, the regime endeavoured to improve material conditions and to raise the self-consciousness of the 'German worker'. These tasks devolved upon the DAF's 'Beauty of Labour' and 'Strength through Joy' organisations. The former adopted environmental and hygienic measures pioneered by progressive industrialists in the 1920s, although for self-interested reasons the DAF preferred to give the impression that ideas for improvements to the workplace stemmed from the factory floor. Although some of the measures adopted were purely cosmetic, like the ubiquitous geraniums which adorned the factory portals, or efforts to bring culture to the workers in the form of symphony orchestras playing Wagner in tram depots, other improvements included the provision of wholesome canteen food, better sanitation, ventilation, and lighting, and greater attention to the physical health of the worker, measures which in contemporary Britain are still associated only with Japanese or North American employers. Severally, these measures were designed to create stronger attachments between the worker and the place of production, a trend further fostered by the introduction of inter-factory competitions, which appealed to the workers' preoccupation with

9.8 Interior of an aircraft factory from a book of German Labour Front propaganda photographs designed to show improvements to the working environment.

competitive team sport. Improved medical care reflected a shift away from health as a concern of each individual towards individual health as a 'duty' to the collective, a notion encapsulated by the chilling slogan 'Your health does not belong to you!' For all the collectivist rhetoric, these measures were designed to atomise and hence control the workforce. A Sopade report from July 1935 subtly analysed the underlying intentions:

> All means are employed to prevent any form of association on the part of the workers. In many factories they are also endeavouring to isolate the individual worker as far as possible during the actual work process. The various departments are kept strictly segregated from one another. Opportunities for discussion, either while working or during breaks, have become very restricted. Instead of factory meetings with the right to speak freely, there is now the factory assembly. The 'Beauty of Labour' organisation is trying to create vast canteens, so that workers can no longer discuss things with their colleagues during breaks. Where it is at all possible, groups of workers are split into the

9.9 A 'Strength through Joy' concert in a tram depot.

smallest viable units. This means that attempts by workers to discuss even the most elementary matters among themselves take on the character of illegal activities. Outside the factories, the Nazi association 'Strength through Joy' attempts to organise their free time, so that they do not get any 'stupid ideas'. The Labour Front is not only an embarrassing solution, but also a large-scale attempt to prevent the worker from associating with others, whether it be privately or in purely social circles or clubs, without being subject to control.[30]

The 'Strength through Joy' (KdF) organisation also endeavoured to introduce the reward for performance principle into the worker's free time. Leisure became State-controlled. The regime extended the number of paid holidays from an average of three days in 1933 to between six and twelve days per annum, depending on the sector of employment. The KdF organised what was bruited as mass tourism, with group excursions to the Black Forest or North Sea coast for the less favoured, and cruises to Norway or Madeira for the lucky. These trips were cheap – employers thought it worthwhile to contribute – with a seven-day cruise to the fjords costing 60RMs, or a week hoping to photograph the Führer at Berchtesgaden for 29RMs. Up to 1939 about seven million Germans had availed themselves of KdF vacations, although it should be noted that only some 17 per cent

9.10 *A poster advertising a 'Strength through Joy' cruise holiday in Norway. The caption reads 'Now you can travel too!'*

9.11 Hitler being presented with a model VW 'Beetle' car by the industrialist Porsche and Robert Ley, leader of the Labour Front. Hitler admired entrepreneurs as winners in 'the economic life struggle'.

of cruise passengers were described as 'workers'. Inevitably, Party functionaries and the middle classes made up most of the holidaymakers. Mass tourism was part of a wider attempt to give the worker the feeling that no doors were barred to him. Although bourgeois establishments put up signs which made it clear the rough and ready were unwelcome, workers gained the impression that in theory they could visit any theatre, dance hall, tennis or riding club. They were also sold the idea that if they worked hard enough they would be able to fulfil such quintessentially modern aspirations as owning their own motor car. Some 360,000 people paid weekly contributions to the DAF in the expectation that one day they would have the 990RMs for a Volkswagen 'Beetle' in which they could speed along at 100kms per hour on one of the new motorways. In reality, the Volkswagen plants, whose contemporary virtues are based upon much past credulity, as well as the labour of Turkish, Yugoslav, and Neapolitan migrant labour, were soon producing military vehicles rather than the 'people's car'. Severally, these policies gave the 'German worker' a feeling of well-being in a society whose class barriers appeared to be falling, even though objective indicators have subsequently shown that this was not

the case. By 1937 the exiled SPD had to concede that these policies
were successful, and that the food-soldiers of the labour movement were
not as stoically self-denying as they liked to imagine: 'The experience
of recent years has unfortunately demonstrated that the petit-bourgeois
inclinations of part of the working class are unfortunately greater than
we had earlier recognised.'[31] This was in the nature of an understate-
ment.

The ambitions of Ley and the DAF bureaucracy, which alone comprised
some 40,000 paid and honorary functionaries, and the necessity of offer-
ing the German workforce concrete compensation for the sacrifices of war
resulted in the DAF's Scientific Labour Institute's plans for a comprehensive welfare system. In a speech delivered in September 1940, Ley grandly
proclaimed that 'the German people will be rewarded for the sacrifices of
war with a carefree old age. In ten years Germany will be transformed
beyond recognition. A nation of proletarians will have become a nation of
rulers. In ten years a German worker will look better than an English lord
does today.'[32] The DAF's plans included a uniform State old age and
disability pensions scheme; improved industrial and family preventative
medicine, with increased patient choice; industrial training programmes;
an expansion of public housing; and more provision for rest and recreation.
Severally these measures have sometimes been compared to the British
Beveridge Report. However, it is vital to note the differences of underlying
objectives, beyond superficially similar integrationary intentions. While the
projected pensions scheme had undeniably egalitarian features, in the sense
that all of those employed were obliged to contribute, those deemed to be
'alien', 'asocial', of 'lesser racial value', or who had been convicted for
'activities inimical to the interests of the state' were simply to be excluded
from entitlements under the system. In other words, old age pensions
became a means of increasing the regime's totalitarian control from the
cradle to the grave. Behind the projected increase in the number of family
and works physicians, sanatoria, and medicinal baths lay a thoroughly
mechanistic and inhuman attitude towards human beings: 'We must
achieve a position whereby each German is overhauled every four or five
years. Just as one periodically services an engine, so human beings must
also be periodically overhauled and maintained in preventative health.' The
object was to extend the worker's labour potential, while synchronising
the decline of his or her productive powers with the onset of physiological
death. Finally, Ley's plans – in his capacity as Reich Commissar for the
Construction of Public Housing – for three- to five-room houses and
apartments, with rents related to income and numbers of children, were

9.12 A poster designed to recruit foreign labour in occupied France. Candidates are being presented with the choice between thriving in Germany or allying themselves with the English, depicted here as on the way to defeat.

designed to encourage larger families, and hence reflected the regime's wider racial preoccupations.

The initial successes of the regime on the far-flung battlefields of Europe were enthusiastically acclaimed by virtually all sections of the population. The SD reported 'a previously unprecedented inner solidarity' and the effective demise of political opposition. The regime's increasing use of concentration camp and foreign forced labour made the working class more or less passive accomplices in Nazi racial policy.[33] The resort to foreign labour, which of course contradicted the regime's ideological fixation with racial purity, was largely conditioned by its reluctance to increase the proportion of women in the workforce. The first 'recruits' were unemployed Polish agricultural labourers, who were soon accompanied by prisoners of war and people abducted en masse from cinemas or churches. These were then followed by the French. By the summer of 1941 there were some three million foreign workers in Germany, a figure which mushroomed to 7.7 million in the autumn of 1944. In terms of national origins, there were almost 2.8 million

Russians, 1.7 million Poles, 1.3 million French, 590,000 Italians, 280,000 Czechs, 270,000 Dutch, and a quarter of a million Belgians. A high proportion of these workers were either young or female. By 1944, a quarter of those working in the German economy were foreigners. Virtually every German worker was thus confronted by the fact and practice of Nazi racism. In some branches of industry, German workers merely constituted a thin, supervisory layer above a workforce of which between 80 and 90 per cent were foreigners. This tends to be passed over by historians of the labour movement.

Treatment of these foreign workers was largely determined by their 'racial' origins. Broadly speaking, the usual hierarchy consisted of 'German workers' at the top, 'west workers' a stage below them, and Poles and 'eastern workers' at the lowest level. This racial hierarchy determined both living conditions and the degree of coercion to which foreign workers were subjected both at the workplace and in society at large. Foreign forced labourers were more liable to be sent to a factory disciplinary camp or a concentration camp than their German colleagues. Work disciplinary camps were established on the basis of an edict issued by Himmler in 1941 and were run by the Gestapo. 'Slackers' could be held there for a maximum of fifty-six days, following which 'recidivists' were sent to concentration camps. Of the 321 people sent to a disciplinary camp for 'slackers' in north Westphalia between February and March 1944, 294 of the victims were foreigners and only twenty-seven Germans. The ratio of foreigners to Germans sent to concentration camps for the same offence was 15:1. Although the presence of SS factory guards and SD spies made 'normal' factory life bad enough, conditions in these work disciplinary camps were appallingly brutal. A German Volkswagen worker recalled what he had seen as an inmate of 'Camp 21' in Hallendorf near Salzgitter.

> During my four months' sojourn in Camp 21 I was repeatedly abused with kicks and blows . . . It is true that every month several foreign workers were hanged in Camp 21, as I witnessed with my own eyes. They were Poles and Russians. I do not remember the names of those hanged. The executions were always ordered by the camp commandant. Mistreatment by the camp's SS guards was a daily occurrence. It was also frequently the case that foreign workers who collapsed because of exhaustion and who were therefore no longer capable of work were beaten to death. In September 1942 I was transferred from Camp 21 to the concentration camp at Sachsenhausen from which I was released in November 1942.[34]

'Eastern workers' were regarded as expendable. Indeed, the decision to deploy Soviet prisoners of war in the German economy was only taken after 60 per cent of the 3,350,000 Soviet POWs had already died of starvation or maltreatment in captivity. Those who survived the POW camps for employment in German factories and mines were often so undernourished and exhausted that heavy manual labour rapidly killed them. As a DAF official complacently explained to a factory manager in Essen: when a hundred thousand of these 'people without souls' expired, there would be another hundred thousand immediately available to take their place. A report on Russian civilian workers in March 1943 revealed deplorable conditions:

> Most of their complaints have to do with long working hours (up to 18 hours a day), and the heavy, dirty work and the absence of days off. They frequently complain that despite the cold they have to work in ragged clothing or in shoes which are falling apart, or with no shoes at all . . . More and more frequently they complain about the thin soup, or unpeeled potatoes, turnips, and inadequate rations of bread (150g, 200g). Since food is inadequate, they secretly purchase cabbage or turnips in the town and eat them raw. If they are caught doing this, they are punished (three days' detention) . . . As a result of this dearth of food there is a flourishing black market, at extortionate prices, in many camps. A kilo of bread costs as much as 15RMs . . . Complaints about cold barracks: 'Lightly-built timber huts which threaten to fall apart at any moment'. Vermin as a result of inadequate sanitation . . . Complaints about poor wages, 1, 2, 3RMs per week and frequently no pay at all (for up to half a year) . . . 'The clothes are new, only the holes are old.' More and more complaints about a lack of clothing and footwear . . . Most of the complaints concern inadequate or perfunctory medical treatment and a refusal to tolerate sickness ('driven away like a dog by the physician'). Having to work, when they do not feel able to do so, in cases of illness the rations are often reduced or withdrawn entirely . . . Many complaints about life behind the barbed wire and barred windows of the camps, about restrictions upon free time and prohibitions on going out on days off . . . Many complaints about the way they are treated: 'Children throw stones at us on the streets, and regard us like dogs.' Complaints about being called 'Russian pigs'. 'People regard us as animals.' 'Since people call us Bolsheviks, that is what we want to be.' Very frequent complaints about being beaten by the landlord ('with a club'), by the foremen ('with a hammer and crowbar') and by the police: 'I know people who have blue and green marks all over their bodies.'[35]

Conditions for Russian workers only improved when diseases in their camps reached epidemic proportions, or when industrialists and the military grew concerned about their low productivity. Inevitably, many foreign workers mentally or physically collapsed because of appalling treatment;

many young women workers also became pregnant. Initially, those who fell ill were simply repatriated once it was apparent that rapid recovery was unlikely. However, the arrival in occupied Poland of trainloads of sick or pregnant passengers was liable to enlighten the local population as to working conditions for foreign workers in the Reich, while burdening such Polish health services as still existed. The running down of the 'euthanasia' programme, and the resultant murderous medical capacity standing idle in the asylums, meant that sick or mentally disturbed foreign workers were no longer repatriated but sent from 'collection camps' to Hadamar or Kaufbeuren, where they were killed with lethal medication. The same fate awaited the 'racially undesirable' children of Russian or Polish female foreign workers. Himmler was especially exercised by sexual relations between Germans and foreign workers. Whereas Polish or Russian men were usually summarily executed for sleeping with German women, Polish or Russian women who became pregnant through German men were taken to special delivery camps for Eastern workers. There, their newborn children were subjected to racial selection. Those babies who failed the test were starved or killed with lethal injections.[36]

'Eastern workers' were subject to harsh discipline at the workplace, and a combination of petty discriminatory measures and lethal sanctions for 'misconduct' outside it. A series of instructions issued by the Dresden Gestapo on 16 November 1942 to those responsible for supervising foreign forced labour gives a clear idea of the discrimination, segregation, and legalised brutality to which these people were subjected:

A. Identification

The following are compelled to wear identificatory markings at all times:

(1) Polish civilian workers from both the Generalgouvernement and the incorporated eastern territories brought to the Reich after 1.9.39 ('P').

(2) Eastern workers ('OST').

No identificatory markings have been introduced for other civilian workers.

B. Accommodation

(1) Poles: civilian Polish workers employed in industry are to be kept in closed camps; those who work on the land are to be kept apart from German national comrades. Common meals between Germans and Poles are prohibited.

Anlage

zu § 1 Abſ. 2 der vorſtehenden Polizeiverordnung über die Kenntlichmachung
im Reich eingeſetzter Zivilarbeiter und =arbeiterinnen polniſchen Volkstums

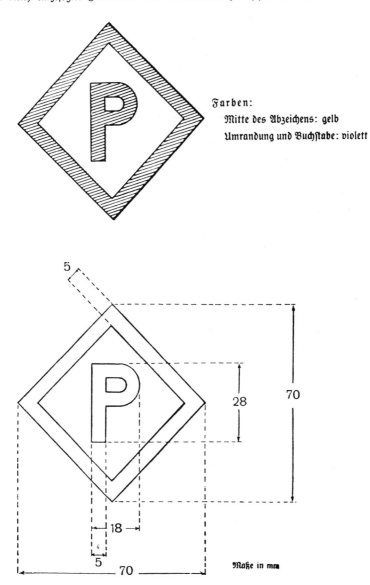

Farben:

   Mitte des Abzeichens: gelb

   Umrandung und Buchſtabe: violett

Maße in mm

*9.13 Diagram (March 1940) showing how to make the 'P' symbol
designating Polish foreign forced labourers. The symbol (violet on yellow)
was to be worn on the right breast area.*

(2) Eastern workers: eastern workers are to be housed in closed and permanently guarded camps. In cases where they are employed individually on the land or in domestic service they are to be kept strictly apart from German and other foreign civilian workers. Their quarters must be capable of being locked. Common meals with Germans and other civilian foreign workers are prohibited.

(3) As far as possible, the remaining civilian foreign workers should be housed in camps in which the camp regulations issued by the DAF apply. In so far as accommodation on an individual basis is unavoidable, members of the Germanic races are to be given precedence.

C. Restrictions on movement

(1) Poles are forbidden to leave their place of employment without the permission of the police.

(2) Eastern workers are forbidden to move outside their camps and place of work while not under guard. Those eastern workers employed as domestic servants are not permitted to leave the home unless for work-related reasons, or for more than three hours per week during daylight for purposes of recreation.

(3) With the exception of those workers from allied or friendly sovereign states, or the Germanic races, the movements of other foreign workers are restricted to the district or town in which their place of employment is located.

D. Use of public transport

(1) Poles are forbidden to use public transport without written permission from the police.

(2) Eastern workers are forbidden to use public transport.

E. Visits to restaurants, places of entertainment, sports places and public events

(1) Poles are forbidden to have any social contacts with Germans, especially visits to theatres, cinemas, restaurants, sporting and other types of event. Polish workers are only permitted to consume alcohol in places which have been designated for their use.

(2) There is no question of eastern workers having access to theatres, cinemas, restaurants, sporting or other types of event.

(3) All remaining civilian workers, and especially those from former enemy states, must conduct themselves with appropriate modesty while visiting any public establishment or gathering. The police will take action in cases of presumptuous behaviour.

F. Religious observance

(1) Poles are only permitted to attend Sunday services, apart from on high feast days, in churches or profane meeting places suited to religious purposes on the first Sunday of the month between 10 a.m. and noon. It is forbidden to use the Polish language in either the service or song. Restrictions on the movement of Poles are to be observed. Subject to police permission, Poles may travel in sealed transportation to religious services held within a radius of up to 5kms.

(2) There is no question of religious services for eastern workers.

G. Sexual relations

(1) Sexual intercourse or other immoral dealings with Germans will be punished with the death penalty in the case of

(i) Poles

(ii) eastern workers and

(iii) workers from the former Baltic states (Lithuanians, Estonians, and Latvians)

(iv) workers from the Generalgouvernement of non-Polish nationality (Ukrainians, White Ruthenians, etc.)

Female workers from the above-mentioned nationalities will be kept in protective custody for an indefinite period of time. All those civilian foreign workers to whom these provisions apply will be informed of the consequences of sexual intercourse upon commencing employment.

(2) Sexual relations between subjects of the Protectorate and Germans is not allowed, unless they have received permission to marry from the President of the governments.

(3) Moreover, sexual relations between civilian foreign workers and Germans in general are undesirable. These relations are to be discouraged through continuous education and enlightenment of German national comrades. The wives and daughters of soldiers serving in the field are to be especially protected.

IV

State police measures will be taken against every German national comrade who fails to exercise the appropriate restraint in relations with civilian foreign workers, and in particular in cases where they are responsible for non-observance of the regulations or where they aid and abet civilian foreign workers in contravention of the regulations restricting their movements and activities.

V

Association with POWs is forbidden under clause 4 of the Decree for the Protection of the Defence of the German People of 25.11.39, and in the case of serious infringements will be punished with a term of imprisonment. This encompasses not only sexual relations but also attempts to cultivate any confidential relations.

Fundamentals: The POW is a member of a nation which forced us into a world war and therefore he is an enemy of the nation.[37]

This legally-sanctioned discrimination, which did indeed result in Poles or Russians being hanged for sleeping with German women, was accompanied by much invidious treatment at the hands of ordinary German employers and workmates. Poles who worked on the land recalled with particular bitterness being directed to separate tables, and commensurately poor food, while the German *Herrenmenschen* ate their fill. Petty farmyard tyrants had to be called 'boss', and only prefaced commands with the word 'please' the day before Allied soldiers arrived. Every German victory seemed to heighten the mean-mindedness of the Poles' peasant masters and mistresses, particularly in areas with a history of nationality conflict. Josef Pieczewski, who was employed on a farm in Hither Pomerania, recalled:

> The Germans triumphed, achieving one victory after another. In June 1940 our situation became desperate. France had surrendered. The Germans went wild with joy. Demmin sank beneath a sea of swastikas, the radio was full of special bulletins and raucous speeches from the Führer of the Third Reich. Chauvinistic songs rang out all over the place. The arrogance and hostility of the German population towards the Poles grew with the victories at the front . . . More and more frequently one saw signs on shop doors saying 'For Germans only' or 'Poles prohibited'. Our 'Frau' Bork joined in the rhythm of increasing anti-Polish chicanery. In addition to the restrictions she had already imposed on us, she added the ban on our drawing water from her well. She informed us that 'there is water enough in the river for the Poles'. We now had to get our water for cooking from the Peene.[38]

Relations between foreign forced workers and German industrial workers were not much better. This was especially the case where the presence of large numbers of foreign workers enabled Germans to move into supervisory positions and thus enjoy a degree of occupational and social mobility which their own modest talents would otherwise have denied them. Even the most incompetent dullard could lord it over the Poles and Russians. Apart from the nation's foremen, and cases of brutality by, for example, miners in the Ruhr towards the Russian sub-class below them, most German workers seem to have been largely indifferent to the fact that they were working alongside an undernourished army which emerged spectrally from freezing camps but was excluded from public air-raid shelters and swimming baths, and which could be strung up for doing things which the rest of the population took for granted. Informed commentators such as Ulrich Herbert have noted that the principal reason for this response was that Nazi racial policy towards foreign workers interacted with the arrogant self-regard, chauvinism, and racism of some sections of the German working class. This suggests that the Nazis' novel efforts to replace class with racial society found a ready response in significant sections of the population. Judging by studies of how many 'German workers' treat their Turkish colleagues in present-day factories or service industries, these attitudes seem to have survived the Nazi period, which for some workers, marginalised by the 'elbow society' of the Federal Republic and attracted to the extreme Republican party, has become an object of nostalgia as a time of strong and successful government. Working-class racism is, of course, not exclusively confined to Germany.

CONCLUSION: NATIONAL SOCIALIST RACIAL AND SOCIAL POLICY

DID the Third Reich pursue modern rather than profoundly reactionary policies? This question is among the most important posed by recent research. If the Third Reich was a modern and modernising regime, then it can hardly be said to have been the culmination of a German separate road of historical development, but rather is to be compared to other modern regimes, whether Communist, Fascist, or democratic. Questions concerning whether Hitler or other agencies and individuals were responsible for particular policies pale into insignificance beside the implications of this thesis. If the modernising theory is correct, then not only do the crimes of Nazi Germany cease to be singular, but they become comparable with the crimes of other regimes, or indeed part of the 'pathology' of advanced societies in general. Just as the highly dubious Milgram psychological tests apparently 'prove' that we are all capable of torture, so the modernisation theorists would like us to believe that all our societies are latently like Nazi Germany. Of course this is not so. Vacuous notions like 'body fascism' and the indiscriminately inflationary use of the term 'fascist' to describe anyone who happens to disagree with a particular point of view compound this (discomforting) delusion.

Although in our opinion the question of the modern or anti-modern character of the Nazi regime is of central importance, it has received relatively little attention in the existing secondary literature, firstly because there has been no comprehensive treatment of Nazi racial and social policy, and secondly because the inner relationships between the different areas of policy have been neglected. Finally, it is often overlooked that social policy was designed to achieve a global remodelling of society in accordance with racial criteria.

The essential elements of the resulting barbaric utopia had been considered long before Hitler achieved political power. Racial ideologies were not solely concerned with a return to some imagined past social order. They also reflected the desire to create a future society based upon the alleged verities of race. Hitler took over existing ideas and converted them into a comprehensive programme for a racial new order. Without doubt, racial anti-Semitism was the key element in a programme designed to achieve the 'recovery' of the 'Aryan Germanic race'. Various racial-hygienic measures were designed to achieve this goal. These ranged from compulsory sterilisation to murdering the sick, the 'asocial', and those designated as being of 'alien race'. The extermination of the Jews was crucial to these policies. In Hitler's mind they were not only 'racial aliens', but also a threat to his plans for the 'racial recovery' of the German people. They were both a 'lesser race' and one bent upon destroying the 'racial properties' of Hitler's 'Aryans'.

Under the Third Reich, this racial-ideological programme became the official dogma and policy of the State. Racism replaced the Weimar Republic's imperfect experiment in political pluralism. Along with the political parties and trade unions, the Nazis also endeavoured to destroy the existing social structure. Although there were undoubtedly social classes in Nazi Germany, it was a society organised increasingly upon racial rather than class lines. The regime's racial policies struck at people whether they were rich or poor, bourgeois, peasants, or workers.

As we have seen, this racial new order was based upon the 'purification of the body of the nation' of all those categorised as being 'alien', 'hereditarily ill', or 'asocial'. That meant Jews, Sinti and Roma, the mentally and physically handicapped, 'community aliens', and homosexuals. Obviously there were major quantitative and qualitative differences in the degree of persecution to which these groups were subjected. Jews, as the racial group whom the Nazis regarded as the greatest threat, undoubtedly constituted the largest single group of victims and were persecuted in the most intensive and brutal manner. Persecution undoubtedly had different specificities. This should not result in attempts either to relativise or to overlook the sufferings of others, let alone a ghoulish and profoundly inhuman competition to claim the right to having been most persecuted. All of these people were persecuted for the same reasons, although the degree of persecution was bound up with how threatening the regime perceived them to be.

The regime's 'national community' was based upon the exclusion and extermination of all those deemed to be 'alien', 'hereditarily ill', or 'asocial'. These 'elements' were subject to constant and escalating forms of selection. The 'national community' itself was categorised in accordance with racial criteria. The criteria included not merely 'racial purity' but also biological health and socio-economic performance. Members of the 'national community' were also compelled to reproduce through a series of measures ranging from financial inducements to criminal sanctions. The inducements contained in the regime's social legislation were also conditional upon an individual's racial 'value', health, and performance.

For biological reasons, women were particularly affected by the regime's attempts at racial selective breeding. Women's worth was assessed in terms of their ability to produce as many Aryan, healthy, and capable children as possible. Women were therefore reduced to the status of mere 'reproductive machines'. Racially-motivated anti-feminism represented a significant departure from traditional Christian–Conservative anti-feminism. The Nazis' hierarchically organised, racist society, with healthy, 'Aryan' German man at the apex, began to rival the existing social order. However, it failed to supersede it for a variety of reasons. The first is that changes on this scale required longer than twelve years to be realised, a fact which makes any generalisations concerning the impact of the regime on German society difficult. Secondly, there were disagreements within the ruling cartel about the forms, radicalism, and tempo with which a consensually approved racial programme should be implemented. Finally, political and military considerations forced the regime to establish priorities and to postpone some of its plans until the post-war period. In other words, social policy was heavily influenced by military, economic, and domestic-political considerations, not least by the desire to integrate and pacify the population in a wartime crisis.

The main object of social policy remained the creation of a hierarchical racial new order. Everything else was subordinate to this goal, including the regime's conduct of foreign affairs and the war. In the eyes of the regime's racial politicians, the Second World War was above all a racial war, to be pursued with immense brutality until the end, that is until the concentration camps were liberated by invading Allied armies. All of these points draw attention to the specific and singular character of the Third Reich. It was not a form of regression to past times, although the regime frequently instrumentalised various ahistorical myths to convey the idea of historical normalcy. Its objects were novel and *sui generis*: to realise an ideal future world, without 'lesser races', without the sick, and without those who they decreed had no place in the 'national community'. The Third Reich was intended to be a racial rather than a class society. This fact in itself makes existing theories, whether based upon modernisation, totalitarianism, or global theories of Fascism, poor heuristic devices for a greater understanding of what was a singular regime without precedent or parallel.

NOTES

1 HOW MODERN, GERMAN, AND
TOTALITARIAN WAS THE THIRD REICH?

1 Cited by Lothar Baier in his afterword to Karl Otten, *Geplante Illusionen. Eine Analyse des Faschismus* (Frankfurt am Main), p. 347.

2 Karl Otten, *A Combine of Aggression: Masses, Elites and Dictatorship in Germany* (London, 1942).

3 Robert Gilbert Vansittart, *Black Record: German Past and Present* (London, 1941), *The German Octopus* (London, 1945).

4 William Montgomery McGovern, *From Luther to Hitler: The History of Fascist-Nazi Philosophy* (New York, 1946).

5 Henry Morgenthau, *Germany is our Problem* (New York, 1945).

6 Theodore N. Kaufmann, *Germany Must Perish* (Newark, 1941).

7 Z. Nejedly, 'Drang nach Osten', in *Vekovaja bar' ba zapadnych i juznich slavajan ptovi germanskoj agressij* (Moscow, 1944); V. D. Koroljuk (ed.), *Germanskaja expansija Central' noj i Vostocnoj Evrope. Sbornik stej po istorii tak nazyvaemogo 'Drang nach Osten'* (Moscow, 1965); 'Drang nach Osten', *Bolsaja Sovetskaja Enciklopedija*, Vol. 15 (Moscow, 1952), pp. 175–7. For further examples see Wolfgang Wippermann, *Der 'Deutsche Drang nach Osten'. Ideologie und Wirklichkeit eines politischen Schlagwortes* (Darmstadt, 1981), pp. 60ff.; Hans-Heinrich Nolte, *'Drang nach Osten'. Sowjetische Geschichtsschreibung der deutschen Ostexpansion* (Frankfurt am Main, 1976).

8 On this theme see: E. Oberländer, *Sowjetpatriotismus und Geschichte. Dokumentation* (Cologne, 1967); Anatole G. Mazour, *Modern Russian Historiography* (Princeton, 1958); Georg von Rauch, 'Grundlinien der sowjetischen Geschichtsforschung im Zeichen des Stalinismus', *Europa Archiv*, 5 (1950), pp. 3383–8; 3423–32; 3489–94.

9 For the following see Wolfgang Wippermann, *Faschismustheorien. Zum Stand der gegenwärtigen Diskussion*, 5th fully revised edition (Darmstadt, 1989), pp. 80ff.; Henry Ashby Turner, 'Fascism and Modernisation', in Turner (ed.), *Reappraisals of Fascism* (New York, 1975), pp. 117–39; Horst

Matzerath and Heinrich Volkmann, 'Modernisierungstheorie und National-sozialismus', in Jürgen Kocka (ed.), *Theorien in der Praxis des Historikers* (Göttingen, 1977), pp. 86–116.

10 Franz Borkenau, 'Zur Soziologie des Faschismus', *Archiv für Sozial-wissenschaft und Sozialpolitik*, 68 (1933), reprinted in Ernst Nolte (ed.), *Theorien über den Faschismus* (Cologne, 1967), pp. 156–81.

11 For orthodox Marxist-Leninist discussions of Fascism, see Wolfgang Wippermann, *Zur Analyse des Faschismus. Die sozialistischen und kommunistischen Faschismustheorien 1921–1945* (Frankfurt am Main, 1981), and *Faschismustheorien*, pp. 11–57.

12 Luigi Sturzo, *Italien und der Faschismus* (Cologne, 1926). Cited here after E. Nolte (ed.), *Faschismustheorien*, pp. 221–34, especially p. 225.

13 Francesco Nitti, *Bolschewismus, Faschismus und Demokratie* (Munich, 1926).

14 Nitti, *Bolschewismus, Faschismus*, p. 53.

15 Friedrich Meinecke, 'Nationalsozialismus und Bürgertum' (21 December 1930), in Friedrich Meinecke, *Werke* (Stuttgart, 1969), Vol. 2, pp. 441–5.

16 Walter Gerhart (= Waldemar Gurian), *Um des Reiches Zukunft. Nationale Wiedergeburt oder politische Reaktion?* (Freiburg, 1932).

17 Hermann Rauschning, *The Revolution of Nihilism* (London, 1938).

18 Rudolf Hilferding, 'Das historische Problem', *Zeitschrift für Politik*, Neue Folge 1 (1954), pp. 293–324. A Russian summary of this essay appeared in *Sotsialisticheskii Vestnik* (April, 1940), pp. 118–20. Hilferding's essay had a considerable influence upon Karl Dietrich Bracher and other West German students of National Socialism.

19 Ernst Fraenkel, *The Dual State* (New York, 1940). A German translation of this important work only appeared in 1974.

20 Franz L. Neumann, *Behemoth: The Structure and Practice of National Socialism 1933–1944* (New York, 1944). A German edition of Neumann's work, with a good introduction, appeared in 1977.

21 Curt Geyer, *Die Partei der Freiheit* (Paris, 1939).

22 Hans Günther, *Der Herren eigener Geist*. Werner Röhr and Simone Barck (eds.), *Ausgewählte Schriften* (Berlin and Weimar, 1981).

23 Ernst Bloch, *Erbschaft dieser Zeit* (Frankfurt am Main, 1962, reprint of 1935 edition).

24 On what follows see Wolfgang Wippermann, '"Deutsche Katastrophe" oder "Diktatur des Finanzkapitals"? Zur Interpretationsgeschichte des Dritten Reiches im Nachkriegsdeutschland', in Horst Denkler, Karl Prümm (eds.), *Die deutsche Literatur im Dritten Reich* (Stuttgart, 1976), pp. 9–43, 'The Post-War German Left and Fascism', *Journal of Contemporary History*, 11 (1976), pp. 185–220, 'Forschungsgeschichte und Forschungsprobleme', in Wippermann (ed.), *Kontroversen um Hitler* (Frankfurt am Main, 1986), pp. 13–116; Gerhard Schreiber, *Hitler. Interpretationen 1923–1983. Ergebnisse, Methoden und Probleme der Forschung* (Darmstadt, 1988); Ian Kershaw, *The Nazi Dictatorship: Problems and Perspectives of Interpretation* (London, 1989, 2nd edition).

25 Friedrich Meinecke, *The German Catastrophe* (Boston, 1950). On this see Wolfgang Wippermann, 'Friedrich Meineckes "Die deutsche Katastrophe" –

Ein Versuch zur deutschen Vergangenheitsbewältigung', in Michael Erbe (ed.), *Friedrich Meinecke Heute* (Berlin, 1982), pp. 110-21.

26 Gerhard Ritter, *Europa und die deutsche Frage. Betrachtungen über die geschichtliche Eigenart des deutschen Staatsdenkens* (Munich, 1948), *Geschichte als Bildungsmacht. Ein Beitrag zur historisch-politischen Neubesinnung* (Stuttgart, 1947), *Das deutsche Problem. Grundfragen deutschen Staatslebens gestern und heute* (Munich, 1962).

27 On the significance of totalitarian theory within research on German National Socialism, see Wippermann, *Faschismustheorien*, pp. 51ff. and 96ff.; Walter Schlangen, *Die Totalitarismustheorie. Entwicklung und Probleme* (Stuttgart, 1976).

28 Alexander Abusch, *Der Irrweg einer Nation. Ein Beitrag zum Verständnis deutscher Geschichte* (Berlin, 1946); Ernst Niekisch, *Deutsche Daseins-verfehlung* (Berlin, 1946); Paul Wandel, *Die junkerlich–imperialistische Politik des 'Dranges nach dem Osten' – ein Unglück für das deutsche und polnische Volk* (Berlin, 1952).

29 On GDR research on Fascism, see A. Dorpalen, *German History in Marxist Perspective* (London, 1985).

30 Edmond Vermeil, *L'Allemagne contemporaine sociale, politique et culturelle*, Vol. 2: *La République de Weimar et la Troisième Reich 1918–1950* (Paris, 1953); A. J. P. Taylor, *The Course of German History* (London, 1945), *The Origins of the Second World War* (London, 1963, 2nd edition); Marian Friedberg, *Kultura polska a niemiecka. Elementy rdozime a wpywie niemiecki w ustroju i kulturze Polski* (Poznań, 1946).

31 See, in general, Christoph Klessmann, *Die doppelte Staatsgründung. Deutsche Geschichte 1945–1955* (Göttingen, 1982); also the apologetic study by Peter Steinbach, *Nationalsozialistische Gewaltverbrechen. Die Diskussion in der deutschen Öffentlichkeit nach 1945* (Berlin, 1981); more critically, Jörg Friedrich, *Freisprüche für die Nazi-Justiz. Die Urteile gegen NS-Richter seit 1948. Eine Dokumentation* (Reinbeck, 1983); Ingo Müller, *Furchtbare Juristen. Die unbewältigte Vergangenheit unser Justiz* (Munich, 1987).

32 On the history of neo-Fascism in the Federal Republic, see Richard Stöss, *Die extreme Rechte in der Bundesrepublik. Entwicklung–Ursachen–Gegenmassnahmen* (Opladen, 1989). Still valuable on the NPD is Wolfgang Benz (ed.), *Rechtsextremismus in der Bundesrepublik. Voraussetzungen, Zusammenhänge, Wirkungen* (Frankfurt am Main, 1984); Peter Dudek and Hans Gerd Jaschke, *Entstehung und Entwicklung des Rechtsextremismus in der Bundesrepublik*, Vols. 1–2 (Opladen, 1984); Reinhard Kühnl et al., *Die NPD. Struktur, Ideologie und Funktion einer neofaschistischen Partie* (Frankfurt am Main, 1969); Lutz Niethammer, *Angepasster Faschismus. Politische Praxis der NPD* (Frankfurt am Main, 1969).

33 On the failure of 'denazification', see: Jürgen Fürstenau, *Entnazifizierung* (Neuwied, 1969); Klaus-Dieter Henke, *Politische Säuberung unter französischer Besatzung. Die Entnazifizierung in Württemberg-Hohenzollern* (Stuttgart, 1981); Lutz Niethammer, *Entnazifizierung in Bayern* (Frankfurt am Main, 1972).

34 Fritz Fischer, *Germany's Aims in the First World War* (New York, 1967). On

the controversy, see Immanuel Geiss, 'Die Fischer-Kontroverse. Ein kritischer Beitrag zum Verhältnis zwischen Historiographie und Politik in der Bundesrepublik', in his *Studien über Geschichte und Geschichtswissenschaft* (Frankfurt am Main, 1972), pp. 107–98.

35 Hans-Ulrich Wehler, *Bismarck und der Imperialismus* (Berlin, 1969), *Krisenherde des Kaiserreiches 1871–1918* (Göttingen, 1970), *Das Deutsche Kaiserreich 1871–1918* (Göttingen, 1973), translated into English as *The German Empire: 1871–1918* (Leamington Spa, 1985).

36 Ernst Nolte, *Der Faschismus in seiner Epoche* (Munich, 1963).

37 These issues are discussed in Bruno Seidel and Siegfried Jenkner (eds.), *Wege der Totalitarismusforschung* (Darmstadt, 1968).

38 Carl Joachim Friedrich and Zbigniew Brzezinski, *Totalitarian Dictatorship and Autocracy* (Cambridge, 1956).

39 Hans Mommsen, 'Nationalsozialismus', in *Sowjetsystem und demokratische Gesellschaft*, Vol. 4 (Freiburg, 1971), pp. 695–713, especially p. 702. See also Georg Hirschfeld and Lothar Kettenacker (eds.), *Der 'Führerstaat': Mythos und Realität. Studien zur Struktur und Politik des Dritten Reiches* (Stuttgart, 1981).

40 Ralf Dahrendorf, *Society and Democracy in Germany* (London, 1968). See also Jeremy Noakes, 'Nazism and Revolution'; N. O'Sullivan (ed.), *Revolutionary Theory and Political Reality* (London, 1983), pp. 73–100; and Jens Alber, 'Nationalsozialismus und Modernisierung', *Kölner Zeitschrift für Soziologie und Sozialpsychologie*, 41 (1989), pp. 346–65 for critical views of the arguments of Dahrendorf and Schoenbaum.

41 David Schoenbaum, *Hitler's Social Revolution* (New York, 1966).

42 Timothy Mason, *Sozialpolitik im Dritten Reich* (Opladen, 1977).

43 Karl Dietrich Bracher, 'Tradition und Revolution im Nationalsozialismus', in his *Zeitgeschichtliche Kontroversen. Zum Faschismus, Totalitarismus, Demokratie* (Munich, 1976), pp. 62–78.

44 Henry Ashby Turner, 'Fascism and Modernisation', in his *Reappraisals of Fascism* (New York, 1975), pp. 117–39.

45 Hans-Dieter Schäfer, *Das gespaltene Bewusstsein. Deutsche Kultur und Lebenswirklichkeit 1933–1945* (Frankfurt am Main, 1984).

46 Detlev Peukert, *Inside Nazi Germany* (London, 1989).

47 Götz Aly, Karl-Heinz Roth, *Die restlose Erfassung. Volkszählen, Identifizieren, Aussondern im Nationalsozialismus* (Berlin, 1984); Karl-Heinz Roth (ed.), *Erfassung zur Vernichtung. Von der Sozialhygiene zum 'Gesetz über Sterbehilfe'* (Berlin, 1984); Hamburger Stiftung für Sozialgeschichte des 20. Jahrhunderts (ed.), *Das Daimler-Benz Buch. Ein Rüstungskonzern im 'Tausendjährigen Reich'* (Nördlingen, 1987); *Beiträge zur nationalsozialistischen Gesundheits – und Sozialpolitik*, eds. Götz Aly, Jochen August, Peter Chroust, Klaus Dörner, Matthias Hamann, Hans-Dieter Heilmann, Susanne Heim, Franz Koch, Christian Pross, Ulrich Schultz, Christine Teller: Vol. 1, *Aussonderung und Tod. Die klinische Hinrichtung der Unbrauchbaren*; Vol. 3, *Herrenmensch und Arbeitsvölker. Ausländische Arbeiter und Deutsche 1939–1945*; Vol. 4, *Biedermann und Schreibtischtäter. Materialien zur deutschen Täter-Biographie*; Vol. 5,

Sozialpolitik und Judenvernichtung. Gibt es eine Ökonomie der Endlösung?; Vol. 6, *Feinderklärung und Prävention. Kriminalbiologie, Zigeunerforschung und Asozialenpolitik* (Berlin, 1987–8).

48 Editorial in *Beiträge zur nationalsozialistischen Gesundheits- und Sozialpolitik*, 1 (Berlin, 1985), p. 9.

50 David Blackbourn, Geoff Eley, *The Peculiarities of German History: Bourgeois Society and Politics in Nineteenth-Century Germany* (Oxford, 1984). For a critique of this, see Hans-Ulrich Wehler, *Preussen ist wieder chic . . . Politik und Polemik in zwanzig Essays* (Frankfurt am Main, 1983), pp. 19ff.

51 Michael Stürmer, *Das ruhelose Reich 1866–1918* (Berlin, 1983), *Dissonanzen des Fortschritts* (Munich, 1986). For Stürmer's career transformations, see Volker Berghahn, 'Geschichtswissenschaften und Grosse Politik', *Aus Politik und Zeitgeschichte*, B 11 (1987), pp. 25–37.

52 Helmut Boockmann *et al.*, *Mitten in Europa. Deutsche Geschichte* (Berlin, 1984); Hagen Schulze, *Wir sind, was wir geworden sind. Vom Nutzen der Geschichte für die deutsche Gegenwart* (Munich, 1987); Klaus Hildebrand, 'Deutscher Sonderweg und "Drittes Reich"', in Wolfgang Michalka (ed.), *Die nationalsozialistische Machtergreifung* (Paderborn, 1984), pp. 392–4, 'Der deutsche Eigenweg', in Manfred Funke (ed.), *Festschrift Karl Dietrich Bracher* (Düsseldorf, 1987), pp. 15–34; Andreas Hillgruber, *Deutschlands Rolle in der Vorgeschichte der beiden Weltkriege* (Göttingen, 1967); David P. Calleo, *The German Problem Reconsidered* (Cambridge, 1978), translated into German as *Deutsche Legende und Wirklichkeit der deutschen Gefahr* (Bonn, 1980).

On these trends see Bernd Faulenbach, 'Die Frage nach den Spezifika der deutschen Entwicklung. Zu neuen Interpretationen des 19. Jahrhunderts', *Neue politische Literatur*, 3 (1986), pp. 69–82; and Hans-Ulrich Wehler, *Entsorgung der deutschen Vergangenheit? Ein polemischer Essay zum 'Historikerstreit'* (Munich, 1988).

53 The most important contributions have been reprinted in *'Historikerstreit'. Die Dokumentation der Kontroverse um die Einzigartigkeit der nationalsozialistischen Judenverfolgung* (Munich, 1987). See also the essays by Dan Diner, Saul Friedländer, and Hans Mommsen in Dan Diner (ed.), *Ist der Nationalsozialismus Geschichte?* (Frankfurt am Main, 1987), and Hans-Ulrich Wehler, *Entsorgung der deutschen Vergangenheit*. For an excellent English contribution, see Richard J. Evans, *In Hitler's Shadow: West German Historians and the Attempt to Escape from the Nazi Past* (London, 1989).

54 Henry Ashby Turner, *Faschismus und Kapitalismus in Deutschland* (Göttingen, 1972), p. 7.

55 Karl Dietrich Bracher, *Zeitgeschichtliche Kontroversen. Um Faschismus, Totalitarismus, Demokratie* (Munich, 1976).

56 Gilbert Allardyce, 'What Fascism is Not: Thoughts on the Deflation of a Concept', *American Historical Review*, 84 (1976), pp. 367–88; Renzo de Felice, *Die Deutungen des Faschismus* (Göttingen, 1980; Italian edition Turin, 1969), *Der Faschismus: An Interview by Michael A. Ledeen* (Stuttgart, 1977); Saul Friedländer, *Kitsch und Tod. Der Widerschein des Nazismus* (Munich, 1984); Klaus Hildebrand, *The Third Reich* (London, 1984); Bernd

Martin, 'Zur Tauglichkeit eines übergreifenden Faschismus-Begriffs. Ein Vergleich zwischen Japan, Italien und Deutschland'. *Vierteljahrsheft für Zeitgeschichte*, 29 (1981), pp. 48–73.

57 The debate is documented in *Der 'Führerstaat': Mythos und Realität. Studien zur Struktur und Politik des Dritten Reiches* (Stuttgart, 1981); Klaus Hildebrand, *Das Dritte Reich* (Munich, 1979); Wolfgang Wippermann (ed.), *Kontroversen um Hitler* (Frankfurt am Main, 1986).

58 Dan Diner, 'Zwischen Aporie und Apologie. Über Grenzen der Historisierbarkeit des Nationalsozialismus' in his (ed.), *Ist der Nationalsozialismus Geschichte?* (Frankfurt am Main, 1987), pp. 62–73.

59 Christopher Browning, 'German Technocrats, Jewish Labour, and the Final Solution: A Reply to Götz Aly and Susanne Heim', in *Remembering the Future* (Oxford, 1988), pp. 2199ff. See also Michael Burleigh, 'Nazi Social Policies', in *Polin: A Journal of Polish-Jewish Studies*, 4 (1989), pp. 460–6; Ernst Köhler, 'Wissenschaft und Massenvernichtung', *Kommune*, 7 (1989), pp. 58–63.

2 BARBAROUS UTOPIAS; RACIAL IDEOLOGIES IN GERMANY

1 Werner Conze, 'Rasse', in Otto Brunner, Werner Conze, Reinhart Koselleck (eds.), *Geschichtliche Grundbegriffe* (Stuttgart, 1984), Vol. 5, pp. 135–78.

2 For the following, see the general surveys by Patrik von zur Mühlen, *Rassenideologien. Geschichte und Hintergründe* (Berlin and Bonn, 1977); George L. Mosse, *Rassimus. Ein Krankheitssymptom in der europäischen Geschichte des 19. und 20. Jahrhundert* (Königstein, 1978), English version *Towards the Final Solution: A History of European Racism* (New York, 1978), *Nationalismus und Sexualität. Bürgerliche Moral und sexuelle Normen* (Munich, 1985), English version *Nationalism and Sexuality: Respectability and Abnormal Sexuality in Modern Europe* (New York, 1985); Michael Banton, *The Idea of Race* (London, 1977); A. James Gregor, *The Ideology of Fascism: The Rationalism of Totalitarianism* (New York, 1969); Leon Poliakov, *The Aryan Myth: A History of Racist and Nationalist Ideas in Europe* (New York, 1974), *Über den Rassimus. Sechzehn Kapitel zur Anatomie, Geschichte und Deutung des Rassenwahns* (Frankfurt am Main, 1984).

3 Immanuel Kant, *Von den verschiedenen Racen der Menschen* (Königsberg, 1775), p. 3.

4 Johann Kaspar Lavater, *Physiognomische Fragmente zur Beförderung der Menschenkenntnis und Menschenliebe*, Vols. 1–4, in *Johann Kaspar Lavaters ausgewählte Schriften*, ed. Johann Kaspar Orelli (Zurich, 1844).

5 Peter Camper, *Dissertation Physique* (Utrecht, 1791); see also Mosse, *Rassimus*, pp. 26ff.

6 Franz Joseph Gall, *Vorlesungen über die Verrichtung des Gehirns* (Berlin, 1805); see also Mosse, *Rassimus*, p. 30, and von zur Mühlen, *Rassenideologien*, p. 44.

7 Christoph Meiners, *Grundriss der Geschichte der Menschheit* (Lemgo, 1978; reprinted Königstein, 1981), p. 89.

8 Carl Gustav Carus, *Über die ungleiche Befähigung der verschiedenen Menschenstämme für höhere geistige Entwicklung* (Leipzig, 1848).

9 Johann Gottfried Herder, *Ideen zur Philosophie der Geschichte der Menschheit* (1785), *Herders Werke in 5 Bänden, ausgewählt und eingeleitet von Wilhelm Dobbeck* (Berlin, 1969), Vol. 4.

10 For the following see George L. Mosse, *The Crisis of German Ideology: Intellectual Origins of the Third Reich* (London, 1964); Klaus von See, *Deutsche Germanen-Ideologie vom Humanismus bis zur Gegenwart* (Frankfurt am Main, 1970), *Die Ideen von 1789 und die Ideen von 1914. Völkisches Denken in Deutschland zwischen Französischer Revolution und Erstem Weltkrieg* (Frankfurt am Main, 1975); Heinz Gollwitzer, 'Zum politischen Germanismus des 19. Jahrhunderts', in *Festschrift Hermann Heimpel* (Göttingen, 1971), pp. 282ff.; Hans-Jurgen Lutzhöft, *Der nordische Gedanke in Deutschland 1920–1940* (Stuttgart, 1970); Wolfgang Emmerisch, *Zur Kritik der Volkstumsideologie* (Frankfurt am Main, 1971).

11 Johann Georg Forster in a letter to his wife dated 1785, *Georg Fosters Sämtliche Schriften*, ed. by his daughter (Leipzig, 1843), Vol. 7, p. 489. On the following see also Wolfgang Wippermann, *Der 'deutsche Drang nach Osten'. Ideologie und Wirklichkeit eines politischen Schlagwortes* (Darmstadt, 1981).

12 Johann Friedrich Reitemeier, *Geschichte der preussischen Staaten vor und nach ihrer Vereinigung in eine Monarchie* (Frankfurt an der Oder, 1801–5), 1, p. 33.

13 Karl Adolf Menzel, *Die Geschichte der Deutschen* (Breslau, 1818), p. 247.

14 Moritz Wilhelm Heffter, *Der Weltkampf der Deutschen und Slawen seit dem Ende des 4. Jahrhunderts nach christlicher Zeitrechnung, nach seinem Ursprunge, Verlaufe und nach seinen Folgen dargestellt* (Hamburg and Gotha, 1847).

15 *Augsburger Allgemeine Zeitung*, 18 April 1846; Heinrich Wuttke, *Polen und Deutsche* (2nd edition, Leipzig, 1848), pp. 13ff.

16 *Stenographischer Bericht über die Verhandlungen der deutschen constituierenden Nationalversammlung zu Frankfurt am Main*, ed. Franz Wigard (Frankfurt am Main, 1848), pp. 1124–233. See also Wolfgang Hallgarten, *Studien über die deutsche Polenfreundschaft in der Periode der Märzrevolution* (Munich and Berlin, 1928), pp. 32ff.; Richard Cromer, 'Die Polenfrage auf den Nationalversammlungen von Frankfurt am Main und Berlin', *Nation und Staat*, 7 (1933–4), pp. 649–66, and 9 (1935–6), pp. 676–707; Horst-Joachim Seepel, *Das Polenbild der Deutschen. Von den Anfängen des 19. Jahrhunderts bis zum Ende der Revolution von 1848* (unpublished thesis, University of Kiel, 1967), pp. 170ff.

17 Heinrich von Treitschke, 'Das deutsche Ordensland Preussen', *Preussische Jahrbücher*, 10 (1862), pp. 95–151.

18 Comte Henri de Boulainvilliers, *Essais sur la noblesse de France* (Amsterdam, 1732).

19 Joseph Arthur de Gobineau, *Essai sur l'inégalité des races humaines* (Paris, 1853–5), pp. 1–4; see also Michael Biddis, *Father of Racist Ideology: The*

Social and Political Thought of Count Gobineau (London, 1970); E. J. Young, *Gobineau und der Rassimus. Eine Kritik der anthropologischen Geschichtstheorie* (Meisenheim, 1968).

20 Gobineau, *Essai*, Vol. 4, pp. 317ff.

21 Charles Darwin, *On the Origin of Species by Means of Natural Selection, or the Preservation of Favoured Races in the Struggle for Life* (London, 1959). For this and the following, see Hedwig Conrad-Martius, *Utopien der Menschenzüchtung. Der Sozialdarwinismus und die Folgen* (Munich, 1955); Hans-Gunther Zmarlik, 'Der Sozialdarwinismus in Deutschland als geschichtliches Problem', *Vierteljahrshefte für Zeitgeschichte*, 11 (1963), pp. 246–73; Hansjoachim W. Koch, *Der Sozialdarwinismus. Seine Genese und sein Einfluss auf das imperialistische Denken* (Munich, 1973); Gunther Mann (ed.), *Biologismus im 19. Jahrhundert* (Stuttgart, 1973); Gisela Bock, *Zwangssterilisation im Nationalsozialismus. Studien zur Rassenpolitik und Frauenpolitik* (Opladen, 1986), 'Racism and Sexism in Nazi Germany: Motherhood, Compulsory Sterilization, and the State', in Renate Bridenthal, Atina Grossmann, Marion Kaplan (eds.), *When Biology Became Destiny: Women in Weimar and Nazi Germany* (New York, 1984), pp. 271–96; Hans Walter Schmuhl, *Rassenhygiene, Nationalsozialismus, Euthanasie* (Göttingen, 1987); Peter Weingart, Jürgen Kroll, Kurt Bayertz, *Rasse, Blut und Gene. Geschichte der Eugenik und Rassenhygiene in Deutschland* (Frankfurt am Main, 1988); Paul Weindling, *Darwinism and Social Darwinism in Imperial Germany* (Stuttgart, 1989), *Health, Race and German Politics between National Unification and Nazism 1870–1945* (Cambridge, 1989).

22 Francis Galton, *Hereditary Genius: Its Laws and Consequences* (London, 1863), *Inquiries into Human Faculty and its Development* (London, 1883), 'Eugenics: Its Definition, Scope and Aims', *Sociological Papers*, 1 (1905), pp. 45–50.

23 On Haeckel see Daniel Gasman, *The Scientific Origins of National Socialism: Social Darwinism in Ernst Haeckel and the German Monist League* (London, 1971). By contrast see Erika Krause, *Ernst Haeckel* (Leipzig, 1984), who celebrates Haeckel as an 'hervorragenden Gelehrten des 19. Jahrhunderts' whose 'Erbe wir in der Deutschen Demokratischen Republik bewahren, pflegen und für unsere Generation nutzbar machen'.

24 Ernst Haeckel, *Natürliche Schöpfungsgeschichte. Gemeinverständliche wissenschaftliche Vorträge über die Entwicklungslehre* (Berlin, 1869); the 1911 edition is cited here.

25 Haeckel, *Natürliche Schöpfungsgeschichte*, p. 752.

26 *Ibid.*, p. 154.

27 Ernst Haeckel, *Die Lebenswunder. Gemeinverständliche Studien über biologische Philosophie* (Leipzig, 1904).

28 Wilhelm Schallmeyer, *Vererbung und Auslese. Grundriss der Gesellschaftsbiologie und der Lehre vom Rassedienst* (Jena, 1903), *Beiträge zu einer Nationalbiologie* (Jena, 1905).

29 Alfred Ploetz, *Die Tüchtigkeit unserer Rasse und der Schutz der Schwachen. Ein Versuch über Rassenhygiene und ihr Verhältnis zu den humanen Ideen, besonders zum Sozialismus* (Berlin, 1895).

30 August Weissmann, *Das Keimplasma. Eine Theorie der Vererbung* (Jena, 1892).

31 Hans-Josef Steinberg, *Sozialismus und deutsche Sozialdemokratie. Zur Ideologie der Partei vor dem ersten Weltkrieg* (Berlin, 4th edition, 1976).

32 On the following themes see especially Paul Weindling, *Health, Race and German Politics between National Unification and Nazism 1870–1945* (Cambridge, 1989), pp. 388ff. and Jeremy Noakes' seminal 'Nazism and Eugenics: The Background to the Nazi Sterilization Law of 14 July 1933', in R. J. Bullen, H. Pogge von Strandmann, A. B. Polonsky (eds.), *Ideas into Politics: Aspects of European History 1880–1950* (Beckenham, Kent, 1984), pp. 75–94.

33 Friedrich Nietzsche, 'Nachgelassene Fragmente Anfang 1880 bis Sommer 1882', in Giorgio Colli and Mazzino Montinare (eds.), *Nietzsches Sämtliche Werke* (Munich, 1980), Vol. 9, p. 250.

34 Nietzsche, 'Nachgelassene Fragmente', p. 189.

35 Willibald Hentschel, *Mittgart. Ein Weg zur Erneurung der germanischen Rasse* (Leipzig, 1904), *Varuna. Eine Welt- und Geschichts-Betrachtung vom Standpunkt des Ariers* (Leipzig, 1901). On Hentschel and the 'Artamanen' see Klaus Bergmann, *Agrarromantik und Grossstadtfeindschaft* (Meisenheim, 1970); Michael H. Kater, 'Die Artamanen–Völkische Jugend in der Weimarer Republik', *Historische Zeitschrift*, 213 (1971), pp. 577–638; Josef Ackermann, *Heinrich Himmler als Ideologe* (Göttingen, 1979); Bradley F. Smith, *Heinrich Himmler: A Nazi in the Making 1900–1926* (Stanford, 1971); Jost Hermand, *Der alte Traum vom neuen Reich. Völkische Utopien und Nationalsozialismus* (Frankfurt am Main, 1988), especially pp. 140ff.

36 Jorg Lanz von Liebenfels, *Theozoologie* (Vienna, 1906). On Lanz see Wilfried Daim, *Der Mann, der Hitler die Ideen gab. Von den religiösen Verirrungen eines Sektierers zum Rassenwahn des Diktators* (Munich, 1958); Jost Hermand, 'Germania germanicissima. Zum präfaschistischen Arierkult um 1900', in his *Der Schein des schönen Lebens. Studien zur Jahrhundertwende* (Frankfurt am Main, 1972), pp. 39–54, and his *Der alte Traum vom neuen Reich*, pp. 73ff. for similar references to ideologies based upon racial selective breeding.

37 From the vast literature on anti-Semitism see Hannah Arendt, *The Origins of Totalitarianism* (London, 1951); Alex Bein, *Die Judenfrage. Biographie eines Weltproblems* (Stuttgart, 1980), Vols. 1 and 2; Peter G. Pulzer, *The Rise of Political Anti-Semitism in Germany and Austria 1867–1914* (New York, 1964); Reinhard Rürup, *Emanzipation und Antisemitismus, Studien zur 'Judenfrage' der bürgerlichen Gesellschaft* (Göttingen, 1975); Norman Cohn, *Die Protokolle der Weisen von Zion. Der Mythos der jüdischen Weltverschwörung* (Cologne, 1969); Herbert A. Strauss, Norbert Kampe (eds.), *Antisemitismus. Von der Judenfeindschaft zum Holocaust* (Frankfurt am Main, 1985). For the by no means uniform views of racial scientists and eugenicists concerning the 'Jewish Question' see Weindling, *Health, Race and German Politics.*

38 Houston Stewart Chamberlain, *Die Grundlagen des neunzehnten Jahrhunderts* (Munich, 1899).

39 For anti-Semitism in Germany see, in addition to the works cited in note 37, Wanda Kampmann, *Deutsche und Juden. Die Geschichte der Juden in Deutschland vom Mittelalter bis zum Beginn des Ersten Weltkrieges* (Frankfurt am Main, 1979); Ismar Elbogen, Eleonore Sterling, *Die Geschichte der Juden in Deutschland* (Frankfurt am Main, 1966); Peter Gay, *Freud, Jews and other Germans: Masters and Victims in Modernist Culture* (New York, 1978); Werner E. Mosse, Arnold Paucker (eds.), *Juden im Wilhelminischen Deutschland 1890–1914* (Tübingen, 1976), *Deutschen Judentum in Krieg und Revolution 1916–1923* (Tübingen, 1971), *Entscheidungsjahr 1932. Zur Judenfrage in der Endphase der Weimarer Republik* (Tübingen, 1965); Monika Richarz (ed.), *Jüdisches Leben in Deutschland. Selbstzeugnisse zur Sozialgeschichte im Kaiserreich 1871–1918* (Stuttgart, 1979), *Jüdisches Leben in Deutschland. Selbstzeugnisse zur Sozialgeschichte 1919–1945* (Stuttgart, 1982); Shulamit Volkov, 'Kontinuität und Diskontinuität im deutschen Antisemitismus 1878–1945', *Vierteljahreshefte für Zeitgeschichte*, 33 (1985), pp. 221–43; Hermann Graml, *Reichskristallnacht. Antisemitismus und Judenverfolgung im Dritten Reich* (Munich, 1988). More specialised areas are covered in Fritz Stern's masterly *Gold and Iron: Bismarck, Bleichröder and the Building of the German Empire* (London, 1977); Steven E. Aschheim, *Brothers and Strangers: The East European Jew in German and German Jewish Consciousness 1800–1923* (Madison, 1982); Jack Wertheimer, *Unwelcome Strangers: East European Jews in Imperial Germany* (Oxford, 1987).

40 Artur Dinter, *Die Sünde wider das Blut* (Leipzig, 1918).

41 For Hitler's racism and anti-Semitism see Alan Bullock, *Hitler: A Study in Tyranny* (revised edition, London, 1967); Joachim C. Fest, *Hitler* (London, 1974); Eberhard Jäckel, *Hitler's World View: A Blueprint for Power* (Cambridge, Mass., 1981); Karl Lange, *Hitlers unbeachtete Maximen. 'Mein Kampf' und die Öffentlichkeit* (Stuttgart, 1968); Wolfgang Wippermann, *Der konsequente Wahn. Ideologie und Politik Adolf Hitlers* (Munich, 1989).

42 *Hitler's Mein Kampf*, translated by Ralph Mannheim with an introduction by D. C. Watt (London, 1974), p. 258.

43 Eugen Fischer, *Die Rehobother Bastards und das Bastardierungsproblem beim Menschen* (Jena, 1913).

44 *Hitler's Mein Kampf*, p. 348.

45 *Ibid.*, p. 368.

46 *Ibid.*, p. 295.

3 BARBARISM INSTITUTIONALISED: RACISM AS A STATE POLICY

1 'Hitlers Testament', *Der Prozess gegen die Hauptkriegsverbrecher vor dem Internationalen Militärgerichtshof*, Nuremberg, 14 November 1945–1 October 1946 (Nuremberg, 1947–9), Vol. 41, p. 552.

2 For a collection of anti-Semitic laws and decrees see Joseph Walk, *Das Sonderrecht für die Juden im NS-Staat. Eine Sammlung der gesetzlichen Massnahmen und Richtlinien* (Karlsruhe, 1981). There are also editions of the major laws and decrees by Helmut Eschwege, *Kennzeichen 'J'. Bilder, Dokumente, Berichte zur Geschichte der Verbrechen des Hitlerfaschismus an den*

deutschen Juden 1933–1945 (Frankfurt am Main, 1979); Kurt Pätzold (ed.), *Verfolgung, Vertreibung, Vernichtung. Dokumente des faschistischen Anti-semitismus 1933–1942* (Leipzig, 1983); Hans-Dieter Schmid *et al.*, *Juden unterm Hakenkreuz. Dokumente und Berichte zur Verfolgung und Vernichtung der Juden durch die Nationalsozialisten 1933–1945* (Düsseldorf, 1983), Vols. 1 and 2.

3 'Gesetz zur Wiederherstellung des Berufsbeamtentums vom 7. April 1933', *Reichsgesetzblatt 1933*, Part 1, p. 175, reprinted in Schmid *et al.*, *Juden unterm Hakenkreuz*, Vol. 1, pp. 78f. For a detailed discussion of this law see Uwe Dietrich Adam, *Judenpolitik im Dritten Reich* (Düsseldorf, 1979), pp. 46ff.

4 'Wehrgesetz vom 21. Mai 1935', *Reichsgesetzblatt 1935*, Part 1, p. 611; reprinted in Schmid *et al.*, *Juden unterm Hakenkreuz*, Vol. 1, p. 86.

5 'Reichsbürgergesetz' and 'Gesetz zum Schutz des deutschen Blutes und der deutschen Ehre vom 15. September 1935', *Reichsgesetzblatt 1935*, Part 1, pp. 146f.; reprinted in Schmid *et al.*, *Juden unterm Hakenkreuz*, Vol. 1, p. 97f.

6 Falk Ruttke, 'Erb- und Rassenpflege in Gesetzgebung und Rechtssprechung des Dritten Reiches', in *Deutsches Recht*, 25 January 1933, pp. 25–7, cited by Karl A. Schleunes, *The Twisted Road to Auschwitz: Nazi Policy toward German Jews 1933–1939* (London, 1970), p. 120.

7 'I. Verordnung zum Reichsbürgergesetz vom 14. November 1935', *Reichs-gesetzblatt 1935*, Part 1, pp. 1333f.; reprinted in Schmid *et al.*, *Juden unterm Hakenkreuz*, Vol. 1, p. 102.

8 As yet there has been no comprehensive study of Nazi racism. In recent years there has been considerable interest in racial hygiene and health policy under the Nazi regime. On this see Kurt Nowak, *Euthanasie und Sterilisation im Dritten Reich. Die Konfrontation der evangelischen und katholischen Kirche mit dem 'Gesetz zur Verhütung erbkranken Nachwuchses' und der 'Euthanasie'-Aktion* (Göttingen, 1978); Gerhard Baader, Ulrich Schultz (eds.), *Medizin und Nationalsozialismus* (Berlin, 1980); Walter Wuttke-Groneberg, *Medizin im Nationalsozialismus. Ein Arbeitsbuch* (Tübingen, 1980); Ernst Klee, *'Euthanasie' im NS-Staat. Die 'Vernichtung lebens-unwerten Lebens'* (Frankfurt am Main, 1983), *Dokumente zur 'Euthanasie'* (Frankfurt am Main, 1985), *Was sie taten – was sie wurden. Ärtze, Juristen und andere Beteiligte am Kranken- oder Judenmord* (Frankfurt am Main, 1986); Benno Müller-Hill, *Murderous Science: Elimination by Scientific Selec-tion of Jews, Gypsies, and Others, Germany 1933–1945* (Oxford, 1988); Peter Weingart, 'Eugenik, eine angewandte Wissenschaft im Dritten Reich'; Peter Lundgreen (ed.), *Wissenschaft im Dritten Reich* (Frankfurt am Main, 1985), pp. 314–49; Gisela Bock, *Zwangssterilisation im Nationalsozialismus* (Opladen, 1986); Alfons Labisch, Florian Tennstedt, *Der Weg zum Gesetz über die Vereinheitlichung des Gesundheitswesens* (Düsseldorf, 1986); Heidrun Kaupen-Haas (ed.), *Der Griff nach der Bevölkerung. Aktualität und Kon-tinuität nazistischer Bevölkerungspolitik. Schriften der Hamburger Stiftung für Sozialgeschichte des 20. Jahrhunderts*, 1 (Nordlingen, 1986); Christian Ganssmüller, *Die Erbgesundheitspolitik des Dritten Reiches* (Cologne, 1987);

Hans Walter Schmuhl, *Rassenhygiene, Nationalsozialismus, Euthanasie* (Göttingen, 1987); Peter Weingart, Jürgen Kroll, Kurt Bayertz, *Rasse, Blut und Gene. Geschichte der Eugenik und Rassenhygiene in Deutschland* (Frankfurt am Main, 1988); Peter Emil Becker, *Zur Geschichte der Rassenhygiene. Wege ins Dritte Reich* (Stuttgart, 1988); Robert N. Proctor, *Racial Hygiene: Medicine under the Nazis* (London, 1988); Paul J. Weindling, *Health, Race and German Politics.*

9 'Gesetz zur Verminderung der Arbeitslosigkeit vom 1. Juni 1933', *Reichsgesetzblatt 1933*, Part 1, pp. 323ff.

10 'Erste Durchführungsverordnung über die Gewährung von Ehestandsdarlehen vom 20. Juni 1933', *Reichsgesetzblatt 1933*, Part 1, pp. 377–88.

11 'Zweite Durchführungsverordnung über die Gewährung von Ehestandsdarlehen vom 26. Juli 1933', *Reichsgesetzblatt 1933*, Part 1, p. 515.

12 'Runderlass des Preussischen Ministers des Innern vom 4. Mai 1934 über Fahrpreisermässigungen für kinderreiche Familien', *Zentralblatt für Jugendrecht und Jugendwohlfahrt. Organ des deutschen Instituts for Vormundschaftswesen*, 26 (1934), pp. 55f.; 'Einkommensteuergesetz vom 16. Oktober 1934', *Reichsgesetzblatt 1934*, Part 1, pp. 1005–31; 'Verordnung über die Gewährung von Kinderbeihilfen an kinderreiche Familien vom 15. September 1935', *Reichsgesetzblatt 1935*, Part 1, p. 1160.

13 'Durchführungsbestimmungen zur Verordnung über die Gewährung von Kinderbeihilfen an kinderreiche Familien vom 26. September 1935', *Reichsgesetzblatt 1935*, Part 1, pp. 1206ff.

14 'Gesetz zur Verhütung erbkranken Nachwuchses vom 14. Juli 1933', *Reichsgesetzblatt 1933*, Part 1, pp. 529ff. Arthur Gütt, Ernst Rüdin, Falk Ruttke, 'Gesetz zur Verhütung erbkranken Nachwuchses vom 14. Juli 1933' (Berlin, 1934).

15 For the following see Patrick Wagner, 'Das Gesetz über die Behandlung Gemeinschaftsfremder', *Feinderklärung und Prävention. Kriminalbiologie, Zigeunerforschung und Asozialenpolitik. Beiträge zur nationalsozialistischen Gesundheits- und Sozialpolitik*, 6 (Berlin, 1988), pp. 75–100; Ernst Klee, *'Euthanasie' im NS-Staat*, pp. 38ff.; Detlev Peukert, 'Arbeitslager und Jugend-KZ. Die "Behandlung Gemeinschaftsfremder" im Dritten Reich', in Detlev Peukert, Jurgen Reulecke (eds.), *Die Reihen fast geschlossen. Beiträge zur Geschichte des Alltags unterm Nationalsozialismus* (Wuppertal, 1981), pp. 413–34; J. Hellmer, *Der Gewohnheitsverbrecher und die Sicherheitsverwahrung 1934–1945* (Berlin, 1961); Karl-Leo Terhorst, *Polizeiliche planmässige Überwachung und polizeiliche Vorbeugungshaft im Dritten Reich* (Heidelberg, 1983).

16 'Gesetz zur Änderung des Gesetzes zur Verhütung erbkranken Nachwuchses vom 26. Juni 1935', *Reichsgesetzblatt 1935*, Part 1, pp. 1035ff.

17 'Gesetz zum Schutze der Erbgesundheit des deutschen Volkes vom 18. Oktober 1935', *Reichsgesetzblatt 1935*, Part 1, pp. 1246ff.

18 '1. Durchführungsverordnung zum Gesetz zum Schutz des deutschen Blutes und der deutschen Ehre vom 14. November 1935', *Reichsgesetzblatt 1935*, Part 1, pp. 1334ff.

19 'Runderlass des Reichs- und Preussischen Ministers des Innern vom

26. November 1935', *Ministerialblatt für die Preussische innere Verwaltung,* 1935, pp. 1429–34. Compare also 'Runderlass des Reichsministers des Innern vom 3. Januar 1936', in Pätzold (ed.), *Verfolgung, Vertreibung, Vernichtung,* pp. 121f.

20 Wilhelm Stuckart, Hans Globke, *Kommentar zur deutschen Rassengesetz-gebung* (Munich, 1936), Vol. 1, p. 55.

21 'Einkommenssteuergesetz vom 27. Februar 1939', *Reichsgesetzblatt 1939,* Part 1, pp. 297–320.

22 'Ausführungsverordnung zum Gesetz der erwerbstätigen Mutter vom 17. Mai 1942', *Reichsgesetzblatt 1942,* Part 1, pp. 324ff.; 'Verordnung zum Schutz von Ehe, Familie und Mutterschaft vom 9. Marz 1943', *Reichsgesetz-blatt 1943,* Part 1, pp. 140f.

23 On the following see Max Weinreich, *Hitler's Professors: The Part of Scholarship in Germany's Crimes Against the Jewish People* (New York, 1946); Alexander Mitscherlich, Fred Mielke (eds.), *Medizin ohne Menschlichkeit. Dokumente des Nürnberger Ärzteprozesses* (Frankfurt am Main, 1960); Gerhard Baader, Ulrich Schultz (eds.), *Medizin und Nationalsozialismus* (Berlin, 1980); Walter Wuttke-Groneberg, *Medizin im Nationalsozialismus. Ein Arbeitsbuch* (Tübingen, 1980); Till Bastian. *Von der Eugenik zur Euthanasie. Ein verdrängtes Kapitel aus der Geschichte der deutschen Psychiatrie* (Wörishofen, 1981); Projektgruppe 'Volk und Gesundheit' (eds.), *Volk und Gesundheit. Heilen und Vernichten im Nationalsozialismus* (Tübingen, 1982); Ernst Klee, *'Euthanasie' im NS-Staat. Die 'Vernichtung lebensunwerten Lebens'* (Frankfurt am Main, 1983). Benno Müller-Hill, *Murderous Science: Elimination by Scientific Selection of Jews, Gypsies, and Others, Germany 1933–1945* (Oxford, 1988); Peter Weingart, 'Eugenik, eine angewandte Wissenschaft im Dritten Reich', in Peter Lundgreen (ed.), *Wissenschaft im Dritten Reich* (Frankfurt am Main, 1985), pp. 314–49; Robert Jay Lifton, *The Nazi Doctors: Medical Killing and the Psychology of Genocide* (London, 1986); Walter Wuttke, 'Heilen und Vernichten in der nationalsozialistischen Medizin', in Jörg Tröger (ed.), *Hochschule und Wissenschaft im Dritten Reich* (Frankfurt am Main, 1986); Klaus Dieter Thomann, Barbara Mausbach-Bromberger, *Medizin, Faschismus und Widerstand. Drei Beiträge* (Cologne, 1985); Gisela Bock, *Zwangssterilisation im Nationalsozialismus* (Opladen, 1986); Walter Schmuhl, *Rassenhygiene, Nationalsozialismus, Euthanasie* (Göttingen, 1987); Peter Weingart, Jurgen Kroll, Kurt Bayertz, *Rasse, Blut und Gene. Geschichte der Eugenik und Rassen-hygiene in Deutschland* (Frankfurt am Main, 1988); Peter Emil Becker, *Zur Geschichte der Rassenhygiene in Deutschland. Wege ins Dritte Reich* (Stuttgart, 1988); Robert N. Proctor, *Racial Hygiene: Medicine under the Nazis* (London, 1988); Paul J. Weindling, *Health, Race and German Politics.*

24 On the following, see Weingart *et al.,* *Rasse, Blut und Gene,* pp. 399ff.

25 For the following, see Weingart *et al.,* *Rasse, Blut und Gene,* pp. 407ff.; Weindling, *Health, Race and German Politics,* pp. 430ff. and 552ff.; Niels C. Lösch, 'Das Kaiser-Wilhelm-Institut für Anthropologie, menschliche Erblehre und Eugenik', (unpublished M.A. dissertation, Freie Universität, Berlin, 1990).

26 Ute Brucker-Boroujerdi, Wolfgang Wippermann, 'Die "Rassenhygienische und Erbbiologische Forschungsstelle in Reichsgesundheitsamt', *Bundesgesetzblatt* 32, March 1989, *Sonderheft*, pp. 13–19.

27 Weingart *et al.*, *Rasse, Blut und Gene*, pp. 445ff.

28 *Ibid.*, pp. 455ff. For Himmler's interest in Vaernet's work, see Hans-Georg Stümke, *Homosexuelle in Deutschland. Eine politische Geschichte* (Munich, 1989), pp. 123ff.

29 Michael Burleigh, *Germany Turns Eastwards: A Study of 'Ostforschung' in the Third Reich* (Cambridge, 1988); 'Albert Brackmann, *Ostforscher* (1871–1952): The Years of Retirement', *Journal of Contemporary History*, 23 (1988), pp. 571–88, 'The Politics of Research in Occupied Poland', *History Today*, 38 (1988), pp. 12–16.

30 On the following see Weingart *et al.*, *Rasse, Blut und Gene*, pp. 407ff. and 460ff.; Heidrun Kaupen-Haas, 'Die Bevölkerungsplaner im Sachverständigenbeirat für Bevölkerungs- und Rassenpolitik', in Kaupen-Haas (ed.), *Der Griff nach der Bevölkerung*, pp. 103–20; *Trials of War Criminals before the Nuernberg Military Tribunals under Control Council Law No. 10* (Nuremberg, 1949), vol. 1, *The Medical Case*, pp. 92ff. for details of 'medical' experiments.

31 Alfons Labisch, Florian Tennstedt, *Der Weg zum Gesetz über die Vereinheitlichung des Gesundheitswesens* (Düsseldorf, 1986); Weingart *et al.*, *Rasse, Blut und Gene*, pp. 480ff.

32 Horst Seidler, Andreas Rett, *Das Reichssippenamt entscheidet. Rassenbiologie im Nationalsozialismus* (Vienna, 1982).

33 Götz Aly, Karl-Heinz Roth, *Die restlose Erfassung. Volkszählen, Identifizieren, Aussondern im Nationalsozialismus* (Berlin, 1984); Weingart *et al.*, *Rasse, Blut und Gene*, pp. 492ff.

34 Klee, *'Euthanasie' im NS-Staat*; Götz Aly (ed.), *Aktion T 4 1939–1945. Die 'Euthanasie' – Zentrale in der Tiergartenstrasse 4* (Berlin, 1987).

35 For Ley and the DAF see now Ronald Smelser, *Robert Ley: Hitler's Labour Front Leader* (Oxford, 1988), and on Rosenberg, Reinhard Bollmus, *Das Amt Rosenberg und seine Gegner. Studien zum Machtkampf im nationalsozialistischen Herrschaftssystem* (Stuttgart, 1970). There is an introduction to these issues in Ian Kershaw, *The Nazi Dictatorship* (London, 1989), pp. 61ff. For a superb recent discussion, see Dieter Rebentisch, *Führerstaat und Verwaltung im Zweiten Weltkrieg. Verfassungsentwicklung und Verwaltungspolitik 1939–1945, Frankfurter Historische Abhandlungen* (Stuttgart, 1989), Vol. 29.

36 On the history and function of the SS in general, see Hans Buchheim *et al.* (eds.), *Anatomie des SS-Staates* (Munich, 1967), Vols. 1 and 2; Heinz Höhne, *The Order of the Death's Head* (London, 1969); Martin Broszat, *The Hitler State: The Foundation and Development of the Internal Structure of the Third Reich* (London, 1981); Klaus Dobisch, 'Über den Terror und seine Organisationen im Nazi-Deutschland', in Dietrich Eichholtz, Kurt Gossweiler (eds.), *Faschismus Forschung. Positionen, Probleme, Polemik* (Berlin, 1980), pp. 157–80; Eberhard Kolb, 'Die Maschinerie des Terrors. Zum Funktionieren des Unterdrückungs- und Verfolgungsapparatus im NS-

System', in Karl-Dietrich Bracher *et al.* (eds.), *Nationalsozialistische Diktatur 1933–1945. Eine Bilanz* (Bonn, 1983), pp. 270–84; Robert L. Koehl, *The Black Corps: The Structure and Power Struggles of the Nazi SS* (Madison, 1983); Johannes Tuchel, Reinhold Schattenfroh, *Zentrale des Terrors. Prinz-Albrecht-Strasse 8. Das Hauptquartier der Gestapo* (Berlin, 1987).

37 For the history of the Gestapo see Jacques Delarue, *Geschichte der Gestapo* (Düsseldorf, 1964); Hans Buchheim, *SS und Polizei im NS-Staat* (Bonn, 1964); Christoph Graf, *Politische Polizei zwischen Demokratie und Diktatur. Die Entwicklung der preussischen politischen Polizei vom Staatsschutzorgan der Weimarer Republik zum Geheimen Staatspolizeiamt des Dritten Reiches* (Berlin, 1983).

38 On the SD see Friedrich Zipfel, *Gestapo und SD* (Berlin, 1960); Shlomo Aronson, *Reinhard Heydrich und die Frühgeschichte von Gestapo und SD* (Stuttgart, 1971). Biographies of Heydrich include Gunther Deschner, *Heydrich: The Pursuit of Total Power* (London, 1981).

39 Heinz Boberach (ed.), *Meldungen aus dem Reich. Die geheimen Lageberichte des Sicherheitsdienstes der SS 1938–1945* (Herrsching, 1984), Vols. 1–18.

40 On the history of the concentration camps see Martin Broszat, 'National-sozialistische Konzentrationslager 1933–1945', in H. Buchheim *et al.* (eds.), *Anatomie des SS-Staates*, pp. 11–136; Heinz Kühnrich, *Der KZ-Staat 1933–1945* (Berlin, 1980); Falk Pingel, *Häftlinge unter SS-Herrschaft. Widerstand, Selbstbehauptung und Vernichtung im Konzentrationslager* (Hamburg, 1978).

41 On the Waffen-SS, see Bernd Wegner, *The Waffen-SS: Organisation, Ideology and Function* (Oxford, 1990). The various economic enterprises of the SS are discussed in Enno Georg, *Die wirtschaftlichen Unternehmungen der SS* (Stuttgart, 1963).

42 For Ritter's SS connections see Reimar Gilsenbach, 'Die Verfolgung der Sinti – ein Weg der nach Auschwitz führte', in *Feinderklärung und Prävention. Kriminalbiologie, Zigeunerforschung und Asozialenpolitik. Beiträge zur nationalsozialistischen Gesundheits- und Sozialpolitik* (Berlin, 1988), vol. 6, pp. 26–7; Michael Zimmermann, 'Von der Diskriminierung zum "Familien-lager" Auschwitz. Die nationalsozialistische Zigeunerverfolgung', *Dachauer Hefte*, 5 (1989), pp. 95ff., and his 'Die nationalsozialistische Vernichtungspolitik gegen Sinti und Roma', *Aus Politik und Zeitgeschichte. Beilage zur Wochenzeitung Das Parlament*, 18 April 1987, pp. 31ff.

43 Hans-Georg Stümke, Rudi Rinkler, *Rosa Winkel, Rosa Listen. Homosexuelle und 'Gesundes Volksempfinden' von Auschwitz bis heute* (Hamburg, 1981), pp. 243–4.

44 Michael H. Kater, *'Das Ahnenerbe' der SS 1935–1945. Ein Beitrag zur Kulturpolitik des Dritten Reiches* (Stuttgart, 1974), pp. 231ff.

45 Georg Lilienthal, *Der 'Lebensborn e.V.'. Ein Instrument nationalsozialistischer Rassenpolitik* (Stuttgart, 1985).

46 Robert Koehl, *RKFDV: German Resettlement and Population Policy 1939–45* (Cambridge, Mass., 1957); see also Christopher Browning, 'Nazi Resettle-ment Policy and the Search for a Solution to the Jewish Question, 1939–1941', *German Studies Review* (1986), pp. 503ff.

47 On the Einsatzgruppen see Heinz Artzt, *Mörder in Uniform. Organis-ationen, die zu Vollstreckern nationalsozialistischer Gewaltverbrechen wurden* (Munich, 1979); Helmut Krausnick, Hans-Heinrich Wilhelm, *Hitlers Einsatzgruppen. Die Truppe des Weltanschauungskrieges. Die Einsatzgruppen der Sicherheitspolizie und des SD 1938–1942* (Stuttgart, 1982).

48 H. Heiber, 'Der Generalplan Ost', *Vierteljahreshefte für Zeitgeschichte*, 6 (1958), pp. 281–325; Karol Marian Pospieszalski, 'Hitlerowska polemika z "Generalplan Ost" Reichsfuhrera SS', *Przeglad Zachodni*, 2 (1958), pp. 346ff.; Dietrich Eichholtz, 'Der Generalplan Ost. Über eine Ausgeburt imperialistischer Denkart und Politik', *Jahrbuch für Geschichte*, 26 (1982), pp. 217ff.; Karl-Heinz Roth, 'Bevölkerungspolitik und Zwangsarbeit im "Generalplan Ost"', *Dokumentationsstelle zur NS-Sozialpolitik*, 1 (1985), pp. 70–93, 'Erster "Generalplan Ost" von Konrad Meyer', *Dokumentationsstelle zur NS-Sozialpolitik*, 1 (1985), pp. 45–52. The last two have contributed to M. Rössler, S. Schleiermacher (eds.), *Der 'Generalplan Ost'* (Nordlingen, 1991).

49 On the NSV see Herwart Vorländer, *Die NSV. Darstellung und Dokumenta-tion einer nationalsozialistischen Organisation* (Boppart, 1988); Peter Zolling, *Zwischen Integration und Segregation. Sozialpolitik im 'Dritten Reich' am Beispiel der 'Nationalsozialistischen Volkswohlfahrt' (NSV) in Hamburg* (Frankfurt am Main, 1986); Adelheid Gräfin zu Castel Ruden-hausen, '"Nicht mitzuleiden, mitzukämpfen sind wir da!". Nationalsozial-istische Volkswohlfahrt im Gau Westfalen-Nord', in Detlev Peukert, Jürgen Reulecke (eds.), *Die Reihen fast geschlossen. Beiträge zur Geschichte des Alltags unterm Hakenkreuz* (Wuppertal, 1981), pp. 223–45.

4 THE PERSECUTION OF THE JEWS

1 For these events, see Comité des Délégations Juives (ed.), *Das Schwarzbuch. Tatsachen und Dokumente. Die Lage der Juden in Deutschland 1933* (Paris, 1934, reprinted Berlin, 1984).

2 For examples from Berlin, see Wolfgang Wippermann, *Steinerne Zeugen. Stätten der Judenverfolgung in Berlin* (Berlin, 1982); Hans Norbert Burkert, Klaus Matussek, Wolfgang Wippermann, *'Machtergriefung' Berlin 1933* (Berlin, 1982, 2nd edition); Wolfgang Wippermann, 'Verfolgung und Widerstand der Berliner Juden 1933–1945', in Christian Pross, Rolf Winau (eds.), *Nicht misshandeln. Das Krankenhaus Moabit* (Berlin, 1984), pp. 15–29; Helmut Bräutigam, Oliver C. Gliech, 'Nationalsozialistische Zwangslager in Berlin I. Die 'wilden Konzentrationslager und Folterkeller 1933/34', in Wolfgang Ribbe (ed.), *Berlin-Forschungen* (Berlin, 1987), Vol. 2, pp. 141–78.

3 For the following, see above all Uwe Dietrich Adam, *Judenpolitik im Dritten Reich* (Düsseldorf, 1972), pp. 49ff.

4 'Gesetz zur Wiederstellung des Berufsbeamtentums vom 7. April 1933', *Reichsgesetzblatt*, 1933, Part 1, pp. 175–7.

5 For examples see Joseph Walk (ed.), *Das Sonderrecht für die Juden in NS-Staat. Eine Sammlung der gesetzlichen Massnahmen und Richtlinien–Inhalt*

und Bedeutung (Karlsruhe, 1981), pp. 12ff. For a good discussion of 'Berufsverbote' policies see Avraham Barkai, *From Boycott to Annihilation: The Economic Struggle of German Jews 1933–1943* (New England, 1989), pp. 25ff.

6 For examples from Frankfurt am Main, see Wolfgang Wippermann, *Das Leben in Frankfurt zur NS-Zeit.* Vol. 1: *Die nationalsozialistische Judenverfolgung* (Frankfurt am Main, 1986), pp. 53ff.

7 'Gesetz gegen die Überfüllung deutscher Schulen und Hochschulen vom 25. April 1933', *Reichsgesetzblatt 1933*, Part 1, p. 225; see also Walk, *Sonderrecht*, pp. 17f.

8 '2. Verordnung zur Durchführung des Gesetzes zur Wiederherstellung des Berufsbeamtentums', *Reichsgesetzblatt 1933*, Part 1, pp. 233–5.

9 '3. Verordnung zur Durchführung des Gesetzes zur Wiederherstellung des Berufsbeamtentums', *Reichsgesetzblatt 1933*, Part 1, pp. 245f.

10 For a detailed account see Ulrich Dunker, *Der Reichsbund jüdischer Frontsoldaten 1919–1938* (Düsseldorf, 1977), pp. 113ff.

11 Wippermann, *Steinerne Zeugen*, pp. 81ff.

12 'Verordnung des Reichsarbeitsministers über die Tätigkeit von Zahnärzten und Zahntechnikern bei den Krankenkassen vom 2. Juni 1933', *Reichsgesetzblatt 1933*, Part 1, pp. 350f.

13 'Verordnung des Reichsarbeitsministers über die Zulassung von Ärzten zur Tätigkeit bei den Krankenkassen vom 17. Mai 1934', *Reichsgesetzblatt 1934*, Part 1, pp. 399–409.

14 'Preussische Assistentenordnung vom 26. Juli 1934'; see Walk, *Sonderrecht*, p. 86.

15 'Reichshabilitationsordnung vom 13. Dezember 1934'; see Walk, *Sonderrecht*, p. 99. For examples from Berlin of how these policies affected the careers of individuals, see Rudolf Schottlaender (ed.), *Verfolgte Berliner Wissenschaftler. Ein Gedenkwerk* (Berlin, 1988). See also Doron Niederland, 'The Emigration of Jewish Academics and Professionals from Germany in the First Years of Nazi Rule', *Leo Baeck Institute Year Book*, 33 (1988), pp. 285ff.

16 For examples see Walk, *Sonderrecht*, pp. 1–129. See also Martin Broszat, 'The "Reichskristallnacht": A Turning Point on the Road to Holocaust', in Konrad Kwiet (ed.), *From the Emancipation to the Holocaust: Essays on Jewish Literature and History in Central Europe* (New South Wales, 1987), pp. 58f.

17 On this theme see the memoirs collected in Monika Richarz (ed.), *Jüdisches Leben in Deutschland. Selbstzeugnisse zur Sozialgeschichte 1918–1945* (Stuttgart, 1982). See also Barkai, *From Boycott to Annihilation*, pp. 25ff.

18 'Gesetz über den Widerruf von Einbürgerungen und die Aberkennung der deutschen Staatsbürgerschaft vom 14. Juli 1933', *Reichsgesetzblatt 1933*, Part 1, p. 480 (not mentioned in Walk, *Sonderrecht*). See also the 'Verordnung zur Durchführung des Gesetzes über den Widerruf von Einbürgerungen und die Aberkennung der deutschen Staatsbürgerschaft vom 26. Juli 1933', *Reichsgesetzblatt 1933*, Part 1, p. 538.

19 Salomon Adler-Rudel, *Ostjuden in Deutschland 1880 bis 1940. Zugleich eine Geschichte ihrer Organisationen, die sie betreuten* (Tübingen, 1959). On 'Ostjuden' in the Berlin 'Scheuenviertel', see Eike Geisel, *Im Scheuenviertel*.

Bilder, Texte und Dokumente (Berlin, 1981). For Frankfurt am Main, see Wippermann, *Leben in Frankfurt*, Vol. 1, pp. 42ff. On 'Ostjuden' in general, see Trude Maurer, *Ostjuden in Deutschland 1918–1933* (Hamburg, 1986); Steven E. Aschheim, *Brothers and Strangers: The East European Jew in German and German Jewish Consciousness 1800–1923* (Madison, 1982); Jack Wertheimer, *Unwelcome Strangers: East European Jews in Imperial Germany* (Oxford, 1987).

20 'Reichserbhofgesetz vom 29. September 1933', *Reichsgesetzblatt 1933*, Part 1, pp. 685–92.

21 'Gesetz zur Ordnung der nationalen Arbeit vom 20. Januar 1934', *Reichsgesetzblatt 1934*, Part 1, pp. 45–56. See also Walk, *Sonderrecht*, p. 69.

22 'Wehrgesetz vom 21 Mai 1935', *Reichsgesetzblatt 1935*, Part 1, pp. 609–14.

23 For the reactions of non-Jews to the persecution of the Jews see Ian Kershaw, 'Antisemitismus und Volksstimmung. Reaktion auf die Judenverfolgung', in Martin Broszat *et al.* (eds.), *Bayern in der NS-Zeit* (Munich, 1979), Vol. 2, pp. 281–348, 'The Persecution of the Jews and German Popular Opinion in the Third Reich', *Leo Baeck Institute Year Book*, 26 (1981), pp. 261–89; Michael H. Kater, 'Everyday Anti-Semitism in Prewar Nazi Germany: The Popular Bases', *Yad Vashem Studies*, 16 (1984), pp. 129–59; Otto Dov Kulka, '"Public Opinion" in Nazi Germany and the "Jewish Question"', *Jerusalem Quarterly*, 25 (1982), pp. 121–44 and 26 (1983), pp. 34–45, 'Die Nürnberger Rassegesetze und die deutsche Bevölkerung im Lichte geheimer NS-Lage- und Stimmungsberichte', *Vierteljahreshefte für Zeitgeschichte*, 32 (1984), pp. 582–624; Otto Dov Kulka, Aron Rodrigue, 'The German Population and the Jews in the Third Reich: Recent Publications and Trends in Research on German Society and the "Jewish Question"', *Yad Vashem Studies*, 16 (1984), pp. 421–35; Sarah Gordon, *Hitler, Germans and the 'Jewish Question'* (Princeton, 1984); Hans Mommsen, 'Was haben die Deutschen vom Völkermord an den Juden gewusst?', in Walter H. Pehle (ed.), *Der Judenpogrom 1938. Von der 'Reichskristallnacht' zum Völkermord* (Frankfurt am Main, 1988), pp. 176ff. For a good discussion of the issues involved, see Michael Marrus, *The Holocaust in History* (London, 1987), pp. 85–94.

24 On the burning of books see Ulrich Walberer (ed.), *10. Mai 1933. Bücherverbrennung in Deutschland und die Folgen* (Frankfurt am Main, 1983). See also Norbert Frei, *Der Führerstaat* (Munich, 1987), pp. 76ff., and Burkert, Matussek, Wippermann, *'Machtergreifung'. Berlin 1933*, pp. 197–8.

25 See Werner Röder, Herbert A. Strauss (eds.), *Biographisches Handbuch der deutschsprachigen Emigration nach 1933/ International Biographical Dictionary of Central European Emigrés 1933–1945* (Munich, 1980–3), Vols. 1–3, *Die jüdische Emigration aus Deutschland 1933–1941. Die Geschichte einer Austreibung* (Frankfurt am Main, 1985). For the following details on actors and film directors see Norbert Frei, *Der Führerstaat*, p. 112.

26 For examples from Frankfurt am Main, see Wippermann, *Leben in Frankfurt*, Vol. 1, pp. 53ff., and for Bremerhaven see his *Jüdisches Leben im Raum Bremerhaven. Eine Fallstudie zur Alltagsgeschichte der Juden vom 18. Jahrhundert bis zur NS-Zeit* (Bremerhaven, 1985), pp. 155ff.

27 'Reichsbürgergesetz' and 'Gesetz zum Schutze des deutschen Blutes und der deutschen Ehre vom 15. September 1935', *Reichsgesetzblatt 1935*, Part 1, pp. 1146–7. These texts are translated and discussed by Jeremy Noakes, Geoffrey Pridham (eds.), *Nazism 1919–1945: A Documentary Reader*, Vol. 2, *State, Economy and Society 1933–1939* (Exeter, 1984), pp. 532ff. See also Adam, *Judenpolitik*, pp. 114ff.

28 Cited by Hermann Graml, *Reichskristallnacht. Antisemitismus und Judenverfolgung im Dritten Reich* (Munich, 1988), p. 162.

29 On the increasingly sterile 'intentionalist' and 'structuralist' controversy see Klaus Hildebrand, *The Third Reich* (London, 1984), pp. 146–51; Wolfgang Wippermann, 'Forschungsgeschichte und Forschungsprobleme', and Wippermann (ed.), *Kontroversen um Hitler* (Frankfurt am Main, 1986), pp. 83ff.; Ian Kershaw, *The Nazi Dictatorship: Problems and Perspectives of Interpretation* (London, 1989), pp. 84ff.

30 'Erste Verordnung zum Reichsbürgergesetz vom 14. November 1935', *Reichsgesetzblatt 1935*, Part 1, pp. 133f. For further examples see Walk, *Sonderrecht*, pp. 131ff. See also Adam, *Judenpolitik*, pp. 132ff.

31 On this see Helmut Genschel, *Die Verdrängung der Juden aus der Wirtschaft im Dritten Reich* (Göttingen, 1966); Klaus Drobisch *et al.*, *Juden unterm Hakenkreuz. Verfolgung und Ausrottung der deutschen Juden 1933–1945* (Frankfurt am Main, 1973), pp. 165f.; Adam, *Judenpolitik*, pp. 145ff.; Avraham Barkai, *From Boycott to Annihilation.*

32 Cited by Martin Broszat, 'The "Reichskristallnacht"', p. 59. A copy of the original letter is in the Wiener Library, London.

33 The first quotation is from an article in the *Zentralblatt für Bibliothekswesen*, 55 (1938), p. 407, the second from a letter of the *Kreisleiter* of the NSDAP to the *Oberbürgermeister* of Frankfurt am Main dated 27 July 1938. The text is reprinted in Wippermann, *Das Leben in Frankfurt*, Vol. 1, p. 185.,

34 'Richtlinien für die Bewilligung von Unterhaltszuschüssen an jüdische Beamte, die im Weltkrieg an der Front für das Deutsche Reich oder für seine Verbündeten gekämpft und ein Ruhegehalt nach den gesetzlichen Vorschriften nicht erdient haben, gemäss c. 2 der II VO zum RBuG (21.12.1935) vom 3. März 1936', in Walk, *Sonderrecht*, p. 155; and 'III. Durchführungs-Verordnung über die Gewährung von Kinderbeihilfen an kinderreiche Familien vom 24. März 1936', *Reichsgesetzblatt 1936*, Part 1, pp. 252–4.

35 'Erste Verordnung zum Gesetz über die Verpachtung und Verwaltung öffentlicher Apotheken vom 26. März 1936', *Reichsgesetzblatt 1936*, Part 1, pp. 317f.

36 'Reichstierärzteordnung vom 3. April 1936', *Reichsgesetzblatt 1936*, Part 1, pp. 347–58.

37 'Verordnung über die geschäftsmässige Hilfeleistung in Devisensachen', *Reichsgesetzblatt 1936*, Part 1, pp. 524–6.

38 'Gesetz über die Befähigung zum höheren bautechnischen Verwaltungsdienst vom 16. Juli 1936', *Reichsgesetzblatt 1936*, Part 1, pp. 563f.

39 'Verordnung über den Handel mit Vieh vom 25. Januar 1937', *Reichsgesetzblatt 1937*, Part 1, pp. 28f.

40 'Reichsnotarordnung vom 13. Februar 1937', *Reichsgesetzblatt 1937*, Part 1, pp. 191–202.

41 'Zweite Durchführungsverordnung zum Reichsjagdgesetz vom 5. Februar 1937', *Reichsgesetzblatt 1937*, Part 1, pp. 179–83.

42 'Allgemeine Verfügung des Reichsministers der Justiz vom 4. November 1937', Walk, *Sonderrecht*, p. 204.

43 See Adam, *Judenpolitik*, pp. 97ff. and 197ff.

44 On this see Hans Robinsohn, *Justiz als politische Verfolgung. Die Rechtssprechung in 'Rassenschändefallen' beim Landgericht Hamburg 1936–1943* (Stuttgart, 1977).

45 Above all see Barkai, *From Boycott to Annihilation*, pp. 114ff. and his '"Schicksalsjahr 1938". Kontinuität und Verschärfung der wirtschaftlichen Ausplünderung der deutschen Juden', in Walter H. Pehle (ed.), *Der Judenpogrom 1938*, pp. 94–117.

46 Graml, *Reichskristallnacht*, p. 11.

47 'Waffengesetz vom 18. März 1938', *Reichsgesetzblatt 1938*, Part 1, pp. 265–9.

48 'Gesetz zur Änderung der Gewerbeordnung für das Deutsche Reich vom 6. Juli 1938", *Reichsgesetzblatt 1938*, Part 1, pp. 823f.

49 'Gesetz zur Ordnung der Krankenpflege vom 28. September 1938', *Reichsgesetzblatt 1938*, Part 1, p. 1309; and 'I. Verordnung über die Krankenpflegeschulen vom 28. September 1938', *Reichsgesetzblatt 1938*, Part 1, pp. 1310–13.

50 'VI. Verordnung zum Reichsbürgergesetz vom 31. Oktober 1938', *Reichsgesetzblatt 1938*, Part 1, pp. 1545f.

51 'Hebammengesetz vom 21. Dezember 1938', *Reichsgesetzblatt 1938*, Part 1, pp. 1893–6.

52 Barkai, *Vom Boykott zur 'Entjudung'*, pp. 168ff.

53 Cited by Barkai, 'Schicksalsjahr 1938', p. 107. 'Jewish' businesses were also systematically ruined by the denial of advertising space or bank credits. For examples from the clothing industry see Angelika Klose, 'Frauenmode im Dritten Reich' (unpublished M.A. dissertation, Freie Universität, Berlin, 1989), pp. 55–6.

54 'Verordnung über die Anmeldung des Vermögens von Juden vom 26. April 1938', *Reichsgesetzblatt 1938*, Part 1, pp. 414f.

55 On German Jewish self-help see Barkai, *From Boycott to Annihilation*, pp. 139ff., also Salomon Adler-Rudel, *Jüdische Selbsthilfe unter dem Naziregime 1933 bis 1939. Im Spiegel der Berichte der Reichsvertretung der Juden in Deutschland* (Tübingen, 1974).

56 'Runderlass des Reichsministers des Innern vom 27. Juli 1938 über "nach Juden und jüdischen Mischlingen benannte Strassen"'; see Walk, *Sonderrecht*, p. 235.

57 'Stenographische Niederschrift der Besprechung über die Judenfrage im Reichsluftfahrtministerium vom 12. November 1938', in Helmut Eschwege (ed.), *Kennzeichen 'J.' Bilder, Dokumente, Berichte zur Geschichte der Verbrechen des Hitlerfaschismus an den deutschen Juden 1933–1945* (Berlin, 1981), pp. 124–30.

58 'Erlass des Reichsministers des Innern vom 18. August 1938', Walk, *Sonder-recht*, p. 237.

59 Victor Klemperer, *LTI. Notizbuch eines Philologen* (Frankfurt am Main, 1982), pp. 177ff.

60 See Götz Aly, Karl Heinz Roth, *Die restlose Erfassung. Volkszählen, Identifizieren, Aussondern im Nationalsozialismus* (Berlin, 1984), pp. 25–6.

61 See Karl A. Schleunes, *The Twisted Road to Auschwitz: Nazi Policy towards German Jews 1933–1939* (London, 1972), pp. 169ff.

62 Drobisch *et al.*, *Juden unterm Hakenkreuz*, pp. 181ff.; Regina Bruss, *Die Bremer Juden unter dem Nationalsozialismus* (Bremen, 1983), pp. 202ff.; Barkai, *From Boycott to Annihilation*, pp. 142ff.

63 Arthur D. Morse, *While Six Million Died: A Chronicle of American Apathy* (New York, 1967); David S. Wyman, *Paper Walls: America and the Refugee Crisis 1938–1941* (Amherst, 1968), *The Abandonment of the Jews: America and the Holocaust* (New York, 1985); Henry Feingold, *The Politics of Rescue* (New Jersey, 1970); Robert W. Ross, *So It Was True: The American Protestant Press and the Nazi Persecution of the Jews* (Minneapolis, 1980); Deborah Lipstadt, *Beyond Belief: The American Press and the Coming of the Holocaust 1933–1945* (New York, 1986); Richard Breitman, Alan M. Kraut, *American Refugee Policy and European Jewry 1933–1945* (Bloomington, 1987); Haskel Lookstein, *Were We Our Brothers' Keepers? The Policy Response of American Jews to the Holocaust 1938–1944* (New York, 1985); Kurt Heitmann, 'National Socialist Racial Policy and the New York Times 1933–1939' (unpublished M.A. thesis, Freie Universität, Berlin, 1989); Bernard Wasserstein, *Britain and the Jews of Europe 1939–1945* (Oxford, 1988); Dov Levin, 'The Attitude of the Soviet Union toward the Rescue of Jews', *Proceedings of the Second Yad Vashem International Historical Conference* (Jerusalem, 1974), pp. 225–36. There is a sensitive discussion of the role of 'bystanders' in Marrus, *The Holocaust in History*, pp. 156ff.

64 For the Polish measures see *Dziennik Ustaw Rzeczyspolitej Polskiiej 1938*, 1 No. 22, p. 340. See also Eliahu Ben Elissar, *La Diplomatie du IIIe Reich et les Juifs* (Paris, 1969), pp. 301–21; Emanuel Melzer, 'Relations between Poland and Germany and their Impact on the Jewish Problem in Poland (1935–1938)', *Yad Vashem Studies*, 12 (1977), pp. 193–229; Sybil Milton, 'The Expulsion of Polish Jews from Germany October 1938 to July 1939: A Documentation', *Leo Baeck Institute Year Book*, 29 (1984), pp. 169–99; Trude Maurer, 'Abschiebung und Attentat. Die Ausweisung der polnischen Juden und der Vorwand für die "Kristallnacht"', in Walter H. Pehle (ed.), *Der Judenpogrom 1938*, pp. 59–61.

65 The most important source collections are Eschwege (ed.), *Kennzeichen 'J.'*, pp. 111ff.; Wolfgang Scheffler, 'Ausgewählte Dokumente zur Geschichte des Novemberpogroms', in Landeszentrale für politische Bildungsarbeit Berlin (ed.), *Judenverfolgung im Dritten Reich. Zur Politik und Zeitgeschichte* (Berlin, 1964), Vol. 4; Hermann Graml, 'Die Reichskristallnacht. Geschichte des Pogroms vom 9.–10. November 1938', Evangelischer Arbeitskreis Kirche und Israel in Hessen-Nassau (ed.), *Reichskristallnacht. Eine Arbeitshilfe für Unterricht und Gemeindearbeit* (Frankfurt am Main, 1978),

pp. 3–18; Kurt Pätzold, Irene Runge, *Kristallnacht. Zum Pogrom 1938* (Cologne, 1988). By far the most outstanding of the recent spate of commemorative books is Walter H. Pehle (ed.), *Der Judenpogrom 1938*. See also Hermann Graml's *Reichskristallnacht. Antisemitismus und Judenverfolgung im Dritten Reich*; Yehuda Bauer, 'Kristallnacht as a Turning Point: Jewish Reactions to Nazi Policies', Jyman H. Legters (ed.), *Western Society After the Holocaust* (Boulder, 1983), pp. 39–68; Peter Loewenberg, 'The Kristallnacht as a Public Degradation Ritual', *Leo Baeck Institute Year Book*, 32 (1987), pp. 309–23.

66 From Wolfgang Benz, 'Der Rückfall in die Barbarei. Bericht über den Pogrom', in Walter H. Pehle, *Der Judenpogrom 1938*, pp. 23–5.

67 William S. Allen, 'Die deutsche Öffentlichkeit und die "Reichskristallnacht" – Konflikte zwischen Werthierarchie und Propaganda im Dritten Reich', in Detlev Peukert, Jürgen Reulecke (eds.), *Die Reihen fast geschlossen. Beiträge zur Geschichte des Alltags unterm Nationalsozialismus* (Wuppertal, 1981), pp. 397–412; on the attitudes of the German resistance towards the persecution of the Jews see Christoph Dipper, 'Der Deutsche Widerstand und die Juden', *Geschichte und Gesellschaft*, 9 (1983), pp. 349–80.

68 Eschwege (ed.), *Kennzeichen 'J.'*, pp. 124–32. For the resulting decrees see 'Verordnung zur Wiederherstellung des Strassenbildes bei jüdischen Gewerbebetrieben vom 12. November 1938', *Reichsgesetzblatt 1938*, Part 1, p. 1581; 'Verordnung über eine Sühneleistung der Juden deutscher Staatsangehörigkeit vom 12. November 1938', *Reichsgesetzblatt 1938*, Part 1, p. 1579. For further decrees see Walk, *Sonderrecht*, pp. 254f.

69 'Runderlass des Reichsminister der Finanzen vom 3. Dezember 1938', Walk, *Sonderrecht*, p. 262; and 'Verordnung über den Einsatz des jüdischen Vermögens', in Walk, *Sonderrecht*. See also Barkai, *From Boycott to Annihilation*, p. 138; and Stefan Mehl, 'Das Reichsfinanzministerium und die Verfolgung der deutschen Juden 1933–1943" (unpublished M.A. thesis, Freie Universität, Berlin, 1989), pp. 124ff.

70 'VII. Verordnung zum Reichsbürgergesetz vom 5. Dezember 1938', *Reichsgesetzblatt 1938*, Part 1, p. 1751.

71 Letter dated 24 February 1939 from the *Reichswirtschaftsministerium* concerning the obligation upon Jews to surrender jewels and valuables, Walk, *Sonderrecht*, p. 283.

72 'Erste Verordnung des Reichsministers des Innern zur Durchführung und Ergänzung des Brieftaubengesetzes vom 29. November 1938', *Reichsgesetzblatt 1938*, Part 1, pp. 1749f.

73 'Erlass des Reichsführers-SS und Chefs der deutschen Polizei im Reichsministerium des Inneren vom 3. Dezember 1938 über die Entziehung der Führerscheine und Zulassungspapiere für Juden', Walk, *Sonderrecht*, p. 262.

74 'Anordnung des Polizeipräsidenten von Berlin vom 3. Dezember 1938', Walk, *Sonderrecht*, p. 262. For further ordinances on the same theme see Walk, *Sonderrecht*, pp. 303ff.

75 Klemperer, *LTI*, pp. 177ff. See also Philip Friedman, 'The Jewish Badge and the Yellow Star in the Nazi Era', *Historia Judaica*, 17 (1955), pp. 41ff.

76 Karl A. Schleunes, *The Twisted Road to Auschwitz*; Adam, *Judenpolitik*; Martin Broszat, 'Hitler und die Genesis der "Endlösung": Aus Anlass der Thesen von David Irving', *Vierteljahreshefte für Zeitgeschichte*, 25 (1977), pp. 739–73; Hans Mommsen, 'The Realization of the Unthinkable: The "Final Solution of the Jewish Question" in the Third Reich', in Gerhard Hirschfeld (ed.), *The Policies of Genocide: Jews and Soviet Prisoners of War in Nazi Germany* (London, 1986), pp. 93ff.; Christopher Browning, 'The Government Experts', in Henry Friedlander, Sybil Milton (eds.), *The Holocaust: Ideology, Bureaucracy, and Genocide* (New York, 1978), pp. 183–97.

77 Lucy Dawidowicz, *The War against the Jews 1933–1945* (London, 1977); Klaus Hildebrand, *The Third Reich*, pp. 146ff.; Andreas Hillgruber, 'Die "Endlösung" und das deutsche Ostimperium als Kernstück des rassenideologischen Programms des Nationalsozialismus', in his *Deutsche Grossmacht- und Weltpolitik im 19. und 20. Jahrhundert* (Düsseldorf, 1977), pp. 252–75; Gerald Fleming, *Hitler and the Final Solution* (Oxford, 1986); Eberhard Jäckel, Jürgen Rohwer (eds.), *Der Mord an den Juden im Zweiten Weltkrieg. Entschlussbildung und Verwirklichung* (Stuttgart, 1985); Eberhard Jäckel, *Hitlers Herrschaft, Vollzug einer Weltanschauung* (Stuttgart, 1986), pp. 89ff. See also Kershaw, *The Nazi Dictatorship*, pp. 83ff.

78 See the works cited in note 76.

79 For a rather too perfunctory dismissal of the victim-centred literature see Kershaw, *The Nazi Dictatorship*, pp. 82ff. The books and films of Bruno Bettelheim, Primo Levi, Alain Renais, and Claude Lanzmann treat the subject in a moving and innovative way.

80 Eschwege (ed.), *Kennzeichen 'J.'*, p. 130.

81 The relevant passage from Hitler's speech on 30 January 1939 can be found in Noakes and Pridham (eds.), *Nazism 1919–1945: A Documentary Reader*, Vol. 3: *Foreign Policy, War and Racial Extermination* (Exeter, 1988), p. 1047.

82 See the works cited in note 76.

83 Kershaw, *The Nazi Dictatorship*, p. 97; on the various 'reservation' plans see Philip Friedman, 'The Lublin Reservation and the Madagascar Plan: Two Aspects of Nazi Jewish Policy during the Second World War', *YIVO. Annual of Jewish Social Science*, 8 (1953), pp. 151–77; Jonny Moser, 'Nisko: The First Experiment in Deportation', *Simon Wiesenthal Centre Annual*, 2 (1985), pp. 1–31; Seev Goschen, 'Eichmann und die Nisko-Aktion im Oktober 1939: Eine Fallstudie zur NS-Judenpolitik in der letzten Etappe vor der "Endlösung"', *Vierteljahreshefte für Zeitgeschichte*, 29 (1981), pp. 74–96.

84 Helmut Kraunsnick, Hans-Heinrich Wilhelm, *Hitlers Einsatzgruppen. Die Truppen des Weltanschauungskrieges 1938–1942* (Frankfurt am Main, 1985).

85 Graml, *Reichskristallnacht*, pp. 193ff.

86 *Ibid.*, p. 193.

87 See Ernst Klee, Willi Dressen, Volker Riess (eds.), *'Schöne Zeiten'. Judenmord aus der Sicht der Täter und Gaffer* (Frankfurt am Main, 1988), pp. 84–5.

88 *Ibid.*, pp. 95ff.

89 The phrase comes from Christopher Browning, *The Final Solution and the German Foreign Office* (New York, 1978), p. 8.

90 *IMT*, Vol. 26, pp. 266f.; cited by Wolfgang Scheffler, *Judenverfolgung im Dritten Reich* (Berlin, 1964), p. 34.

91 The text of the minutes is reprinted by Noakes and Pridham in their *Nazism 1919–1945: A Documentary Reader*, Vol. 3, pp. 1127ff.

92 *Ibid.*, p. 1135, citing Fleming, *Hitler and the Final Solution*, pp. 91–2.

93 Klee, Dressen, Riess, '*Schöne Zeiten*', pp. 208ff.

94 *Ibid.*, pp. 234–5.

95 *Ibid.*, p. 245. On Hoess see Martin Broszat (ed.), *Kommandant in Auschwitz. Autobiographische Aufzeichnungen* (Stuttgart, 1958).

96 Claude Lanzmann interview with Filip Müller reprinted in *Shoah: An Oral History of the Holocaust* (New York, 1985), pp. 125–6.

97 *Hitler's Table-Talk*, translated by N. Cameron and R. H. Stevens (Oxford, 1988), p. 332.

98 See Konrad Kwiet, Helmut Eschwege, *Selbstbehauptung und Widerstand. Deutsche Juden im Kampf um Existenz und Menschenwürde 1933 bis 1945* (Hamburg, 1984); Helmut Eschwege, 'Resistance of German Jews against the Nazi Regime', *Leo Baeck Institute Year Book*, 15 (1970), pp. 134–80; Konrad Kwiet, 'Gehen oder bleiben?', in Walter H. Pehle (ed.), *Der Judenpogrom 1938*, pp. 132ff.

99 Konrad Kwiet, 'The Ultimate Refuge: Suicide in the Jewish Community Under the Nazis', *Leo Baeck Institute Year Book*, 29 (1984), pp. 135–68.

100 These statistics are from Konrad Kwiet, 'Gehen oder bleiben?', pp. 139–40.

101 Wolfgang Wippermann, *Die Berliner Gruppe Baum und der jüdische Widerstand. Beiträge zum Thema Widerstand* (Berlin, 1981), p. 19.

102 Nathan Stoltzfus, '"Jemand war für mich da." Der Aufstand der Frauen in der Rosenstrasse', *Die Zeit*, 30 (1989), pp. 9–13.

5 THE PERSECUTION OF SINTI AND ROMA, AND OTHER ETHNIC MINORITIES

1 See Romani Rose, *Bürgerrechte für Sinti und Roma. Das Buch zum Rassismus in Deutschland* (Heidelberg, 1987), pp. 9ff. For a description of the present situation of Sinti and Roma in West Germany see the article by Annelie Stankau in the *Kölner Stadt-Anzeiger*, 18 February 1989, reprinted and translated as 'Living at the Edges of Society: Life Remains Tough for the Modern Gypsy', in *The German Tribune* (1989), No. 1362, p. 15.

2 According to another version, the term 'Egyptian' refers to the Peloponnese, which in the later Middle Ages was known as 'Little Egypt'. There was apparently a Sinti and Roma settlement near the town of 'Gyppe', or Methone as it is called today.

3 Rüdiger Vossen, *Zigeuner, Roma, Sinti, Gitanos, Gypsies zwischen Verfolgung und Romantisierung* (Frankfurt am Main, 1983).

4 For collected contemporary chronicles see Reimer Gronemeyer, *Zigeuner im Spiegel früherer Chroniken und Abhandlungen. Quellen vom 15. bis 18. Jahrhundert* (Giessen, 1987).

5 See Joachim S. Hohmann, *Geschichte der Zigeunerverfolgung in Deutschland* (Frankfurt am Main, 1981), pp. 13ff.

6 See Hohmann, *Geschichte der Zigeuneverfolgung*, pp. 48ff.; on the persecution of Sinti and Roma in the late nineteenth and early twentieth centuries, see Wolfgang Günther, *Zur preussischen Zigeunerpolitik seit 1871. Eine Untersuchung am Beispiel des Landkreises Neustadt am Rübenberge und der Haupstadt Hannover* (Hanover, 1895); Rainer Hehemann, *Die 'Bekämpfung des Zigeunerunwesens' im Wilhelminischen Deutschland und in der Weimarer Republik 1871–1933* (Frankfurt am Main, 1987).

7 See the contemporary dissertation by Werner-Kurt Höhne, 'Die Vereinbarkeit der deutschen Zigeunergesetze und Verordnungen mit dem Reichsrecht, insbesondere der Reichsverfassung' (University of Heidelberg, 1929). Höhne came to the conclusion that the 'Gypsy' legislation of the various *Länder* was not compatible with the constitution of the Weimar Republic. See also Hehemann, *Die 'Bekämpfung des Zigeunerunwesens'*, and Bernhard Streck, 'Die "Bekämpfung des Zigeunerunwesens". Ein Stück moderner Rechtsgeschichte', in Tilman Zülch (ed.), *In Auschwitz vergast, bis heute verfolgt. Zur Situation der Roma (Zigeuner) in Deutschland* (Reinbeck, 1979), pp. 64–88.

8 Bavarian 'Gesetz zur Bekämpfung von Zigeunern, Landfahrern und Arbeitsscheuen vom 16. Juli 1926', *Gesetz- und Verordnungsblatt für den Freistaat Bayern 1926*, pp. 359ff.

9 'Ausführungsbestimmungen zum (bayerischen) Zigeuner- und Arbeitsscheuen-Gesetz vom 16. Juli 1926', reprinted in Höhne, 'Die Vereinbarkeit der deutschen Zigeunergesetze', pp. 146–53. See also the contemporary legal commentary by Hermann Reich, 'Das bayerische Zigeuner- und Arbeitsscheuengesetz', *Juristische Rundschau*, 2 (1926), pp. 834–7.

10 Streck, 'Die "Bekämpfung des Zigeunerunwesens"', p. 85.

11 The first moves towards this were made in 1936. See 'Runderlass des Reichs- und Preussischen Ministers des Innern vom 5. Juni 1936, betr. "Bekämpfung der Zigeunerplage"', *Ministerialblatt für die Preussische Innere Verwaltung*, 1, No. 17 (1936), p. 783. See also Michael Zimmermann, *Verfolgt, vertrieben, vernichtet. Die nationalsozialistische Vernichtungspolitik gegen Sinti und Roma* (Essen, 1989), pp. 23f.

12 For examples see Wolfgang Wippermann, *Das Leben in Frankfurt zur NS-Zeit*, Vol. 2: *Die nationalsozialistische Zigeunerverfolgung* (Frankfurt am Main, 1986), pp. 66f.; Zimmermann, *Verfolgt, vertrieben, vernichtet*, pp. 19f.

13 'Runderlass des Reichs- und Preussischen Ministers des Innern vom 26. November 1935 über das "Verbot von Rassenmischehen"', *Ministerialblatt für die innere Verwaltung*, 49 (1935), pp. 1429–34.

14 Wilhelm Stuckart, Hans Globke, *Kommentar zur deutschen Rassengesetzgebung* (Munich, 1936), Vol. 1, pp. 55f.

15 Reprinted in Wippermann, *Das Leben in Frankfurt*, Vol. 2, pp. 55f.

16 Oberbürgermeister of Frankfurt am Main, draft letter dated 27 September 1930, reprinted in Wippermann, *Das Leben in Frankfurt*, Vol. 2, pp. 55f.

17 For a detailed account see Ute Brucker-Boroujerdi, Wolfgang Wippermann, 'Gutachten über den Zwangscharakter des "Zigeunerlagers" Berlin-Marzahn in der NS-Zeit' (MS, Freie Universität, Berlin, 1988), and their 'National-

sozialistische Zwangslager in Berlin III. Das "Zigeunerlager" Marzahn', in Wolfgang Ribbe (ed.), *Berlin-Forschungen II* (Berlin, 1987), pp. 189–201; Wippermann, 'Das "Zigeunerlager" Berlin-Marzahn 1936–1945', *Pogrom. Zeitschrift für bedrohte Völker*, 18 (1987), pp. 77–80.

18 On Ritter see Benno Müller-Hill, *Murderous Science: Elimination by Scientific Selection of Jews, Gypsies, and Others, Germany 1933–1945* (Oxford, 1988); Ute Brucker-Boroujerdi, Wolfgang Wippermann, 'Die "Rassenhygienische und Erbbiologische Forschungsstelle" im Reichsgesundheitsamt', *Bundesgesundheitsblatt*, 32 (1989), pp. 13–19. This essay is largely based upon publications by Ritter, his personal file in the Berlin Document Centre and the so-called 'Forschungsakte Ritter' in the Bundesarchiv Koblenz, R 73/ 14.005. See also Zimmermann, *Verfolgt, vertrieben, vernichtet*, and Reimar Gilsenbach, 'Die Verfolgung der Sinti – ein Weg, der nach Auschwitz führte' and 'Wie Lolitschai zur Doktorwürde kam', *Beiträge zur nationalsozialistischen Gesundheits- und Sozialpolitik*, Vol. 6: *Feinderklärung und Prävention. Kriminalbiologie, Zigeunerforschung und Asozialenpolitik* (Berlin, 1988), pp. 11–41 and 101–34.

19 Bundesarchiv Koblenz R 73/ 14.005.

20 For Ritter's working hypotheses see Robert Ritter, *Ein Menschenschlag. Erbärztliche und erbgeschichtliche Untersuchungen über die – durch 10 Geschlechterfolgen erforschten – Nachkommen von 'Vagabunden, Jauern und Räubern'* (Leipzig, 1937), *'Zigeuner und Landfahrer', Der nichtsesshafte Mensch. Ein Beitrag zur Neugestaltung der Raum- und Menschenordnung im Grossdeutschen Reich* (Munich, 1939), pp. 71–88, 'Zur Frage der Rassenbiologie und Rassenpsychologie der Zigeuner in Deutschland', *Reichsgesundheitsblatt*, 12 (1938), pp. 425ff., 'Die Zigeunerfrage und das Zigeunerbastardproblem', *Fortschritte der Erbpathologie*, 3 (Leipzig, 1939), pp. 1–10, 'Die Bestandsaufnahme der Zigeuner und Zigeunermischlinge in Deutschland', *Der Öffentliche Gesundheitsdienst* (5 February 1941), 6, pp. 477–89, 'Arbeitsbericht' (MS), BDC, Ritter file, and in Bundesarchiv Koblenz BA ZSg 142/ 2.923.

21 Letter from Himmler dated 16 July 1937 cited by Hans-Joachim Döring, *Die Zigeuner im nationalsozialistischen Staat* (Hamburg, 1964), p. 33.

22 'Runderlass des Reichsführers-SS und Chefs der Deutschen Polizei im Reichsministerium des Inneren vom 8. Dezember 1938, betr. "Bekämpfung der Zigeunerplage"', *Ministerialblatt des Reichs- und Preussischen Ministers des Innern*, 99, no. 51 (1938), 14 December 1938, p. 2105, partially reprinted in Wippermann, *Das Leben in Frankfurt*, Vol. 2, pp. 70f.

23 'Ausführungsanweisungen des Reichskriminalpolizeiamt vom 1.3.1939 zum Runderlass des Reichsführers-SS und Chefs der Deutschen Polizei im Reichsministerium des Innern vom 8. Dezember 1938', *Deutsches Kriminalpolizeiblatt*, 12 (1939), reprinted in Wippermann, *Das Leben in Frankfurt*, Vol. 2, pp. 72–5.

24 Unfortunately the detailed minutes of this meeting have not been found. For what was discussed see Ritter's letter to the DFB dated 15 June 1940, BA R 73/ 14.005, and the testimony of Adolf Würth in Müller-Hill, *Murderous Science*, p. 145.

25 'Schnellbrief des Reichssicherheitshauptamtes vom 17. Oktober 1939 an die Staatlichen Kriminalpolizei leit stellen, bez. "Zigeunererfassung"', Erlassammlung des Reichskriminalpolizeiamtes – Vorbeugende Verbrechensbekämpfung, Institut für Zeitgeschichte, Munich, Dc 17.02, reprinted in Wipperman, *Das Leben in Frankfurt*, Vol. 1, pp. 80f.

26 On the 'Zigeunerlager' in Frankfurt see Wippermann, *Das Leben in Frankfurt*, Vol. 2, pp. 28ff. On the camp at Marzahn, see Brucker-Boroujerdi, Wippermann, 'Nationalsozialistische Zwangslager in Berlin III'; for the 'Zigeunerlager' at Lackenbach see Erika Thurner, *Nationalsozialismus und Zigeuner in Österreich* (Salzburg, 1983).

27 See Hans Buchheim, 'Die Aktion "Arbeitsscheu Reich"', *Gutachten des Instituts für Zeitgeschichte*, 2 (Munich, 1966), pp. 196–201; Wolfgang Ayass, '"Ein Gebot nationaler Arbeitsdisziplin". Die Aktion "Arbeitsscheu Reich" 1938', *Beiträge zur nationalsozialistischen Gesundheits- und Sozialpolitik*, 6 (Berlin, 1988), pp. 43–74.

28 'Schnellbrief des Reichssicherheitshauptamtes vom 20. November 1939'. Erlassammlung des Reichskriminalpolizeiamtes – Vorbeugende Verbrechensbekämpfung, Institut für Zeitgeschichte, Munich, Dc 17.02.

29 'Schnellbrief Des Reichssicherheitshauptamtes vom 18. Juni 1940, betr. "Haftprüfung der gemäss Erlass vom 1. Juni 1938 festgenommenen Personen"', Erlassammlung des Reichskriminalpolizeiamtes – Vorbeugende Verbrechensbekämpfung, Institut für Zeitgeschichte, Munich Dc 17.02.

30 See Donald Kenrick, Grattan Puxon, *Sinti und Roma. Die Vernichtung eines Volkes im NS-Staat* (Göttingen, 1981), p. 67.

31 For a detailed discussion of the deportations see Wippermann, *Das Leben in Frankfurt*, Vol. 2, pp. 82ff. See also Zimmermann, *Verfolgt, vertrieben, vernichtet*, pp. 43ff.

32 'Protokoll der Besprechung Heydrichs mit Seyss-Inquart und anderen SS- und Polizeiführern am 30. Januar 1940', *Nürnberger Dokumente* No. 5322, reprinted in Kurt Pätzold (ed.), *Verfolgung, Vertreibung, Vernichtung. Dokumente des faschistischen Antisemitismus 1933 bis 1942* (Leipzig, 1983), pp. 258f. See also Zimmermann, *Verfolgt, vertrieben, vernichtet*, p. 48.

33 See note 17 above.

34 Michael Zimmermann, 'Von der Diskriminierung zum "Familienlager" Auschwitz. Die nationalsozialistische Zigeunerverfolgung', *Dachauer Hefte*, 5 (1989), p. 103.

35 See for example 'Bericht des Kommandeurs der 281. Sicherungsdivision vom 23. Juni 1942 über die Erschiessung von 127 Zigeunern in Nororschew durch die geheime Feldpolizei', *Nürnberger Dokumente* NOKW 2072, also *Nürnberger Dokumente* NOKW 2535, 2022, 802 and 1486; 'Schreiben der 339. Infanterie Division an die Befehlshaber rückwärtigen Heeres-Gebiet Mitte vom 5. November 1941', *Bundesarchiv Militärarchiv Freiburg* RH 26-339/5. For detailed accounts see Kenrick, Puxon, *Sinti und Roma*, pp. 93ff.; Helmut Krausnick, *Die Truppen des Weltanschauungskrieges 1938–1942* (Frankfurt am Main, 1985), pp. 135ff.; Raul Hilberg, *Die Vernichtung der europäischen Juden. Die Gesamtgeschichte des Holocaust* (Berlin, 1982), pp. 197ff.; Martin Gilbert, *Atlas of the Holocaust* (London, 1988).

36 'Schreiben des Reichssicherheitshauptamtes vom 13. Oktober 1942, betr. "Zigeunerhäuptlinge", Erlassammlung des Reichskriminalpolizeiamtes – Vorbeugende, Verbrechensbekämpfung', *Institut für Zeitgeschichte*, Munich, Dc 17.02, reprinted in Wippermann, *Das Leben in Frankfurt*, Vol. 1, pp. 106f. See also Michael H. Kater, *Das 'Ahnenerbe' der SS 1935–1945. Ein Beitrag zur Kulturpolitik des Dritten Reiches* (Stuttgart, 1974), pp. 206f.; Thurner, *Nationalsozialismus und Zigeuner in Österreich*, pp. 143f.

37 The decree has not been found. See however 'Schnellbrief des Reichssicherheitshauptamtes vom 29. Januar 1943 betr. "Einweisung von Zigeunermischlingen, Ròm-Zigeunern und balkanischen Zigeunern in ein Konzentrationslager"', Erlassammlung des Reichskriminalpolizeiamtes- Vorbeugende Verbrechensbekämpfung, *Institut für Zeitgeschichte*, Munich, Dc 17.02, reprinted in Wippermann, *Das Leben in Frankfurt*, 1, pp. 109–14.

38 Martin Broszat (ed.), Rudolf Höss, *Kommandant in Auschwitz. Autobiographische Aufzeichnungen* (Stuttgart, 1958), pp. 105f.

39 See the reports by Elisabeth Guttenberger, 'Das Zigeunerlager', in H. G. Adler, Hermann Langbein, Ella Lingens-Reiner, *Auschwitz. Zeugnisse und Berichte* (Frankfurt am Main, 1965), pp. 159ff.; Hermann Langbein, *Der Auschwitz-Prozess. Eine Dokumentation* (Frankfurt am Main, 1965), pp. 106f.; Lucy Adelsberger, *Auschwitz – Ein Tatsachenbericht* (Berlin, 1965), also the accounts by Kenrick, Puxon, *Sinti und Roma* , pp. 106ff.; Bernhard Streck, 'Zigeuner in Auschwitz, Chronik des Lagers BIIe', in B. Streck, Mark Münzel (eds.), *Kumpania und Kontrolle. Moderne Behinderungen zigeunerischen Lebens* (Giessen, 1981), pp. 69ff.; Zimmermann, *Verfolgt, vertrieben, vernichtet*, pp. 75ff.

40 Gilsenbach, 'Wie Lolitschai zur Doktorwürde kam', p. 109.

41 'Anordnung des Reichsarbeitsministers vom 14. März 1942, betr. "Beschäftigung von Zigeunern"', *Reichsgesetzblatt 1942*, Part 1, p. 138.

42 'Dritte Verordnung des Reichsministers der Finanzen vom 26. März 1942 zur Durchführung der Verordnung über die Erhebung einer Sozialausgleichsabgabe vom 23 März 1942', *Reichsgesetzblatt 1943*, Part 1, pp. 268f.

43 'Zwölfte Verordnung zum Reichsbürgergesetz vom 25. April 1943', *Reichsgesetzblatt 1943*, Part 1, pp. 268f.

44 'Anordnung der Reichsleitung der NSDAP – Hauptamt für Volkswohlfahrt vom 21. Mai 1942, betr. arbeitsrechtliche Gleichstellung von "Vollzigeunern und Zigeunermischlingen mit vorwiegend oder gleichem zigeunerischen Blutanteil" mit Juden', Erlassammlung des Reichskriminalpolizeiamtes, *Institut für Zeitgeschichte*, Munich, Dc 17.02.

45 'Urteil des Bundesgerichtshofes vom 7. Januar 1956', partly reprinted in Zülch (ed.), *In Auschwitz vergast*, pp. 168f.

46 See Rose, *Bürgerrechte für Sinti und Roma*, pp. 31ff. See also Mathias Winter, 'Kontinuitäten in der deutschen Zigeunerforschung und Zigeunerpolitik', *Beiträge zur nationalsozialistischen Gesundheits- und Sozialpolitik*, 6 (Berlin, 1988), pp. 135ff.

47 Rose, *Bürgerrechte für Sinti und Roma*, pp. 114ff.

48 On the following see Reiner Pommerin, *Sterilisierung der Rheinland-bastarde. Das Schicksal einer farbigen deutschen Minderheit 1918–1937* (Düsseldorf, 1979); Paul Weindling, *Health, Race and German Politics between National Unification and Nazism 1870–1945* (Cambridge, 1989), pp. 385ff.

49 Reich Chancellor Hermann Müller speaking in the Reichstag on 12 April 1920, *Verhandlungen der verfassunggebenden Deutschen National-versammlung*, Vol. 333: *Stenographische Berichte von der 15. Sitzung* (Berlin, 1920), p. 5048.

50 Friedrich Ebert in a speech delivered in Darmstadt in February 1923, Friedrich Ebert, *Schriften, Aufzeichnungen, Reden* (Dresden, 1926), Vol. 2, p. 290.

51 Sally Marks, 'Black Watch on the Rhine: A Study in Propaganda, Prejudice and Prurience', *European Studies Review*, 13 (1983), pp. 297–334. See also Gisela Lebzelter, 'Die "Schwarze Schmach". Vorurteile – Propaganda – Mythos', *Geschichte und Gesellschaft*, 11 (1985), pp. 37–58; K. Nelson, ' "The Black Horror on the Rhine": Race as a Factor in Post World War I Diplomacy', *Journal of Modern History*, 42 (1970), pp. 606–27.

52 *Hitler's Mein Kampf*, with an introduction by D. C. Watt (London, 1974), p. 295.

53 Dr Rosenberger, *Ärztliche Rundschau*, 47 (1920), cited by Pommerin, '*Rheinlandbastarde*', p. 24.

54 *Ibid.*, pp. 29ff.

55 *Ibid.*, pp. 56ff.

56 *Ibid.*, pp. 46ff; see also Niels C. Losch, 'Das Kaiser-Wilhelm-Institut für Anthropologie, menschliche Erblehre und Eugenik' (unpublished M.A. thesis, Freie Universität, Berlin, 1990), pp. 147ff.

57 Hans Macco, *Rassenprobleme im Dritten Reich* (Berlin, 1933).

58 Pommerin, *Rheinlandbastarde*, pp. 56ff. and 71ff. See also Heidrun Kaupen-Haas, 'Die Bevölkerungsplaner im Sachverständigenbeirat für Bevölkerungs- und Rassenpolitik', in Kaupen-Haas (ed.), *Der Griff nach der Bevölkerung. Aktualität und Kontinuität nazistischer Bevölkerungspolitik* (Nördlingen, 1986), pp. 112–13.

59 *Ibid.*, pp. 78ff.

60 On Nazi policy towards Slavic minorities see Michael Burleigh, *Germany Turns Eastwards: A Study of 'Ostforschung' in the Third Reich* (Cambridge, 1989).

61 *Ibid.*, pp. 184ff. On Nazi population policy in Poland, see Czeslaw Madajczyk, *Die Okkupationspolitik Nazideutschlands in Polen 1939–1945* (Cologne, 1988), pp. 454ff.; Martin Broszat, *Nationalsozialistische Polenpolitik* (Frankfurt am Main, 1965, 2nd edition), pp. 119ff.

62 BA Koblenz R153/280 'Sonderbericht zur Kaschubenfrage', 15 October 1939, p. 4.

63 Jan Solta, Klaus Schiller, Martin Kasper, Frido Mětšk, *Geschichte der Sorben* (Bautzen, 1977–9), Vols. 1–4; Gerald Stone, *The Smallest Slavonic Nation: The Sorbs of Lusatia* (London, 1972), for the history of the Sorbs.

64 On Prussian and Saxon policy towards Sorbian education see Wolfgang Wippermann, 'Wendische Gefahr und deutsche Angst. Sorbenbild und Sorbenpolitik im deutschen Kaiserreich' (unpublished MS), pp. 24ff.

65 *Ibid.*

66 Martin Kasper (ed.), *Geschichte der Sorben*, Vol. 3, pp. 27ff. for an account of the negotiations in Versailles.

67 On this see Todd Heubner, 'Ethnicity Denied: Nazi Policy Towards the Lusatian Sorbs, 1933–1945', *German History*, 6 (1988), pp. 253–4.

68 *Ibid.*, pp. 258ff.

69 BA Koblenz R153/1455 Reich Ministry of the Interior to the North-East German Research Community 'Thesen zur Wendenfrage', 26 April 1937; on this see Burleigh, *Germany Turns Eastwards*, pp. 122ff.

70 Huebner, 'Ethnicity Denied', p. 266.

71 Heinz Boberach (ed.), *Meldungen aus dem Reich. Die geheimen Lageberichte des Sicherheitsdienstes der SS 1938–1945* (Herrsching, 1984), Vol. 4, p. 1196.

72 Helmut Heiber, 'Denkschrift Himmler über die Behandlung der Fremdvölkischen im Osten', *Vierteljahrshefte für Zeitgeschichte*, 2 (1957), pp. 198ff.; Burleigh, *Germany Turns Eastwards*, pp. 217–18.

6 THE PERSECUTION OF THE 'HEREDITARILY ILL',
   THE 'ASOCIAL', AND HOMOSEXUALS

1 On the so-called 'hereditarily ill', compulsory sterilisation and the murder of the sick ('euthanasia'), see Alexander Mitscherlich, Fred Mielke (eds.), *Medizin ohne Menschlichkeit. Dokumente des Nürnberger Ärzteprozesses* (Stuttgart, 1948, reprinted Frankfurt am Main, 1989); Klaus Dörner, 'Nationalsozialismus und Lebensvernichtung', *Vierteljahrshefte für Zeitgeschichte*, 15 (1968), pp. 121ff.; Karl Dietrich Erdmann, '"Lebensunwertes Leben". Totalitäre Lebensvernichtung und das Problem der Euthanasie', *Geschichte in Wissenschaft und Unterricht*, 26 (1975), pp. 215–25; Lothar Gruchmann, '"Euthanasie" und Justiz im Dritten Reich', *Vierteljahreshefte für Zeitgeschichte*, 20 (1971), pp. 235–79; Kurt Nowak, *Euthanasie und Sterilisierung im Dritten Reich. Die Konfrontation der evangelischen und katholischen Kirche mit dem 'Gesetz zur Verhütung erbkranken Nachwuchses' und der 'Euthanasie' Aktion* (Göttingen, 1987); Ernst Klee, *'Euthanasie' im NS-Staat. Die 'Vernichtung lebensunwerten Lebens'* (Frankfurt am Main, 1983); Achim Thom, Horst Spaar (eds.), *Medizin im Faschismus* (East Berlin, 1985); Gisela Bock, *Zwangssterilisation im Nationalsozialismus* (Opladen, 1986); Heidrun Kaupen-Haas, *Der Griff nach der Bevölkerung* (Nördlingen, 1986); Christian Ganssmüller, *Die Erbgesundheitspolitik des Dritten Reiches* (Cologne, 1987); Hans Walter Schmuhl, *Rassenhygiene, Nationalsozialismus, Euthanasie* (Göttingen, 1987), Götz Aly *et al.*, *Aussonderung und Tod. Die klinische Hinrichtung der Unbrauchbaren. Beiträge zur nationalsozialistischen Gesundheits- und Sozialpolitik* (Berlin, 1987, 2nd edition), Vol. 1, and *Reform und Gewissen. 'Euthanasie' im Dienst des Fortschritts. Beiträge zur nationalsozialistischen Gesundheits- und Sozialpolitik* (Berlin, 1985), Vol. 2; Robert Jay Lifton, *The Nazi Doctors: A*

Study in the Psychology of Evil (London, 1986); Benno Müller-Hill, *Murderous Science: Elimination by Scientific Selection of Jews, Gypsies, and Others, Germany 1933–1945* (Oxford, 1988); Robert Proctor, *Racial Hygiene: Medicine under the Nazis* (Cambridge, Mass., 1988); Paul J. Weindling, *Health, Race and German Politics Between National Unification and Nazism 1870–1945* (Cambridge, 1989); Dorothea Sick, *'Euthanasie' im Nationalsozialismus am Beispiel des Kalmenhofs in Idstein im Taunus* (Frankfurt am Main, 1983); Manfred Klüppel, *'Euthanasie' und Lebensvernichtung am Beispiel der Landesheilanstalten Haina und Merxhausen. Eine Chronik der Ereignisse 1933–1945* (Kassel, 1984); Gerhard Kneuker, Wulf Steglich, *Begegnungen mit der Euthanasie in Hadamar* (Rehberg-Loccum, 1985); Dorothee Roer, Dieter Henkel (eds.), *Psychiatrie im Faschismus. Die Anstalt Hadamar 1933–1945* (Bonn, 1986); Landeswohlfahrtsverbandes Hessen (ed.), *Psychiatrie im Nationalsozialismus* (Kassel, 1989); Peter Chroust *et al.*, *Soll nach Hadamar überführt werden. Den Opfern der Euthanasiemorde 1939 bis 1945* (Frankfurt am Main, 1989) for an excellent catalogue of the memorial exhibition at Hadamar. For a moving biographical account of a victim of the 'euthanasia' programme see Hans-Ulrich Dapp, *Emma Z. Ein Opfer der Euthanasie* (Stuttgart, 1990). Michael Burleigh, 'Euthanasia in the Third Reich', *Social History of Medicine* (1991), 4 surveys this and other relevant literature. Helmuth Sorg, ' "Euthanasie" in den evangelischen Heilanstalten in Württemberg im Dritten Reich' (unpublished M.A. thesis, Freie Universität, Berlin, 1987) is an excellent local study.

2 'Gesetz zur Verhütung erbkranken Nachwuchses vom 14.7.1933', *Reichsgesetzblatt 1933*, Part 1, pp. 529ff.; see also the commentary on this by Arthur Gütt, Ernst Rüdin, Falk Ruttke, *Gesetz zur Verhütung erbkranken Nachwuchses vom 14. Juli 1933 nebst Ausführungsverordnungen* (Munich, 1936). For the prehistory and content of the law see Michael Meixner *et al.*, 'Das Gesetz zur Verhütung erbkranken Nachwuchses. Seine wissenschaftlichen und politischen Voraussetzungen und Folgewirkungen', in Achim Thom, Horst Spaar (eds.), *Medizin im Faschismus* (Berlin, 1985), pp. 152ff.; Joachim Müller, *Sterilisation und Gesetzgebung bis 1933* (Husum, 1985); Bock, *Zwangssterilisation*, pp. 55ff.

3 From *Reichsgesetzblatt 1933*, Part 1, pp. 529ff.

4 'Verordnung zur Ausführung des Gesetzes zur Verhütung erbkranken Nachwuchses vom 5. Dezember 1933', *Reichsgesetzblatt 1933*, Part 1, pp. 1021ff.

5 Bock, *Zwangssterilisation*, pp. 230ff.

6 *Reichsgesetzblatt 1933*, Part 1, pp. 1032ff.

7 Bock, *Zwangssterilisation*, pp. 97ff.

8 'Gesetz zur Änderung des Gesetzes zur Verhütung erbkranken Nachwuchses vom 26.6.1935', *Reichsgesetzblatt 1935*, Part 1, p. 196.

9 *Ibid.*

10 Karl Binding, Alfred Hoche, *Die Freigabe der Vernichtung lebensunwerten Lebens. Ihr Mass und ihre Form* (Leipzig, 1920).

11 Hitler's speech to the Nuremberg Party Rally on 5 August 1929, cited by Bock, *Zwangssterilisation*, p. 24.

12 See Klee, *'Euthanasie'*, p. 52 and Johannes Tuchel (ed.), *'Kein Recht auf Leben'. Beiträge und Dokumente zur Entrechtung und Vernichtung 'lebensunwerten Lebens' im Nationalsozialismus* (Berlin, 1984).

13 Klee *'Euthanasie'*, pp. 78f.

14 *Ibid.*, pp. 82ff. On the following see also Götz Aly (ed.), *Aktion T-4 1939–1945. Die 'Euthanasie' Zentrale in der Tiergartenstrasse 4* (Berlin, 1987).

15 Klee, *'Euthanasie'*, pp. 100f.

16 J. Noakes, G. Pridham (eds.), *Nazism 1919–1945: A Documentary Reader* (Exeter, 1988), Vol. 3, p. 1010.

17 Klee, *'Euthanasie'*, pp. 115ff.

18 Questionnaire 1 dated 1941, reprinted from Tuchel (ed.), *'Kein Recht auf Leben'*, p. 57. See also Ernst Klee (ed.), *Dokumente zur 'Euthanasie'* (Frankfurt am Main, 1985).

19 Reprinted from Tuchel (ed.), *'Kein Recht auf Leben'*, pp. 64f.

20 Noakes, Pridham (eds.), *Nazism 1919–1945: A Documentary Reader*, Vol. 3, p. 1021.

21 See Götz Aly, 'Der saubere und schmutzige Fortschritt', *Beiträge zur nationalsozialistischen Gesundheits- und Sozialpolitik*, 2 (Berlin, 1985), pp. 9–78; Klee, *'Euthanasie'*, pp. 95gg.

22 See above all Götz Aly (ed.), *Aktion T-4 1939–1945*, pp. 11–20.

23 For examples see Noakes, Pridham (eds.), *Nazism 1919–1945: A Documentary Reader*, Vol. 3, pp. 1028–9.

24 Ernst Klee, *Was sie taten – Was sie werden. Ärzte, Juristen und andere Beteiligte am Kranken- oder Judenmord* (Frankfurt am Main, 1986), p. 204.

25 Klee, *'Euthanasie'*, p. 249 for several examples.

26 *Ibid.*, p. 240.

27 On Kreyssig, see Klee *'Euthanasie'*, pp. 209f.

28 On Braune, see Klee, *'Euthanasie'*, pp. 211f.

29 For Galen's sermon see Noakes and Pridham, *Nazism 1919–1945: A Documentary Reader*, Vol. 3, pp. 1036ff.; see also Peter Löffler (ed.), *Bishof Clemens August Graf von Galen. Akten*, Vols. 1–2 (Mainz, 1988), 2, nr. 341, pp. 874ff.; Klee, *'Euthanasie'*, pp. 334ff.

30 Noakes, Pridham, *Nazism 1919–1945: A Documentary Reader*, Vol. 3, p. 1038.

31 Klee, *'Euthanasie'*, pp. 33ff.

32 R. Dorner (ed.), *Mathematische Aufgaben aus der Volks-Gelände und Wehrkunde*, 1. Teil (*Mittelstufe*) (Frankfurt am Main, 1936), p. 21; reprinted in Tuchel (ed.), *'Kein Recht auf Leben'*, p. 47. See also Klee, *'Euthanasie'*, p. 53.

33 For the background to these films see, above all, the definitive study by Ludwig Rost, *Sterilisation und Euthanasie im Film des 'Dritten Reiches'. Nationalsozialistische Propaganda in ihrer Beziehung zu rassenhygienischen Massnahmen des NS-Staates* (Husum, 1987); Karl-Heinz Roth, 'Filmpropaganda für die Vernichtung der Geisteskranken und Behinderten im 'Dritten Reich', *Beiträge zur nationalsozialistischen Gesundheits- und Sozialpolitik*, Vol. 2 (Berlin, 1985), pp. 125ff. In English see Erwin Leiser, *Nazi Cinema* (London, 1974), pp. 89ff.; David Welch, *Propaganda and the German*

Cinema 1933–1945 (Oxford and London, 1983), pp. 121–34; Michael Burleigh, '"Euthanasia" and the Cinema in Nazi Germany', *History Today*, 40 (1990), pp. 11–16. Both authors would like to thank Ludwig Rost for advising us on this subject. Copies of the earlier Racial Political Office of the NSDAP documentary films, e.g. *Sünden der Väter* and *Erbkrank*, are in our possession. We would like to thank the Filmarchiv, Koblenz and the Filmarchiv der DDR, East Berlin.

34 Roth, 'Filmpropaganda', pp. 135–6.

35 *Ibid.*

36 Rost, *Sterilisation und Euthanasie*, p. 255. Michael Burleigh would like to thank Ludwig Rost for copies of Liebeneiner's script for *I Accuse* and other documents connected with the film.

37 *Ibid.*, p. 269.

38 Heinz Boberach (ed.), *Meldungen aus dem Reich. Die geheimen Lagerberichte des Sicherheitsdienstes der SS 1938–1945* (Herrsching, 1984), Vol. 9, pp. 3175–8.

39 Klee, 'Euthanasie', pp. 345ff.; see also Stanislaw Kłodzinski, 'Die Aktion 14f13. Der Transport von 575 Häftlingen von Auschwitz in das "Sanatorium Dresden"', in Götz Aly (ed.), *Aktion T-4*, pp. 136ff.

40 Klee, 'Euthanasie', pp. 345ff.

41 Noakes, Pridham, *Nazism 1919–1945: A Documentary Reader*, Vol. 3, p. 1045.

42 Peter Chroust, 'Friedrich Mennecke. Innenansichten eines medizinischen Täters im Nationalsozialismus', in *Biedermann und Schreibtischtäter. Materialien zur deutschen Täter-Biographie* (Berlin, 1987), Vol. 4, pp. 81ff.

43 Klee, 'Euthanasie', pp. 401ff.

44 For the extension of the 'euthanasia' programme after Hitler's 'halt order', see *inter alia* Götz Aly, 'Medizin gegen Unbrauchbare' and Matthias Hamann, 'Die Morde an polnischen und sowjetischen Zwangsarbeitern in deutschen Anstalten', in *Aussonderung und Tod. Die klinische Hinrichtung der Unbrauchbaren. Beiträge zur nationalsozialistischen Gesundheits- und Sozialpolitik*, Vol. 1 (Berlin, 1987, 2nd edition). The quotation here is from Hamann, pp. 134–5. See also Klee, 'Euthanasie', pp. 356ff.

45 Klee, 'Euthanasie', pp. 367ff., 'Vom der "T-4" zur Judenvernichtung. Die "Aktion Reinhard" in den Vernichtungslagern Belzec, Sobibor und Treblinka', in Götz Aly (ed.), *Aktion T-4*, pp. 147ff.

46 Gitta Sereny, *Into that Darkness* (London, 1976) includes Stangl's account of his activities in Hartheim. There is a documentary film *Tod und Leben im Schloss Hartheim* (ORF), for which we are grateful to the director, Andreas Grüber, for a copy.

47 On the ways in which medical murderers evaded justice, see above all Ernst Klee, *Was sie taten – Was sie werden* (Frankfurt am Main, 1985).

48 Roth, 'Filmpropaganda', pp. 188–9.

49 *Brockhaus Enzyklopädie* (Wiesbaden, 1966, 17th revised edition), p. 792.

50 Nazi policy towards the 'asocial' was heavily influenced by the criminal-biological presuppositions of the Italian racial ideologist Cesare Lombroso, whose works were translated and popularised by Hans Kurella. See Cesare

Lombroso, *Die Ursachen und Bekämpfung des Verbrechens*, authorised translation by Hans Kurella and E. Jentzsch (Berlin, 1902), and his *Der Verbrecher in anthropologischer, ärztlicher und juristischer Beziehung* (Hamburg, 1890–6), 3 vols.; C. Lombroso and G. Ferrero, *Das Weib als Verbrecherin und Prostituierte. Anthropologische Studien*, authorised translation by Hans Kurella (Hamburg, 1894). Although Lombroso's theories were rarely directly cited because of his Jewish origins, his influence on the work of leading 'criminal-biologists' in the Third Reich was unmistakable. See Robert Ritter, *Ein Menschenschlag. Erbärztliche Untersuchungen über die – durch 10 Geschlechtserfolgen erforschten – Nachkommen von Vagabunden, Jaunern und Räubern* (Leipzig, 1937); Ferdinand von Neureiter, *Kriminalbiologie* (Berlin, 1940). The persecution of the 'asocial' is usually only treated peripherally in works dealing with the Nazi period. The literature on this theme is very scanty. Among the most important works are Detlev Peukert, 'Arbeitslager und Jugend-KZ. Die Behandlung "Gemeinschaftsfremder" im Dritten Reich', D. Peukert, Jürgen Reulecke (eds.), *Die Reihen fast geschlossen. Beiträge zur Geschichte des Alltags unterm Nationalsozialismus* (Wuppertal, 1981), pp. 413–43; Heidrun Kaupen-Haas (ed.), *Der Griff nach der Bevölkerung. Aktualität und Kontinuität nazistischer Bevölkerungspolitik* (Nördlingen, 1986); Jeremy Noakes, 'Social Outcasts in the Third Reich', in Richard Bessel (ed.), *Life in the Third Reich* (Oxford, 1987), pp. 83–96; Patrick Wagner, 'Das Gesetz über die Behandlung Gemeinschaftsfremder', *Beiträge zur nationalsozialistischen Gesundheits- und Sozialpolitik*, Vol. 6 (Hamburg, 1988), pp. 75–100; Wolfgang Ayass, 'Ein Gebot der nationalen Arbeitsdisziplin. Die Aktion "Arbeitsscheu Reich" 1938', *Beiträge zur nationalsozialistischen Gesundheits- und Sozialpolitik*, Vol. 6 (Hamburg, 1988), pp. 43–77, and his 'Vagrants and Beggars in Hitler's Reich', in Richard J. Evans (ed.), *The German Underworld: Deviants and Outcasts in German History* (London, 1988), pp. 210–37.

51 Hans Frank in the *Nationalsozialistische Monatshefte*, 1 (1930), p. 298.

52 For examples see Ernst Klee, *'Euthanasie'*, pp. 34ff.; the definitive study of compulsory sterilisation is Gisela Bock, *Zwangssterilisation im Nationalsozialismus. Studien zur Rassenpolitik und Frauenpolitik*; see also Karl-Heinz Roth (ed.), *Erfassung zur Vernichtung. Von der Sozialhygiene zum 'Gesetz über Sterbehilfe'* (Berlin, 1984) and Hans-Walter Schmuhl, *Rassenhygiene, Nationalsozialismus, Euthanasie* (Göttingen, 1987), pp. 151ff. For an interesting local study see Sabine Krause, 'Zwangssterilisation in Bremerhaven (1934–1945). Eine Fallstudie' (unpublished M.A. thesis, Freie Universität, Berlin, 1989).

53 For examples see Bock, *Zwangssterilisation*, pp. 401ff.

54 Klee, *'Euthanasie'*, pp. 34ff.

55 Ayass, 'Vagrants and Beggars', p. 213.

56 *Ibid.*, pp. 213–14.

57 *Ibid.*, pp. 225ff.

58 Karl-Heinz Roth, 'Städtesanierung und "ausmerzende" Soziologie. Der Fall Andreas Walther und die "Notarbeit 51" der "Notgemeinschaft der Deutschen Wissenschaft" 1934–1935 in Hamburg', in Carsten Klingemann

(ed.), *Rassenmythos und Sozialwissenschaften in Deutschland* (Opladen, 1987), pp. 370ff.

59 'Gesetz gegen gefährliche Gewohnheitsverbrecher vom 24.11.1933', *Reichsgesetzblatt 1933*, Part 1, p. 995.

60 See Klee, *'Euthanasie'*, pp. 37ff.

61 'Jugendstrafvollzugsordnung 22.1.1937'. See also Martin Guse *et al.*, 'Das Jugendschutzlager Moringen – ein Jugendkonzentrationslager', in Hans-Uwe Otto, Heinz Sünker (eds.), *Soziale Arbeit und Faschismus. Volkspflege und Aussonderung in der Fürsorgeerziehung in Westfalen von 1933–1945* (Weinheim, 1989).

62 On the following see Peukert, 'Arbeitslager und Jugend-KZ', pp. 418ff., and Ayass, 'Ein Gebot der nationalen Arbeitsdisziplin', pp. 44f.

63 'Grundlegender Erlass über die vorbeugende Verbrechensbekämpfung durch die Polizei des Reichs- und Preussischen Ministers des Innern vom 14.12.1937', Reichssicherheitshauptamt-Amt V (ed.), *Vorbeugende Verbrechensbekämpfung* (Berlin, 1942), p. 41.

64 See Ayass, 'Ein Gebot der nationalen Arbeitsdisziplin', pp. 45ff.

65 Hauptarchiv der von Bodelschwingschen Anstalten, Bestand 2, No. 12–45, cited by Ayass, 'Ein Gebot der nationalen Arbeitsdisziplin', p. 57.

66 *Ibid.*

67 Talk by SS-Oberführer Ulrich Greifelt delivered in January 1939. *Nürnberger Dokumente*, No. 5591, pp. 104ff.

68 See Peukert, 'Arbeitslager und Jugend-KZ', p. 415; Wagner, 'Das Gesetz über die Behandlung Gemeinschaftsfremder', pp. 80ff.

69 BA Koblenz R 22/944, pp. 228f., cited by Norbert Frei, *Der Führerstaat* (Munich, 1987), pp. 203–8.

70 See also Diemut Majer, *'Fremdvölkische' im Dritten Reich* (Boppard, 1981).

71 Letter from Reich Justice Minister Thierack to Bormann dated 13 October 1942, cited by Bruno Blau, *Das Ausnahmerecht für die Juden in Deutschland* (Düsseldorf, 1954), p. 116.

72 *'Richterbrief'*, 1 June 1943, cited by Heinz Boberach (ed.), *Richterbriefe. Dokumente zur Beeinflussung der deutschen Rechtssprechung 1942 bis 1944* (Boppard, 1975).

73 *'Richterbriefe'*, 1 January 1943 and 1 June 1943, cited in *ibid.*.

74 'Runderlass des Reichsministers des Innern 18.7.1940, "Richtlinien für die Beurteilung der Erbgesundheit"', *Ministerialblatt des Reichs- und Preussischen Ministers des Innern*, 5 (4 July 1940), p. 1591.

75 Interview with an anonymous subject, published in Hans-Georg Stümke, Rudi Finkler, *Rosa Winkel, Rosa Listen. Homosexuelle und 'Gesundes Volksempfinden' von Auschwitz bis heute* (Hamburg, 1981), p. 238. See also Burkhard Jellonek, *Homosexuelle unter dem Hakenkreuz. Verfolgung von Homosexuellen im Dritten Reich* (Paderborn, 1990) for a regional study of the persecution of homosexuals.

76 For an informed discussion of the issue of compensation, see Hans-Georg Stümke, *Homosexuelle in Deutschland. Eine politische Geschichte* (Munich, 1989), pp. 132ff. See also S. Romey, 'Zu Recht verfolgt? Zur Geschichte der ausgebliebenen Entschädigung', Projektgruppe für die vergessen Opfer des

NS-Regimes in Hamburg e.V. (eds.), *Verachtet – Verfolgt – Vernichtet zu den vergessenen Opfern des NS-Regimes* (Hamburg, 1986), pp. 220–45.

77 Stümke, *Homosexuelle in Deutschland*, pp. 166ff.; H. W. Wieland, 'Realer Sozialismus: DDR integriert Homosexuelle', *Du & Ich*, 19 (1987), pp. 71–3.

78 Reprinted in Richard Plant, *The Pink Triangle: The Nazi War against Homosexuals* (Edinburgh, 1987), p. 206.

79 For these remarks on the homosexual 'scene' see Stümke, *Homosexuelle in Deutschland*, pp. 22ff. and the catalogue *'Eldorado'. Homosexuelle Frauen und Männer in Berlin 1850–1950* (Berlin, 1984).

80 On Hirschfeld see Charlotte Wolff, *Magnus Hirschfeld: A Portrait of a Pioneer in Sexology* (London, 1986).

81 Stümke, *Homosexuelle in Deutschland*, pp. 40ff. See also B. Engelmann, *Krupp, Legenden und Wirklichkeit* (Frankfurt, 1970); for the Eulenburg affair see also E. Ebermayer, 'Glanz und Gloria verblasst. Der Fall Fürst Philipp zu Eulenburg-Hertefeld', *Der neue Pitaval*, Vol. 14: *Skandale* (Munich, 1967), pp. 115–64.

82 For attempts to reform paragraph 175 see Stümke, *Homosexuelle in Deutschland*, pp. 53ff. and Stümke, Finkler, *Rosa Winkel, Rosa Listen*, pp. 39ff.

83 On this theme see W. U. Eissler, *Arbeiterparteien und Homosexualität. Zur Sexualpolitik von SPD und KPD in der Weimarer Republik* (Berlin, 1980).

84 *Deutschland-Berichte der Sozialdemokratischen Partei Deutschlands (Sopade)* (1934), Vol. 1, p. 198. See also Ian Kershaw, *The 'Hitler Myth'. Image and Reality in the Third Reich* (Oxford, 1987), pp. 84ff.

85 Stümke, Finkler, *Rosa Winkel, Rosa Listen*, pp. 163–6.

86 Plant, *The Pink Triangle*, p. 206.

87 Stümke, *Homosexuelle in Deutschland*, p. 112.

88 For Himmler's speech, see Stümke, Finkler, *Rosa Winkel, Rosa Listen*, pp. 217–21.

89 Stümke, *Homosexuelle in Deutschland*, pp. 115–16.

90 For Vaernet, see Stümke, *Homosexuelle in Deutschland*, pp. 123ff.

91 BA (Koblenz) NS 4 Bu/50, Carl Vaernet to the Reichsführer-SS, 30 October 1944, with attached notes on Patient No. 1 (No. 21,686).

92 Stümke, *Homosexuelle in Deutschland*, p. 127.

93 Stümke, Finkler, *Rosa Winkel, Rosa Listen*, p. 286.

7 YOUTH IN THE THIRD REICH

1 *Adolf Hitler's Mein Kampf*, with an introduction by D. C. Watt (London, 1974), pp. 390ff. On the programmatic nature of these statements, see Wolfgang Wippermann, *Der konsequente Wahn. Ideologie und Politik Adolf Hitlers* (Munich, 1989), pp. 171ff. and 'Das Berliner Schulwesen in der NS-Zeit', in Benno Schmoldt (ed.), *Schule in Berlin. Gestern und heute* (Berlin, 1989), pp. 57–74; Hubert Steinhaus, *Hitlers pädagogische Maximen. 'Mein Kampf' und die Destruktion der Erziehung im Nationalsozialismus* (Frankfurt am Main, 1981).

Curiously enough, National Socialist policy towards youth has received scant attention in the context of the 'internationalists' versus 'revisionists' debate. The same applies to the debate about 'modernisation' theories. Apart from a few works from the GDR, which are more or less stuck in the rut of discussing the influence of big business, most older research is essentially Hitlercentric. Recent research tends to stress struggles over competence while treating the racial aims behind Nazi youth policy in a peripheral fashion.

The best survey of policy towards youth is Arno Klönne, *Jugend im Dritten Reich. Die Hitler-Jugend und ihre Gegner* (Cologne, 1984). There is also a fine collection of documents in Peter D. Stachura, *The German Youth Movement 1900–1945: An Interpretative Documentary History* (London, 1981).

2 Hitler, *Mein Kampf*, p. 454.

3 *Ibid.*, p. 277.

4 *Ibid.*, p. 451.

5 On the history of the HJ before 1933 see Klönne, *Jugend im Dritten Reich*, pp. 15ff.; Peter D. Stachura, *Nazi Youth in the Weimar Republic* (Santa Barbara, 1975); Hans-Christian Brandenburg, *Die Geschichte der HJ. Wege und Irrwege einer Generation* (Cologne, 1968).

6 See Anselm Faust, *Der nationalsozialistische Studentenbund. Studenten und Nationalsozialismus in der Weimarer Republik*, Vols. 1 and 2 (Düsseldorf, 1973).

7 For an enthusiastic account of this event see Hannsjoachim W. Koch, *Geschichte der Hitlerjugend* (Percha, 1975).

8 On the BDM see Martin Klaus, *Mädchen in der Hitlerjugend. Die Erziehung zur 'deutschen Frau'* (Cologne, 1980), and *Mädchen im Dritten Reich. Der Bund Deutscher Mädel (BDM)* (Cologne, 1983); Dagmar Rese, 'Bund Deutscher Mädel. Zur Geschichte der weiblichen Jugend im Dritten Reich', in Frauengruppe Faschismusforschung (ed.), *Mutterkreuz und Arbeitsbuch. Zur Geschichte der Frauen in der Weimarer Republik und im National-sozialismus* (Frankfurt, 1981), pp. 163–87.

9 Various examples in *Deutschland-Berichte (Sopade)*.

10 On the Kommunistischen Jugendverband Deutschland, see Karl Heinz Jahnke, *Jungkommunisten im Widerstandskampf gegen den Hitlerfaschismus* (Berlin, 1977). And on the relationship between the HJ and working-class youth organisations in general, see Karl Heinz Jahnke, Michael Buddrus, *Deutsche Jugend 1933–1945. Eine Dokumentation* (Hamburg, 1989).

11 There is a considerable literature on the *bündisch* youth movement, which is mainly concerned with the question of whether the latter was a precursor of the Hitler Youth. See Walter Z. Laqueur, *Die deutsche Jugendbewegung. Eine historische Studie* (Cologne, 1962); Harry Pross, *Jugend–Eros–Politik. Die Geschichte der deutschen Jugendverbände* (Berne, 1964); Felix Raabe, *Die Bündische Jugend. Ein Beitrag zur Geschichte der Weimarer Republik* (Stuttgart, 1961); Hermann Giesecke, *Vom Wandervogel bis zur Hitler-jugend* (Munich, 1981). For a valuable collection of sources see Werner Kindt (ed.), *Grundschriften der deutschen Jugendbewegung* (Düsseldorf, 1963) and, especially useful, Michael H. Kater, 'Bürgerliche Jugend-

bewegung und Hitlerjugend von 1926 bis 1939', *Archiv für Sozialgeschichte*, 17 (1977), and Klönne, *Jugend im Dritten Reich*, pp. 20ff.

12 'Vernichtet die Bünde!', *Junge Nation* (Mai 1933), reprinted in Klönne, *Jugend im Dritten Reich*, p. 106.

13 On the Artamanen League see George L. Mosse, *The Crisis of German Ideology: Intellectual Origins of the Third Reich* (London, 1964), pp. 116ff.; Klaus Bergmann, *Agrarromantik und Grosstadtfeindschaft* (Meisenheim, 1970), pp. 247–97; Michael H. Kater, 'Die Artamanen – Völkische Jugend in der Weimarer Republik', *Historische Zeitschrift*, 213 (1971), pp. 577–638; Wolfgang Schlicker, 'Die Artamanenbewegung – eine Frühform des Arbeitsdienstes und Kaderzelle des Faschismus auf dem Lande', *Zeitschrift für Geschichtswissenschaft*, 18 (1970), pp. 66–75.

14 See the apologetic, pro-Roman Catholic study by Barbara Schellenberger, *Katholische Jugend und Drittes Reich* (Mainz, 1975).

15 'Anordnung des "Reichsführers SS" und Inspekteur der Preussischen Geheimen Staatspolizei, Heinrich Himmler, von 1935', concerning confessional youth work; reprinted in Klönne, *Jugend im Dritten Reich*, p. 167.

16 Klaus Gotto, *Die Wochenzeitung Junge-Front/Michael* (Mainz, 1970).

17 Klönne, *Jugend im Dritten Reich*, pp. 185ff.

18 'Gesetz über die Hitler-Jugend vom 1.12.1936', reprinted in Jahnke, Buddrus, *Deutsche Jugend 1933–1945*, p. 121.

19 From a speech by Hitler on 4 December 1938 in Reichenberg; extracts reprinted in Klönne, *Jugend im Dritten Reich*, p. 30.

20 On the following: Klönne, *Jugend im Dritten Reich*, pp. 15ff.; Brandenburg, *Geschichte der HJ*; Heinz Boberach, *Jugend unter Hitler* (Düsseldorf, 1982); Karl-Heinz Huber, *Jugend unterm Hakenkreuz* (Berlin, 1982).

21 On Nazi education policy: Rolf Eilers, *Die nationalsozialistische Schulpolitik* (Cologne, 1963); Hans-Jürgen Gamm, *Führung und Verführung. Pädagogik des Nationalsozialismus* (Munich, 1900); Elke Nyssen, *Schule in Nationalsozialismus* (Weinheim, 1979), and especially Harald Scholtz, *Erziehung und Unterricht unterm Hakenkreuz* (Göttingen, 1985).

22 Wolfgang Wippermann, 'Das Berliner Schulwesen in der NS-Zeit. Fragen, Thesen und methodische Bemerkungen', in Benno Schmoldt (ed.), *Schule in Berlin. Gestern und heute* (Berlin, 1989), pp. 57–73; pp. 61f.

23 On the history of these schools see Gerd Radde, Fritz Karsen, *Ein Berliner Schulreformer der Weimarer Zeit* (Berlin, 1973).

24 *Berliner Lehrerzeitung*, 27 April 1933.

25 Wippermann, 'Das Berliner Schulwesen in der NS-Zeit', pp. 58–60.

26 See, for examples, Arbeitsgruppe Pädagogisches Museum (ed.), *Heil Hitler, Herr Lehrer. Volksschule 1933–1945* (Reinbeck, 1983).

27 On the so-called 'Crucifix struggle' in Oldenburg, see Jeremy Noakes, 'The Oldenburg Crucifix Struggle of November 1936: A Case Study of Opposition in the Third Reich', in Peter Stachura (ed.), *The Shaping of the Nazi State* (London, 1978), and for Bavaria, see Ian Kershaw's excellent *Popular Opinion and Political Dissent in the Third Reich, Bavaria 1933–1945* (Oxford, 1983), pp. 205ff. and pp. 340–57. Barbara Imbusch is preparing a dissertation on this issue.

28 See above, and also Ute Frevert, *Frauengeschichte. Zwischen bürgerlicher Verbesserung und Neuer Weiblichkeit* (Frankfurt am Main, 1986), pp. 200ff.

29 This is apparent from a case study of a Gymnasium in Göttingen. See Ulrich Popplow, 'Schulalltag im Dritten Reich. Fallstudie über ein Göttinger Gymnasium', *Aus Politik und Zeitgeschichte*, B 18 (1980), pp. 33–69. Other studies of individual schools have reached very contradictory results. 'The' schoolday in the Third Reich seems to have been so variable as to make any generalisations impossible. See especially Kurt-Ingo Flessau, *Schule der Diktatur. Lehrpläne und Schulbücher des Nationalsozialismus* (Frankfurt am Main, 1979).

30 Wippermann, 'Das Berliner Schulwesen', p. 65. This study is based on the early reports concerning Berlin schools in the Archiv des Pädagogischen Zentrums, Berlin.

31 'Gesetz zur Wiederherstellung des Berufsbeamtentums vom 7.4.1933', Hans-Dieter Schmid *et al.*, *Juden unterm Hakenkreuz* (Düsseldorf, 1983), Vol. 1, pp. 78f.

32 'Gesetz gegen die Überfüllung deutscher Schulen und Hochschulen vom 25.4.1933', Schmid *et al.*, *Juden unterm Hakenkreuz*, Vol. 1, p. 83.

33 Letter from the Reichsminister für Wissenschaft und Erziehung dated 15 December 1938, concerning 'Schulunterricht an Juden', Schmid *et al.*, *Juden unterm Hakenkreuz*, Vol. 1, pp. 152f.; 'Erlass des Ministers für Wissenschaft, Erziehung und Volksbildung, 20.6.1942 (7.7.)', reprinted in Joseph Walk, *Das Sonderrecht für die Juden im NS-Staat* (Heidelberg, 1981), p. 379.

34 Report by the *Manchester Guardian*, 21 August 1933; reprinted in Comité des Délégations Juives (ed.), *Die Lage der Juden in Deutschland 1933. Das Schwarzbuch – Tatsachen und Dokumente* (Paris, 1934, reprinted Frankfurt, 1983), p. 266.

35 For the exclusion of Jewish teachers and children from schools and separate Jewish schools in the Third Reich, see Salomon Adler-Rudel, *Jüdische Selbsthilfe unter dem Nazi-Regime 1933–1939* (Tübingen, 1979); Wolfgang Wippermann, 'Verfolgung und Widerstand der Berliner Juden 1933–45', in Christian Pross, Rolf Winau (eds.), *Nicht misshandeln. Das Krankenhaus Moabit* (Berlin, 1984), pp. 15–20, and *Das Leben in Frankfurt zur NS-Zeit*, Vol. 1: *Die nationalsozialistische Judenverfolgung* (Frankfurt am Main, 1986), especially pp. 83ff.

36 'Runderlass des Reichsministers für Wissenschaft, Erziehung und Volks-bildung vom 22.3.1941', 'Zulassung von Zigeunern und Negermischlingen zum Besuch öffentlicher Volksschulen', reprinted in Wolfgang Wippermann, *Das Leben in Frankfurt zur NS-Zeit*, Vol. 2: *Die nationalsozialistische Zigeunerverfolgung* (Frankfurt am Main, 1986), p. 106. For the discussion about whether Sinti and Roma should be admitted to schools see *ibid.*, pp. 42 and 95–101. On the 'Gypsy school' in the 'Gypsy camp' at Berlin-Marzahn see Wippermann, *Das Berliner Schulwesen zur NS-Zeit*, pp. 68ff.

37 See Manfred Höck, *Die Hilfsschule im Dritten Reich* (Berlin, 1977). For examples of racial selection practised in schools for backward children, see Ernst Klee, *'Euthanasie' im NS-Staat. Die 'Vernichtung lebensunwerten Lebens'* (Frankfurt am Main, 1983).

38 Article in the (Frankfurter) *Städtischen Anzeigenblatt* (9 April 1936), reprinted in Wolfgang Wippermann, *Das Leben in Frankfurt*, Vol. 2, pp. 131f.

39 See the outstanding study by Michael H. Kater, 'Hitlerjugend und Schule im Dritten Reich', *Historische Zeitschrift*, 228 (1979), pp. 572–623; Scholtz, *Erziehung und Unterricht unterm Hakenkreuz*, pp. 56ff.

40 Horst Überhorst (ed.), *Elite für die Diktatur. Die nationalpolitischen Erziehungsanstalten 1933–1945* (Düsseldorf, 1969).

41 Harald Scholtz, *NS-Ausleseschulen* (Göttingen, 1973).

42 Harald Scholtz, 'Die NS-Ordensburgen', *Vierteljahrshefte für Zeitgeschichte*, 15 (1967), pp. 269–98. For their relationship to the historical Teutonic Knights, see Wolfgang Wippermann, *Der Ordensstaat als Ideologie. Das Bild des Deutschen Ordens in der deutschen Geschichtsschreibung und Publizistik* (Berlin, 1979), pp. 253ff.

43 'Führers of the Future', *Manchester Guardian*, 17 November 1937; see also E. Hearst, 'Finishing Schools for Nazi Leaders', *Wiener Library Bulletin*, 19 (1965), pp. 35ff.; Harald Scholtz, 'Die "NS-Ordensburgen"', *Vierteljahreshefte für Zeitgeschichte*, 15 (1967), especially pp. 273–9.

44 See Gerhard Dabel, *KLV. Die erweiterte Kinder-Land-Verschickung. KLV-Lager 1940–1945* (Freiburg, 1981). Scholtz, in *Erziehung und Unterricht unterm Hakenkreuz*, pp. 103ff., places great significance on this, because it represented the first success that the Nazi regime had in achieving the total ideological control of young persons.

45 This aspect of Nazi youth policy has received a great deal of attention in recent years. One of the key issues dividing historians is the extent to which the sort of 'deviant' behaviour described here can be termed 'resistance' – a word which has heavy moral and ideological overtones. See Detlev Peukert, *Die Edelweisspiraten. Protestbewegung jugendlicher Arbeiter im Dritten Reich. Eine Dokumentation* (Cologne, 1980); Detlev Peukert and Michael Winter, *Edelweisspiraten in Duisburg. Eine Fallstudie zum subkulturellen Verhalten von Arbeiterjugendlichen* (Duisburg, 1982); Peukert, 'Youth in the Third Reich', in Richard Bessel (ed.), *Life in the Third Reich* (Oxford, 1987), pp. 25–40; Matthias von Hellfeld, *Edelweisspiraten in Köln. Die Jugendrebellion gegen das Dritte Reich. Das Beispiel Köln-Ehrenfeld* (Cologne, 1981); Klönne, *Jugend im Dritten Reich*, pp. 228ff. Peter Rosumek's dissertation caused much controversy even before it appeared by stressing the criminal backgrounds of the Edelweiss Pirates in Cologne.

46 Detlev Peukert, *Edelweisspiraten*, pp. 146ff.; and Klönne, *Jugend im Dritten Reich*, pp. 242ff. There is a good Yorkshire TV documentary on 'Jazz in the Third Reich'.

47 Report by the Reich Youth Leadership on 'Cliquen- und Bandenbildung unter Jugendlichen', September 1942, reprinted in Peukert, *Edelweisspiraten*, pp. 160–229, p. 202.

48 On this see Klönne, *Jugend im Dritten Reich*, pp. 228ff.; and Lothar Gruchmann, 'Jugendopposition und Justiz im Dritten Reich. Die Probleme bei der Verfolgung der "Leipziger Meuten" durch die Gerichte', in

Wolfgang Benz (ed.), *Miscellanea. Festschrift für Helmut Krausnick* (Stuttgart, 1980).

49 See note 47; reprinted in Peukert, *Edelweisspiraten*, pp. 220–3.

50 'Polizeiverordnung zum Schutze der Jugend vom 9.3.1940', reprinted in Arno Klönne (ed.), *Jugendkriminalität und Jugendopposition im NS-Staat* (Münster, 1981).

51 On this see Klönne, *Jugend im Dritten Reich*, pp. 234ff.; and Detlev Peukert, 'Arbeitslager und Jugend-KZ. Die "Behandlung Gemeinschaftsfremder" im Dritten Reich', in Detlev Peukert, Jürgen Reulecke (eds.), *Die Reihen fast geschlossen. Beiträge zur Geschichte des Alltags unterm Nationalsozialismus* (Wuppertal, 1981), pp. 413–34; Christa Hasenclever, *Jugendhilfe und Jugendgesetzgebung seit 1900* (Göttingen, 1978); Rolf Landwehr, Rüdiger Baron (eds.), *Geschichte der Sozialarbeit* (Weinheim, 1983); Carole Kuhlmann, *Erbkrank oder erziehbar? Jugendhilfe als Vorsorge und Aussonderung in der Fürsorgeerziehung in Westfalen von 1933–1945* (Weinheim, 1989).

52 On Robert Ritter's involvement in the registration and persecution of Sinti and Roma, see especially Peukert, 'Arbeitslager und Jugend-KZ', pp. 422ff.

53 See the report by the Essen Landgerichtspräsident to the Reich Ministry of Justice, 31 July 1944, on the 'police detention camp at Moringen', in Peukert, *Edelweisspiraten*, pp. 137–45.

54 'Erlass des Reichsführers-SS und Chefs der Deutschen Polizei, Heinrich Himmler', 25 October 1944; reprinted in Peukert, *Edelweisspiraten*, pp. 123–33; p. 124.

55 See note 45 above for further literature.

56 Reprinted in Klönne, *Jugend im Dritten Reich*, p. 22.

57 Reprinted in *ibid.*, , p. 120.

58 Reprinted in *ibid.*, p. 167, and Jahnke, Buddrus, *Deutsche Jugend*, p. 101.

59 Reprinted in *ibid.*, p. 28, and Jahnke, Buddrus, *Deutsche Jugend*, p. 121.

60 Reprinted in *ibid.*, p. 35.

61 From the 'Gesetz gegen die Überfüllung deutscher Schulen und Hochschulen', 25 April 1933, *Reichsgesetzblatt 1933*, Part 1, p. 225.

62 'Erlass des Reichsministers für Wissenschaft, Erziehung und Volksbildung über die Einrichtung besonderer jüdischer Schulen', 10 September 1935, in Michalka (ed.), *Das Dritte Reich*, p. 156.

63 'Anordnung des Reichsministers für Wissenschaft, Erziehung und Volksbildung über die sofortig Entlassung jüdischer Schüler von deutschen Schulen' 14 November 1938, in J. Hohlfeld (ed.), *Dokumente der deutschen Politik von 1848 bis zur Gegenwart*, Vol. 4 (Berlin, 1953), pp. 501ff.

64 Speech by Frick on 9 May 1935, cited by P. Meier-Benneckenstein (ed.), *Dokumente der Deutschen Politik* (Berlin, 1937), no. 96, p. 301.

65 From 'Erziehung und Unterricht in der Volksschule', 15 December 1939, *Deutsche Wissenschaft, Erziehung und Volksbildung, Amtsblatt des Reichsministerium* (Berlin, 1939).

66 From 'Bestimmungen über Erziehung und Unterricht in der Mittelschule',

15 December 1939 (Berlin, 1939), *Sonderdruck des Zentralverlags der NSDAP.*

67 From 'Erziehung und Unterricht in der Höhern Schule', 29 January 1938 (Berlin, 1939).

68 Reprinted in Klönne, *Jugend im Dritten Reich*, p. 58.

69 Reprinted in Klönne, *Jugend im Dritten Reich*, p. 83.

70 'Führers of the Future: The Chosen Few', *Manchester Guardian* (17 November 1937).

71 Reprinted in Peukert, *Edelweisspiraten*, pp. 50f.

72 Peukert, *Edelweisspiraten*, pp. 123ff.

8 WOMEN IN THE THIRD REICH

1 Hitler's speech to the *NS-Frauenschaft* on 8 September 1934 in Max Domarus (ed.), *Hitler. Reden und Proklamationen 1932–1945* (Munich, 1965), Vol. 1, pp. 449–52. *Mein Kampf* lacks extended statements on the subject of women. He did however remark that 'The goal of female education must invariably be the future mother'; see *Hitler's Mein Kampf*, with an introduction by D. C. Watt (London, 1974), p. 377.

2 Renate Wiggershausen, *Frauen unterm Nationalsozialismus* (Wuppertal, 1984), pp. 15f.

3 This particularly applies to Goebbels, Alfred Rosenberg, and Alfred Bäumler. Their anti-feminist and reactionary utterances were frequently picked up by contemporary Social Democratic critics.

4 Apart from the (false) assumption that women were particularly responsible for bringing Hitler to power, research on women under Nazism has concentrated upon the following issues. The sociologist and ex-politician Dahrendorf and the American social historian Schoenbaum claim that Nazism had a modernising impact upon the position of women, a view largely endorsed by the late Tim Mason. See T. W. Mason, 'Zur Lage der Frauen in Deutschland 1930–1940. Wohlfahrt, Arbeit und Familie', *Gesellschaft. Beiträge zur Marxschen Theorie*, 6 (Frankfurt am Main, 1976), pp. 118–930 and his 'Women in Nazi Germany', *History Workshop Journal*, 1 (1976), pp. 74ff. and 2, pp. 5ff. Most historians stress the reactionary and anti-feminist character of Nazi policy towards women. See especially Frauengruppe Faschismusforschung (ed.), *Mutterkreuz und Arbeitsbuch* (Frankfurt am Main, 1981); Maruta Schmidt *et al.* (eds.), *Frauen unterm Hakenkreuz* (Berlin, 1983); Rita Thalmann, *Frauensein im Dritten Reich* (Munich, 1984); Renate Wiggershaus, *Frauen unterm Nationalsozialismus* (Wuppertal, 1984); Renate Bridenthal *et al.* (eds.), *When Biology Became Destiny: Women in Weimar and Nazi Germany* (New York, 1984); Claudia Koonz, *Mothers in the Fatherland: Women, the Family and Nazi Politics* (New York, 1986); Gisela Bock, *Zwangssterilisation im Nationalsozialismus. Studien zur Rassenpolitik und Frauenpolitik* (Opladen, 1986). The best survey in English of these issues is Jill Stephenson, *Women in Nazi Society* (London, 1976). In what follows, we have attempted to demonstrate the obvious point, namely that Nazi policy towards women was neither

exclusively 'modernistic' nor simply reactionary and anti-feminist, but rather the result of racial-political and socially-integrative considerations. Like men, women were integrated into the 'national community' by a combination of repression and inducements. For simple biological reasons they were more likely to be affected by the regime's concern with 'purifying' the body of the nation. Policy towards women can therefore only be fully understood within the broader context of racial policy as a whole. Women were not merely inferior subjects, but also the objects of racial policies.

5 This is expressed particularly crassly in Joachim C. Fest, *Hitler* (London, 1974). The idea that German women found Hitler erotically attractive is perpetuated in books and documentaries which show Hitler being 'adored' by 'hysterical' screaming women without any attempt to examine the context in which the pictures were taken.

6 See Gisela Bremme, *Die politische Rolle der Frau in Deutschland. Eine Untersuchung über den Einfluss der Frauen bei Wahlen und ihre Teilnahme in Partei und Parlament* (Göttingen, 1963). Since there were no opinion polls, the following information is based on voting patterns in the few constituencies where the votes of men and women were counted separately. What is said concerning the gradual evening out of the male and female vote should be regarded with caution since the data base is very fragmentary. It is however a fact that women voted more conservatively then men, although the reasons for this are not clear.

7 See Renate Bridenthal, Claudia Koonz, 'Beyond Kinder, Küche, Kirche: Weimar Women in Politics and Work', in B. A. Carroll (ed.), *Liberating Women's History* (Urbana, 1976), pp. 301–29. For a good survey of recent research see Ute Frevert, *Frauen-Geschichte. Zwischen bürgerlicher Verbesserung und Neuer Weiblichkeit* (Frankfurt am Main, 1986), pp. 163ff. On KPD attitudes towards the 'women's question', see the rather rosy study by Hans-Jürgen Arndt, 'Das Schutzprogramm der KPD für die arbeitende Frau vom 15.10.1931', *Beiträge zur Geschichte der Arbeiterbewegung*, 11 (1969), pp. 291–311, and his 'Zur Frauenpolitik der KPD und zur Rolle der werktätigen Frau im antifaschistischen Kampf im Frühjahr und Sommer 1932', *Beiträge zur Geschichte der Arbeiterbewegung*, 14 (1972), pp. 805–18.

8 See the essay by the contemporary Social Democrat Judith Grünfeld, 'Frauenarbeit und Faschismus', *Die Arbeit*, 9 (1932), pp. 424–35. The SPD voted in favour of Brüning's proposals, much to the disgust of many female members and supporters of the Party. On this, see Wolfgang Wippermann, *Zur Analyse des Faschismus. Die sozialistischen und kommunistischen Faschismustheorien 1921–1945* (Frankfurt am Main, 1981), pp. 20ff.

9 KPD and SPD brochures; Central Committee of the KPD (ed.), *Die Nationalsozialisten und die werktätigen Frauen* (Berlin, 1930); Wilhelm Hoegner, *Die Frau im Dritten Reich* (Berlin, 1933); K. Kern, *Der soll dein Herr sein? Frauen entscheidet euch!* (Berlin, 1931); *Ihr dummen Ziegen! Bilder vom Frauenparadies im Dritten Reich* (Vienna, 1932); Werbeabteilung der SPD (ed.), *Nationalsozialismus und Frauenfragen: Material zur Information und Bekämpfung* (Berlin, 1932). Further material,

especially illustrations and cartoons, can be found in SPD journals and newspapers. The Nazis reacted by publishing brochures such as Sonja Rabe's *Die Frau im nationalsozialistischen Staate* (Berlin, 1932) and G. Diehl's *Die Frau im Dritten Reich* (Berlin, 1931).

10 See Jill Stephenson, *The Nazi Organisation of Women* (London and New York, 1981), pp. 23ff.; Michael H. Kater, 'Frauen in der NS-Bewegung', *Vierteljahrshefte für Zeitgeschichte*, 31 (1983), pp. 102–239.

11 See Rita Thalmann, *Frauensein im Dritten Reich* (Munich, 1984), pp. 89ff.

12 See her memoirs: Gertrud Scholtz-Klink, *Die Frau im Dritten Reich* (Tübingen, 1978).

13 Jill Stephenson, *Women in Nazi Society*, p. 118.

14 See Stephenson, *The Nazi Organisation of Women*; Martin Klaus, *Mädchen im Dritten Reich. Der Bund Deutscher Mädel* (Cologne, 1983); Dagmar Reese, 'Bund Deutscher Mädel. Zur Geschichte der weiblichen Jugend im Dritten Reich', in Frauengruppe Faschismusforschung (ed.), *Mutterkreuz und Arbeitsbuch* (Frankfurt am Main, 1981), pp. 163–87.

15 See above all, Stephenson, *Women in Nazi Society*, pp. 61ff.

16 For sources and further information, see Frevert, *Frauen-Geschichte*, pp. 225ff.

17 Stephenson, *The Nazi Organisation of Women*, pp. 45 and 165ff.

18 On Nazi policy towards women in employment, see Dörte Winkler, *Frauenarbeit im 'Dritten Reich'* (Hamburg, 1977); Stefan Bajohr, *Die Hälfte der Fabrik. Geschichte der Frauenarbeit in Deutschland 1914–1945* (Marburg, 1979); Carola Sachse, 'Hausarbeit im Betrieb. Betriebliche Sozialarbeit unter dem Nationalsozialismus', in Sachse (ed.), *Angst, Belohnung, Zucht und Ordnung. Herrschaftsmechanismen im Nationalsozialismus* (Opladen, 1982), pp. 209–74.

19 Frevert, *Frauen-Geschichte*, pp. 227ff.

20 Stephenson, *Women in Nazi Society*, p. 65.

21 On what follows, see Georg Lilienthal, *Der 'Lebensborn e.V.'. Ein Instrument nationalsozialistischer Rassenpolitik* (Stuttgart, 1985).

22 See note 21 above.

23 Heidrun Kaupen-Haas, 'Die Bevölkerungsplaner im Sachverständigenbeirat für Bevölkerungs- und Rassenpolitik', in Kaupen-Haas (ed.), *Der Griff nach der Bevölkerung. Aktualität und Kontinuität nazistischer Bevölkerungspolitik* (Nördlingen, 1986), pp. 103ff.

24 On what follows, see Gisela Bock, *Zwangssterilisation im Nationalsozialismus*.

25 Since there are no social-statistical studies of the sterilisation programme our remarks are based upon impressionistic evidence collected by Gisela Bock and local studies such as Wilfent Dalicho, *Sterilisationen in Köln auf Grund des Gesetzes zur Verhütung erbkranken Nachwuchses vom 14. Juli 1933 nach den Akten des Erbgesundheitsgerichte von 1943 bis 1945* (Cologne, 1971) and Sabine Krause, 'Zwangssterilisation in Bremerhaven (1934–1945). Eine Fallstudie' (unpublished M.A. thesis, Freie Universität, Berlin, 1989).

26 Bock, *Zwangssterilisation*, pp. 211ff.

27 *Ibid.*, pp. 225ff.
28 *Ibid.*, pp. 222ff.
29 *Ibid.*, pp. 222–3.
30 *Hitler's Mein Kampf*, pp. 185ff. For a detailed account see Timothy W. Mason, *Sozialpolitik im Dritten Reich* (Opladen, 1978), pp. 15ff.
31 Frevert, *Frauen-Geschichte*, pp. 211ff.
32 *Ibid.*, p. 212.
33 Winkler, *Frauenarbeit im Dritten Reich*, pp. 66ff., 'Frauenarbeit versus Frauenideologie. Probleme der Weiblichen Erwerbstätigkeit in Deutschland 1930–1945', *Archiv für Sozialgeschichte*, 17 (1977), pp. 99–126; Leila Rupp, 'Klassenzugehörigkeit und Arbeitseinsatz der Frauen im Dritten Reich', *Soziale Welt*, 31 (1980), pp. 191–205.
34 Timothy W. Mason, 'Zur Lage der Frauen in Deutschland 1930–1940. Wohlfahrt, Arbeit und Familie', *Gesellschaft*, 6 (Frankfurt am Main, 1976), pp. 118–93.
35 Ulrich Herbert, *Fremdarbeiter im Dritten Reich. Politik und Praxis des 'Ausländer-Einsatzes' in der deutschen Kriegswirtschaft* (Berlin, 1985); Ingrid Schupetta, 'Jeder das Ihre – Frauenerwerbstätigkeit und Einsatz vom Fremdarbeitern/arbeiterinnen im Zweiten Weltkrieg', in Frauengruppe Faschismusforschung (ed.), *Mutterkreuz und Arbeitsbuch* (Frankfurt am Main, 1981), pp. 292–318. For a growing literature on 'Fremdarbeiter' see Barbara Kasper, Lothar Schuster, Christof Watkinson, *Arbeiten für den Krieg. Deutsche und Ausländer in der Rüstungsproduktion bei Rheinmetall-Borsig 1943–1945* (Hamburg, 1987); Klaus-Jörg Siegfried, *Rüstungs-produktion und Zwangsarbeit im Volkswagenwerk 1939–1945* (Frankfurt am Main, 1986), 2 vols. Predictably enough, the huge 'official' history of Siemensstadt in Berlin – by a reputable West German academic – does not mention foreign forced labour.
36 Christoph U. Schminck-Gustavus (ed.), *Hungern für Hitler. Erinnerungen polnischer Zwangsarbeiter im Deutschen Reich 1940–1945* (Hamburg, 1984), pp. 197ff.
37 *Ibid.*, p. 208.
38 On what follows see note 35 above and also Barbara Bromberger, Hans Mausbach, *Feinde des Lebens. NS-Verbrechen an Kindern* (Frankfurt am Main, 1987); Roman Hrabar, Zofia Torkarcz, Jazek Wichzur, *Kinder im Krieg – Krieg gegen Kinder 1939–1945* (Reinbeck, 1981); Georg Lilienthal, *Der 'Lebensborn e.V.'*; Kirye Sosnowsky, *The Tragedy of Children under Nazi Rule* (Warsaw, 1962).
39 Heinz Boberach (ed.), *Meldungen aus dem Reich. Die geheimen Lageberichte des Sicherheitsdienstes der SS 1938–1945* (Herrsching, 1984), Vol. 9, pp. 3200ff.
40 *Ibid.*, extracts from pp. 3202–4.
41 For this, see the literature cited in note 38 above.
42 'Stimmungs- und Gerüchteerfassung der Kreisleitung der NSDAP Frankfurt vom 12.2.1944', reprinted in Wolfgang Wippermann, *Das Leben in Frankfurt*, Vol. 3, pp. 159ff.
43 Boberach (ed.), *Meldungen aus dem Reich*, Vol. 16, pp. 6481–8.

9 MEN IN THE THIRD REICH

1 Many socio-psychological theories of Fascism stress the close connections between Fascism and 'machismo'. See Klaus Theweleit, *Male Fantasies* (Minneapolis, 1989), 2 vols. Further details on this subject can be found in Wolfgang Wippermann, *Faschismustheorien. Zum Stand der gegenwärtigen Diskussion* (Darmstadt, 1989, 5th edition), pp. 76ff. The subject of 'men' has been largely neglected in empirical research. Work on Nazi social policy runs along well-worn lines. Orthodox Marxists tend either to ignore Nazi social policy altogether or to treat it as a form of cosmetic irrelevance organised by 'elements of finance capital'. So-called 'bourgeois' historians have concentrated upon two questions: firstly, whether social policy was based upon a programme developed by Hitler or was the result of improvisational initiatives on the part of several individuals and agencies, and secondly, whether Nazi social policy represents a consciously conceived attempt at 'modernisation' or a profound form of social reaction. These rather laboured debates are carefully rehearsed in Ian Kershaw, *The Nazi Dictatorship: Problems and Perspectives of Interpretation* (London, 1989, 2nd edition), chapters 3 and 7. What follows represents the first attempt to use anthropological, rather than class, categories in order to stress the pervasiveness of racial-ideological factors. The notes have been kept to a minimum.

2 See chapter above on 'the hereditarily ill'.

3 See chapter above on 'women'.

4 See chapter above on 'Sinti and Roma'.

5 See chapter above on 'Jews'.

6 The relationship between the German upper classes and the NSDAP has hitherto received insufficient attention. Orthodox Marxist research in the former GDR has laboured an instrumental analysis of Fascism, whereby the NSDAP received material support from 'imperialist and reactionary elements of finance capital'. See Wolfgang Wippermann, *Faschismustheorien. Zum Stand der gegenwärtigen Diskussion*, pp. 57ff.; there is important material on this subject in Martin Broszat, Klaus Schwabe (eds.), *Die deutschen Eliten und der Weg in den Zweiten Weltkrieg* (Munich, 1989), and recently, Jeremy Noakes, 'German Conservatives and the Third Reich: An Ambiguous Relationship', in Martin Blinkhorn (ed.), *Fascists and Conservatives* (London, 1990), pp. 71ff.

7 This thesis is in line with Marx's model of Bonapartism. On this see Wippermann, *Faschismustheorien*, pp. 65ff., and his *Die Bonapartismustheorie von Marx und Engels* (Stuttgart, 1983).

8 On the relationship between industry and the NSDAP see Dick Geary's outstanding survey, 'The Industrial Elite and the Nazis in the Weimar Republic', in Peter D. Stachura (ed.), *The Nazi Machtergreifung* (London, 1983), pp. 85–100; Klaus Hildebrand, *The Third Reich* (London, 1984), pp. 124ff.; Richard Saage, *Faschismustheorien* (Munich, 1971), pp. 72ff.; Hans-Erich Volkmann, 'Zum Verhältnis von Grosswirtschaft und NS-Regime im Zweiten Weltkrieg', in K.-D. Bracher *et al.* (eds.), *Nationalsozialistische Diktatur 1933–1945. Eine Bilanz* (Bonn, 1983), pp. 480–508; Wilhelm

Deist *et al.*, *Das Deutsche Reich und der Zweite Weltkrieg* (Stuttgart, 1979), 2 vols., Vol. 1, pp. 208ff.; Kershaw, *The Nazi Dictatorship*, pp. 43ff.; Ludolf Herbst, 'Der Krieg und die Unternehmersstrategie deutscher Industrie-Konzerne in der Zwischenkriegszeit', in Broszat, Schwabe (eds.), *Die deutschen Eliten*, pp. 72ff.

9 On what follows see Heinz Höhne, *The Order of the Death's Head* (London, 1969); Robert L. Koehl, *The Black Corps: The Structure and Power Struggles of the Nazi SS* (Madison, 1983); Bernd Wegner, *The Waffen-SS: Organisation, Ideology and Function* (Oxford, 1990); Helmut Krausnick, Hans-Heinrich Wilhelm, *Die Truppe des Weltanschauungskrieges. Die Einsatzgruppen der Sicherheitspolizei und des SD 1938–1941* (Stuttgart, 1982).

10 Josef Ackermann, *Heinrich Himmler als Ideologe* (Göttingen, 1970); Wolfgang Wippermann, *Der Ordensstaat als Ideologie* (Berlin, 1979), pp. 253ff.; Peter Padfield, *Himmler. Reichsführer-SS* (London, 1990).

11 *Wewelsburg 1933 bis 1945. Kult und Terrorstätte der SS. Eine Dokumentation* (Paderborn, 1982).

12 Höhne, *Order of the Death's Head*, pp. 123ff. See also Gunnar C. Boehnert, 'The Third Reich and the Problem of "Social Revolution": German Officers and the SS', in V. H. Berghahn, M. Kitchen (eds.), *Germany in the Age of Total War* (London, 1981), pp. 203ff.; Ruth Bettina Birn, *Die Höheren SS- und Polizeiführer* (Düsseldorf, 1986).

13 See Klaus Jürgen Müller, *Das Heer und Hitler. Armee und national-sozialistisches Regime 1933–1940* (Stuttgart, 1969), and his *Armee, Politik und Gesellschaft in Deutschland 1933–1945* (Paderborn, 1970) and 'Deutsche Militär-Elite in der Vorgeschichte des Zweiten Weltkrieges', in Broszat, Schwabe (eds.), *Die deutschen Eliten*, pp. 226ff.; Reinhard Absolon, *Die Wehrmacht im Dritten Reich* (Boppard, 1969–75), 3 vols.; Manfred Messerschmidt, *Die Wehrmacht im NS-Staat. Zeit der Indoktrination* (Hamburg, 1969).

14 Peter Hoffmann, *Widerstand, Staatsstreich, Attentat. Der Kampf der Opposition gegen Hitler* (Munich, 1970, 2nd edition); Gerd van Roon, *Widerstand im Dritten Reich. Ein Überblick* (Munich, 1979); Jürgen Schmädeke, Peter Steinbach (eds.), *Der Widerstand gegen den National-sozialismus* (Munich, 1985); Hermann Graml, Hans Mommsen, Hans-Joachim Reichhardt, Ernst Wolf (eds.), *The German Resistance to Hitler* (London, 1970); Hermann Graml (ed.), *Widerstand im Dritten Reich* (Frankfurt am Main, 1984).

15 The literature on Allied plans for post-war Germany is vast. For a good survey see Christoph Klessmann, *Die doppelte Staatsgründung. Deutsche Geschichte 1945–1955* (Göttingen, 1982), pp. 19ff.; and Hermann Graml, *Die Alliierten und die Teilung Deutschlands. Konflikte und Entscheidungen 1941–1948* (Frankfurt am Main, 1985); Rudolf Morsey, *Die Bundesrepublik Deutschland. Entstehung und Entwicklung bis 1969* (Munich 1987), pp. 1ff.

16 On NSDAP policy towards the 'Mittelstand' before 1933, see Dietrich Orlow, *The History of the Nazi Party*, Vol. 1, 1919–33 (Pittsburgh, 1969);

Max H. Kele, *Nazis and Workers: National Socialist Appeals to German Labour 1919–1933* (Chapel Hill, 1972); Reinhard Kühnl, *Die nationalsozialistische Linke 1925–1930* (Meisenheim, 1966); Horst Gies, 'NSDAP und landwirtschaftliche Organisationen in der Endphase der Weimarer Republik', *Vierteljahrshefte für Zeitgeschichte*, 15 (1967), pp. 341–76.

17 The emphasis upon lower-middle-class support for the NSDAP can be found in Theodor Geiger, 'Panik im Mittelstand', *Die Arbeit*, 7 (1930), pp. 553–637; Seymour Martin Lipset, 'Der "Faschismus", die Linke, die Rechte und die Mitte', *Kölner Zeitschrift für Soziologie und Sozialpsychologie*, 11 (1959), pp. 401–44; Arthur Schweitzer, *Die Nazifizierung des Mittelstandes* (Stuttgart, 1970). the following are critical of this theory: Heinrich August Winkler, 'Extremismus der Mitte?', *Vierteljahrshefte für Zeitgeschichte*, 20 (1972), pp. 175–91, and his *Mittelstand, Demokratie und Nationalsozialismus. Die politische Entwicklung von Handwerk und Kleinhandel in der Weimarer Republik* (Cologne, 1972) and 'Mittelstandsbewegung oder Volkspartei? Zur sozialen Basis der NSDAP', in Wolfgang Schieder (ed.), *Faschismus als soziale Bewegung. Deutschland und Italian im Vergleich* (Hamburg, 1976), pp. 25–68; Richard F. Hamilton, *Who Voted for Hitler?* (Princeton, 1982); Thomas Childers, *The Nazi Voter: The Social Foundations of Fascism in Germany 1919–1933* (Chapel Hill, 1983); Childers (ed.), *The Formation of the Nazi Constituency 1919–1933* (London, 1986); Michael H. Kater, *The Nazi Party: A Social Profile of the Members and Leaders 1919–1945* (Oxford, 1983).

18 On the following, see Heinrich August Winkler, 'Der entbehrliche Stand. Zur Mittelstandspolitik im "Dritten Reich"', *Archiv für Sozialgeschichte*, 17 (1977), pp. 1–40; Adelheid von Saldern, *Mittelstand im III. Reich. Handwerker – Einzelhändler – Bauern* (Frankfurt am Main, 1979); Detlev Peukert, *Inside Nazi Germany: Conformity, Opposition and Racism in Everyday Life* (London, 1987), pp. 86ff.; Werner Abelshauser, Anselm Faust, 'Wirtschafts- und Sozialpolitik. Eine nationalsozialistische Sozialrevolution?', in Deutsches Institut für Fernstudien an der Universität Tübingen (ed.), *Nationalsozialismus im Unterricht. Studieneinheit*, 4 (Tübingen, 1983), pp. 92–114.

19 Heinrich Uhlig, *Die Warenhäuser im Dritten Reich* (Cologne, 1956).

20 Marxist historians have stressed the connections between Nazi persecution of the Jews and socio-economic policies. See Klaus Drobisch *et al.*, *Juden unterm Hakenkreuz. Verfolgung und Ausrottung der deutschen Juden 1933–1945* (Frankfurt am Main, 1973); Kurt Pätzold, *Faschismus, Rassenwahn, Judenverfolgung* (Berlin, 1975). There is an original and interesting study of this subject by the Israeli Avraham Barkai, *From Boycott to Annihilation: The Economic Struggle of German Jews 1933–1945* (New England, 1989).

21 For the following, see Friedrich Grundmann, *Agrarpolitik im 'Dritten Reich'. Ansprüche und Wirklichkeit des Reichserbhofgesetzes* (Hamburg, 1979); John E. Farquharson, *The Plough and the Swastika: The NSDAP and Agriculture in Germany 1928–1945* (London, 1976).

22 *Deutschland-Berichte der Sozialdemokratischen Partei Deutschlands (Sopade)*, Erster Jahrgang (1934), p. 232.

23   See Hans-Erich Volkmann's excellent contribution, 'Deutsche Agrareliten auf Revisions- und Expansionskurs', in Broszat, Schwabe (eds.), *Die deutschen Eliten*, especially p. 359.

24   See the works cited in note 16 above.

25   On resistance in the (divided) labour movement, see the relevant sections in Christoph Klessmann, Falk Pingel (eds.), *Gegner des Nationalsozialismus* (Frankfurt am Main, 1980); Richard Löwenthal, Patrick von zur Mühlen (eds.), *Widerstand und Verweigerung in Deutschland 1933 bis 1945* (Bonn, 1982); Jürgen Schmädeke, Peter Steinbach (eds.), *Der Widerstand gegen den Nationalsozialismus* (Munich, 1985); Anthony Glees, 'The SPD in Emigration and Resistance 1933–1945', in Roger Fletcher (ed.), *Bernstein to Brandt: A Short History of German Social Democracy* (London, 1987), pp. 183ff.; Allan Merson, *Communist Resistance in Nazi Germany* (London, 1985); T. W. Mason, 'The Workers' Opposition in Nazi Germany', *History Workshop*, 11 (1981), pp. 120–37, and his 'Injustice and Resistance: Barrington Moore and the Reaction of German Workers to Nazism', in R. J. Bullen, H. Pogge von Strandmann, A. B. Polonsky (eds.), *Ideas into Politics* (Beckenham, 1984), pp. 106ff. Local and regional studies have corrected the exaggerated accounts of the significance of working-class resistance emanating (not exclusively) from the GDR. See Detlev Peukert, *Die KPD im Widerstand. Verfolgung und Untergrundarbeit an Rhein und Ruhr 1933 bis 1945* (Wuppertal, 1980); Harmut Mehringer, 'Die KPD in Bayern 1918–1945. Vorgeschichte, Verfolgung und Widerstand', in Martin Broszat (ed.), *Bayern in der NS-Zeit* (Munich, 1983), Vol. 5, pp. 1–286, and his 'Die bayerische Sozialdemokratie bis zum Ende des NS-Regimes. Vorgeschichte, Verfolgung und Widerstand', in *ibid.*, pp. 287–432.

26   For the following survey of Nazi policy towards the working class, see David Schoenbaum, *Hitler's Social Revolution* (London, 1966); T. W. Mason, *Sozialpolitik im Dritten Reich* (Opladen, 1977), and 'Labour in the Third Reich', *Past and Present*, 33 (1966), pp. 112–41; Thomas Berger, 'NS-Sozialpolitik als Mittel der Herrschaftssicherung', in Peter Meyer, Dieter Riesenberger (eds.), *Der Nationalsozialismus in der historisch-politischen Bildung* (Göttingen, 1979), pp. 71–93; Heinz Lampert, 'Staatliche Sozialpolitik im Dritten Reich', in K.-D. Bracher *et al.* (eds.), *Nationalsozialistische Diktatur 1933–1945. Eine Bilanz* (Bonn, 1983), pp. 177–205; Carola Sachse *et al.* (eds.), *Angst, Belohnung, Zucht und Ordnung. Herrschaftsmechanismen im Nationalsozialismus* (Opladen, 1982); Marie Luise Recker, *Nationalsozialistische Sozialpolitik im Zweiten Weltkrieg* (Munich, 1985); Tilla Siegel, *Leistung und Lohn in der nationalsozialistischen 'Ordnung der Arbeit'* (Opladen, 1989).

27   On the DAF see now Ronald Smelser, *Robert Ley* (Oxford, 1988); and Günther Mei, 'Warum steht der deutsche Arbeiter zu Hitler? Zur Rolle der Deutschen Arbeitsfront im Herrschaftssystem des Dritten Reiches', *Geschichte und Gesellschaft*, 12 (1986), pp. 212ff.

28   See the literature cited in note 25 above. From a vast literature see also Richard Overy, *The Nazi Economic Recovery 1931–1938* (London, 1982); Harald James, *The German Slump: Politics and Economics 1924–1936*

(Oxford, 1986), especially pp. 343ff.; Ludolf Herbst, *Der totale Krieg und die Ordnung der Wirtschaft. Die Kriegswirtschaft im Spannungsfeld von Politik, Ideologie und Propaganda 1939–1945* (Stuttgart, 1982) and Avraham Barkai, *Das Wirtschaftssystem des Nationalsozialismus* (Frankfurt am Main, 1988).

29 Richard Grunberger, *A Social History of the Third Reich* (London, 1971), p. 256.

30 *Deutschland-Berichte (Sopade)*, Zweiter Jahrgang (1935), pp. 885–6.

31 *Deutschland-Berichte (Sopade)*, Vierter Jahrgang (1937), p. 1259.

32 Speech by Ley to the foreign press on 15 September 1940, reproduced in *Dokumentation 'Versorgungswerk des Deutschen Volkes. Die Neuordnungspläne der Deutschen Arbeitsfront zur Sozialversicherung 1935–1943', Dokumentationstelle zur NS-Sozialpolitik* (Hamburg, 1985), Vol. 1, document 4. For a short discussion of these plans see Norbert Frei, *Der Führerstaat* (Munich, 1987), pp. 139ff.

33 On this rather neglected theme, i.e. working-class racism, see Ulrich Herbert, *Fremdarbeiter im Dritten Reich. Politik und Praxis des 'Ausländer-Einsatzes' in der deutschen Kriegswirtschaft* (Berlin, 1985), and his 'Arbeiterschaft im "Dritten Reich". Zwischenbilanz und offene Fragen', *Geschichte und Gesellschaft*, 15 (1989), especially pp. 350ff.

34 Cited in Klaus-Jörg Siegfried, *Rüstungsproduktion und Zwangsarbeit im Volkswagenwerk 1939–1945* (Frankfurt am Main, 1986), p. 104.

35 Ulrich Herbert, 'Der "Ausländereinsatz". Fremdarbeiter und Kriegsgefangene in Deutschland 1939–1945 – Ein Überblick', *Herrenmensch und Arbeitsvölker. Ausländische Arbeiter und Deutsche 1939–1945. Beiträge zur nationalsozialistischen Gesundheits- und Sozialpolitik* (Berlin, 1986), Vol. 3, p. 39.

36 Matthias Hamann, 'Die Morde an polnischen und Sowjetischen Zwangsarbeitern in deutschen Anstalten', in *Aussonderung und Tod. Die klinische Hinrichtung der Unbrauchbaren. Beiträge zur nationalsozialistischen Gesundheits- und Sozialpolitik*, Vol. 1 (Berlin, 1987, 2nd edition), pp. 121ff.

37 'Merkblatt für die Beauftragten der NSDAP bei der Überwachung fremdvölkischer Arbeitskräfte zur Begegnung volkspolitischer Gefahren' (16 November 1942), *'Dokumentation', Herrenvolk und Arbeitsvölker*, pp. 136–8.

38 Jochen August, 'Erinnern an Deutschland. Berichte polnischer Zwangsarbeiter', *ibid*, p. 124.

BIBLIOGRAPHICAL ESSAY

BIBLIOGRAPHICAL AND HISTORIOGRAPHICAL SURVEYS OF RESEARCH ON
THE HISTORY OF THE NATIONAL SOCIALIST REGIME

Bibliographies on the period include Thilo Vogelsang, Helmut Auerbach (eds.), *Bibliographie zur Zeitgeschichte 1953–1980* (Munich, 1982–3), Vols. 1–3; Peter Huttenberger (ed.), *Bibliographie zum Nationalsozialismus* (Göttingen, 1980); Helen Kehr, Janet Langmaid, *The Nazi Era 1919–1945: A Select Bibliography of Published Works from the Early Roots to 1980* (London, 1982). Recent surveys of the literature include Wolfgang Wippermann, ' "Deutsche Katastrophe" oder "Diktatur des Finanzkapitals"? Zur Interpretationsgeschichte des Dritten Reichs im Nachkriegsdeutschland', in Horst Denkler, Karl Prumm (eds.), *Die deutsche Literatur im Dritten Reich* (Stuttgart, 1976), pp. 9–43, 'The Post-War German Left and Fascism', *Journal of Contemporary History*, 11 (1976), pp. 185–220, 'Forschungsgeschichte und Forschungsprobleme', in Wippermann (ed.), *Kontroversen um Hitler* (Frankfurt am Main, 1986), pp. 13–116, *Faschismustheorien. Zum Stand der gegenwärtigen Diskussion* (5th fully revised edition, Darmstadt, 1989); Pierre Ayçoberry, *The Nazi Question: An Essay on the Interpretations of National Socialism (1922–1975)* (London, 1981); Klaus Hildebrand, *The Third Reich* (London, 1984); Gerhard Schreiber, *Hitler Interpretationen 1923–1983* (Darmstadt, 1983); John Hiden, John Farquharson, *Explaining Hitler's Germany: Historians and the Third Reich* (London, 1983); Ian Kershaw, *The Nazi Dictatorship: Problems and Perspectives of Interpretation* (2nd edition, London, 1989). See also the bibliographic sections of the relevant volumes by Martin Broszat, Hermann Graml, Bernd-Jürgen Wendt, Lothar Gruchmann, and Norbert Frei in Martin Broszat, Wolfgang Benz, Hermann Graml (eds.), *Deutsche Geschichte der neuesten Zeit vom 19. Jahrhundert bis zur Gegenwart*. Ayçoberry and Kershaw contain the best and most cogently argued surveys of the development of the literature, and of the present controversies and debates surrounding problems of interpretation. Kershaw's book is especially strong on the respective merits of general theories of fascism and theories of totalitarianism; on the relationship between the State and economy in the Third Reich; and on the part played by

Hitler in Nazi foreign policy and the 'Final Solution'. Klaus Hildebrand's *The Third Reich* contains surveys of the literature on National Socialism. He either ignores or dismisses both Marxist and so-called 'revisionist' historians of the period. The recent West German 'Historikerstreit' is lucidly discussed by Richard J. Evans, *In Hitler's Shadow: West German Historians and the Attempt to Escape from the Nazi Past* (London, 1989). The relevant texts in the controversy have been collected as *'Historikerstreit'. Die Dokumentation der Kontroverse um die Einzigartigkeit der nationalsozialistischen Judenvernichtung* (Munich, 1987).

SURVEYS AND STANDARD WORKS

Ernst Fraenkel, *The Dual State* (New York, 1940); Franz L. Neumann, *Behemoth: The Structure and Practice of National Socialism 1933–1944* (New York, 1944); Hannah Arendt, *The Origins of Totalitarianism* (New York, 1951). These three works undoubtedly constitute the 'classics' on the history of National Socialism, and in many respects have not been superseded so far. Karl-Dietrich Bracher, *The German Dictatorship: The Origins, Structure and Consequences of National Socialism* (London, 1971) is a standard work which relies heavily on totalitarian theory, and which has not been revised in terms of recent research. Martin Broszat, *The Hitler State: The Foundation and Development of the Internal Structure of the Third Reich* (London, 1981) is concerned with the 'polycratic' character of the Nazi regime, rather than with the monocracy of Hitler as the main title misleadingly suggests. Kurt Pätzold, Manfred Weissbecker, *Geschichte der NSDAP 1920–1945* (Cologne, 1981) is a GDR standard work which relies heavily on an 'agental' interpretation of the relationship between big business and politics, and which adopts a reductionist approach to both ideology and racism in so far as these subjects are treated at any length. Klaus Hildebrand, *The Third Reich* (London, 1984) neglects both domestic and social issues and the whole subject of working-class resistance. Hildebrand is a confirmed advocate of the view that Nazi policies were an attempt to implement a programme conceived by Hitler. Hans-Ulrich Thamer, *Verführung und Gewalt. Deutschland 1933–1945* (Berlin, 1986) is a well-written and thoughtfully illustrated survey which attempts to steer a middle course through the controversies on the nature of the regime. Discussion of Nazi racial and social policy is rather perfunctory. Norbert Frei, *Der Führerstaat* (Munich, 1987) is a short, interesting, and intelligent survey which gives adequate coverage to social history and the history of everyday life. The best single work on the period is J. Noakes and G. Pridham's *Nazism 1919–1945: A Documentary Reader* (Exeter, 1983–8), Vols. 1–3. A fourth volume will deal with the 'home front'.

THE HISTORY OF RACISM IN GERMANY

Earlier studies, relying on a history of ideas approach, have now been augmented by the products of the history of science as an institutionalised academic discipline. Older general surveys include Patrik von zur Mühlen, *Rassenideologien. Geschichte und Hintergründe* (Berlin and Bonn, 1977); Georg L. Mosse, *Rassimus. Ein Krankheitssymptom in der europäischen Geschichte des 19. und 20. Jahrhundert* (Königstein, 1978), English version *Towards the Final Solution: A History of*

European Racism (New York, 1978), and his *The Crisis of German Ideology: Intellectual Origins of the Third Reich* (New York, 1981); Michael Banton, *The Idea of Race* (London, 1977); Leon Poliakov, *The Aryan Myth: A History of Racist and Nationalist Ideas in Europe* (New York, 1974). The rather undifferentiated approach towards the history of German racism reflected in many of the preceding titles has been corrected by Daniel Gasman, *The Scientific Origins of National Socialism: Social Darwinism in Ernst Haeckel and the German Monist League* (London, 1971); Peter Weingart, Jürgen Kroll, Kurt Bayertz, *Rasse, Blut und Gene. Geschichte der Eugenik und Rassenhygiene in Deutschland* (Frankfurt am Main, 1988); Robert N. Proctor, *Racial Hygiene: Medicine under the Nazis* (Cambridge, Mass., 1988); and Paul J. Weindling, *Health, Race and German Politics between National Unification and Nazism 1870–1945* (Cambridge, 1989). The literature on the history of anti-Semitism is discussed separately below.

NAZI RACIAL POLICY

General surveys of institutions responsible for racial policy include Hans Buchheim *et al.*, *Anatomie des SS-Staates* (Munich, 1967), Vols. 1 and 2; Klaus Drobisch, 'Über den Terror und seine Organisationen im Nazi-Deutschland', in Dietrich Eichholtz, Kurt Gossweiler (eds.), *Faschismus Forschung. Positionen, Probleme, Polemik* (Berlin, 1980), pp. 157–80; Eberhard Kolb, 'Die Maschinerie des Terrors. Zum Funktionieren des Unterdrückungs- und Verfolgungsapparates im NS-System', in Karl-Dietrich Bracher *et al.* (eds.), *Nationalsozialistische Diktatur 1933–1945. Eine Bilanz* (Bonn, 1983), pp. 270–84; Johannes Tuchel, Reinhold Schattenfroh, *Zentrale des Terrors. Prinz-Albrecht-Strasse 8. Das Hauptquartier der Gestapo* (Berlin, 1987); Helmut Fischer, *Hitlers Apparat. Namen, Ämter, Kompetenzen. Ein Strukturanalyse des III. Reiches* (Kiel, 1988). General histories of the SS include Heinz Höhne's *The Order of the Death's Head* (London, 1969); Robert L. Koehl's *The Black Order: The Structure and Power Struggles of the Nazi SS* (Madison, 1983); Herbert G. Ziegler, *Nazi Germany's New Aristocracy: The SS Leadership, 1925–1939* (Princeton, 1989) for the sociological composition of the higher echelons of the organisation. For the history of the Gestapo see Friedrich Zipfel, *Gestapo und SD* (Berlin, 1960); Shlomo Aronson, *Reinhard Heydrich und die Frühgeschichte von Gestapo und SD* (Stuttgart, 1971); Jacques Delarue, *Geschichte der Gestapo* (Düsseldorf, 1964); Christoph Graf, *Politische Polizei zwischen Demokratie und Diktatur. Die Entwicklung der preussischen Politischen Polizei vom Schutzorgan der Weimarer Republik zum Geheimen Staatspolizeiamt des Dritten Reiches* (Berlin, 1983); Robert Gellately, *The Gestapo and German Society: Enforcing Racial Policy 1933–1945* (Oxford, 1990). For the history of the concentration camps see Eugen Kogon, *Der SS-Staat. Das System der deutschen Konzentrationslager* (Frankfurt am Main, 1946); Martin Broszat, 'Nationalsozialistische Konzentrationslager 1933–1945', in Buchheim *et al.*, *Anatomie des SS-Staates* (Munich, 1967), Vol. 2, pp. 11–136; Heinz Kühnrich, *Der KZ-Staat 1933–1945* (Berlin, 1980); Falk Pingel, *Häftlinge unter SS-Herrschaft. Widerstand, Selbstbehauptung und Vernichtung im Konzentrationslager* (Hamburg, 1978); Yisrael Gutman, Avital Saf, *The Nazi Concentration Camps: Structure and Aims, The Image of the Prisoner, The Jews in the Camps, Proceedings of the Fourth Yad Vashem*

International Historical Conference (Jerusalem, 1980). On the history of the Einsatzgruppen see Heinz Artzt, *Mörder in Uniform. Organisationen, die zu Vollstreckern nationalsozialistischer Gewaltverbrechen wurden* (Munich, 1979); Helmut Krausnick, Hans-Heinrich Wilhelm, *Die Truppen des Weltanschauungskrieges. Die Einsatzgruppen der Sicherheitspolizei und des SD 1938–1942* (Stuttgart, 1982); Alfred Streim, 'The Tasks of the SS Einsatzgruppen' in *Simon Wiesenthal Center Annual*, 4 (1987), pp. 309–28; for diaries, letters, and photographs concerning the Einsatzgruppen see Ernst Klee, Willi Dressen, Volker Riess (eds.), *'Schöne Zeiten'. Judenmord aus der Sicht der Täter und Gaffer* (Frankfurt am Main, 1988) and *'Gott mit uns'. Der deutsche Vernichtungskrieg im Osten 1939–1945* (Frankfurt am Main, 1989). On the Waffen-SS see Bernd Wegner, *The Waffen-SS: Organisation, Ideology and Function* (Oxford, 1990). Other studies of SS agencies include Robert Koehl, *RKFDV: German Resettlement and Population Policy 1939–45* (Cambridge, Mass., 1957); Christopher Browning, 'Nazi Resettlement Policy and the Search for a Solution to the Jewish Question, 1939–1941', *German Studies Review*, 9 (1986), pp. 503ff.; Michael H. Kater, *'Das Ahnenerbe' der SS 1935–1945. Ein Beitrag zur Kulturpolitik des Dritten Reiches* (Stuttgart, 1974); Larry V. Thompson, 'Lebensborn and the Eugenics Policy of the Reichsführer-SS', *Central European History*, 4 (1971), pp. 57–71; Georg Lilienthal, *Der 'Lebensborn e.V.'. Ein Instrument nationalsozialistischer Rassenpolitik* (Stuttgart, 1985). The SS was not the sole agency responsible for institutionalised terror. Recent studies have also examined the part played by the judiciary and legal profession. They have revised an earlier picture centred on the allegedly heroic stance adopted by individual lawyers (whose effect was to distract attention from the culpability of the majority), while simultaneously questioning the idea that the legal system was totally 'co-ordinated' or subject to central control by the Nazi regime. Important studies include Hubert Schorn, *Der Richter im Dritten Reich. Geschichte und Dokumente* (Frankfurt am Main, 1959), and his *Die Gesetzgebung des Nationalsozialismus als Mittel der Machtpolitik* (Frankfurt am Main, 1963); Hermann Weinkauff, *Die deutsche Justiz und der Nationalsozialismus. Ein Überblick* (Stuttgart, 1968); Walter Wagner, *Der Volksgerichtshof im NS-Staat* (Stuttgart, 1974); Heinz Boberach, *Richterbriefe. Dokumente zur Beeinflussung der deutschen Rechtssprechung 1942 bis 1944* (Boppard, 1975); Hans Robinsohn, *Justiz als politische Verfolgung. Die Rechtssprechung in 'Rassenschandefällen' beim Landgericht Hamburg 1936–1943* (Stuttgart, 1977); Ilse Staff (ed.), *Justiz im Dritten Reich. Eine Dokumentation* (Frankfurt am Main, 1978); Heinz Hillermeier (ed.), *'Im Namen des Deutschen Volkes'. Todesurteile des Volksgerichtshofes* (Darmstadt, 1980); Institut für Zeitgeschichte, Munich (ed.), *NS-Recht in historischer Perspektive* (Munich, 1981); Peter Hüttenberger, 'Heimtückefalle vor dem Sondergericht München 1933–1939', in Martin Broszat *et al.* (eds.), *Bayern in der NS-Zeit* (Munich, 1981), Vol. 4, pp. 435–526; Redaktion Kritische Justiz (ed.), *Der Unrechts-Staat* (Baden-Baden, 1983–4), Vols. 1 and 2; Gerhard Fieberg, *Justiz im nationalsozialistischen Deutschland* (Cologne, 1984); Martin Hirsch, Diemut Majer, Jurgen Meinck (eds.), *Recht, Verwaltung und Justiz im Nationalsozialismus. Ausgewählte Schriften, Gesetze und Gerichtsentscheidungen von 1933–1945* (Cologne, 1984); Gotthart Jasper, 'Zur Rolle der Justiz von Weimar bis Bonn. Neuere Publikationen zur Justizgeschichte nach 1918',

Politische Vierteljahrsschrift, 25 (1984), pp. 143–51; Günter Spendel, *Rechtsbeugung durch Rechtsprechung* (Berlin, 1984); Niedersächsische Landeszentrale für politische Bildung (ed.), *Justiz und Nationalsozialismus* (Hanover 1985); Diemut Majer, *Grundlagen des nationalsozialistischen Rechtssystems* (Stuttgart, 1987); Ingo Müller, *Furchtbare Juristen. Die unbewältigte Vergangenheit unserer Justiz* (Munich, 1987). Lother Gruchmann, *Justiz im Dritten Reich 1933–1940. Anpassung und Unterwerfung in der Ära Gürtner* (Munich, 1988) is the most substantial work on the subject to date. See also Ralf Dreier, Wolfgang Sellert (eds.), *Recht und Justiz im 'Dritten Reich'* (Munich, 1989) and the exhibition catalogue *'In Namen des Deutschen Volkes'. Justiz und Nationalsozialismus* (Cologne, 1989). English readers are poorly served by H. W. Koch's tendentious and unreliable *In the Name of the Volk: Political Justice in Hitler's Germany* (London, 1989). The contribution of demographers and population planners to racial policy is investigated by, *inter alia*, Götz Aly, Karl-Heinz Roth, *Die restlose Erfassung. Volkszählen, Identifizieren, Aussondern im Nationalsozialismus* (Berlin, 1984); Heidrun Kaupen-Haas (ed.), *Der Griff nach der Bevölkerung. Aktualität und Kontinuität nazistischer Bevölkerungspolitik* (Hamburg, 1986); Götz Aly, Susanne Heim, *Vordenker der Vernichtung* (Hamburg, 1991). For the culpable involvement of academics and scientists with the Nazi regime, see Max Weinreich, *Hitler's Professors: The Part of Scholarship in Germany's Crimes against the Jewish People* (New York, 1946); Peter Lundgreen (ed.), *Wissenschaft im Dritten Reich* (Frankfurt am Main, 1985); Benno Müller-Hill, *Murderous Science: Elimination by Scientific Selection of Jews, Gypsies, and Others, Germany 1933–1945* (Oxford, 1988); Michael Burleigh, *Germany Turns Eastwards: A Study of 'Ostforschung' in the Third Reich* (Cambridge, 1988).

THE PERSECUTION OF THE JEWS

Surveys of the vast literature on this subject include Klaus Hildebrand, *The Third Reich* (London, 1984), pp. 146ff.; Konrad Kwiet, 'Zur historiographischen Behandlung der Judenverfolgung im Dritten Reich', *Militärgeschichtliche Mitteilungen*, 27 (1980), pp. 149–92, and his 'Historians of the German Democratic Republic on Antisemitism and Persecution', *Leo Baeck Institute Year Book*, 21 (1976), pp. 173–98; Otto Dov Kulka, 'Major Trends and Tendencies of German Historiography on National Socialism and the "Jewish Question" (1924–1984)', *Leo Baeck Institute Year Book*, 30 (1985), pp. 215–42; Yehuda Bauer, *The Holocaust in Historical Perspective* (Seattle, 1978), and his 'On the Place of the Holocaust in Contemporary History', *Journal of Contemporary Jewry*, 1 (1984), pp. 201–24; Michael Marrus, *The Holocaust in History* (London, 1987), and his 'The History of the Holocaust: A Survey of Recent Literature', *Journal of Modern History*, 59 (1987), pp. 114–60; Wolfgang Wippermann, 'Forschungsgeschichte und Forschungsprobleme', in Wippermann (ed.), *Kontroversen um Hitler* (Frankfurt am Main, 1986), pp. 83ff.; Ian Kershaw, *The Nazi Dictatorship* (London, 1989, 2nd edition), pp. 82ff. The following historians subscribe to the view that Nazi policy towards the Jews represented the implementation of Hitler's preconceived 'programme': Lucy Dawidowicz, *The War Against the Jews 1933–1945* (London, 1977); Klaus Hildebrand, *The Third Reich* (London, 1984), pp. 69ff.; Andreas Hillgruber, 'Die "Endlösung" und das deutsche Ostimperium als Kernstück des rassenideologischen Programms des Nationalsozialismus', in Hillgruber (ed.), *Deutsche Grossmacht- und Weltpolitik im 19. und 20. Jahrhundert* (Düsseldorf, 1977), pp. 252–75; Eberhard Jäckel, *Hitler's World View: A Blueprint for Power* (Cambridge, Mass., 1981), and his *Hitlers Herrschaft. Vollzug einer Weltanschauung* (Stuttgart, 1986); Gerald Fleming, *Hitler and the Final Solution* (Oxford, 1986). The following historians argue, with varying degrees of emphasis, that policy towards the Jews was made unsystematically by various persons and agencies in the 'polyocracy' of the Third Reich, and that it did not simply represent the implementation of the ideological obsessions of Adolf Hitler: Karl A. Schleunes, *The Twisted Road to Auschwitz: Nazi Policy towards German Jews 1933–1939* (London, 1972); Uwe Dietrich Adam, *Judenpolitik im Dritten Reich* (Düsseldorf, 1972), and his 'An Overall Plan for Anti-Jewish Legislation in the Third Reich?', *Yad Vashem Studies*, 11 (1976), pp. 33–55; Martin Broszat, 'Hitler und die Genesis der "Endlösung". Aus Anlass der Thesen von David Irving', *Vierteljahreshefte für Zeitgeschichte*, 26 (1977), pp. 739–75; Hans Mommsen, 'The Realization of the Unthinkable: The "Final Solution of the Jewish Question" in the Third Reich', in Gerhard Hirschfeld (ed.), *The Policies of Genocide: Jews and Soviet Prisoners of War in Nazi Germany* (London, 1986), pp. 97–145. East German historians claim that Nazism was primarily anti-socialist and that the Jews were persecuted principally for economic reasons; see Klaus Drobisch *et al.*, *Juden unterm Hakenkreuz. Verfolgung und Ausrottung der deutschen Juden 1933–1945* (Frankfurt am Main, 1973); Kurt Pätzold, *Faschismus, Rassenwahn, Judenverfolgung* (Berlin, 1975), and his 'Von der Vertreibung zum Genozid. Zu den Ursachen, Triebkräften und Bedingungen der antijüdischen Politik im faschistischen deutschen Imperialismus', in Dietrich Eichholtz, Kurt Gossweiler (eds.), *Faschismusforschung. Positionen, Probleme, Polemik* (Berlin, 1980), pp. 181–208. The best overall surveys of the subject include Helmut Krausnick, 'Judenverfolgung', in Hans Buchheim *et al.* (eds.), *Anatomie des SS-Staates* (Munich, 1979), Vol. 2, pp. 233–366; Wolfgang Scheffler, *Judenverfolgung im Dritten Reich* (Berlin, 1964); ; Klaus Drobisch *et al.*, *Juden unterm Hakenkreuz. Verfolgung und Ausrottung der deutschen Juden 1933–1945* (Frankfurt am Main, 1973); Yehuda Bauer, *A History of the Holocaust* (New York, 1982); Raul Hilberg, *The Destruction of the European Jews* (New York, 1983); Avraham Barkai, *From Boycott to Annihilation: The Economic Struggle of German Jews 1933–1945* (New England, 1989). The most comprehensive recent work on the 'Final Solution' is undoubtedly *Remembering for the Future*, International Scholars Conference in Oxford (Oxford, 1988), Vols. 1–3. The following works deal with the reaction of German Jews to Nazi persecution: Herbert Freeden, *Jüdisches Theater in Nazideutschland* (Tübingen, 1964); Jizchak Schwerzenz, Edith Wolff, 'Jüdische Jugend im Untergrund. Eine zionistische Gruppe in Deutschland während des Zweiten Weltkrieges', *Bulletin des Leo-Baeck-Instituts*, 12 (1969), pp. 1–100; Lucien Steinberg, *La Révolte des Justes. Les Juifs contre Hitler 1933–1945* (Paris, 1970); Salomon Adler-Rudel, *Jüdische Selbsthilfe unter dem Naziregime 1933 bis 1939. Im Spiegel der Berichte der Reichsvertretung der Juden in Deutschland* (Tübingen, 1974); Ulrich Dunker, *Der Reichsbund jüdischer Frontsoldaten 1919–1938* (Düsseldorf, 1977); Monika Richarz (ed.), *Jüdisches*

Leben in Deutschland. Selbstzeugnisse zur Sozialgeschichte 1918–1945 (Stuttgart, 1982); Marion Kaplan, *Die jüdische Frauenbewegung in Deutschland. Organisation und Ziele des Jüdischen Frauenbundes 1904–1938* (Hamburg, 1981); Konrad Kwiet, Helmut Eschwege, *Selbstbehauptung und Widerstand. Deutsche Juden im Kampf um Existenz und Menschenwürde 1933 bis 1945* (Hamburg, 1984); Konrad Kwiet, 'Problems of Jewish Resistance Historiography', *Leo Baeck Institute Year Book*, 24 (1979), pp. 37–57; Herbert A. Strauss, 'Jewish Emigration from Germany: Nazi Policies and Jewish Response', *Leo Baeck Institute Year Book*, 25 (1980), pp. 313–61 and 26 (1981), pp. 343–409. The responses, of the German population to the persecution of the Jews are discussed by Otto Dov Kulka, Aron Rodrigue, 'The German Population and the Jews in the Third Reich: Recent Publications and Trends in Research on German Society and the "Jewish Question"', *Yad Vashem Studies*, 16 (1984), pp. 421–35; Lawrence Stokes, 'The German People and the Destruction of the European Jews', *Central European History*, 6 (1973), pp. 167–91; Ian Kershaw, 'The Persecution of the Jews and German Popular Opinion in the Third Reich', *Leo Baeck Institute Year Book*, 26 (1981), pp. 261–89; Michael H. Kater, 'Everyday Anti-Semitism in Prewar Nazi Germany: The Popular Bases', *Yad Vashem Studies*, 16 (1984), pp. 129–59; Otto Dov Kulka, '"Public Opinion" in Nazi Germany and the "Jewish Question"', *Jerusalem Quarterly*, 25 (1982), pp. 121–44 and 26 (1983), pp. 34–45; these essays have been collected in Michael Marrus (ed.), *The Nazi Holocaust*, Vols. 1–15 (Westport, 1989), Vol. 5. See also Hans Mommsen, 'Was haben die Deutschen vom Völkermord an den Juden gewusst?', in Walter H. Pehle (ed.), *Der Judenpogrom 1938. Von der 'Reichskristallnacht' zum Völkermord* (Frankfurt am Main, 1988), pp. 176–200.

THE PERSECUTION OF ETHNIC MINORITIES

Sinti and Roma

It has been estimated that as many as 500,000 Sinti and Roma were killed by the Nazis. This subject has been virtually neglected by both German and non-German historians. The Nazi mass murder of Sinti and Roma was not dealt with at the Nuremberg War Crimes Trials, although various documents were collected on the subject which were used in a few publications immediately after the war. See Mateo Maximoff, 'Germany and the Gypsies from the Gypsies' Point of View', *Journal of Gypsy Lore Society*, 25 (1946), pp. 104ff.; J. Molitor, 'The Fate of a German Gypsy', *Journal of Gypsy Lore Society*, 26 (1947), pp. 48ff.; Otto Pankok, 'The Gypsies in Germany Today', *Journal of Gypsy Lore Society*, 32 (1953), pp. 152ff. International public opinion seems to have remained unexercised by the fact that surviving Sinti and Roma have been denied compensation by West German courts and compensation agencies. This practice has been 'justified' with the argument that prior to the 1943 Auschwitz deportation order, Sinti and Roma had been 'legitimately' persecuted by the Nazi authorites for being 'asocial'. This scandalous state of affairs was confirmed by a Federal Court judgement of 7 January 1956. The judgement is partially reprinted in Tilman Zulch (ed.), *In Auschwitz vergast, bis heute verfolgt. Zur Situation der Roma (Zigeuner) in Deutschland und Europa* (Reinbeck, 1979), pp. 169f.; the judgement itself gave the impetus to two further publications on the deportations of May 1940: Hans Buchheim, 'Die Zigeunerdeportation vom Mai 1940', in *Gutachten des Instituts für Zeitgeschichte* (Munich, 1958), pp. 51–61; Hans-Joachim Döring, 'Die Motive der Zigeunerdeportation vom Mai 1940', *Vierteljahrshefte für Zeitgeschichte*, 7 (1959), pp. 418–28. While Buchheim regarded the deportations of May 1940 as being illegal and racially motivated, Döring argued that 'crime-prevention' and 'political security' motives were determinative. He developed this misleading and justificatory view in an otherwise richly researched, if one-sided and prejudiced, book entitled *Zigeuner im national-sozialistischen Staat* (Hamburg, 1964). Similarly prejudiced and indeed racist views are apparent in Hermann Arnold's various publications: *Vaganten, Komödianten, Fieranten und Briganten. Untersuchungen zum Vagantenproblem an vagierenden Bevölkerungsgruppen vorwiegend in der Pfalz* (Stuttgart, 1958); *Die Zigeuner. Herkunft und Leben im deutschen Sprachgebiet* (Olten, 1965). Arnold, who passes for an authority on 'Gypsy matters' in official circles, has materially contributed to the perpetuation of misleading stereotypes about Sinti and Roma among the West German population. Following criticism in the 1970s (!) of racist overtones in Arnold's writings, he made himself the spokesman and defender of the racially-motivated 'research on Gypsies' conducted during the Third Reich, and called upon the government of the Federal Republic – in a neo-fascist periodical – to adopt 'an active population policy': Hermann Arnold, 'Ein Menschenalter danach. Anmerkungen zur Geschichtsschreibung der Zigeuner-verfolgung', *Mitteilungen zur Zigeunerkunde* (Alzenau, March 1977), *Beiheft* 4; 'Bevölkerungspolitik? Fehlanzeige!' in *Nation Europa* (1976), pp. 35f. For a critical discussion of Arnold's alleged expertise, see Mathias Winter, 'Kontinuitäten in der deutschen Zigeunerforschung und Zigeunerpolitk', *Beiträge zur national-sozialistischen Gesundheits- und Sozialpolitik* (Berlin, 1988), Vol. 6, pp. 135–52. The first serious academic studies of the persecution of Sinti and Roma in the Nazi period were by non-German historians: Jerzy Ficowski, *Cyganie Polscy. Skice historyczno-obyczajowe* (Warsaw, 1953), *Cyganie na polskich drogach* (Kraków, 1965); Donald Kenrick, Grattan Puxon, *The Destiny of Europe's Gypsies* (London, 1982). Along with public protests by Sinti and Roma in the Federal Republic, this last title was the occasion for a further spate of publications which however have little new to offer in terms of content: Wolf In der Maur, *Die Zigeuner. Wanderer zwischen den Welten* (Vienna, 1978); Joachim S. Hohmann, Ronald Schopf (eds.), *Zigeunerleben. Beiträge zur Sozialgeschichte einer Verfolgung* (Darmstadt, 1979); Joachim S. Hohmann, *Zigeuner und Zigeunerwissenschaft. Ein Beitrag zur Grund-lagenforschung und Dokumentation des Völkermordes im 'Dritten Reich'* (Marburg, 1980), and his *Geschichte der Zigeunerverfolgung in Deutschland* (Frankfurt am Main, 1981); Kirsten Martins-Heuss, *Zur mythischen Figur des Zigeuners in der deutschen Zigeunerforschung* (Frankfurt am Main, 1983); Rüdiger Vossen, *Zigeuner, Roma, Sinti, Gitanos, Gypsies zwischen Verfolgung und Romantisierung. Katalog zur Ausstellung des Hamburgischen Museums für Völkerkunde* (Frankfurt am Main, 1983); Tilman Zülch (ed.), *In Auschwitz vergast – bis heute verfolgt* (Reinbeck, 1979, 2nd edition 1983). Other studies, whose main emphasis is upon the history of Sinti and Roma after 1945, deal with the preceding period in greater or lesser detail: Lukrezia Jochimsen, *Zigeuner heute. Untersuchung einer Aussen-*

seitergruppe in einer deutschen Mittelstadt (Stuttgart, 1963); Anita Geigges,
Bernhard Wette, *Zigeuner heute. Verfolgung und Diskriminierung in der BRD*
(Bornheim-Merten, 1979); Andreas Hundsalz, *Stand der Forschung über Zigeuner
und Landfahrer* (Stuttgart, 1979); George V. Soest, *Zigeuner zwischen Verfolgung
und Integration. Geschichte, Lebensbedingungen und Eingliederungsversuche*
(Weinheim, 1979); Margret Weiler, 'Zur Frage der Integration der Zigeuner in
der Bundesrepublik Deutschland. Eine Untersuchung der gegenwärtigen Situation der Zigeuner und der sozialpolitischen und sozialarbeiterischen Massnahmen
für Zigeuner' (unpublished thesis, University of Cologne, 1979). None of these
titles has contributed much to our understanding of the origins, course, and
consequences of genocide against Sinti and Roma. The same applies to the
Giessen-based project 'Kulturelle Alternativen und Integration – das Beispiel der
Zigeuner'. The latter attributes to Sinti and Roma a 'stubbornness' whereby they
allegedly refuse to allow themselves to be integrated into society. Rejection of this
assumption by representatives of the Sinti and Roma, who argue that they have
been rejected by West German society, has resulted in hostile pronouncements by
the academics involved, up to and including denials of racially-motivated genocide:
Reimer Gronemeyer (ed.), *Eigensinn und Hilfe. Zigeuner in der Sozialpolitik
heutiger Leistungsgesellschaften* (Giessen, 1983); Mark Münzel, Bernhard Streck
(eds.), *Kumpania und Kontrolle. Moderne Behinderungen zigeunerischen Lebens*
(Giessen, 1981); Bernhard Streck, 'Die nationalsozialistischen Methoden zur
"Lösung" des Zigeunerproblems', *Tribune*, 20 (1981), pp. 53ff. The Sinti and
Roma civil rights movement has initiated a number of oral history works. See
Romani Rose (ed.), *Bürgerrechte für Sinti und Roma. Das Buch zum Rassismus in
Deutschland* (Heidelberg, 1987); Michael Krausnick, *Die Zigeuner sind da. Roma
und Sinti zwischen gestern und heute* (Würzburg, 1981), *'Da wollten wir frei sein!'
Eine Sinti-Familie erzählt* (Weinheim, 1983), and 'Das Leben des Herrn Stein-
berger', *Aus Politik und Zeitgeschichte*, B 12 (1981); Karin Bott-Bodenhausen,
H. Tommen (eds.), *Erinnerungen an 'Zigeuner'. Menschen aus Ostwestfalen-Lippe
erzählen von Sinti und Roma* (Düsseldorf, 1988). In the last few years professional
historians have at last discovered the persecution of Sinti and Roma as a subject for
study. For the participation of academics in the definition and persecution of Sinti
and Roma, see Benno Müller-Hill, *Murderous Science: Elimination by Scientific
Selection of Jews, Gypsies, and Others, Germany 1933–1945* (Oxford, 1988); Reimer
Gilsenbach, 'Wie Lolitschai zur Doktorwürde kam', *Beiträge zur nationalsozialistischen Gesundheits- und Sozialpolitik* (Berlin, 1988), Vol. 6, pp. 101–52;
Ute Brucker-Boroujerdi, Wolfgang Wippermann, 'Die Rassenhygienische und
Erbbiologische Forschungsstelle im Reichsgesundheitsamt', *Bundesgesundheits-
blatt*, 32 (1989), pp. 13–19. For the 'pre-history' of Nazi persecution of Sinti and
Roma see Wolfgang Günther, *Zur preussischen Zigeunerpolitik seit 1871. Eine
Untersuchung am Beispiel des Landkreises Neustadt am Rübenberge und der Haupt-
stadt Hannover* (Hanover, 1985); Rainer Hehemann, *Die 'Bekämpfung des
Zigeunerunwesens' im Wilhelminischen Deutschland und in der Weimarer Repub-
lik 1871–1933* (Frankfurt am Main, 1987). For regional and local studies of the
persecution of Sinti and Roma, see Siegfried Wölffling, 'Zur Verfolgung und
Vernichtung der mitteldeutschen Zigeuner unter dem Nationalsozialismus',
Wissenschaftliche Zeitschrift der Martin-Luther-Universität Halle-Wittenberg, 14

(1965), pp. 501–8; Inge Marssolek, Reiner Ott, *Bremen im 3. Reich. Anpassung–Widerstand–Verfolgung* (Bremen, 1986), pp. 334–7; Rudko Kawcznski, 'Hamburg soll "Zigeunerfrei" werden', in Angelika Ebbinghausen *et al.* (eds.), *Heilen und Vernichten im Mustergau Hamburg. Bevölkerungs- und Gesundheitspolitik im Dritten Reich* (Hamburg, 1984), pp. 45ff.; Johannes Meister, *Schicksale der 'Zigeunerkinder' aus der St. Josefspflege in Mulfingen* (Sigmaringen, 1984), and his 'Die "Zigeunerkinder" von der St. Josefspflege in Mulfingen', *1991 Zeitschrift für die Sozialgeschichte des 20. und 21. Jahrhunderts*, 2 (1987), pp. 14–51; Wolfgang Wippermann, *Das Leben in Frankfurt zur NS-Zeit*, Vol. 2: *Die nationalsozialistische Zigeunerverfolgung* (Frankfurt am Main, 1986); on forced labour camps for 'Gypsies' in the Third Reich, see the local studies, Erika Thurner, *Nationalsozialismus und Zigeuner in Österreich* (Salzburg, 1983); Ute Brucker-Boroujerdi, Wolfgang Wippermann, 'Nationalsozialistische Zwangslager in Berlin III. Das "Zigeunerlager" Marzahn', in Wolfgang Ribbe (ed.), *Berlin-Forschungen II* (Berlin, 1987), pp. 187–201, and 'Das "Zigeunerlager" Berlin-Marzahn 1936–1945. Zur Geschichte und Funktion eines nationalsozialistischen Zwangslagers', *Pogrom. Zeitschrift für bedrohte Völker*, 18 (1987), pp. 77–80. Michael Zimmermann has recently published a short survey on the persecution of Sinti and Roma based on archival materials in the Bundesarchiv and the publications mentioned above: *Verfolgt, vertrieben, vernichtet. Die nationalsozialistische Vernichtungspolitik gegen Sinti und Roma* (Essen, 1989). See also Ulrich König, *Sinti und Roma unterm Nationalsozialismus* (Bochum, 1989). Future research might investigate the reactions of Sinti and Roma to persecution in Germany and the German-occupied territories. Important studies on these last questions include Miriam Novitch, *Le Génocide des Tsiganes sous le régime Nazi* (Paris, 1968); Ch. Bernadac, *L'Holocauste oublié. Le Massacre des Tsiganes* (Paris, 1979); B. A. Sijes *et al.*, *Verfolging van Zigeuners in Nederland 1940–1945* (s'Gravenhage, 1979); J. Beckers, *Me hum Sinthu, Gesprekken met Zigeuners over de verfolging in der periode 40–45 en de jaren daanach* (The Hague, 1980); Vladimir Zerjaric, *Gubici Stanovinistva na territoriji Jugoslavijie n Drugom Svetslean ratu* (Zagreb, 1989); Tadeusz Szymański, Danuta Szymańska, Tadeusz Snieszko, 'Das "Spital" im Zigenuer-Familienlager in Auschwitz-Birkenau', *Die Auschwitz-Hefte*, 1 (1987), pp. 199–207; B. Gorcznśka, 'Das Schicksal des Zigeunervolkes in der Naziokkupation in Polen 1939–1945', *Studia Historiae Oeconomicae*, 9 (1976), pp. 185–92; for information regarding current persecution of Sinti and Roma see Grattan Puxon, 'Roma: Europe's Gypsies', *Minority Rights Group Report* no. 14 (London, 1987, 4th edn) and David Crowe and John Holsti (eds.), *The Gypsies of Eastern Europe* (New York, 1991).

Rhineland 'Bastards'

Studies include Reiner Pommerin, *'Sterilisierung der Rheinlandbastarde'. Das Schicksal einer farbigen deutschen Minderheit 1918–1937* (Düsseldorf, 1979); Gisela Lebzelter, 'Die "Schwarze Schmach". Vorurteile – Propaganda – Mythos', *Geschichte und Gesellschaft*, 11 (1985), pp. 37–58; K. Nelson, ' "The Black Horror on the Rhine": Race as a Factor in Post World War I Diplomacy', *Journal of*

Modern History, 42 (1970), pp. 606–27; E. D. Reinders, 'Racialism on the Left: E. D. Morel and the 'Black Horror on the Rhine''', *International Review of Social History*, 12 (1968), pp. 1–28; Sally Marks, 'Black Watch on the Rhine: A Study in Propaganda, Prejudice and Prurience', *European Studies Review*, 13 (1983), pp. 297–334. For the involvement of academics in the subsequent sterilisations see Niels C. Lösch, *Das Kaiser-Wilhelm-Institut für Anthropologie, menschliche Erblehre und Eugenik* (unpublished M.A. thesis, Freie Universität, Berlin, 1990), pp. 147ff.; Benno Müller-Hill, *Murderous Science: Elimination by Scientific Selection of Jews, Gypsies, and Others, Germany 1933–1945* (Oxford, 1988); Paul Weindling, *Health, Race and German Politics between National Unification and Nazism 1870–1945* (Cambridge, 1989), pp. 386ff.; Georg Lilienthal, '"Rheinlandbastarde". Rassenhygiene und das Problem der rassenideologischen Kontinuität', *Medizinhistorisches Journal*, 15 (1980), pp. 426–37.

Sorbs

Tschechisches Schrifttum über die Lausitzer Wenden, translated by the Johann-Gottfried-Herder Instituts No. 6 (Marburg, 1951); Martin Kasper, J. Softa (eds.), *Aus Geheimakten nazistischer Wendenpolitik* (Bautzen, 1960); Gerald Stone, *The Smallest Slavonic Nation: The Sorbs of Lusatia* (London, 1972); Martin Kasper, *Geschichte der Sorben* (Bautzen, 1976), Vol. 3; Hartmut Zwahr (ed.), *Meine Landsleute. Die Sorben und die Lausitz im Zeugnis deutscher Zeitgenossen* (Bautzen, 1984); Michael Burleigh, *Germany Turns Eastwards: A Study of 'Ostforschung' in the Third Reich* (Cambridge, 1988), pp. 117ff. and 299ff.; Todd Huebner, 'Ethnicity Denied: Nazi Policy Towards the Lusatian Sorbs, 1933–1945', *German History*, 6 (1988), pp. 250–77.

THE PERSECUTION OF THE 'HEREDITARILY ILL', THE 'ASOCIAL', AND HOMOSEXUALS

The 'hereditarily ill'

On 20 August 1947 fifty German physicians were convicted by an American Military Court at Nuremberg for their involvement in the Nazi 'euthanasia' programme. Courts in both the Federal Republic and the GDR subsequently convicted further medical personnel for similar offences. Others, however, were able to continue practising medicine up to the 1980s. Moreover, physicians and psychiatric 'experts' who recommended compulsory sterilisations have not been prosecuted by either Allied or German courts.

This can be explained by the widespread public indifference in West Germany towards the persecution of the so-called 'hereditarily' ill during the Third Reich. Representatives of West German medical associations, some of whom were themselves culpably involved in compulsory sterilisations and 'euthanasia' killings, actively tried to obstruct research on the subject. For example, they managed to limit the distribution of the first edition of Alexander Mitscherlich and Fred Mielke's *Dokumente des Nürnberger Ärzteprozesses* to members of the West German Medical Council. This ensured that the book – Alexander Mitscherlich,

Fred Mielke, *Das Diktat der Menschenverachtung* (Heidelberg, 1947) – was virtually unknown to the public at large.

In 1960 Mitscherlich and Mielke were able to bring out a paperback: Alexander Mitscherlich, Fred Mielke, *Medizin ohne Menschlichkeit* (Frankfurt am Main, 1960), which, however, failed to generate further research. Up to the late 1970s only a few articles and books appeared on this subject, including Klaus Dörner, 'Nationalsozialismus und Lebensvernichtung', *Vierteljahrshefte für Zeitgeschichte*, 15 (1968), pp. 121ff., reprinted in Klaus Dörner *et al.* (eds.), *Der Krieg gegen die psychisch Kranken* (Rehburg-Loccum, 1980); Karl Dietrich Erdmann, '"Lebensunwertes Leben". Totalitäre Lebensvernichtung und das Problem der Euthanasie', *Geschichte in Wissenschaft und Unterricht*, 26 (1975), pp. 215–25; Lothar Gruchmann, '"Euthanasie" und Justiz im Dritten Reich', *Vierteljahrshefte für Zeitgeschichte*, 20 (1972), pp. 235–79.

Intensive research on the subject only began in the early 1980s with the publication of the Leipzig ecclesiastical historian Kurt Nowak's pioneering studies on the relationship between 'euthanasia' and compulsory sterilisation: Kurt Nowak, *Euthanasie und Sterilisierung im Dritten Reich. Die Konfrontation der evangelischen und katholischen Kirche mit dem 'Gesetz zur Verhütung erbkranken Nachwuchses' und der 'Euthanasie'-Aktion* (Göttingen, 1978). Critically-minded German physicians also began to examine the past criminal activities of their own colleagues: Gerhard Baader, Ulrich Schultz (eds.), *Medizin und Nationalsozialismus* (Berlin, 1980); Walter Wuttke-Groneberg, *Medizin im Nationalsozialismus. Ein Arbeitsbuch* (Tübingen, 1980).

Wider interest in the subject was awakened by two remarkable books by the journalist Ernst Klee, who has made a lifetime study of Nazi persecution of the sick and of the failure of West German courts to punish the guilty. The books are meticulously researched. Ernst Klee, *'Euthanasie' in NS-Staat. Die 'Vernichtung lebensunwerten Lebens'* (Frankfurt am Main, 1983), *Was sie taten – Was sie werden* (Frankfurt am Main, 1985). See also Benno Müller-Hill, *Murderous Science: Elimination of Jews, Gypsies and Others, Germany 1933–1945* (Oxford, 1988).

Since then a number of important works have appeared on racial hygiene, eugenics, and medicine under the Nazi regime. See Peter Weingart, 'Eugenik, eine angewandte Wissenschaft im Dritten Reich', in Peter Lundgreen (ed.), *Wissenschaft im Dritten Reich* (Frankfurt am Main, 1985), pp. 314–49; Gisela Bock, *Zwangssterilisation im Nationalsozialismus* (Opladen, 1986); Alfons Labisch, Florian Tennstedt, *Der Weg zum Gesetz über die Vereinheitlichung des Gesundheitswesens* (Düsseldorf, 1986); Heidrun Kaupen-Haas (ed.), *Der Griff nach der Bevölkerung* (Nördlingen, 1986); Christian Ganssmüller, *Die Erbgesundheitspolitik des Dritten Reiches* (Cologne, 1987); Hans Walter Schmuhl, *Rassenhygiene, Nationalsozialismus, Euthanasie* (Göttingen, 1987); Peter Weingart, Jürgen Kroll, Kurt Bayertz, *Rasse, Blut und Gene. Geschichte der Eugenik und Rassenhygiene in Deutschland* (Frankfurt am Main, 1988); Peter Emil Becker, *Zur Geschichte der Rassenhygiene. Wege ins Dritte Reich* (Stuttgart, 1988); Robert Jay Lifton, *The Nazi Doctors: A Study in the Psychology of Evil* (London, 1986); Robert N. Proctor, *Racial Hygiene: Medicine under the Nazis* (London, 1988); Paul J. Weindling, *Health, Race and German Politics between National Unification and Nazism 1870–1945* (Cambridge, 1989). For a survey of this literature see

Michael Burleigh, 'Euthanasia in the Third Reich', *Social History of Medicine* (1991), 4. Films on medical issues including 'euthanasia' are dealt with in Erwin Leiser, *Nazi Cinema* (London, 1974); David Welch, *Propaganda and the German Cinema 1933–1945* (Oxford, 1983); Michael Burleigh, 'Euthanasia and the Cinema in the Third Reich', *History Today*, 40 (1990), pp. 11–16; and Burleigh, 'Racism and Social Policy', *Ethnic Studies* (1991), 14, pp. 453–73. See also Ludwig Rost, *Sterilisation und Euthanasie im Film des 'Dritten Reiches'. Nationalsozialistische Propaganda in ihrer Beziehung zu rassenhygienischen Massnahmen des NS-Staates* (Husum, 1987).

The 'asocial'

The so-called 'asocial' are not included among the recognised (and compensated) victims of Nazi racism. Some lawyers and sociologists in the Federal Republic have actually managed to defend Nazi policy towards the 'asocial'. For example, see Hans W. Jürgens, *Asozialität als biologisches und sozialbiologisches Problem* (Stuttgart, 1961); Karl-Leo Terhorst, *Polizeiliche planmässige Überwachung und polizeiliche Vorbeugungshaft im Dritten Reich* (Heidelberg, 1983).

Academics have only very recently begun to write about the history of the 'asocial' in the Third Reich. See Hans Buchheim, 'Die Aktion "Arbeitsscheu Reich"', *Gutachten des Instituts für Zeitgeschichte, München*, 2 (Munich, 1966), pp. 194ff.; Helmut Auerbach, 'Arbeitserziehungslager 1940–1944', *Gutachen des Instituts für Zeitgeschichte, München*, 2 (Munich, 1966), pp. 196–201. Wolfgang Fritz Werner, 'Die Arbeitserziehungslager als Mittel nationalsozialistischer "Sozialpolitik" gegen deutsche Arbeiter', in Wacław Długoborski (ed.), *Zweiter Weltkrieg und sozialer Wandel* (Göttingen, 1981), pp. 138–50; Detlev Peukert, 'Arbeitslager und Jugend-KZ. Die "Behandlung Gemeinschaftsfremder" im Dritten Reich', in Detlev Peukert, Jürgen Reulecke (eds.), *Die Reihen fast geschlossen. Beiträge zur Geschichte des Alltags unterm Nationalsozialismus* (Wuppertal, 1981), pp. 413–43; Ernst Klee, *'Euthanasie' im NS-Staat. Die 'Vernichtung lebensunwerten Lebens'* (Frankfurt am Main, 1983), pp. 38ff.; Patrick Wagner, 'Das Gesetz über die Behandlung Gemeinschaftsfremder', *Beiträge zur nationalsozialistischen Gesundheits- und Sozialpolitik*, 6 (1988), pp. 75–100; Wolfgang Ayass, '"Ein Gebot nationaler Arbeitsdisziplin". Die Aktion "Arbeitsscheu Reich" 1938', *Beiträge zur nationalsozialistischen Gesundheits- und Sozialpolitik*, 6 (1988), pp. 43–74, and his 'Vagrants and Beggars in Hitler's Reich', in Richard J. Evans (ed.), *The German Underworld: Deviants and Outcasts in German History* (London, 1988), pp. 210–37. There is an excellent short discussion of Sinti and Roma, vagrants, and the 'hereditarily ill' by Jeremy Noakes, 'Social Outcasts in the Third Reich', in Richard Bessel (ed.), *Life in the Third Reich* (Oxford, 1987), pp. 83–96. For a recent comprehensive treatment see Klaus Scherer, *'Asozial' im Dritten Reich* (Münster, 1990).

Homosexuals

The Nazis' 1935 tightening of Paragraph 175 of the 1871 Reich Criminal Code was only abrogated in 1969 in the Federal Republic. This partly explains why the Nazi persecution of homosexuals was virtually ignored by the German public until the 1970s. Professional historians in Germany usually chose to ignore the subject entirely. Surveys of the history of the Third Reich usually fail to mention the fate of homosexuals.

The available sources for the subject are scanty. The records of the SS Reich Central Office for the Combating of Homosexuality and Abortion have not been located. It is possible that they are held by the West or former East German security services for more or less legitimate purposes. There is also a paucity of autobiographical accounts, largely because survivors are reluctant to acknowledge their homosexuality publicly. An exception is Heinz Heger, *The Men with the Pink Triangle* (London, 1980). This means that there are few books to recommend on the subject. They include Rüdiger Lautmann (ed.), *Seminar: Gesellschaft und Homosexualität* (Frankfurt, 1977), and his '"Hauptdevise: bloss nicht anecken". Das Leben homosexueller Männer unter dem Nationalismus', in Johannes Beck *et al.* (eds.), *Terror und Hoffnung in Deutschland 1933–1945. Leben im Faschismus* (Reinbeck, 1980), pp. 366–90, and *Der Zwang zur Tugend. Die gesellschaftliche Kontrolle der Sexualität* (Frankfurt, 1984); Hans-Georg Stümke, Rudi Finkler, *Rosa Winkel, Rosa Listen. Homosexuelle und 'Gesundes Volksempfinden' von Auschwitz bis heute* (Reinbeck, 1981); Berlin Museum (ed.), *Eldorado. Homosexuelle Frauen und Männer in Berlin 1850–1950* (Berlin, 1984); Heinz-Dieter Schilling (ed.), *Schwule und Faschismus* (Berlin, 1983); Richard Plant, *The Pink Triangle: The Nazi War against Homosexuals* (New York, 1986); Hans-Georg Stümke, *Homosexuelle in Deutschland. Eine politische Geschichte* (Munich, 1989); G. Grau, 'Die Verfolgung und "Ausmerzung" Homosexueller zwischen 1933 und 1945', in A. Thom, G. I. Zaregorodzew (eds.), *Medizin unterm Hakenkreuz* (Berlin, 1989); K.-H. Roth, 'Die "Behandlung" von Homosexuellen im National-sozialismus', in H. L. Gremliza, V. Sigusch (eds.), *Konkret Sexualität* (Hamburg, 1985), pp. 26–9; Ruediger Lautmann, 'Gay Prisoners in Concentration Camps', in Michael Berenbaum (ed.), *A Mosaic of Victims: Non-Jews Persecuted and Murdered by the Nazis* (London, 1990), pp. 200–21.

YOUTH

While some members of the generation which grew up in the Third Reich, notably Chancellor Helmut Kohl, like to congratulate themselves on the 'blessing of being born late', matters were regarded differently in the immediate post-war period. The generation which had grown up during the Nazi period found itself under the suspicion that it had been indoctrinated by National Socialist propaganda. This accusation was made by members of the older generation, many of whom now occupied senior positions, but only a few of whom (such as Adenauer) were themselves free from suspicion. In view of these charges it is understandable why members of the so-called Hitler Youth generation were so concerned to prove the existence of a specific 'youth resistance movement'. In the Federal Republic this resulted in an emphasis upon the role of bourgeois groups like the 'Weisse Rose' or the activities of confessional youth groups. By contrast, in the GDR research concentrated upon the activities of the KJVD or Communist Youth League. Only recently has this bipolar approach been modified. There has been increased interest in both the former GDR and the Federal Republic in bourgeois and proletarian, organised and unorganised forms of youth resistance. Since the 1960s there has also been growing interest in Nazi policies towards education and schools. This has been followed by interest in the Hitler Youth and the League of German Maidens, and latterly in the social history of youth in general. There has also been a spate of autobiographical accounts of what it was like to grow up in Nazi Germany.

Most of these themes are evident in general studies of youth in the Third Reich. The most important are Heinz Boberach, *Jugend unter Hitler* (Düsseldorf, 1982); Karl-Heinz Huber, *Jugend unterm Hakenkreuz* (Berlin, 1982); Karl-Heinz Jahnke, Michael Buddrus, *Deutsche Jugend 1933–1945. Eine Dokumentation* (Hamburg, 1989); Arno Klönne, *Jugend im Dritten Reich. Die Hitler-Jugend und ihre Gegner* (Düsseldorf, 1982); Peter D. Stachura, *The German Youth Movement 1900–1945: An Interpretative Documentary History* (London, 1981). The subject of youth resistance is dealt with by Egon Boesten, *Jugendwiderstand im Faschismus* (Cologne, 1983), and *Die junge Garde. Arbeiterjugendbewegung in Frankfurt am Main 1904–1945* (Giessen, 1980); Lothar Gruchmann, 'Jugendopposition und Justiz im Dritten Reich. Die Probleme bei der Verfolgung der "Leipziger Meuten" durch die Gerichte', in Wolfgang Benz (ed.), *Miscellanea. Festschrift für Helmut Krausnick* (Stuttgart, 1980); Matthias von Hellfeld, *Edelweisspiraten in Köln. Die Jugendrebellion gegen das Dritte Reich. Das Beispiel Köln-Ehrenfeld* (Cologne, 1981), and *Bündische Jugend und Hitlerjugend. Zur Geschichte von Anpassung und Widerstand 1930–1939* (Cologne, 1987); Karl-Heinz Jahnke, *Weisse Rose contra Hakenkreuz* (Frankfurt am Main, 1969), and his *Jungkommunisten im Widerstandskampf gegen den Hitlerfaschismus* (Berlin, 1977), and *Jugend im Widerstand* (Frankfurt am Main, 1985); Inge Jens (ed.), *Hans Scholl. Sophie Scholl. Briefe und Aufzeichnungen* (Frankfurt am Main, 1984); Arno Klönne, *Gegen den Strom. Bericht über den Jugendwiderstand im Dritten Reich* (Hanover, 1957); Christian Petry, *Studenten aufs Schafott. Die Weisse Rose und ihr Scheitern* (Munich, 1968); Detlev Peukert, *Die Edelweisspiraten. Protestbewegung jugendlicher Arbeiter im Dritten Reich. Eine Dokumentation* (Cologne, 1980); Barbara Schellenberger, *Katholische Jugend und Drittes Reich* (Mainz, 1975); Inge School, *Die Weisse Rose* (Frankfurt am Main, 1982).

Nazi youth organisations are discussed by Hans-Christian Brandenburg, *Die Geschichte der HJ. Wege und Irrwege einer Generation* (Cologne, 1968); Anselm Faust, *Der nationalsozialistische Studentenbund. Studenten und Nationalsozialismus in der Weimarer Republik*, Vols. 1 and 2 (Düsseldorf, 1973); Hermann Giesecke, *Vom Wandervogel bis zur Hitlerjugend* (Munich, 1981); Ludwig Helbig, *Und sie werden nicht mehr frei, ihr ganzes Leben* (Weinheim, 1982); Michael H. Kater, 'Bürgerliche Jugendbewegung und Hitlerjugend in Deutschland vom 1926 bis 1939', *Archiv für Sozialgeschichte*, 17 (1977), pp. 127–74; Martin Klaus, *Mädchen in der Hitlerjugend. Die Erziehung zur 'deutschen Frau'* (Cologne, 1980), and his *Mädchen im Dritten Reich. Der Bund Deutscher Mädel (BDM)* (Cologne, 1983); Arno Klönne, *Hitlerjugend. Die Jugend und ihre Organisation im Dritten Reich* (Hanover, 1955); Dagmar Reese, 'Bund Deutscher Mädel. Zur Geschichte der weiblichen Jugend im Dritten Reich, in Frauengruppe Faschismusforschung (ed.), *Mutterkreuz und Arbeitsbuch. Zur Geschichte der Frauen in der Weimarer Republik und im Nationalsozialismus* (Frankfurt am Main, 1981), pp. 163–87; Jutta Rüdiger, *Die Hitler-Jugend und ihr Selbstverständnis* (Linden-horst, 1983); Rolf Schörken, *Luftwaffenhelfer und Drittes Reich* (Stuttgart, 1984); Jurgen Schultz, *Die Akademie für Jugendführung der Hitlerjugend in Braunschweig* (Brunswick, 1978); Peter D. Stachura, *Nazi Youth in the Weimar Republic* (Santa Barbara, 1975).

On Nazi education and school policies see Gerhard Dabel, *KLV. Die erweiterte Kinder-Land-Verschickung. KLV-Lager 1940–1945* (Freiburg, 1981); Rolf Eilers, *Die nationalsozialistische Schulpolitik* (Cologne, 1963); Kurt-Ingo Flessau, *Schule der Diktatur. Lehrpläne und Schulbücher des Nationalsozialismus* (Munich, 1977); Hans-Jurgen Gamm, *Führung und Verführung. Pädagogik des Nationalsozialismus* (Munich, 1977); Manfred Heinemann (ed.), *Erziehung und Schulung im Dritten Reich*, Vols. 1 and 2 (Stuttgart, 1980); Manfred Hock, *Die Hilfsschule im Dritten Reich* (Berlin, 1977); Wolfgang Keim (ed.), *Pädagogen und Pädagogik im Nationalsozialismus* (Frankfurt am Main, 1988); Karl Christoph Lingelbach, *Erziehung und Erziehungstheorien im nationalsozialistischen Deutschland* (Wein-heim, 1970); Edith Niehus, *Das Landjahr. Eine Jugenderziehungseinrichtung in der Zeit des Nationalsozialismus* (Nörten-Hardenberg, 1984); Elke Nyssen, *Schule im Nationalsozialismus* (Heidelberg, 1977); Otwilm Ottweiler, *Die Volksschule im Nationalsozialismus* (Weinheim, 1979); Harald Scholtz, *Erziehung und Unterricht unterm Hakenkreuz* (Göttingen, 1985), and his *Nationalsozialistische Ausleseschulen. Internatsschulen als Herrschaftsmittel des Führerstaates* (Göttingen, 1973); Horst Ueberhorst, *Elite für die Diktatur. Die nationalpolitischen Erziehungsanstalten 1933–1945. Ein Dokumentarbericht* (Königstein, 1980). The following autobiographical accounts and collections of reminiscences contain use-ful material: Arbeitsgemeinschaft Pädagogisches Museum (ed.), *Heil Hitler, Herr Lehrer. Volksschule 1933–1945* (Reinbeck, 1983); Peter Brücker, *Das Abseits als sicherer Ort. Kindheit und Jugend zwischen 1933 und 1945* (Berlin, 1980); Werner Klose, *Generation im Gleichschritt. Die Hitlerjugend. Ein Dokumentarbericht* (Oldenburg, 1982); Peter Kohrs, *Kindheit und Jugend unter dem Hakenkreuz* (Stuttgart, 1983); Melitta Maschmann, *Fazit. Mein Weg in die Hitlerjugend* (Munich, 1980); Eva Sternheim-Peters, *Die Zeit der grossen Täuschungen. Mädchenleben im Faschismus* (Bielefeld 1989, 2nd edition). Social histories of the situation of youth in the Third Reich include Christa Hasenclever, *Jugendhilfe und Jugendgesetzgebung seit 1900* (Göttingen, 1978); Ulrich Herrmann (ed.), '*Die Formung der Volksgenossen*'. *Der 'Erziehungsstaat' des Dritten Reiches* (Weinheim, 1985); Arno Klönne, *Jugendkriminalität und Jugendopposition im NS Staat. Dokumentation des Lageberichts des RJF vom 1.1.1941* (Münster, 1981); David Kramer, 'Die Fürsorgeerziehung im Dritten Reich', in Rolf Landwehr, Rüdiger Baron (eds.), *Geschichte der Sozialarbeit* (Weinheim, 1983), pp. 173ff.; Carola Kuhlmann, *Erbkrank oder erziehbar? Jugendhilfe als Vorsorge und Aussonderung in der Fürsorgeerziehung in Westfalen von 1933–1945* (Weinheim, 1989); Hans-Uwe Otto, Heinz Sünker (eds.), *Soziale Arbeit und Faschismus* (Frankfurt am Main, 1989); Detlev Peukert, 'Arbeitslager und Jugend-KZ. Die "Behandlung Gemeinschaftsfremder" im Dritten Reich', in Detlev Peukert, Jürgen Reulecke (eds.), *Die Reihen fast geschlossen. Beiträge zur Geschichte des Alltags unterm Nationalsozialismus* (Wuppertal, 1981), pp. 413–34, and his 'Youth in the Third Reich', in Richard Bessel (ed.), *Life in the Third Reich* (Oxford, 1987), pp. 25–40, and *Inside Nazi Germany: Conformity, Opposition and Racism in Everyday Life* (London, 1987), pp. 145–74; Herwart Vorländer, *Die NSV. Darstellung und Dokumentation einer nationalsozialistischen Organisation* (Boppard, 1988); Peter Zolling, *Zwischen Integration und Segregation. Sozialpolitik im 'Dritten Reich' am Beispiel der Nationalsozialistischen Volkswohlfahrt (NSV) in Hamburg* (Frankfurt am Main, 1986).

WOMEN

Most general histories and surveys of Nazi Germany either hardly mention women at all, or depict them as enthusiastic worshippers of Adolf Hitler. This is particularly evident in illustrated histories of the period, and indeed in works such as Joachim C. Fest's *Hitler* (London, 1974). Since the 1970s some research has been done on women in Nazi Germany. An excellent starting point for those interested in this subject is Jill Stephenson, *Women in Nazi Society* (London, 1975) and her *Nazi Organisation of Women* (London and New York, 1981). See also Dörte Winkler, *Frauenarbeit im 'Dritten Reich'* (Hamburg, 1977); Stephenson's pioneering work on Nazi women's organisations has been supplemented by Martin Klaus, *Mädchen in der Hitlerjugend. Die Erziehung zur 'deutschen Frau'* (Cologne, 1980), and his *Mädchen im Dritten Reich. Der Bund Deutscher Mädel (BDM)* (Cologne, 1983); Dagmar Reese, 'Bund Deutscher Mädel. Zur Geschichte der weiblichen Jugend im Dritten Reich', in Frauengruppe Faschismusforschung (ed.), *Mutterkreuz und Arbeitsbuch* (Frankfurt am Main, 1981), pp. 163–87; Susanna Dammer, 'Kinder, Küche, Kriegsarbeit – Die Schulung der Frauen durch die NS-Frauenschaft', in Frauengruppe Faschismusforschung (ed.), *Mutterkreuz und Arbeitsbuch* (Frankfurt am Main, 1981), pp. 215–345; Stefan Bajohr, 'Weiblicher Arbeitsdienst im "Dritten Reich". Ein Konflikt zwischen Ideologie und Ökonomie', *Vierteljahrshefte für Zeitgeschichte*, 28 (1980), pp. 331–57; Michael H. Kater, 'Frauen in der NS-Bewegung', *Vierteljahrshefte für Zeitgeschichte*, 31 (1983), pp. 102–239; Dorothee Klinksiek, *Die Frau im NS-Staat* (Stuttgart, 1982). Work begun by Dörte Winkler on women in the labour market was developed by the late Tim Mason. See his 'Women in Nazi Germany', *History Workshop Journal*, 1 (1976), pp. 74ff., and his 'Zur Lage der Frauen in Deutschland 1930–1940', *Gesellschaft. Beiträge zur Marxschen Theorie*, 6 (1976), pp. 118–93. Mason's claim that the position of women was 'modernised' under National Socialism has been criticised by various women historians working on the situation of female workers, servants, civil servants, students, and teachers. See Frauengruppe Faschismusforschung (ed.), *Mutterkreuz und Arbeitsbuch*, and also Stefan Bajohr, *Die Hälfte der Fabrik. Geschichte der Frauenarbeit in Deutschland 1914–1945* (Marburg, 1979); Carola Sachse, 'Hausarbeit im Betrieb. Betriebliche Sozialarbeit unter dem Nationalsozialismus', in Sachse (ed.), *Angst, Belohnung, Zucht und Ordnung. Herrschaftsmechanismen im Nationalsozialismus* (Opladen, 1982), pp. 209–74. There has been considerable interest in how Nazi propaganda depicted women. See the various contributions on this theme in Frauengruppe Faschismusforschung (ed.), *Mutterkreuz und Arbeitsbuch*; Maruta Schmidt *et al.* (eds.), *Frauen unterm Hakenkreuz* (Berlin, 1983); Christel Wittrock, *Weiblichkeitsmythen. Das Frauenbild im Faschismus und seine Vorläufer in der*

Frauenbewegung der 20. Jahre (Frankfurt am Main, 1983); Rita Thalmann, *Frauensein im Dritten Reich* (Munich, 1984); Renate Wiggershausen, *Frauen unterm Nationalsozialismus* (Wuppertal, 1984). An interesting, if not entirely convincing, attempt to argue that the racial-hygienic measures taken by the Nazi State were primarily anti-feminist can be found in Gisela Bock's *Zwangssterilisation im Nationalsozialismus. Studien zur Rassenpolitik und Frauenpolitik* (Opladen, 1986) and in Renate Bridenthal, Anita Grossmann, Marion Kaplan (eds.), *When Biology Became Destiny: Women in Weimar and Nazi Germany* (New York, 1984); Claudia Koonz, *Mothers in the Fatherland: Women, the Family and Nazi Politics* (New York, 1986) is rather unreliable. An excellent survey of the literature to date is Ute Frevert, *Women in German History* (Oxford, 1989), pp. 200–43. For a good collection of source material see Annette Kuhn, *Frauen im deutschen Faschismus* (Düsseldorf, 1982).

MEN

The upper classes

In discussions on the nature of Fascism one frequently encounters the claim that Fascism was an instrument or agent of particular elements in 'finance capital' or of 'the bourgeoisie'. This idea, which reflects more or less crude forms of economic reductionism, is particularly evident in the work of orthodox Marxist-Leninists, who dwell upon the role of industry and big business before and during the Nazi regime. For historiographical discussions of both the Marxist and non-Marxist literature see Wolfgang Wippermann, *Faschismustheorien. Zum Stand der gegenwärtigen Diskussion* (Darmstadt, 1989, 5th edition), pp. 58ff.; and Ian Kershaw, *The Nazi Dictatorship* (London, 1989), pp. 42ff. Although there is a large literature on the part played by big business in the Nazi 'seizure of power', to which the best guides are Dick Geary, 'The Industrial Elite and the Nazis in the Weimar Republic', in Peter Stachura (ed.), *The Nazi Machtergreifung* (London, 1983), and Ian Kershaw (ed.), *Weimar: Why did German Democracy Fail?* (London, 1990) there have been relatively few social histories of industrialists and other members of the upper classes in Nazi Germany. Most of the standard social histories of the Third Reich more or less fail to mention them. See, for example, David Schoenbaum, *Hitler's Social Revolution* (London, 1966); Richard Grunberger, *A Social History of the Third Reich* (London, 1971); Detlev Peukert, *Inside Nazi Germany: Conformity, Opposition and Racism in Everyday Life* (London, 1987). A recent attempt to redress this is Martin Broszat, Klaus Schwabe (eds.), *Die deutschen Eliten und der Weg in den Zweiten Weltkrieg* (Munich, 1989). There is also much suggestive material in J. Noakes, 'Nazism and Revolution', in N. O'Sullivan (ed.), *Revolutionary Theory and Political Reality*, and Michael H. Kater, 'Hitler in a Social Context', *Central European History*, 14 (1981), pp. 243–72. There have been a number of studies of what are generally termed 'functional elites'. These include studies of lawyers: for example, see Hans Robinsohn, *Justiz als politische Verfolgung. Die Rechtsprechung in 'Rasseschande-fällen' beim Landgericht Hamburg 1936–1943* (Stuttgart, 1977); Kritische Justiz (ed.), *Der Unrechts-Staat* (Baden-Baden, 1983–4), Vols. 1 and 2; Gerhard

Fieberg, *Justiz im nationalsozialistischen Deutschland* (Cologne, 1984); Martin Hirsch *et al.* (eds.), *Recht, Verwaltung und Justiz im Nationalsozialismus* (Cologne, 1984); Ingo Muller, *Furchtbare Juristen. Die unbewältigte Vergangenheit unserer Justiz* (Munich, 1987); on the role of civil servants see Jane Caplan, *Government Without Administration* (Oxford, 1988); Dieter Rebentisch, *Führerstaat und Verwaltung im Zweiten Weltkrieg* (Frankfurt am Main, 1989); on the military, R. Absolon, *Die Wehrmacht im Dritten Reich* (Boppard, 1960–85), Vols. 1–3; Manfred Messerschmidt, *Die Wehrmacht im NS-Staat. Zeit der Indoktrination* (Hamburg, 1969); Klaus-Jürgen Müller, *Das Heer und Hitler. Armee und nationalsozialistisches Regime 1933–1940* (Stuttgart, 1969); on the Churches see John S. Conway, *Die NS-Kirchenpolitik 1933–1945. Ihre Ziele, Widersprüche und Fehlschläge* (Munich, 1969); Friedrich Zipfel, *Kirchenkampf in Deutschland 1933–1945* (Berlin, 1965); Kurt Meier, *Der Evangelische Kirchenkampf, Gesamtdarstellung in drei Bänden* (Halle, 1976–84); Klaus Scholder, *Die Kirchen und das Dritte Reich*, Vol. 1 (Frankfurt am Main, 1977); Hans Prolingheuer, *Kleine politische Kirchengeschichte. 50 Jahre evangelischer Kirchenkampf von 1919 bis 1969* (Cologne, 1984).

The 'Mittelstand' in the Third Reich

Contemporary observers were the first to argue that the middle classes were particularly susceptible to Nazi ideology and propaganda and that they constituted the main social constituency for Fascist movements. See Theodor Geiger, 'Panik im Mittelstand', *Die Arbeit*, 7 (1930), pp. 553–637, and his 'Die Mittelschichten und die Sozialdemokratie', *Die Arbeit*, 8 (1931), pp. 619–35; Svend Riemer, 'Mittelstand und sozialistische Politik', *Die Arbeit*, 9 (1932), pp. 265–72. After 1945 this claim was generalised into the argument that the *Mittelstand* constituted 'the' social basis of Fascism, and that the latter phenomenon represented the 'extremism of the middle'. See Seymour Lipset, 'Der "Faschismus", die Linke, die Rechte und die Mitte', *Kölner Zeitschrift für Soziologie und Sozialpsychologie*, 11 (1959), pp. 401–4; Arthur Schweitzer, *Die Nazifizierung des Mittelstandes* (Stuttgart, 1970). This argument has increasingly been questioned in recent research, which has concentrated upon the question of the social composition of the Nazi party and its electoral base. See Heinrich August Winkler, 'Extremismus der Mitte?', *Vierteljahrshefte für Zeitgeschichte*, 20 (1970), pp. 175–91, and his *Mittelstand, Demokratie und Nationalsozialismus. Die politische Entwicklung von Handwerk und Kleinhandel in der Weimarer Republik* (Cologne, 1972), and 'Mittelstandsbewegung oder Volkspartei? Zur sozialen Basis der NSDAP', in Wolfgang Schieder (ed.), *Faschismus als soziale Bewegung. Deutschland und Italien im Vergleich* (Hamburg, 1976), pp. 25–68; Richard F. Hamilton, *Who Voted for Hitler?* (Princeton, 1982); Thomas Childers, *The Nazi Voter: The Social Foundations of Fascism in Germany 1919–1933* (Chapel Hill, 1983); Michael H. Kater, *The Nazi Party: A Social Profile of Members and Leaders 1919–1945* (Oxford, 1983); Mathilde Jamin, *Zwischen den Klassen. Zur Sozialstruktur der SA-Führerschaft* (Wuppertal, 1984). These authors have argued that while members of the *Mittelstand* were certainly disproportionately represented among both the members and voters of the NSDAP, the Party itself was by no means a specifically middle-class party, but rather a 'negative people's party'. They also stress that the Nazi regime pursued policies which were far from being in the interests of the middle class. See Heinrich August Winkler, 'Der entbehrliche Stand. Zur Mittelstandspolitik im "Dritten Reich"', *Archiv für Sozialgeschichte*, 17 (1977), pp. 1–40; Adelheid von Saldern, *Mittelstand im 'III. Reich'. Handwerker – Einzelhändler – Bauern* (Frankfurt am Main, 1979); Detlev Peukert, *Inside Nazi Germany: Conformity, Opposition and Racism in Everyday Life* (London, 1987), pp. 86–100; Werner Abelshauser, Anselm Faust, 'Wirtschafts- und Sozialpolitik: Eine national-sozialistische Sozialrevolution?', Deutsches Institut für Fernstudien an der Universität Tübingen, Nationalsozialismus im Unterricht, *Studieneinheit*, 4 (Tübingen, 1983), pp. 92–114. See also Heinrich Uhlig, *Die Warenhäuser im Dritten Reich* (Cologne, 1956); Friedrich Grundmann, *Agrarpolitik im 'Dritten Reich'. Anspruch und Wirklichkeit des Reichserbhofgesetzes* (Hamburg, 1979); John E. Farquharson, *The Plough and the Swastika: The NSDAP and Agriculture in Germany 1928–1945* (London, 1976); Bernhard Keller, *Das Handwerk im faschistischen Deutschland. Zum Problem der Massenbasis* (Cologne, 1980).

Workers

Research on the position of the working class in Nazi Germany concentrates upon two areas; accounts of organised working-class resistance, and the social history of the working class. For a long time, research on working-class resistance was a preserve of historians in the GDR, whose aim – as laid down by politicians and educational bureaucrats – was to glorify the role of the KPD in the past as a means of legitimising the dictatorship of the SED in the present. This meant that while the published product was often well researched, its ideological character and objectives were all too apparent. Examples of this would include Klaus Mammach, *Die KPD und die deutsche antifaschistische Widerstandsbewegung 1933–1945* (Frankfurt am Main, 1974). By contrast, West German historians discovered this theme relatively late in the day. This was because many of them had concentrated on the history of bourgeois and aristocratic-military resistance groups, a subject which of course was also instrumentalised in the service of politics in the Federal Republic. Although the Moltkes and Trotts still have their devotees, most West German historians now manage to give due attention to the history of working-class resistance. See Christoph Klessmann, Falk Pingel (eds.), *Gegner des Nationalsozialismus* (Frankfurt am Main, 1980); Richard Löwenthal, Patrik von zur Mühlen (eds.), *Widerstand und Verweigerung in Deutschland 1933 bis 1945* (Bonn, 1982); Jürgen Schmädeke, Peter Steinbach (eds.), *Der Widerstand gegen den Nationalsozialismus. Die deutsche Gesellschaft und der Widerstand gegen Hitler* (Munich, 1985); Manfred Geis *et al.*, *Widerstand und Exil der deutschen Arbeiterbewegung 1933–1945. Grundlagen und Materien* (Bonn, 1982). Local and regional studies have done much to correct the *parti pris* findings of East German historians. See Detlev Peukert, *Die KPD im Widerstand. Verfolgung und Untergrundarbeit an Rhein und Ruhr 1933 bis 1945* (Wuppertal, 1980); Hartmut Mehringer, 'Die KPD in Bayern 1918–1945. Vorgeschichte, Verfolgung und Widerstand', in Martin Broszat *et al.* (eds.), *Bayern in der NS-Zeit* (Munich and Vienna, 1983), Vol. 5, pp. 1–286, and his 'Die bayerische Sozialdemokratie bis zum Ende des NS-Regimes. Vorgeschichte, Verfolgung und Widerstand', in *ibid.*, pp. 287–432; Wolfgang Wippermann, *Das Leben in Frankfurt zur NS-Zeit*, Vol. 4, *Der Widerstand* (Frankfurt am Main, 1986). There is still no synthesis of the findings of local and regional studies of working-class resistance to the regime. Studies of working-class resistance usually fail to take account of the social situation of the working class under Nazism. Orthodox Marxist-Leninist research still argues the old anti-fascist line on the progressive impoverishment of the working class under Nazism. See Jürgen Kuczynski, *Darstellung der Lage der Arbeiter in Deutschland von 1933–1945. Die Geschichte der Lage der Arbeiter unter dem Kapitalismus* (Berlin, 1964), Vol. 6. This line is opposed by those who stress the 'modernising' impact of the Nazi regime, particularly in the field of social policy. See David Schoenbaum, *Hitler's Social Revolution* (London, 1966). This 'modernisation thesis' was endorsed by those like Tim Mason, who claimed, on the basis of much empirical research, that the real wages of workers in the armaments industry rose under National Socialism. However, Mason attributed this phenomenon less to the 'modernising' or 'revolutionary' policies of the regime than to a form of covert 'class struggle' waged by the workers themselves. This 'class struggle' assumed such proportions that the Nazi leadership was finally obliged to essay a 'flight forwards', or in other words to bring about a war for domestic political reasons. See Timothy W. Mason, 'Labour in the Third Reich 1933–1939', *Past and Present*, 33 (1966), pp. 112–41; *Arbeiterklasse und Volksgemeinschaft. Dokumente und Materialien zur deutschen Arbeiterpolitik 1936–1939* (Opladen, 1975), *Sozialpolitik im Dritten Reich. Arbeiterklasse und Volksgemeinschaft* (Opladen, 1977), 'Zur Entstehung des Gesetzes zur Ordnung der nationalen Arbeit vom 20. Januar 1934. Ein Versuch über das Verhältnis "archaischer" und "moderner" Momente in der neuesten deutschen Geschichte', in Hans Mommsen *et al.* (eds.), *Industrielles System und politische Entwicklung in der Weimarer Republik* (Düsseldorf, 1974), pp. 322–51, and 'Innere Krise und Angriffskrieg 1938/1939', in Friedrich Forstmeier, Hans-Erich Volkmann (eds.), *Wirtschaft und Rüstung am Vorabend des Zweiten Weltkrieges* (Düsseldorf, 1975), pp. 158–88. Schoenbaum and Mason's various arguments have encountered considerable criticism. Firstly, considerable doubt has been cast upon the utility of 'modernisation' theories for the study of the period. See Horst Matzerath, Heinrich Volkmann, 'Modernisierungstheorie und Nationalsozialismus', in Jürgen Kocka (ed.), *Theorien in der Praxis des Historikers* (Göttingen, 1977), pp. 36–116. Secondly, greater emphasis has been laid upon the differences in wages between the various branches and sectors of industry. See Werner Abelshauser, Dietmar Petzina, 'Krise und Rekonstruktion. Zur Interpretation der gesamtwirtschaftlichen Entwicklung Deutschlands im 20. Jahrhundert', in Abelsshauser and Petzina (eds.), *Deutsche Wirtschaftsgeschichte im Industriezeitalter* (Königstein, 1981), pp. 47–93; Werner Abelshauser, Anselm Faust, 'Wirtschafts- und Sozialpolitik: eine nationalsozialistische Sozialrevolution', Nationalsozialismus im Unterricht, *Studieneinheit*, 4 (ed.), Deutsches Institut für Fernstudien an der Universität Tübingen (Tübingen, 1983). Thirdly, Mason's 'flight forwards' interpretation of the origins of the Second World War has been criticised for seriously underestimating the elements of diplomatic, economic, military, and political calculation in Hitler's decision to go to war. See above all Richard Overy's excellent contributions, *The Nazi Economic Recovery 1932–1938* (London, 1982), 'Hitler's War and the German Economy: A Reinterpretation', *Economic History Review*, 35 (1982), pp. 272–91, 'Germany, "Domestic Crisis" and War in 1939', *Past and Present*, 116 (1987), pp. 138–68, and the ensuing debate with Mason in *Past and Present*, 122 (1989), pp. 200–40; Ludolf Herbst, 'Die Krise des national-sozialistischen Regimes am Vorabend des Zweiten Weltkrieges und die forcierte Aufrüstung. Ein Kritik', *Vierteljahrshefte für Zeitgeschichte*, 26 (1978), pp. 347–92, and his *Der totale Krieg und die Ordnung der Wirtschaft. Die Kriegswirtschaft im Spannungsfeld von Politik, Ideologie und Propaganda 1939–1945* (Stuttgart, 1982); Alan S. Milward, *War, Economy and Society 1939–1945* (London, 1977). Fourthly, historians have also criticised Mason's overestimation of working-class 'opposition' or 'resistance', and his underestimation of the success enjoyed by the Nazis' combination of repression and inducements in the socio-economic sphere. See Thomas Berger, 'NS-Sozialpolitik als Mittel der Herrschaftssicherung', in Peter Meyers, Dieter Riesenberger (eds.), *Der Nationalsozialismus in der historisch-politischen Bildung* (Göttingen, 1979), pp. 71–93; Heinz Lampert, 'Staatliche Sozialpolitik in Dritten Reich', in Karl Dietrich Bracher (ed.), *National-sozialistische Diktatur 1933–1945. Eine Bilanz* (Bonn, 1983), pp. 177–205; Carole Sachse *et al.* (eds.), *Angst, Belohnung, Zucht und Ordnung. Herrschaftsmech-anismen im Nationalsozialismus* (Opladen, 1982); Tilla Siegel, *Leistung und Lohn in der nationalsozialistischen 'Ordnung der Arbeit'* (Opladen, 1989); Marie Louise Recker, *Nationalsozialistische Sozialpolitik im Zweiten Weltkrieg* (Munich, 1985); Hasso Spode, '"Der deutsche Arbeiter reist". Massentourismus im Dritten Reich', in Gerhard Huck (ed.), *Sozialgeschichte der Freizeit* (Wuppertal, 1980), pp. 281–306; Gunther Mai, 'Warum steht der deutsche Arbeiter zu Hitler? Zur Rolle der Deutschen Arbeitsfront im Herrschaftssystem des Dritten Reiches', *Geschichte und Gesellschaft*, 12 (1986), pp. 212–34; Herbert Vorländer, *Die NSV. Darstellung und Dokumentation einer nationalsozialistischen Organisation* (Boppard, 1988); Robert Smelser, *Robert Ley: Hitler's Labour Front Leader* (Oxford, 1989). Ulrich Herbert, 'Arbeiterschaft im "Dritten Reich". Zwischen-bilanz und offene Fragen', *Geschichte und Gesellschaft*, 15 (1989), pp. 320–60 is an excellent survey based on recent research. Working class conformity is also implicit in Omer Bartov's outstanding social history of the military, *Hitler's Army* (Oxford 1991). Finally, those who stress the modernising impact of the Nazi regime have been implicitly criticised by those who have studied the close connections between Nazi racial and social policies. This would include studies of foreign forced labour and the exploitation of prisoners of war. See Edward L. Homze, *Foreign Labor in Nazi Germany* (Princeton, 1967); Ulrich Herbert, *Fremdarbeiter im Dritten Reich. Politik und Praxis des 'Ausländer-Einsatzes' in der deutschen Kriegswirtschaft* (Berlin, 1985); Christian Streit, *Keine Kameraden. Die Wehrmacht und die Sowjetischen Kriegsgefangenen 1941–1945* (Stuttgart, 1978), and his 'The German Army and the Policies of Genocide', in Gerhard Hirschfeld (ed.), *The Policies of Genocide: Jews and Soviet Prisoners of War in Nazi Germany* (London, 1986), pp. 1–14; Diemut Majer, *Fremdvölkische im Dritten Reich* (Boppard, 1981); and detailed local studies of foreign workers in particular plants such as Klaus-Jorg Siegfried, *Rüstungs-produktion und Zwangsarbeit im Volkswagenwerk 1939–1945* (Frankfurt am Main, 1986), and his *Das Leben der Zwangsarbeiter im Volkswagenwerk 1939–1945* (Frankfurt am Main, 1988).

INDEX